contents

黒鷺死体宅配便
the KUROSAGI corpse delivery service

4

story
EIJI OTSUKA

art
HOUSUI YAMAZAKI

original cover design
BUNPEI YORIFUJI

translation
TOSHIFUMI YOSHIDA

editor and english adaptation
CARL GUSTAV HORN

lettering and touch-up
IHL

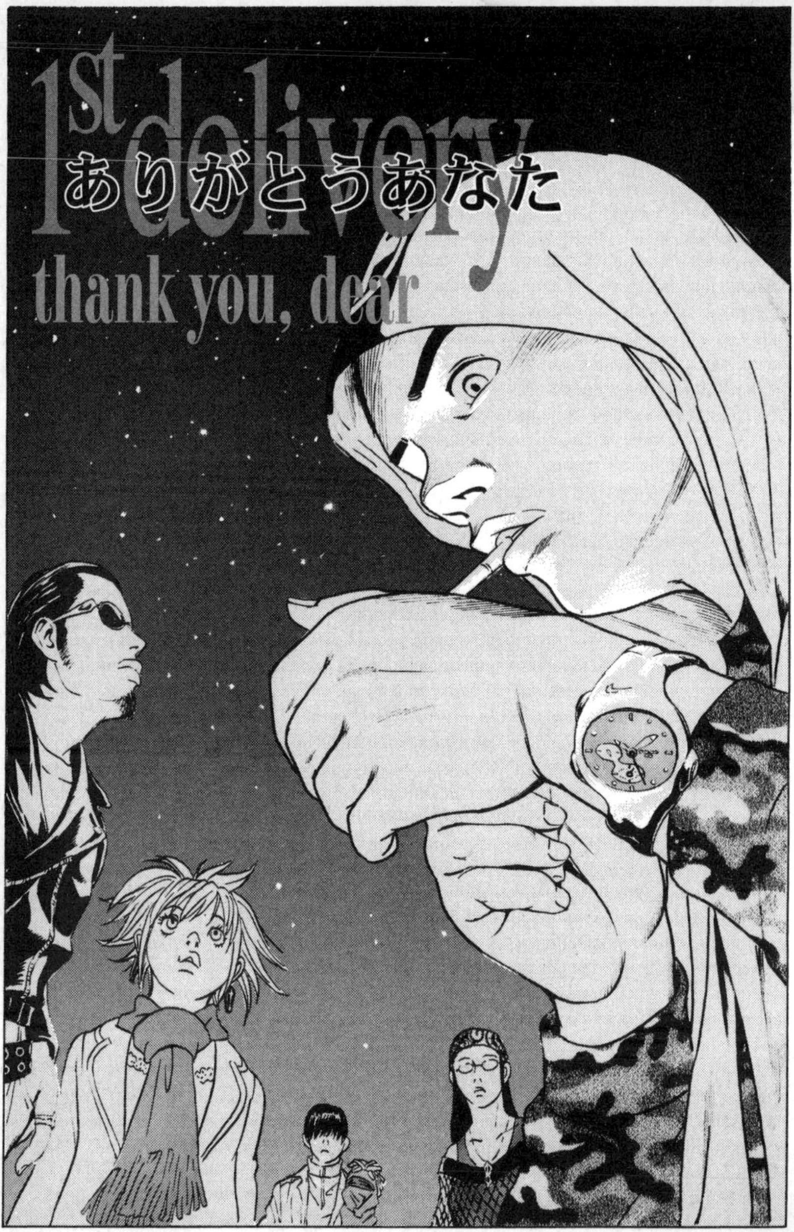
1st delivery
ありがとうあなた
thank you, dear

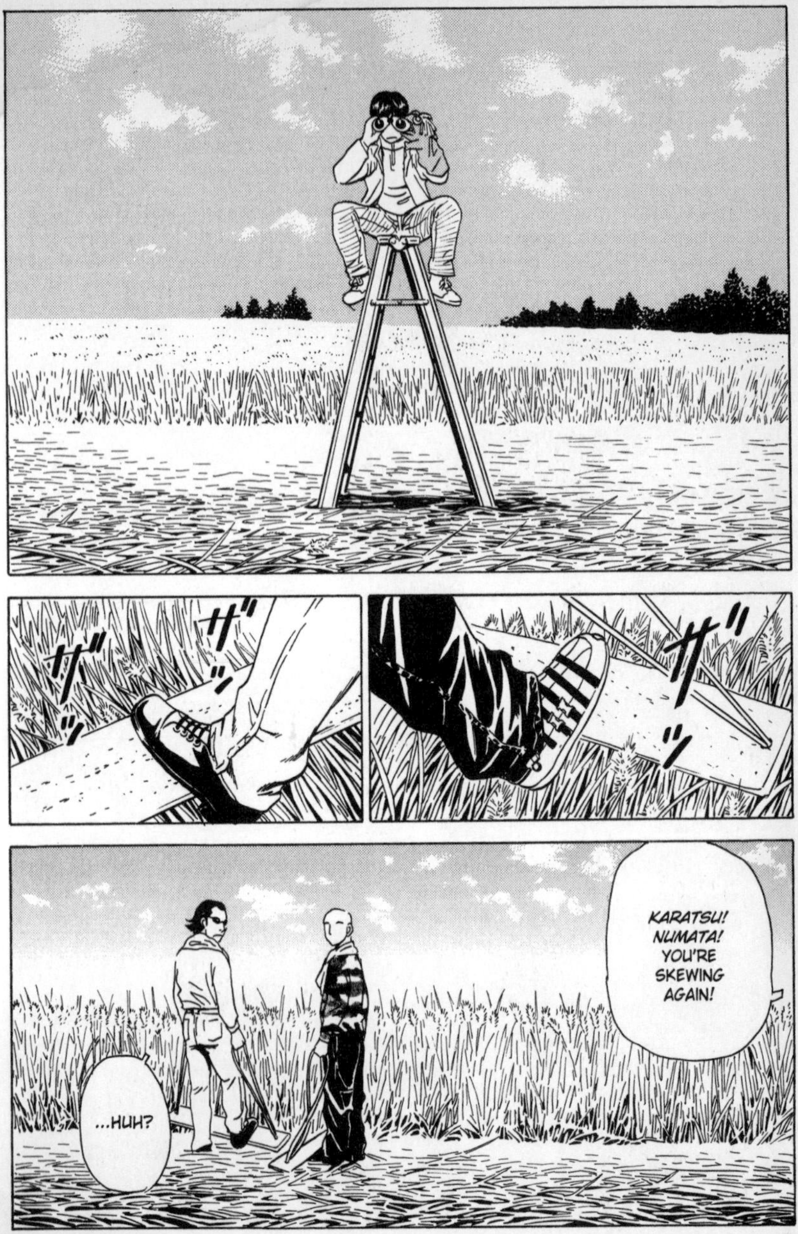
ザッ
ザッ
ザッ
KARATSU! NUMATA! YOU'RE SKEWING AGAIN!
...HUH?

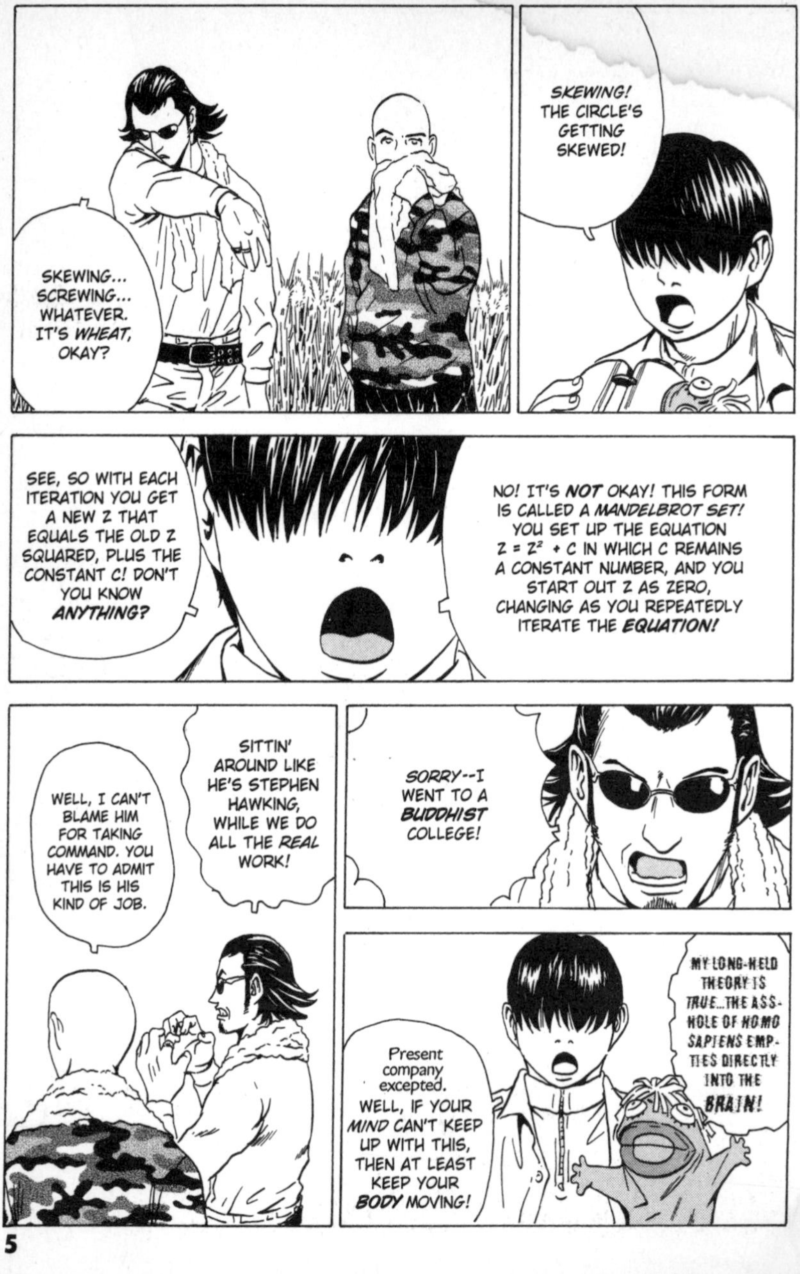
SKEWING! THE CIRCLE'S GETTING SKEWED!
SKEWING... SCREWING... WHATEVER. IT'S *WHEAT,* OKAY?
NO! IT'S ***NOT*** OKAY! THIS FORM IS CALLED A *MANDELBROT SET!* YOU SET UP THE EQUATION $Z = Z^2 + C$ IN WHICH C REMAINS A CONSTANT NUMBER, AND YOU START OUT Z AS ZERO, CHANGING AS YOU REPEATEDLY ITERATE THE ***EQUATION!***
SEE, SO WITH EACH ITERATION YOU GET A NEW Z THAT EQUALS THE OLD Z SQUARED, PLUS THE CONSTANT C! DON'T YOU KNOW ***ANYTHING?***
SORRY--I WENT TO A ***BUDDHIST*** COLLEGE!
MY LONG-HELD THEORY IS *TRUE*...THE ASS-HOLE OF *HOMO SAPIENS* EMPTIES DIRECTLY INTO THE ***BRAIN!***
Present company excepted.
WELL, IF YOUR *MIND* CAN'T KEEP UP WITH THIS, THEN AT LEAST KEEP YOUR ***BODY*** MOVING!
SITTIN' AROUND LIKE HE'S STEPHEN HAWKING, WHILE WE DO ALL THE *REAL* WORK!
WELL, I CAN'T BLAME HIM FOR TAKING COMMAND. YOU HAVE TO ADMIT THIS IS HIS KIND OF JOB.

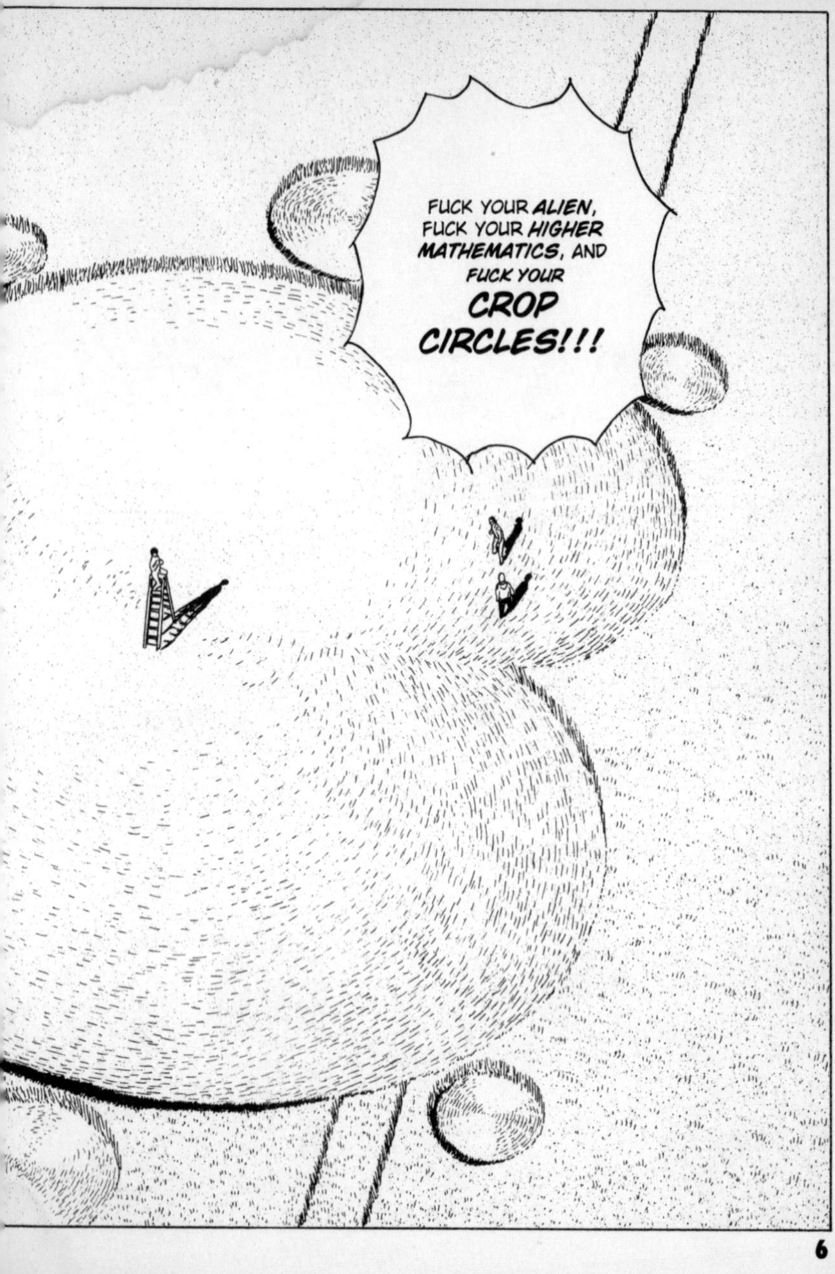
FUCK YOUR ALIEN, FUCK YOUR HIGHER MATHEMATICS, AND FUCK YOUR CROP CIRCLES!!!

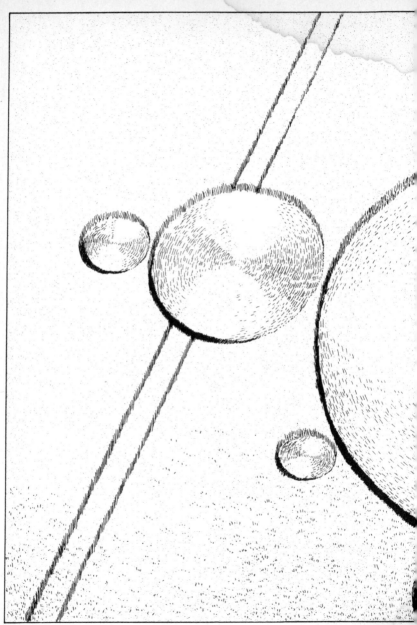

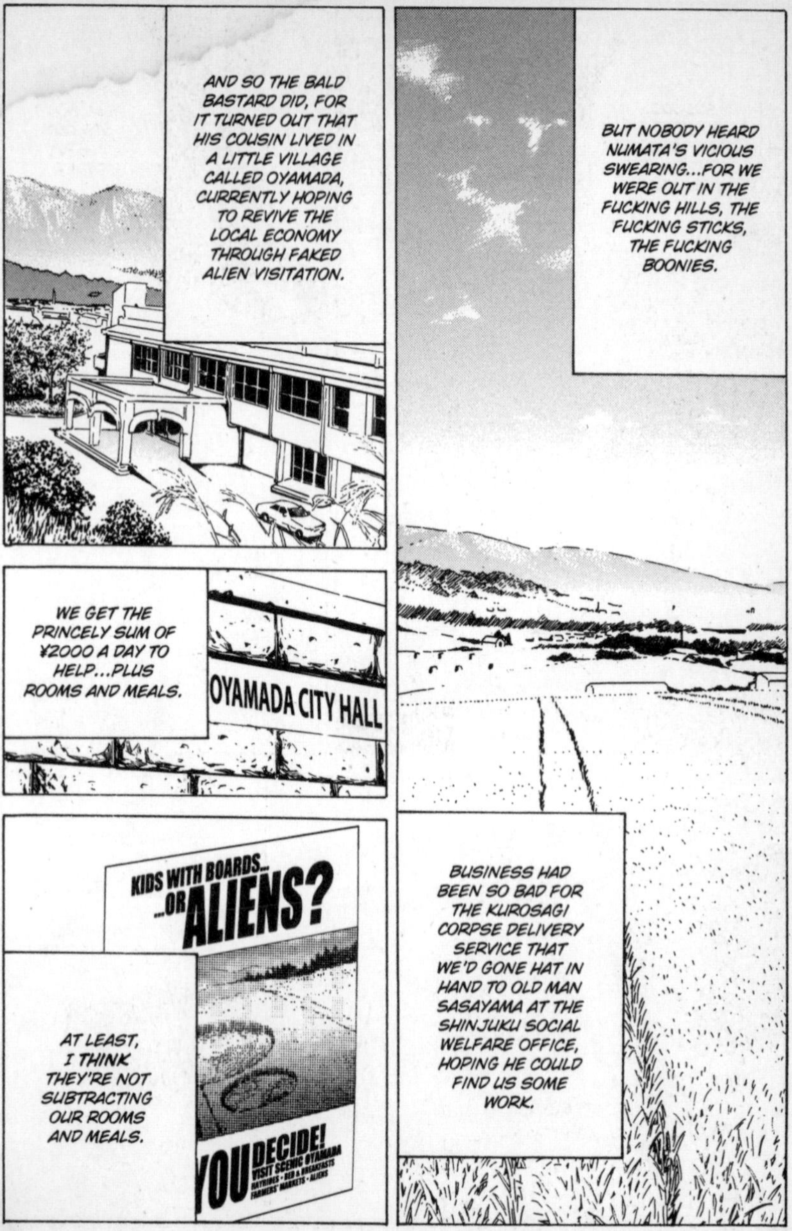
BUT NOBODY HEARD NUMATA'S VICIOUS SWEARING...FOR WE WERE OUT IN THE FUCKING HILLS, THE FUCKING STICKS, THE FUCKING BOONIES.
BUSINESS HAD BEEN SO BAD FOR THE KUROSAGI CORPSE DELIVERY SERVICE THAT WE'D GONE HAT IN HAND TO OLD MAN SASAYAMA AT THE SHINJUKU SOCIAL WELFARE OFFICE, HOPING HE COULD FIND US SOME WORK.
AND SO THE BALD BASTARD DID, FOR IT TURNED OUT THAT HIS COUSIN LIVED IN A LITTLE VILLAGE CALLED OYAMADA, CURRENTLY HOPING TO REVIVE THE LOCAL ECONOMY THROUGH FAKED ALIEN VISITATION.
OYAMADA CITY HALL
WE GET THE PRINCELY SUM OF ¥2000 A DAY TO HELP...PLUS ROOMS AND MEALS.
KIDS WITH BOARDS... ...OR ALIENS?
YOU DECIDE!
VISIT SCENIC OYAMADA
HAYRIDES • BED & BREAKFASTS
FARMERS' MARKETS • ALIENS
AT LEAST, I THINK THEY'RE NOT SUBTRACTING OUR ROOMS AND MEALS.

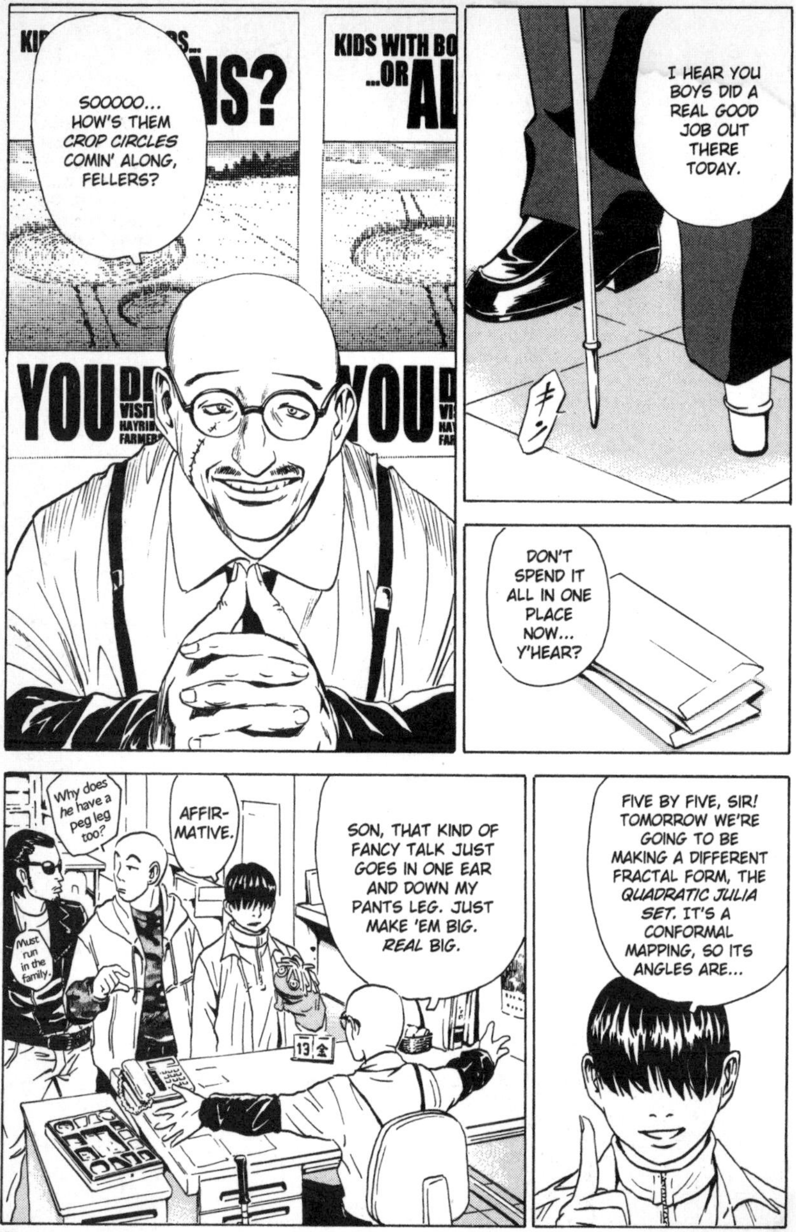
I HEAR YOU BOYS DID A REAL GOOD JOB OUT THERE TODAY.
DON'T SPEND IT ALL IN ONE PLACE NOW... Y'HEAR?
SOOOOO... HOW'S THEM *CROP CIRCLES* COMIN' ALONG, FELLERS?
FIVE BY FIVE, SIR! TOMORROW WE'RE GOING TO BE MAKING A DIFFERENT FRACTAL FORM, THE *QUADRATIC JULIA SET*. IT'S A CONFORMAL MAPPING, SO ITS ANGLES ARE...
SON, THAT KIND OF FANCY TALK JUST GOES IN ONE EAR AND DOWN MY PANTS LEG. JUST MAKE 'EM BIG. *REAL* BIG.
AFFIRMATIVE.
Why does he have a peg leg too?
Must run in the family.

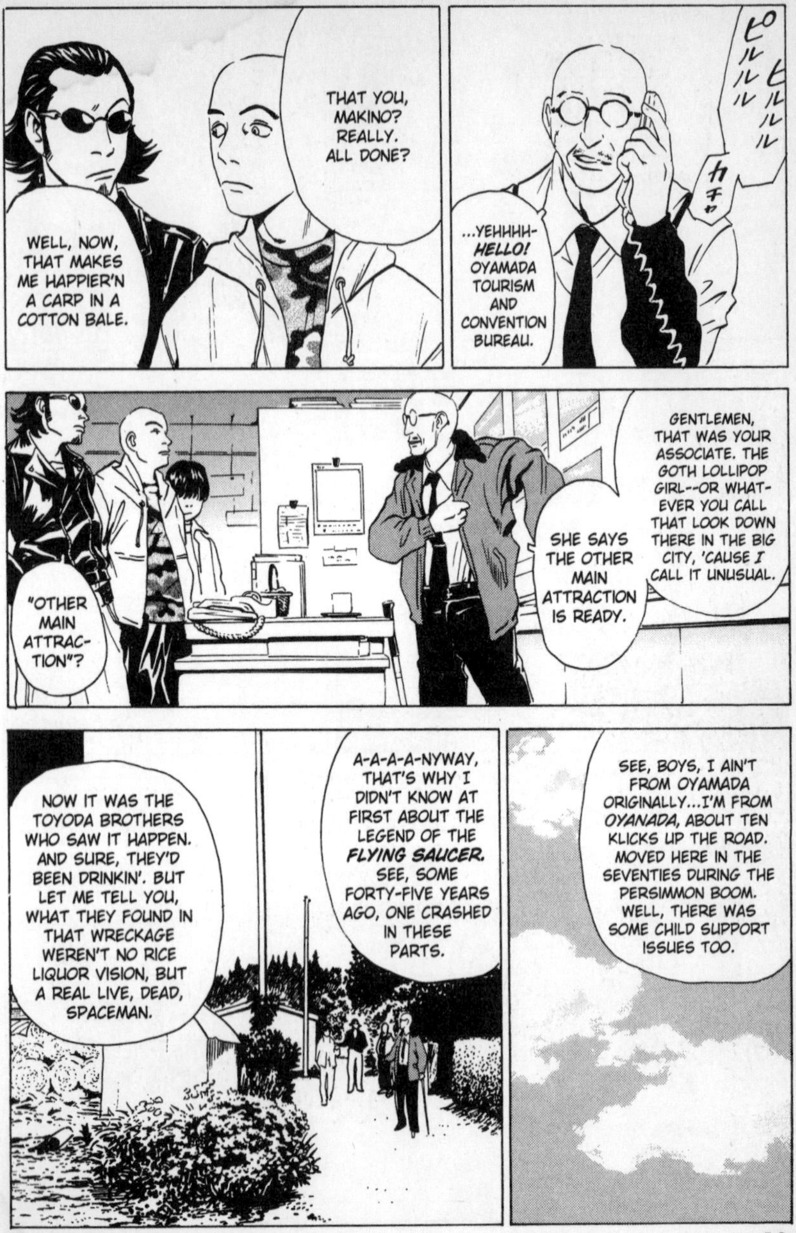
ピルルル ピルルル
カチャ
...YEHHHH- **HELLO!** OYAMADA TOURISM AND CONVENTION BUREAU.
THAT YOU, MAKINO? REALLY. ALL DONE?
WELL, NOW, THAT MAKES ME HAPPIER'N A CARP IN A COTTON BALE.
GENTLEMEN, THAT WAS YOUR ASSOCIATE. THE GOTH LOLLIPOP GIRL--OR WHATEVER YOU CALL THAT LOOK DOWN THERE IN THE BIG CITY, 'CAUSE *I* CALL IT UNUSUAL.
SHE SAYS THE OTHER MAIN ATTRACTION IS READY.
"OTHER MAIN ATTRACTION"?
SEE, BOYS, I AIN'T FROM OYAMADA ORIGINALLY...I'M FROM *OYANADA*, ABOUT TEN KLICKS UP THE ROAD. MOVED HERE IN THE SEVENTIES DURING THE PERSIMMON BOOM. WELL, THERE WAS SOME CHILD SUPPORT ISSUES TOO.
A-A-A-A-NYWAY, THAT'S WHY I DIDN'T KNOW AT FIRST ABOUT THE LEGEND OF THE ***FLYING SAUCER.*** SEE, SOME FORTY-FIVE YEARS AGO, ONE CRASHED IN THESE PARTS.
NOW IT WAS THE TOYODA BROTHERS WHO SAW IT HAPPEN. AND SURE, THEY'D BEEN DRINKIN'. BUT LET ME TELL YOU, WHAT THEY FOUND IN THAT WRECKAGE WEREN'T NO RICE LIQUOR VISION, BUT A REAL LIVE, DEAD, SPACEMAN.

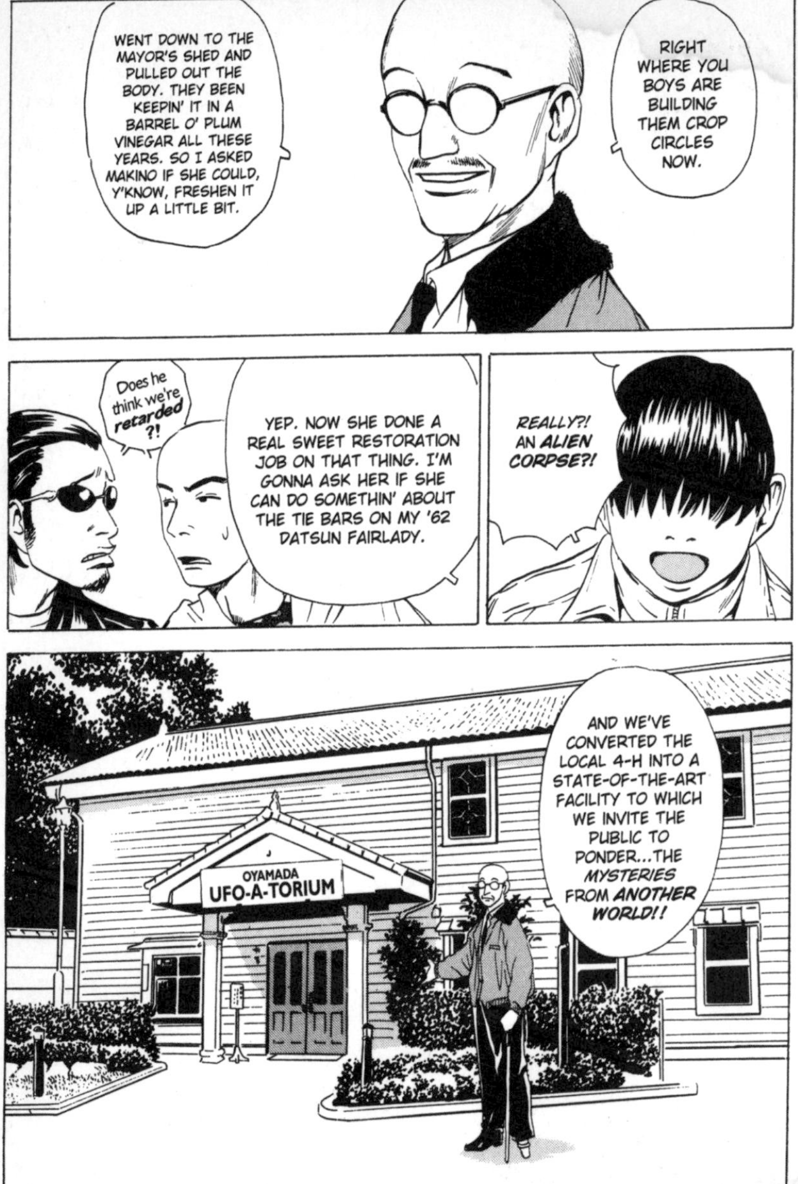

RIGHT WHERE YOU BOYS ARE BUILDING THEM CROP CIRCLES NOW.
WENT DOWN TO THE MAYOR'S SHED AND PULLED OUT THE BODY. THEY BEEN KEEPIN' IT IN A BARREL O' PLUM VINEGAR ALL THESE YEARS. SO I ASKED MAKINO IF SHE COULD, Y'KNOW, FRESHEN IT UP A LITTLE BIT.
REALLY?! AN ALIEN CORPSE?!
YEP. NOW SHE DONE A REAL SWEET RESTORATION JOB ON THAT THING. I'M GONNA ASK HER IF SHE CAN DO SOMETHIN' ABOUT THE TIE BARS ON MY '62 DATSUN FAIRLADY.
Does he think we're retarded?!
OYAMADA UFO-A-TORIUM
AND WE'VE CONVERTED THE LOCAL 4-H INTO A STATE-OF-THE-ART FACILITY TO WHICH WE INVITE THE PUBLIC TO PONDER...THE MYSTERIES FROM ANOTHER WORLD!!

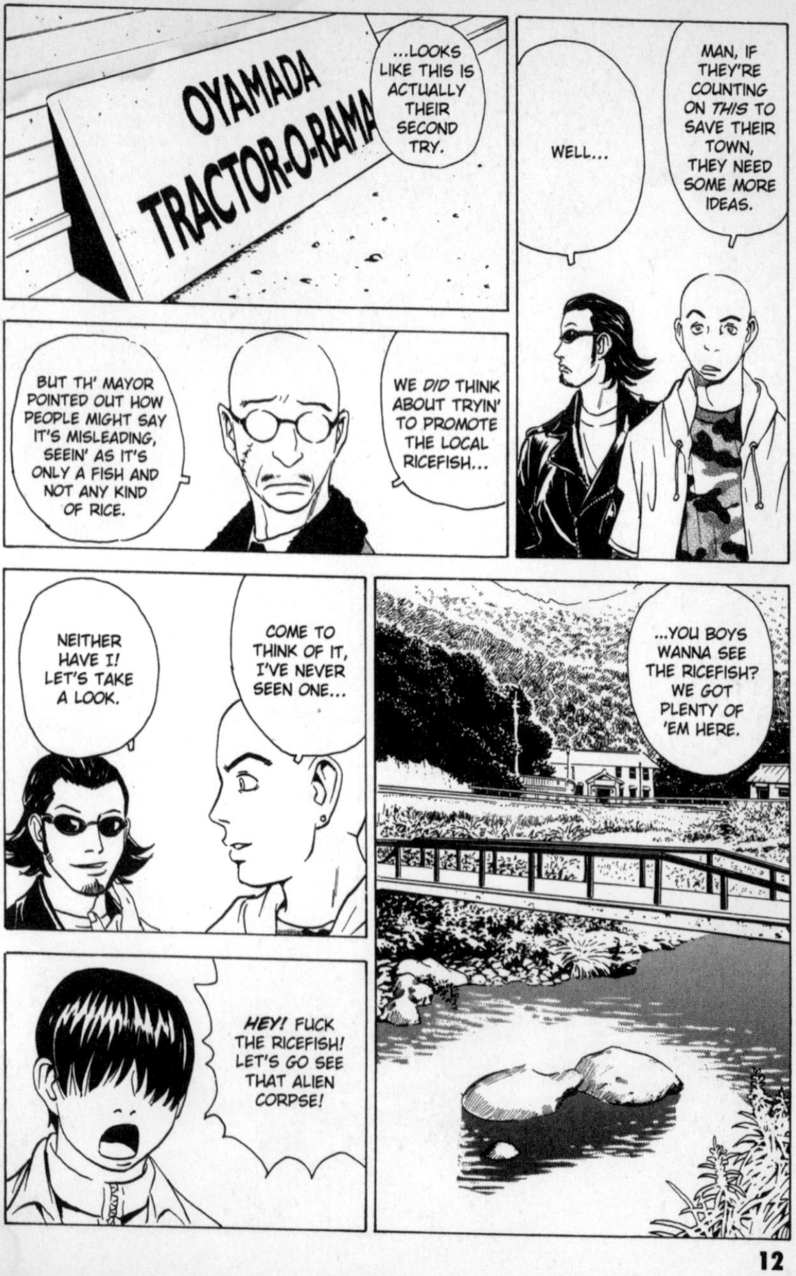

MAN, IF THEY'RE COUNTING ON *THIS* TO SAVE THEIR TOWN, THEY NEED SOME MORE IDEAS.
WELL...
...LOOKS LIKE THIS IS ACTUALLY THEIR SECOND TRY.
OYAMADA TRACTOR-O-RAMA
WE *DID* THINK ABOUT TRYIN' TO PROMOTE THE LOCAL RICEFISH...
BUT TH' MAYOR POINTED OUT HOW PEOPLE MIGHT SAY IT'S MISLEADING, SEEIN' AS IT'S ONLY A FISH AND NOT ANY KIND OF RICE.
...YOU BOYS WANNA SEE THE RICEFISH? WE GOT PLENTY OF 'EM HERE.
COME TO THINK OF IT, I'VE NEVER SEEN ONE...
NEITHER HAVE I! LET'S TAKE A LOOK.
HEY! FUCK THE RICEFISH! LET'S GO SEE THAT ALIEN CORPSE!

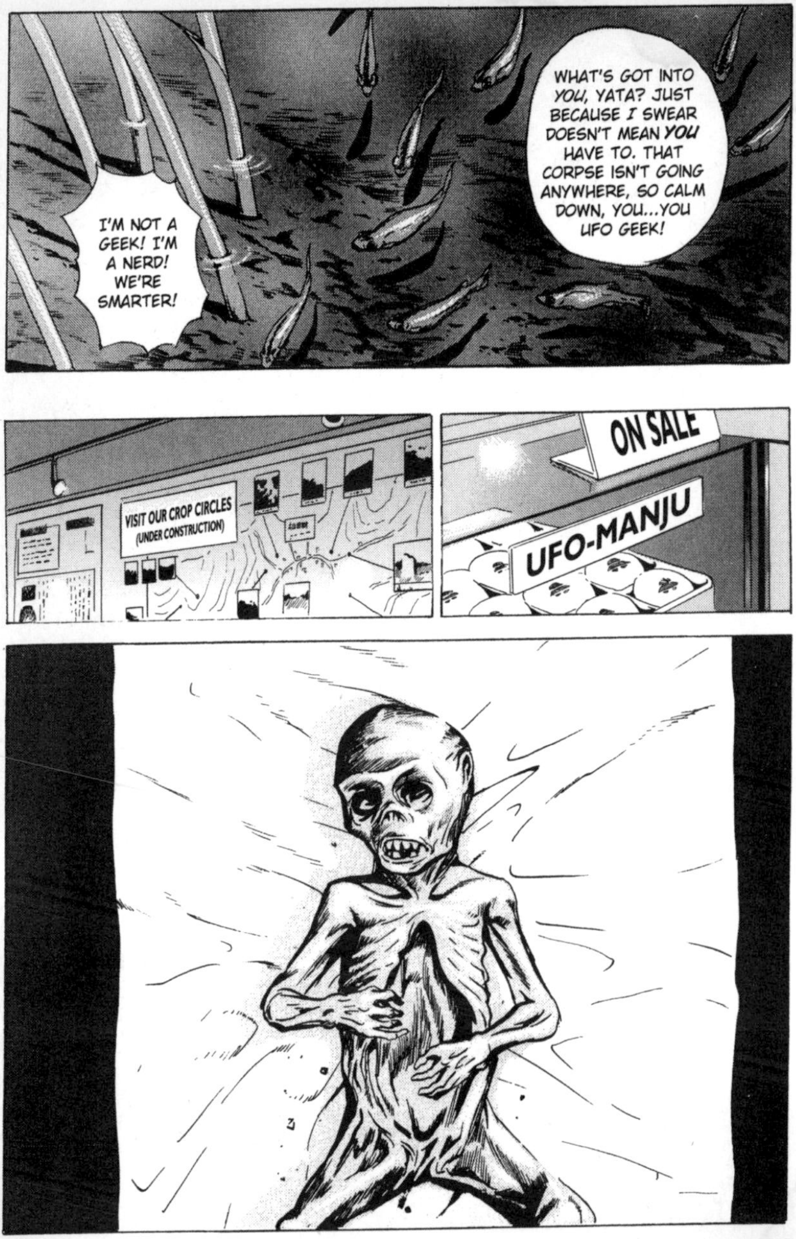
WHAT'S GOT INTO YOU, YATA? JUST BECAUSE I SWEAR DOESN'T MEAN YOU HAVE TO. THAT CORPSE ISN'T GOING ANYWHERE, SO CALM DOWN, YOU...YOU UFO GEEK!
I'M NOT A GEEK! I'M A NERD! WE'RE SMARTER!
ON SALE
UFO-MANJU
VISIT OUR CROP CIRCLES
(UNDER CONSTRUCTION)

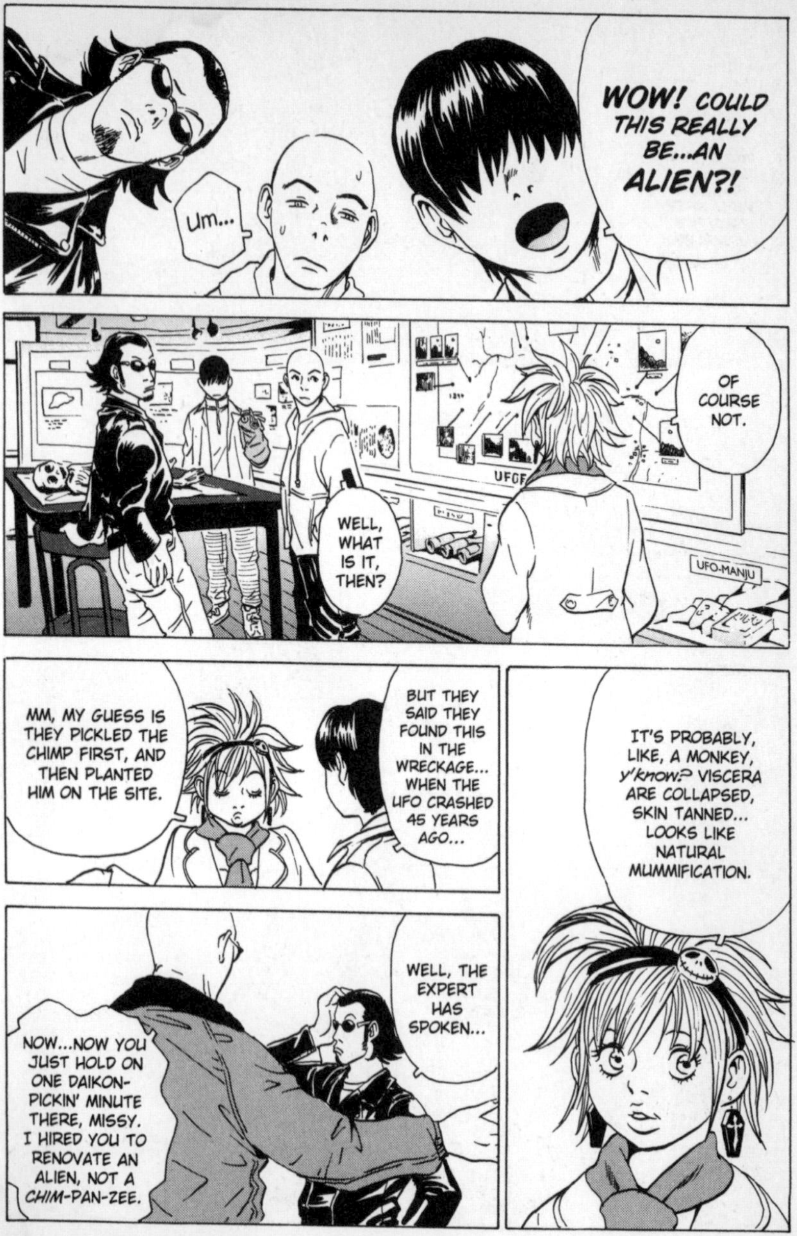
WOW! COULD THIS REALLY BE...AN ALIEN?!
Um...
OF COURSE NOT.
UFO-MANJU
WELL, WHAT IS IT, THEN?
IT'S PROBABLY, LIKE, A MONKEY, y'know? VISCERA ARE COLLAPSED, SKIN TANNED... LOOKS LIKE NATURAL MUMMIFICATION.
BUT THEY SAID THEY FOUND THIS IN THE WRECKAGE... WHEN THE UFO CRASHED 45 YEARS AGO...
MM, MY GUESS IS THEY PICKLED THE CHIMP FIRST, AND THEN PLANTED HIM ON THE SITE.
WELL, THE EXPERT HAS SPOKEN...
NOW...NOW YOU JUST HOLD ON ONE DAIKON-PICKIN' MINUTE THERE, MISSY. I HIRED YOU TO RENOVATE AN ALIEN, NOT A CHIM-PAN-ZEE.

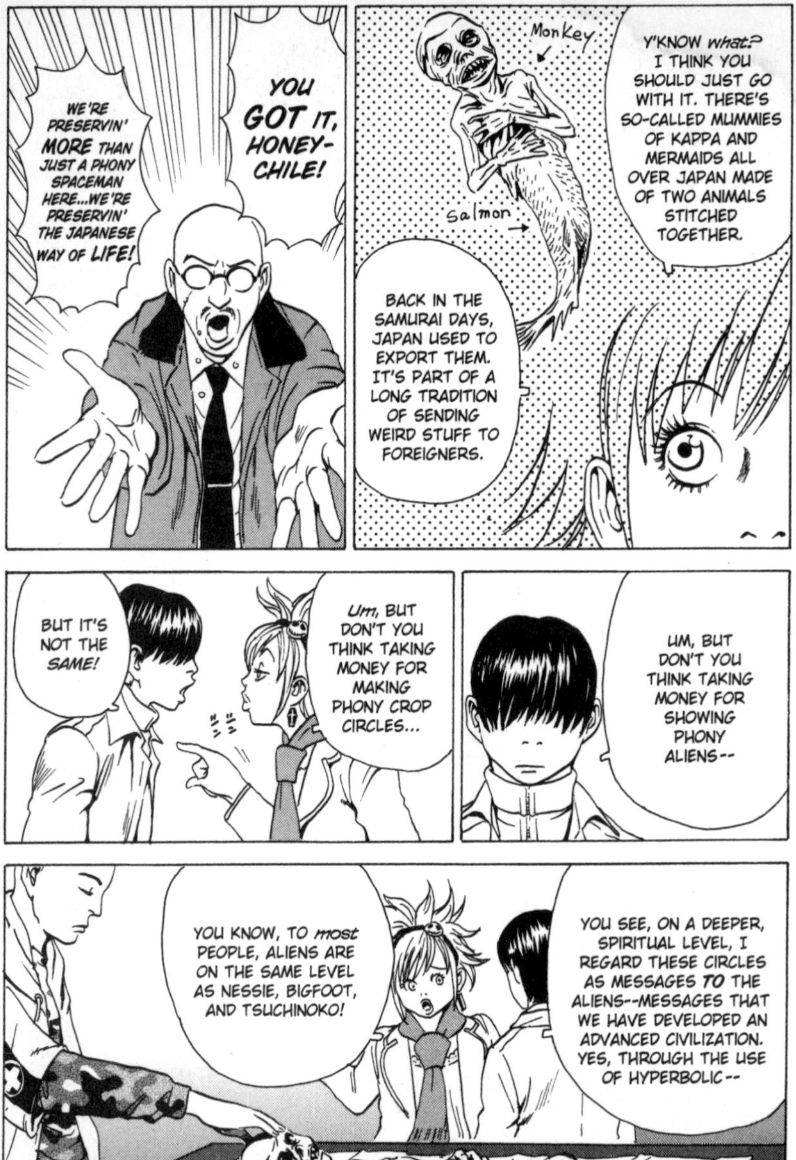
Y'KNOW *what?* I THINK YOU SHOULD JUST GO WITH IT. THERE'S SO-CALLED MUMMIES OF KAPPA AND MERMAIDS ALL OVER JAPAN MADE OF TWO ANIMALS STITCHED TOGETHER.
Monkey
Salmon
BACK IN THE SAMURAI DAYS, JAPAN USED TO EXPORT THEM. IT'S PART OF A LONG TRADITION OF SENDING WEIRD STUFF TO FOREIGNERS.
YOU GOT IT, HONEY-CHILE!
WE'RE PRESERVIN' MORE THAN JUST A PHONY SPACEMAN HERE...WE'RE PRESERVIN' THE JAPANESE WAY OF LIFE!
UM, BUT DON'T YOU THINK TAKING MONEY FOR SHOWING PHONY ALIENS--
Um, BUT DON'T YOU THINK TAKING MONEY FOR MAKING PHONY CROP CIRCLES...
BUT IT'S NOT THE *SAME!*
YOU SEE, ON A DEEPER, SPIRITUAL LEVEL, I REGARD THESE CIRCLES AS MESSAGES *TO* THE ALIENS--MESSAGES THAT WE HAVE DEVELOPED AN ADVANCED CIVILIZATION. YES, THROUGH THE USE OF HYPERBOLIC--
YOU KNOW, TO *most* PEOPLE, ALIENS ARE ON THE SAME LEVEL AS NESSIE, BIGFOOT, AND TSUCHINOKO!

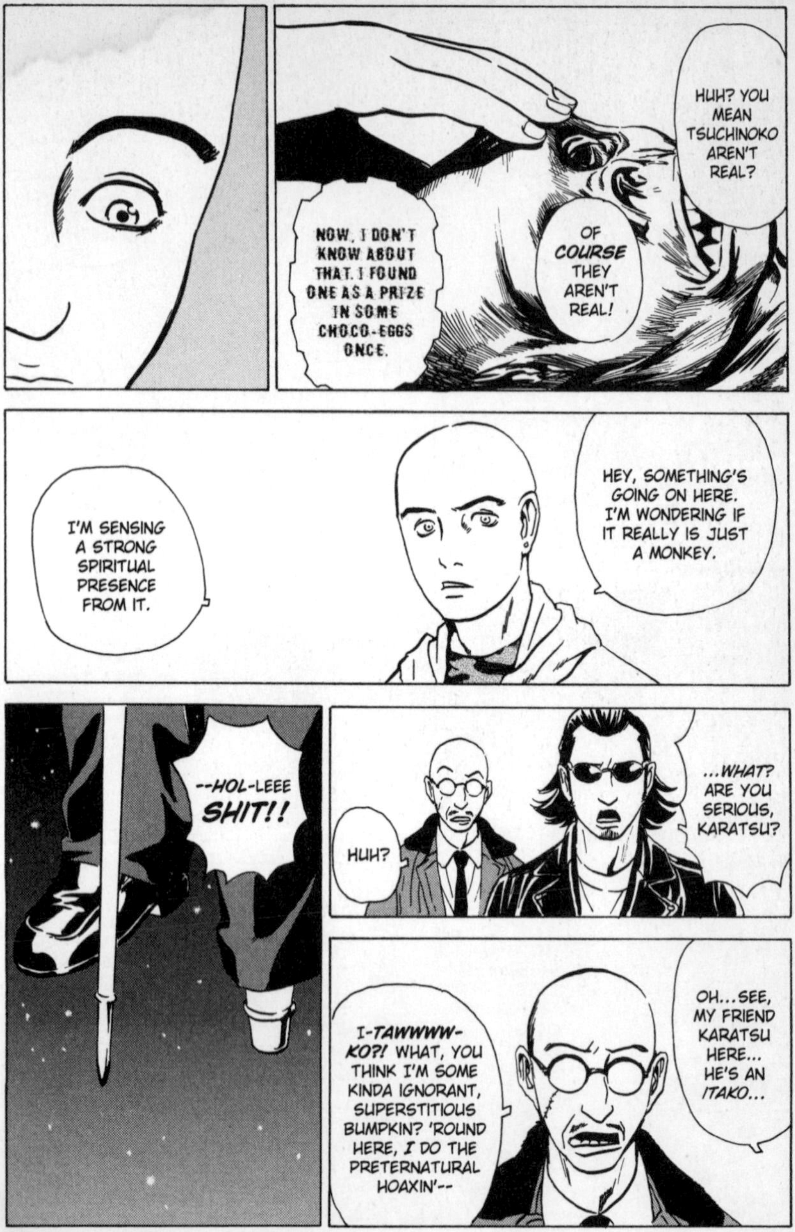
HUH? YOU MEAN TSUCHINOKO AREN'T REAL?
OF COURSE THEY AREN'T REAL!
NOW, I DON'T KNOW ABOUT THAT. I FOUND ONE AS A PRIZE IN SOME CHOCO-EGGS ONCE.
HEY, SOMETHING'S GOING ON HERE. I'M WONDERING IF IT REALLY IS JUST A MONKEY.
I'M SENSING A STRONG SPIRITUAL PRESENCE FROM IT.
...WHAT? ARE YOU SERIOUS, KARATSU?
HUH?
OH...SEE, MY FRIEND KARATSU HERE... HE'S AN ITAKO...
I-TAWWWW-KO?! WHAT, YOU THINK I'M SOME KINDA IGNORANT, SUPERSTITIOUS BUMPKIN? 'ROUND HERE, I DO THE PRETERNATURAL HOAXIN'--
--HOL-LEEE SHIT!!

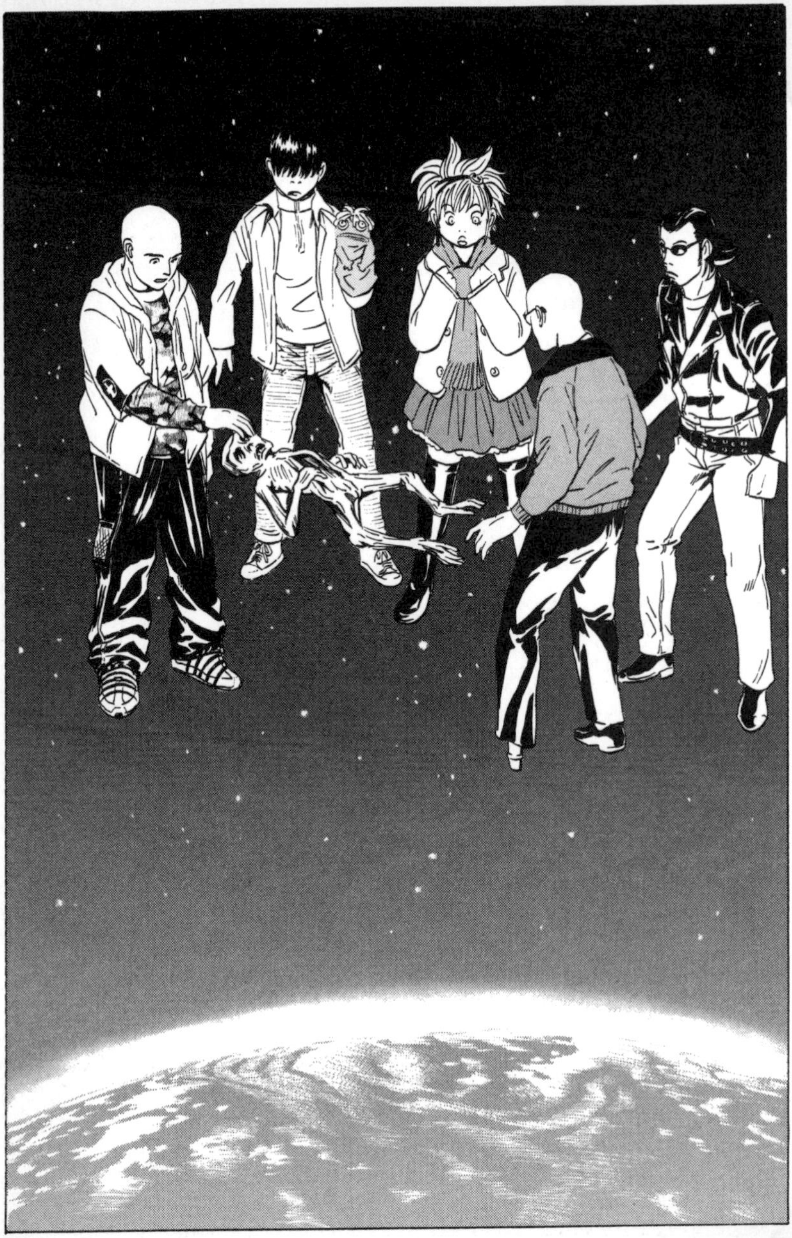

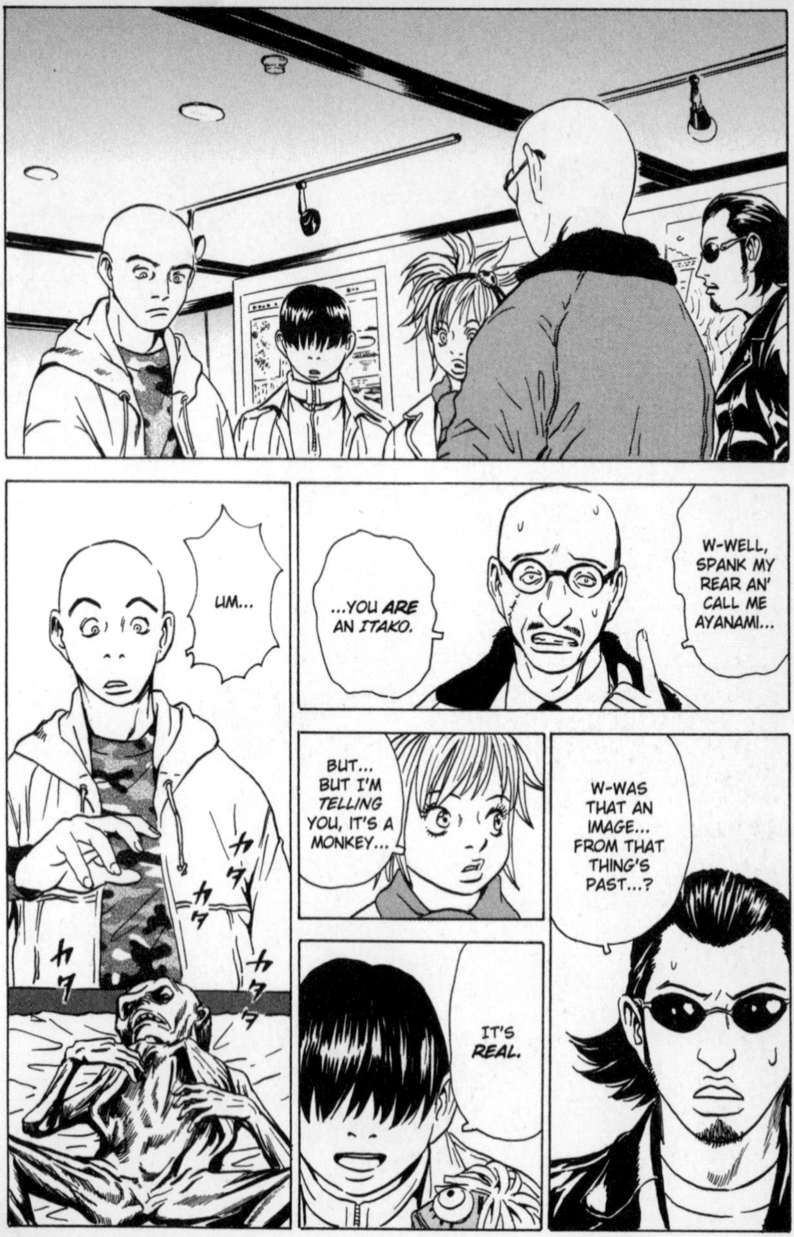
W-WELL, SPANK MY REAR AN' CALL ME AYANAMI...
...YOU *ARE* AN *ITAKO.*
W-WAS THAT AN IMAGE... FROM THAT THING'S PAST...?
BUT... BUT I'M *TELLING* YOU, IT'S A MONKEY...
IT'S *REAL.*
UM...
カタ
カタ
カタ
カタタ

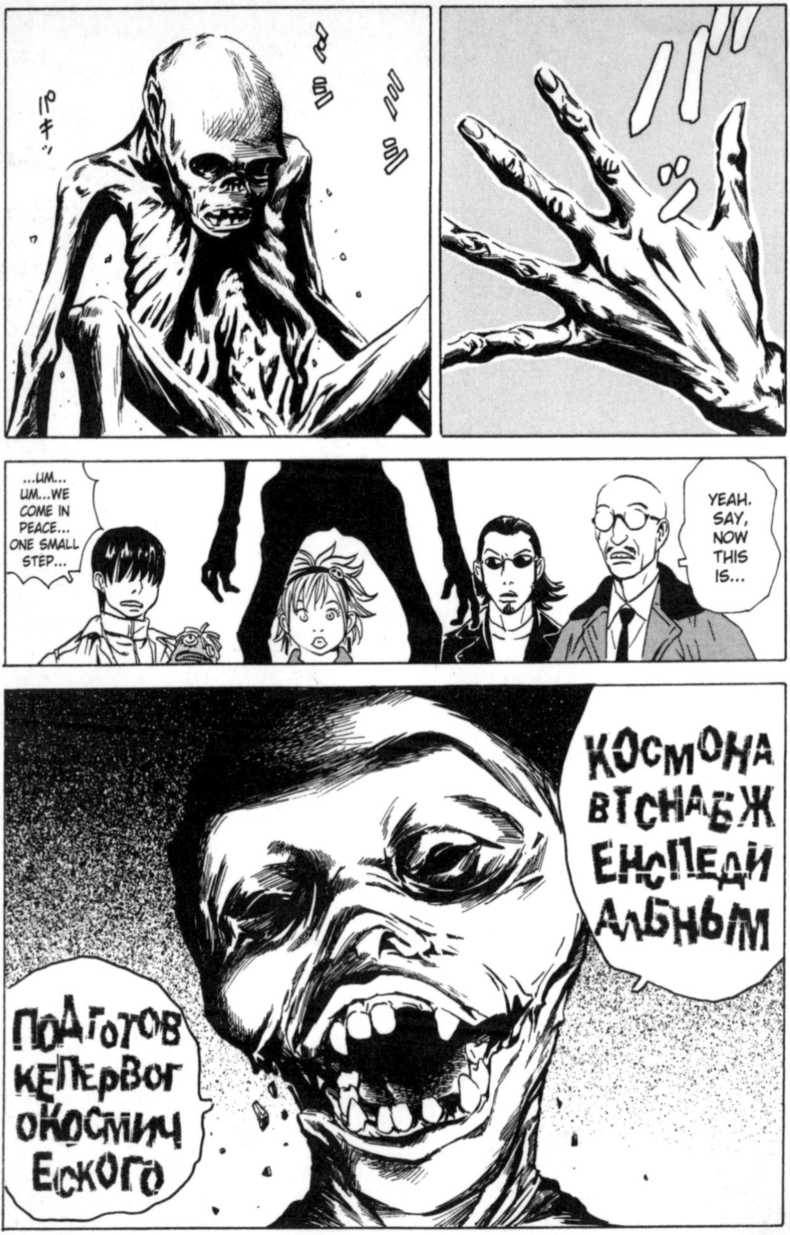
パキッ
YEAH. SAY, NOW THIS IS...
...UM... UM...WE COME IN PEACE... ONE SMALL STEP...
КОСМОНА ВТСНАБЖ ЕНСПЕДИ АЛБНЫМ
ПОДГОТОВ КЕПЕРВОГ ОКОСМИЧ ЕСКОГО

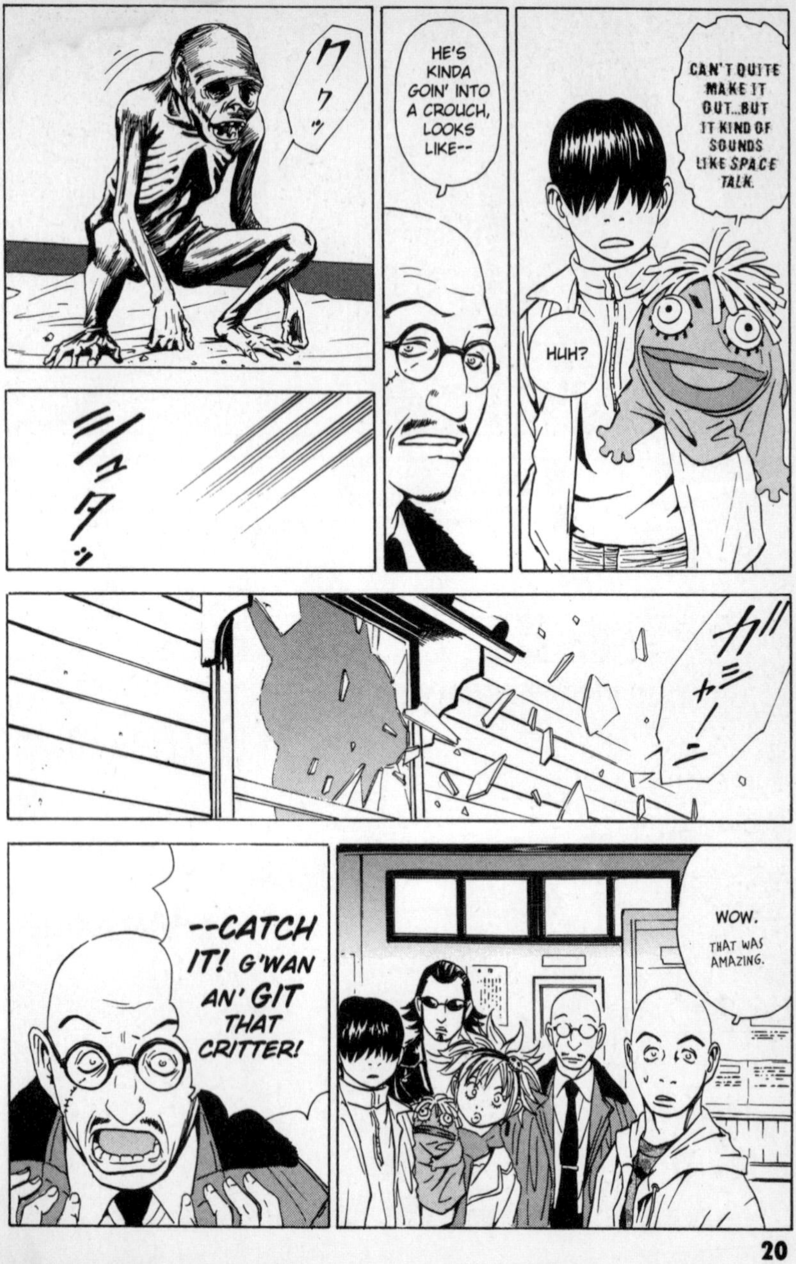
CAN'T QUITE MAKE IT OUT...BUT IT KIND OF SOUNDS LIKE SPACE TALK.
HUH?
HE'S KINDA GOIN' INTO A CROUCH, LOOKS LIKE--
シュタッ
ガシャーン
WOW. THAT WAS AMAZING.
--CATCH IT! G'WAN AN' GIT THAT CRITTER!

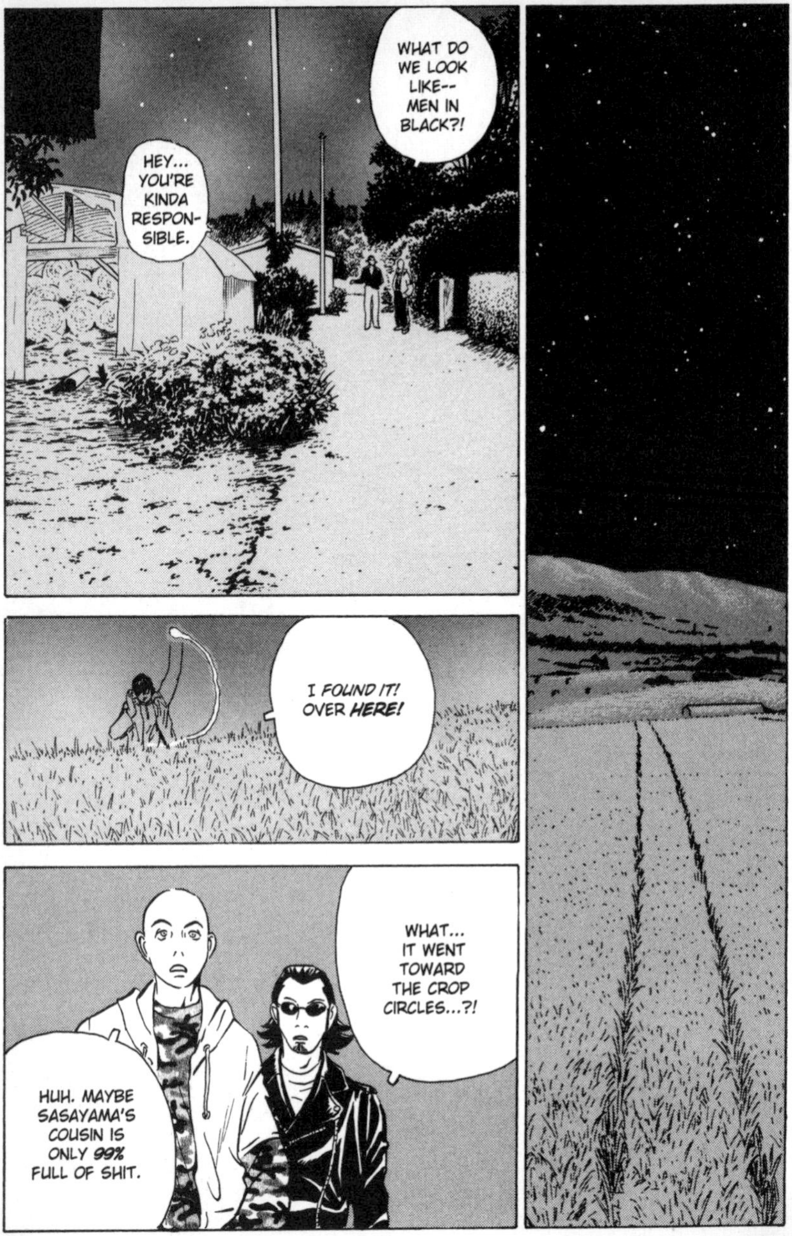
WHAT DO WE LOOK LIKE-- MEN IN BLACK?!
HEY... YOU'RE KINDA RESPON-SIBLE.
I *FOUND IT!* OVER ***HERE!***
WHAT... IT WENT TOWARD THE CROP CIRCLES...?!
HUH. MAYBE SASAYAMA'S COUSIN IS ONLY ***99%*** FULL OF SHIT.

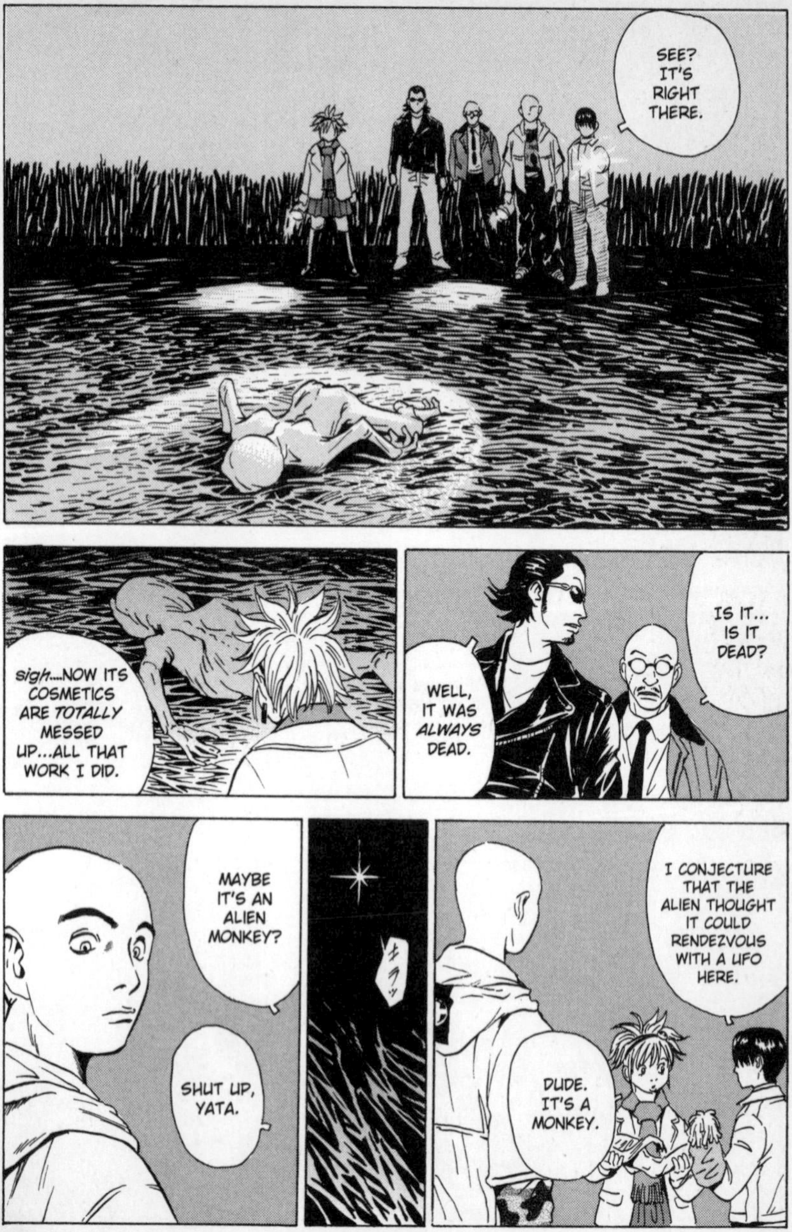
SEE? IT'S RIGHT THERE.
IS IT... IS IT DEAD?
WELL, IT WAS *ALWAYS* DEAD.
sigh....NOW ITS COSMETICS ARE *TOTALLY* MESSED UP...ALL THAT WORK I DID.
I CONJECTURE THAT THE ALIEN THOUGHT IT COULD RENDEZVOUS WITH A UFO HERE.
DUDE. IT'S A MONKEY.
キラッ
MAYBE IT'S AN ALIEN MONKEY?
SHUT UP, YATA.

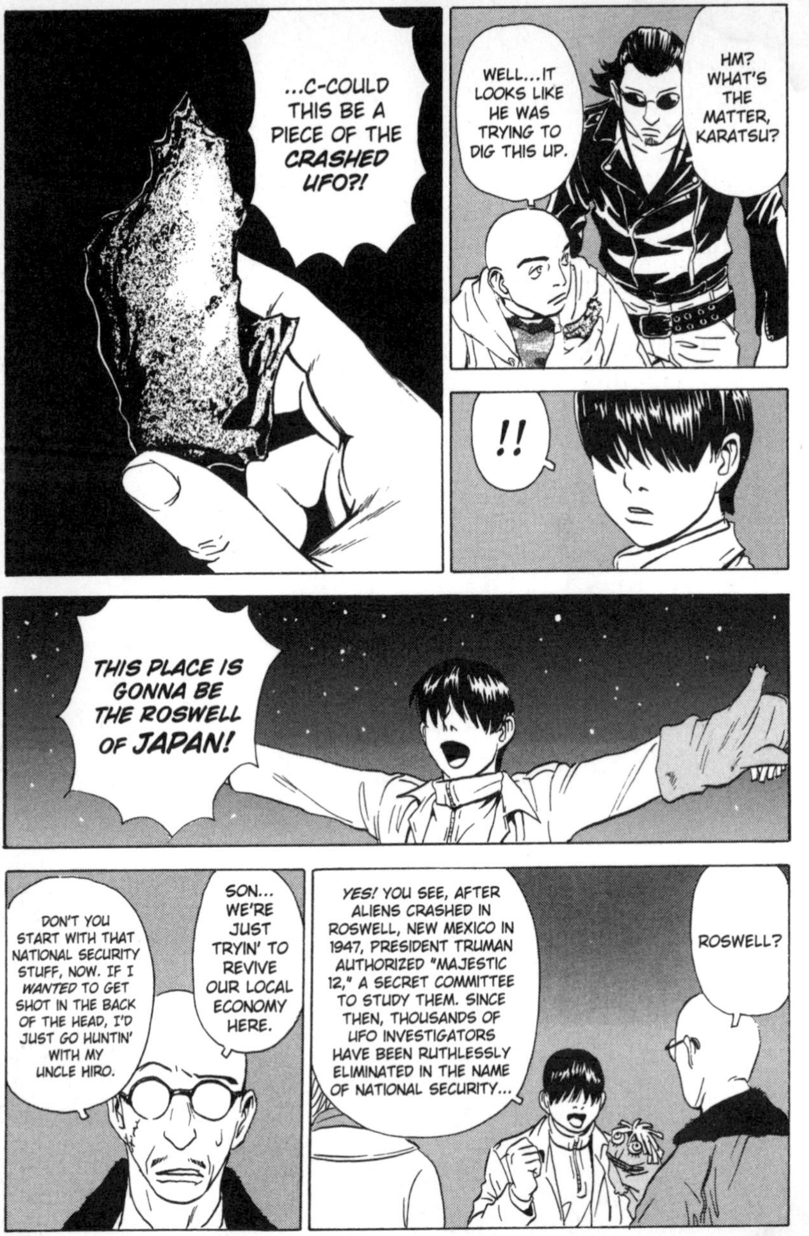
HM? WHAT'S THE MATTER, KARATSU?
WELL...IT LOOKS LIKE HE WAS TRYING TO DIG THIS UP.
!!
...C-COULD THIS BE A PIECE OF THE CRASHED UFO?!
THIS PLACE IS GONNA BE THE ROSWELL OF JAPAN!
ROSWELL?
YES! YOU SEE, AFTER ALIENS CRASHED IN ROSWELL, NEW MEXICO IN 1947, PRESIDENT TRUMAN AUTHORIZED "MAJESTIC 12," A SECRET COMMITTEE TO STUDY THEM. SINCE THEN, THOUSANDS OF UFO INVESTIGATORS HAVE BEEN RUTHLESSLY ELIMINATED IN THE NAME OF NATIONAL SECURITY...
SON... WE'RE JUST TRYIN' TO REVIVE OUR LOCAL ECONOMY HERE.
DON'T YOU START WITH THAT NATIONAL SECURITY STUFF, NOW. IF I WANTED TO GET SHOT IN THE BACK OF THE HEAD, I'D JUST GO HUNTIN' WITH MY UNCLE HIRO.

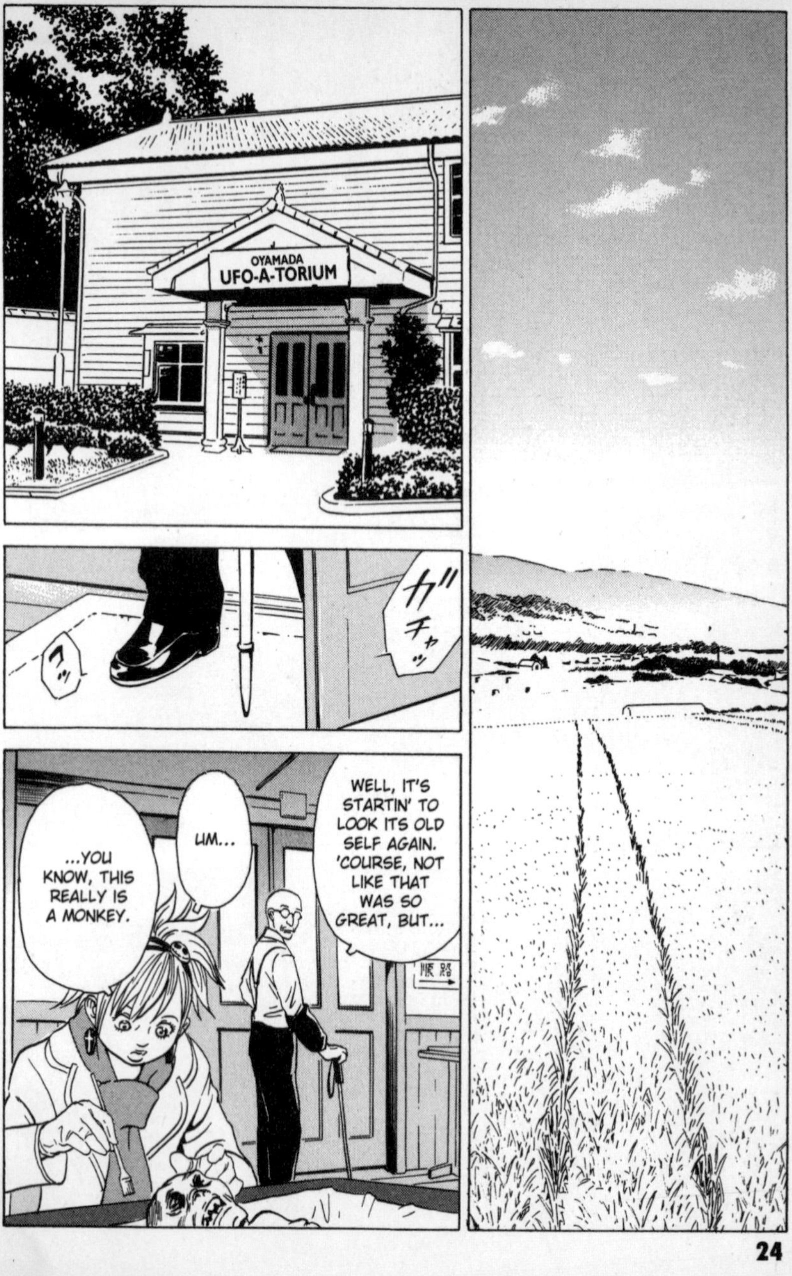
OYAMADA
UFO-A-TORIUM
ガチャッ
フッ
WELL, IT'S STARTIN' TO LOOK ITS OLD SELF AGAIN. 'COURSE, NOT LIKE THAT WAS SO GREAT, BUT...
UM...
...YOU KNOW, THIS REALLY IS A MONKEY.
順路

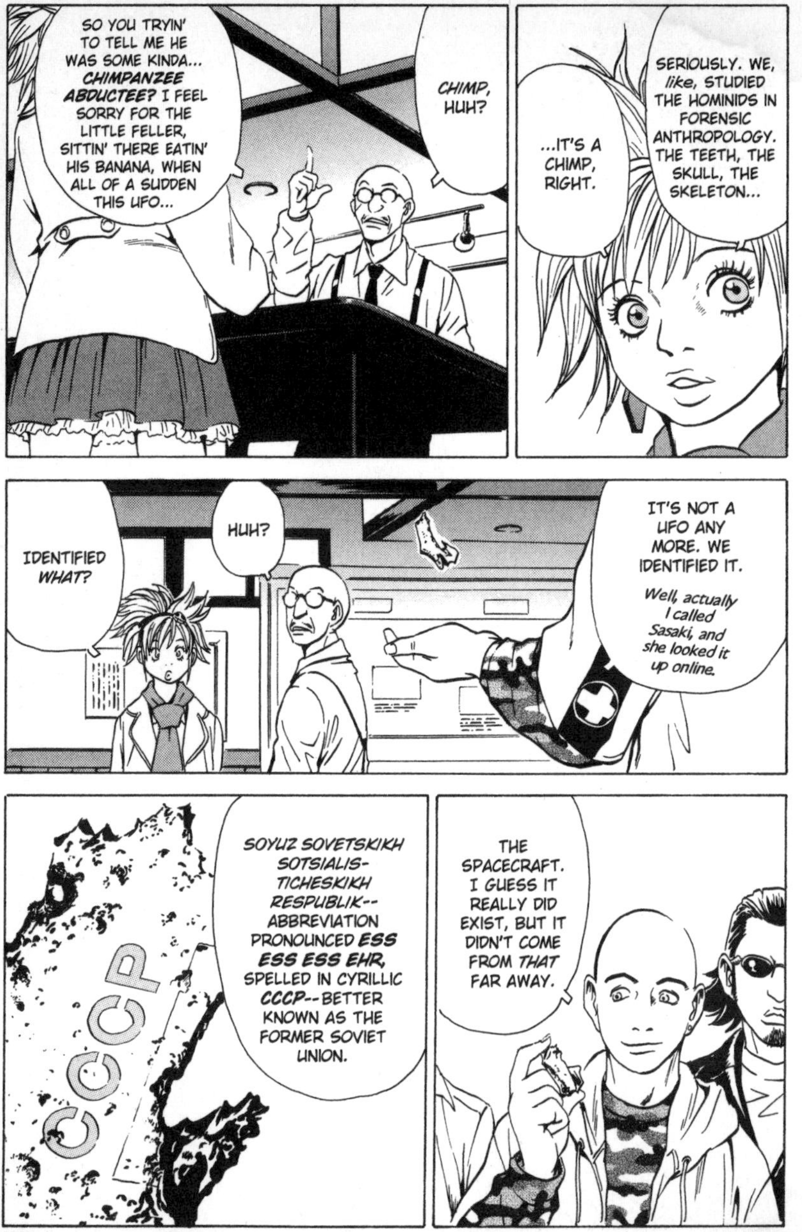
SERIOUSLY. WE, *like*, STUDIED THE HOMINIDS IN FORENSIC ANTHROPOLOGY. THE TEETH, THE SKULL, THE SKELETON...
...IT'S A CHIMP, RIGHT.
CHIMP, HUH?
SO YOU TRYIN' TO TELL ME HE WAS SOME KINDA... ***CHIMPANZEE ABDUCTEE?*** I FEEL SORRY FOR THE LITTLE FELLER, SITTIN' THERE EATIN' HIS BANANA, WHEN ALL OF A SUDDEN THIS UFO...
IT'S NOT A UFO ANY MORE. WE IDENTIFIED IT.
Well, actually I called Sasaki, and she looked it up online.
HUH?
IDENTIFIED *WHAT?*
THE SPACECRAFT. I GUESS IT REALLY DID EXIST, BUT IT DIDN'T COME FROM *THAT* FAR AWAY.
SOYUZ SOVETSKIKH SOTSIALIS-TICHESKIKH RESPUBLIK--ABBREVIATION PRONOUNCED ***ESS ESS ESS EHR,*** SPELLED IN CYRILLIC ***CCCP***--BETTER KNOWN AS THE FORMER SOVIET UNION.
CCCP

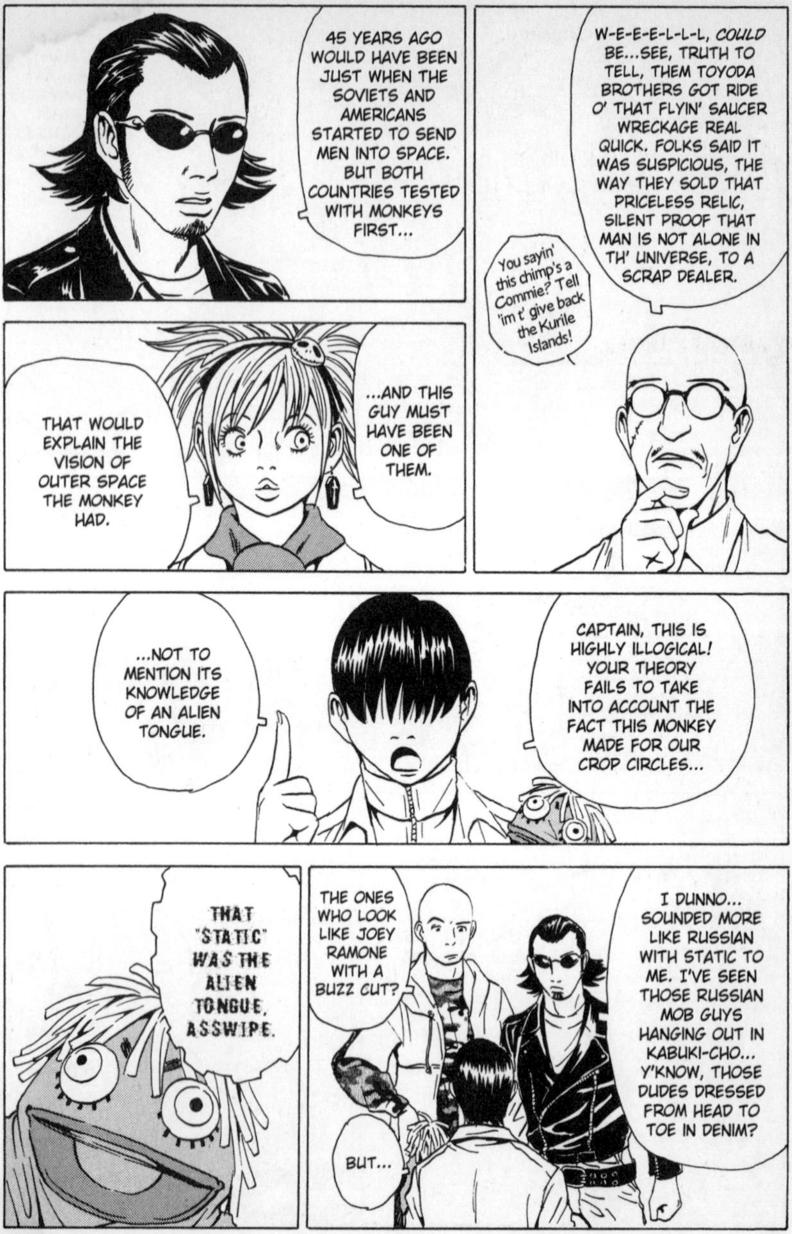
W-E-E-E-L-L-L, *COULD* BE...SEE, TRUTH TO TELL, THEM TOYODA BROTHERS GOT RIDE O' THAT FLYIN' SAUCER WRECKAGE REAL QUICK. FOLKS SAID IT WAS SUSPICIOUS, THE WAY THEY SOLD THAT PRICELESS RELIC, SILENT PROOF THAT MAN IS NOT ALONE IN TH' UNIVERSE, TO A SCRAP DEALER.
You sayin' this chimp's a Commie? Tell 'im t' give back the Kurile Islands!
45 YEARS AGO WOULD HAVE BEEN JUST WHEN THE SOVIETS AND AMERICANS STARTED TO SEND MEN INTO SPACE. BUT BOTH COUNTRIES TESTED WITH MONKEYS FIRST...
...AND THIS GUY MUST HAVE BEEN ONE OF THEM.
THAT WOULD EXPLAIN THE VISION OF OUTER SPACE THE MONKEY HAD.
CAPTAIN, THIS IS HIGHLY ILLOGICAL! YOUR THEORY FAILS TO TAKE INTO ACCOUNT THE FACT THIS MONKEY MADE FOR OUR CROP CIRCLES...
...NOT TO MENTION ITS KNOWLEDGE OF AN ALIEN TONGUE.
I DUNNO... SOUNDED MORE LIKE RUSSIAN WITH STATIC TO ME. I'VE SEEN THOSE RUSSIAN MOB GUYS HANGING OUT IN KABUKI-CHO... Y'KNOW, THOSE DUDES DRESSED FROM HEAD TO TOE IN DENIM?
THE ONES WHO LOOK LIKE JOEY RAMONE WITH A BUZZ CUT?
BUT...
THAT "STATIC" WAS THE ALIEN TONGUE, ASSWIPE.

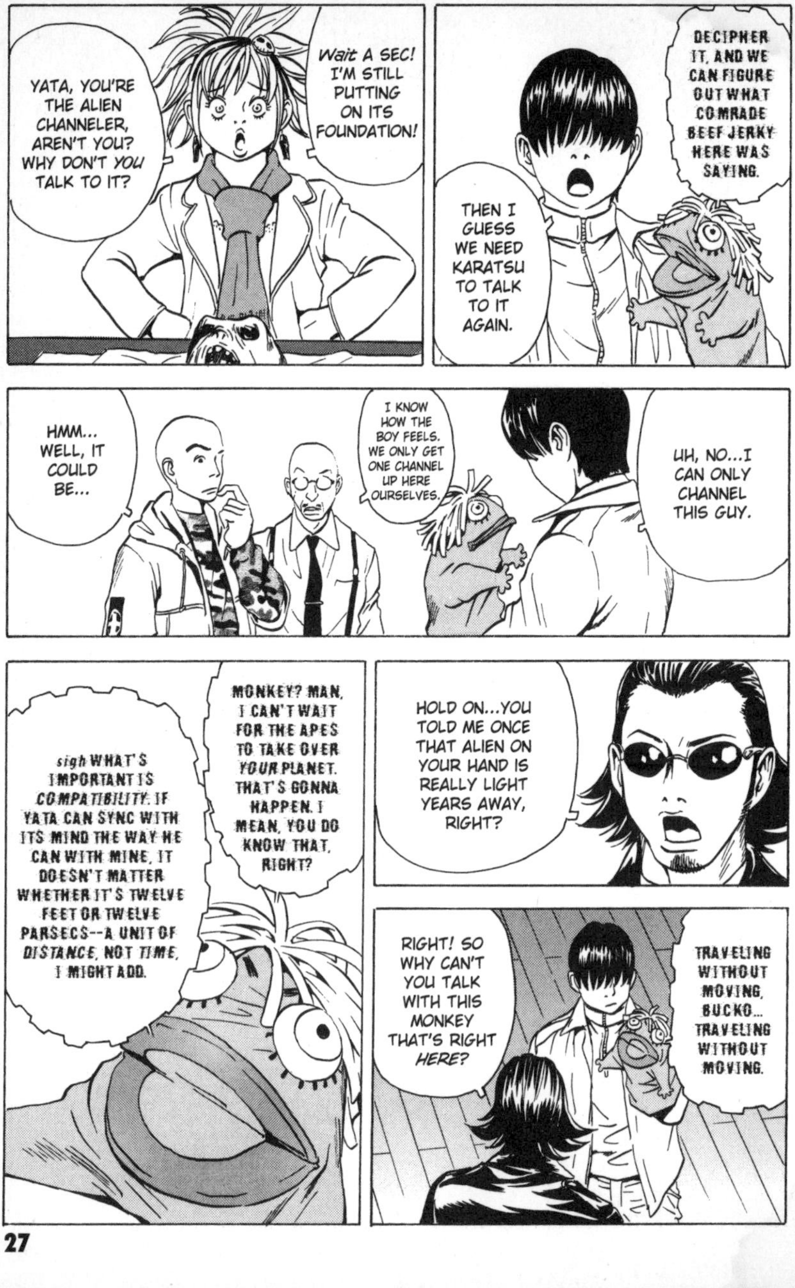
DECIPHER IT, AND WE CAN FIGURE OUT WHAT COMRADE BEEF JERKY HERE WAS SAYING.
THEN I GUESS WE NEED KARATSU TO TALK TO IT AGAIN.
Wait A SEC! I'M STILL PUTTING ON ITS FOUNDATION!
YATA, YOU'RE THE ALIEN CHANNELER, AREN'T YOU? WHY DON'T *YOU* TALK TO IT?
UH, NO...I CAN ONLY CHANNEL THIS GUY.
I KNOW HOW THE BOY FEELS. WE ONLY GET ONE CHANNEL UP HERE OURSELVES.
HMM... WELL, IT COULD BE...
HOLD ON...YOU TOLD ME ONCE THAT ALIEN ON YOUR HAND IS REALLY LIGHT YEARS AWAY, RIGHT?
TRAVELING WITHOUT MOVING, BUCKO... TRAVELING WITHOUT MOVING.
RIGHT! SO WHY CAN'T YOU TALK WITH THIS MONKEY THAT'S RIGHT *HERE*?
MONKEY? MAN, I CAN'T WAIT FOR THE APES TO TAKE OVER *YOUR* PLANET. THAT'S GONNA HAPPEN. I MEAN, YOU DO KNOW THAT, RIGHT?
sigh WHAT'S IMPORTANT IS *COMPATIBILITY*. IF YATA CAN SYNC WITH ITS MIND THE WAY HE CAN WITH MINE, IT DOESN'T MATTER WHETHER IT'S TWELVE FEET OR TWELVE PARSECS--A UNIT OF *DISTANCE*, NOT *TIME*, I MIGHT ADD.

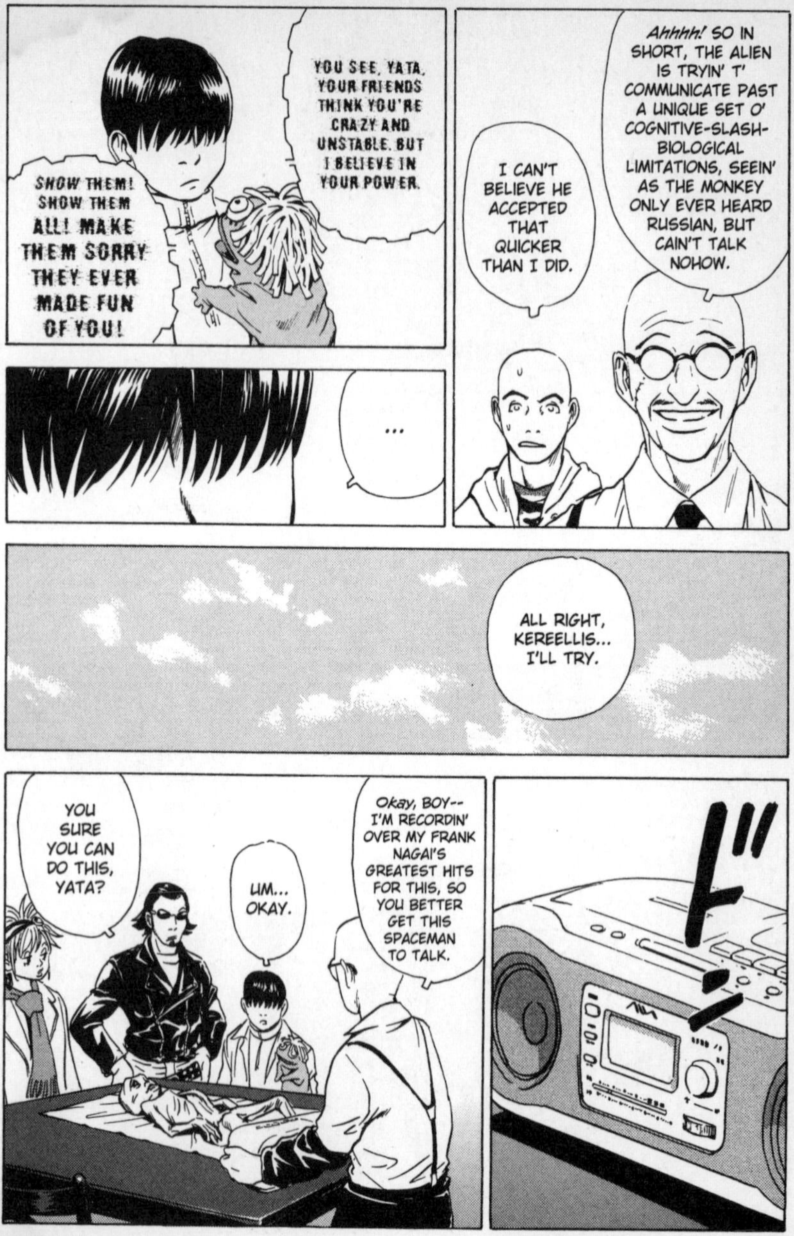

Ahhhh! SO IN SHORT, THE ALIEN IS TRYIN' T' COMMUNICATE PAST A UNIQUE SET O' COGNITIVE-SLASH-BIOLOGICAL LIMITATIONS, SEEIN' AS THE MONKEY ONLY EVER HEARD RUSSIAN, BUT CAIN'T TALK NOHOW.
I CAN'T BELIEVE HE ACCEPTED THAT QUICKER THAN I DID.
YOU SEE, YATA, YOUR FRIENDS THINK YOU'RE CRAZY AND UNSTABLE. BUT I BELIEVE IN YOUR POWER.
SHOW THEM! SHOW THEM ALL! MAKE THEM SORRY THEY EVER MADE FUN OF YOU!
...
ALL RIGHT, KEREELLIS... I'LL TRY.
ド
Okay, BOY-- I'M RECORDIN' OVER MY FRANK NAGAI'S GREATEST HITS FOR THIS, SO YOU BETTER GET THIS SPACEMAN TO TALK.
UM... OKAY.
YOU SURE YOU CAN DO THIS, YATA?

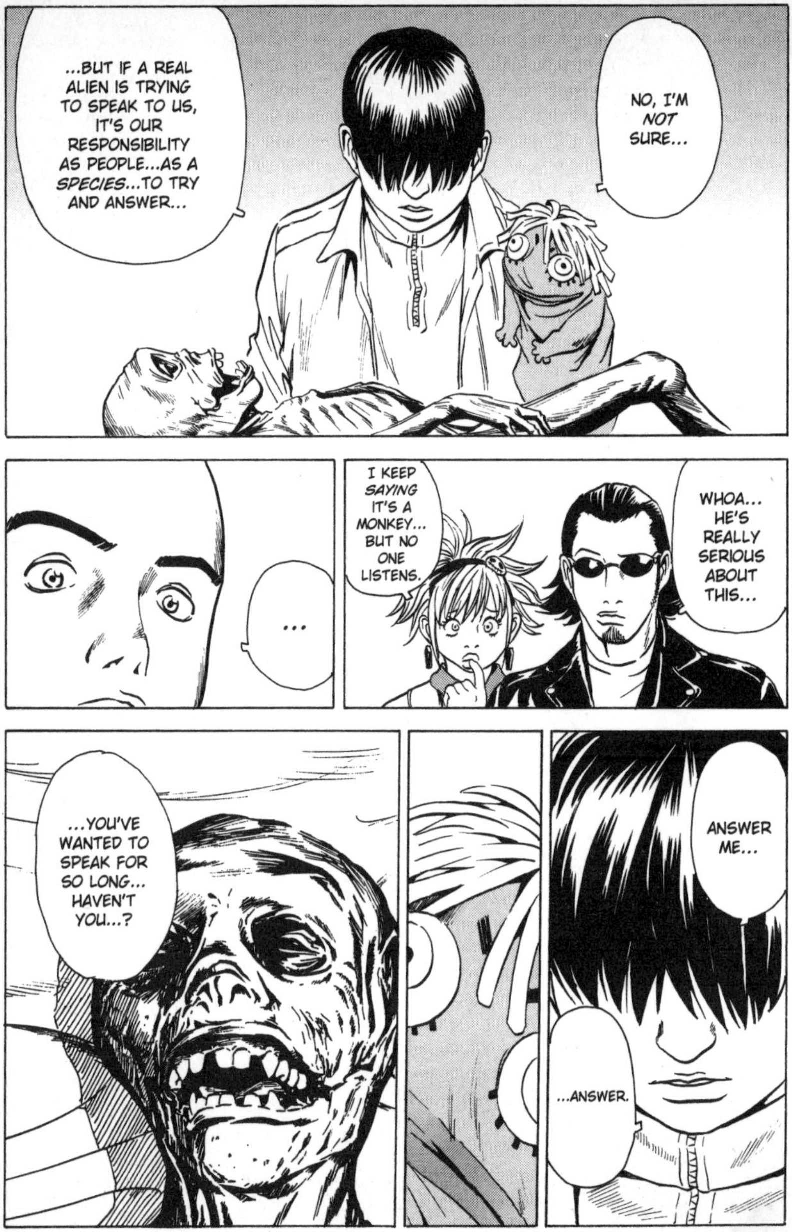
NO, I'M NOT SURE...
...BUT IF A REAL ALIEN IS TRYING TO SPEAK TO US, IT'S OUR RESPONSIBILITY AS PEOPLE...AS A SPECIES...TO TRY AND ANSWER...
WHOA... HE'S REALLY SERIOUS ABOUT THIS...
I KEEP SAYING IT'S A MONKEY... BUT NO ONE LISTENS.
...
ANSWER ME...
...ANSWER.
...YOU'VE WANTED TO SPEAK FOR SO LONG... HAVEN'T YOU...?

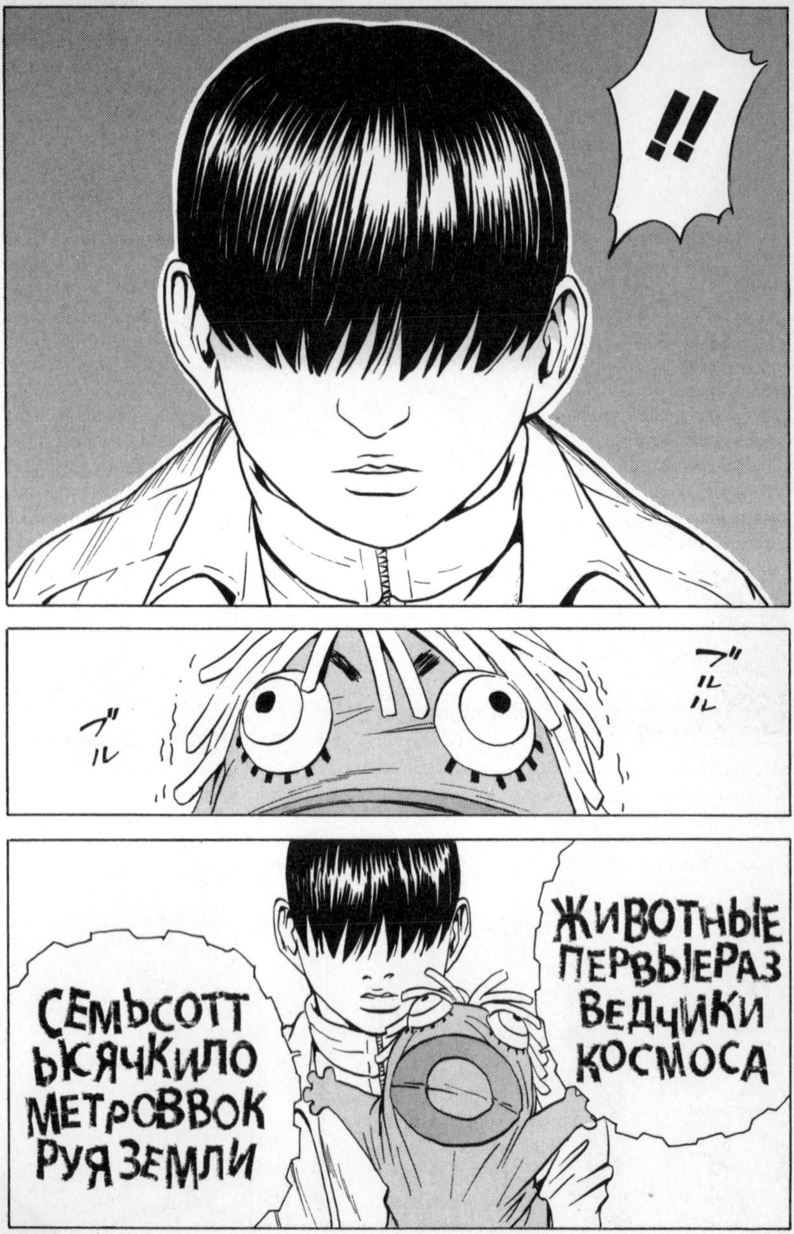
!!
ブルル
ブル
ЖИВОТНЫЕ ПЕРВЫЕРАЗ ВЕДЧИКИ КОСМОСА
СЕМЬСОТТ ЫСЯЧКИЛО МЕТРОВВОК РУЯЗЕМЛИ

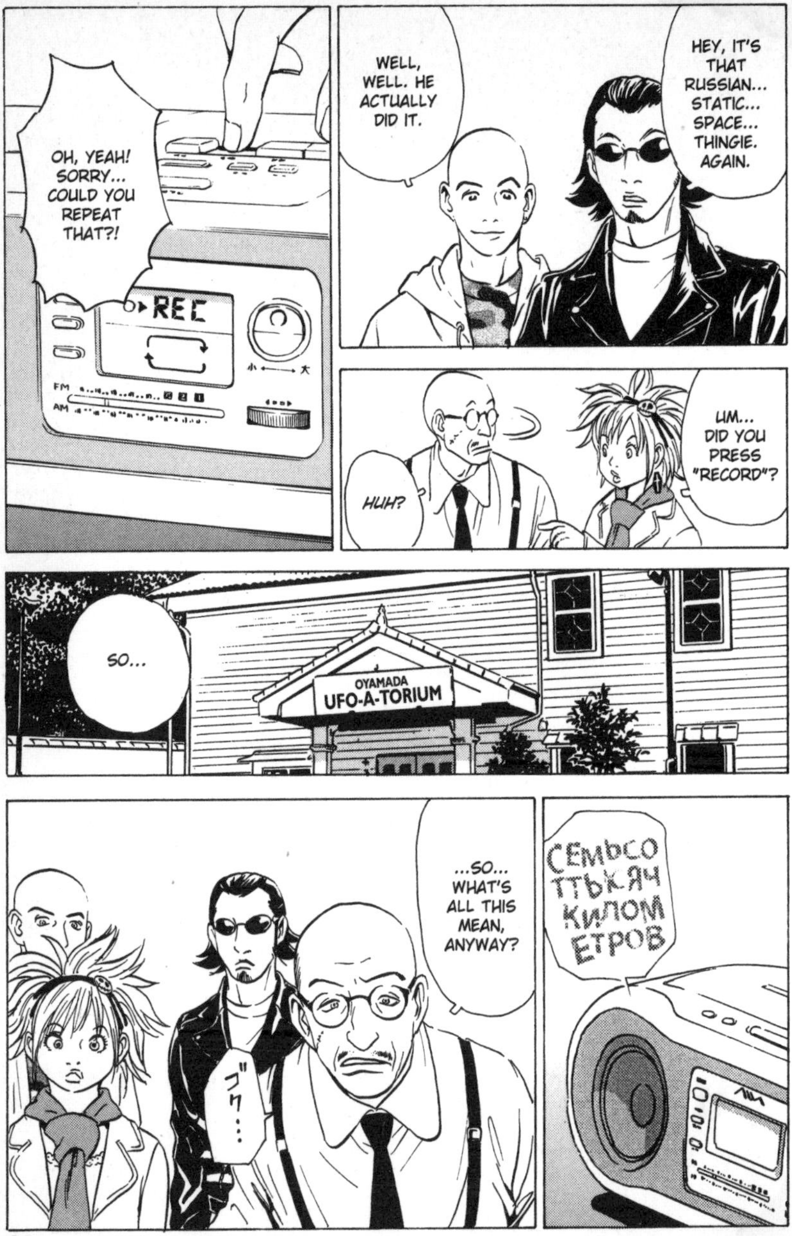
HEY, IT'S THAT RUSSIAN... STATIC... SPACE... THINGIE. AGAIN.
WELL, WELL. HE ACTUALLY DID IT.
UM... DID YOU PRESS "RECORD"?
HUH?
OH, YEAH! SORRY... COULD YOU REPEAT THAT?!
REC
SO...
OYAMADA UFO-A-TORIUM
СЕМЬСО ТТЬКЯЧ КИЛОМ ЕТРОВ
...SO... WHAT'S ALL THIS MEAN, ANYWAY?
ゴク…

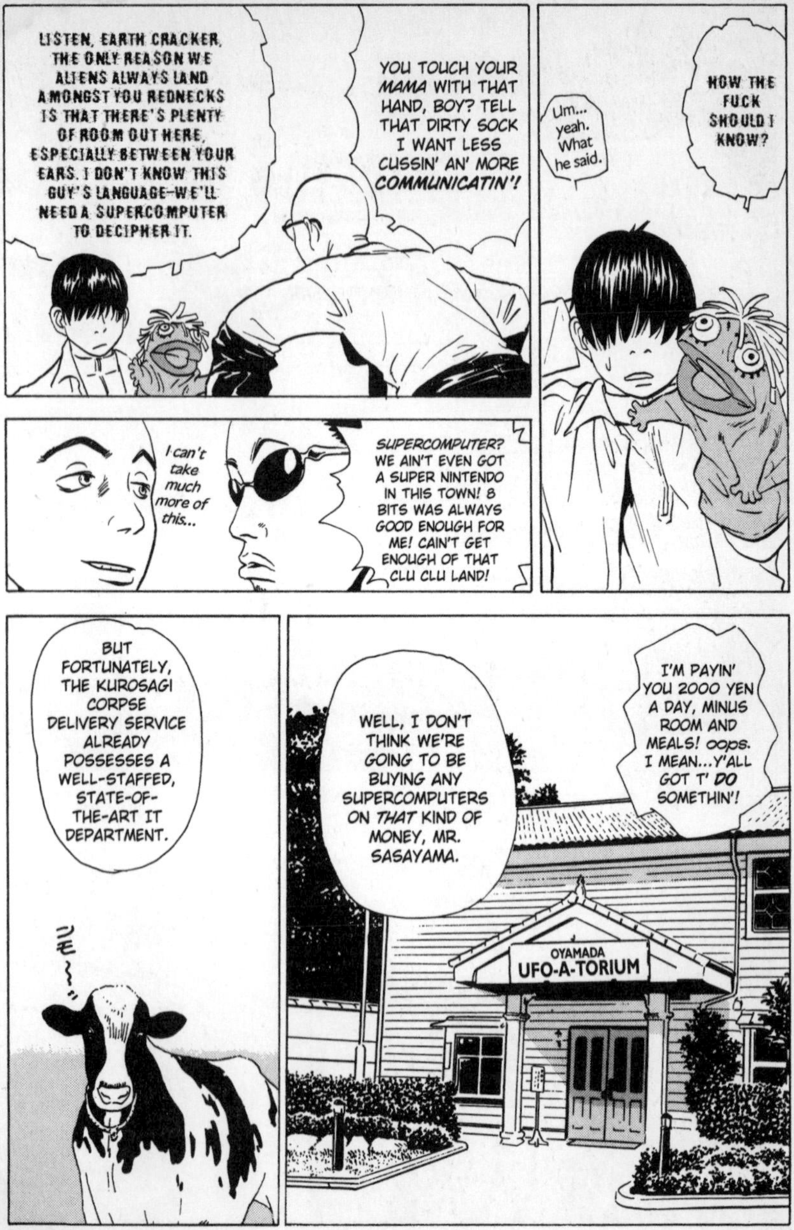

HOW THE FUCK SHOULD I KNOW?
Um... yeah. What he said.
YOU TOUCH YOUR *MAMA* WITH THAT HAND, BOY? TELL THAT DIRTY SOCK I WANT LESS CUSSIN' AN' MORE **COMMUNICATIN'**!
LISTEN, EARTH CRACKER, THE ONLY REASON WE ALIENS ALWAYS LAND AMONGST YOU REDNECKS IS THAT THERE'S PLENTY OF ROOM OUT HERE, ESPECIALLY BETWEEN YOUR EARS. I DON'T KNOW THIS GUY'S LANGUAGE—WE'LL NEED A SUPERCOMPUTER TO DECIPHER IT.
SUPERCOMPUTER? WE AIN'T EVEN GOT A SUPER NINTENDO IN THIS TOWN! 8 BITS WAS ALWAYS GOOD ENOUGH FOR ME! CAIN'T GET ENOUGH OF THAT CLU CLU LAND!
I can't take much more of this...
I'M PAYIN' YOU 2000 YEN A DAY, MINUS ROOM AND MEALS! *oops.* I MEAN...Y'ALL GOT T' *DO* SOMETHIN'!
WELL, I DON'T THINK WE'RE GOING TO BE BUYING ANY SUPERCOMPUTERS ON *THAT* KIND OF MONEY, MR. SASAYAMA.
OYAMADA
UFO-A-TORIUM
BUT FORTUNATELY, THE KUROSAGI CORPSE DELIVERY SERVICE ALREADY POSSESSES A WELL-STAFFED, STATE-OF-THE-ART IT DEPARTMENT.
ンモ～～

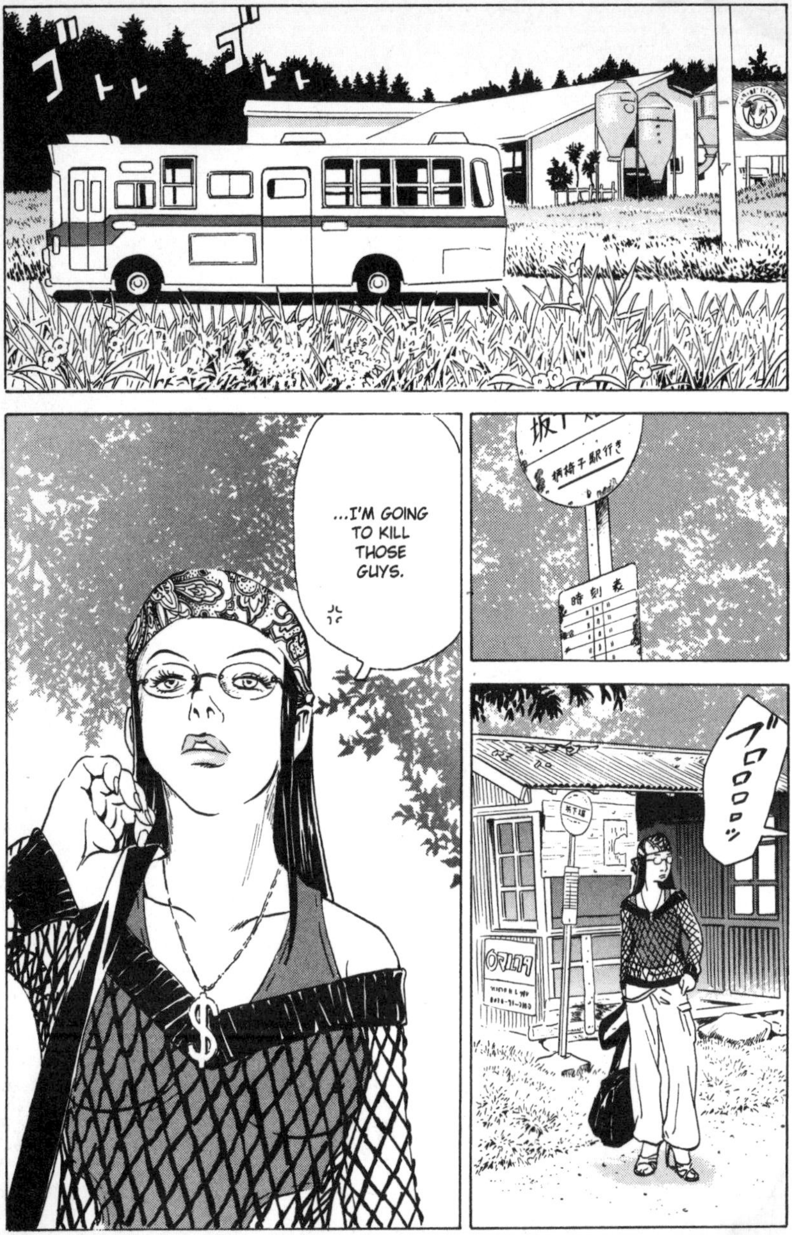
ゴトト
ゴトト
時刻表
ブロロロロッ
...I'M GOING TO KILL THOSE GUYS.

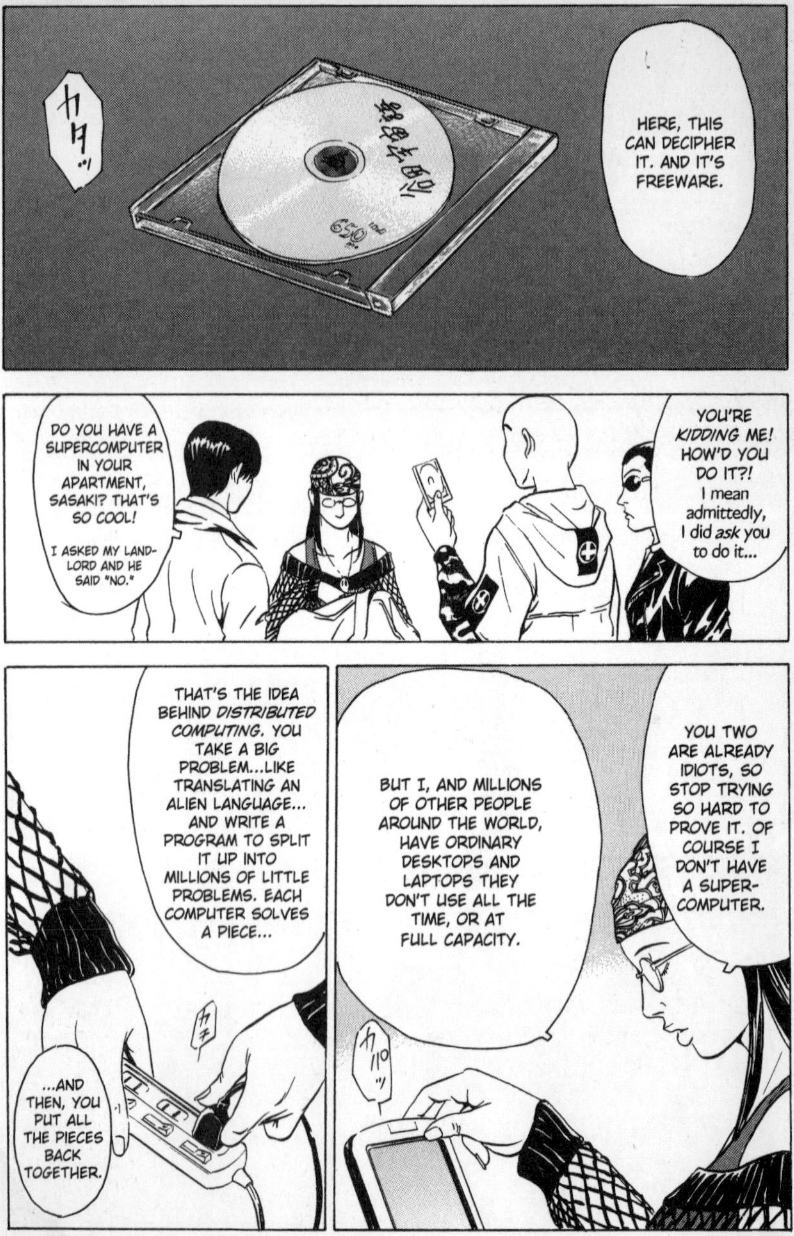

HERE, THIS CAN DECIPHER IT. AND IT'S FREEWARE.
カタッ
YOU'RE *KIDDING* ME! HOW'D YOU DO IT?! I mean admittedly, I did *ask* you to do it...
DO YOU HAVE A SUPERCOMPUTER IN YOUR APARTMENT, SASAKI? THAT'S SO COOL!
I ASKED MY LANDLORD AND HE SAID "NO."
YOU TWO ARE ALREADY IDIOTS, SO STOP TRYING SO HARD TO PROVE IT. OF COURSE I DON'T HAVE A SUPER-COMPUTER.
BUT I, AND MILLIONS OF OTHER PEOPLE AROUND THE WORLD, HAVE ORDINARY DESKTOPS AND LAPTOPS THEY DON'T USE ALL THE TIME, OR AT FULL CAPACITY.
THAT'S THE IDEA BEHIND *DISTRIBUTED COMPUTING*. YOU TAKE A BIG PROBLEM...LIKE TRANSLATING AN ALIEN LANGUAGE... AND WRITE A PROGRAM TO SPLIT IT UP INTO MILLIONS OF LITTLE PROBLEMS. EACH COMPUTER SOLVES A PIECE...
...AND THEN, YOU PUT ALL THE PIECES BACK TOGETHER.

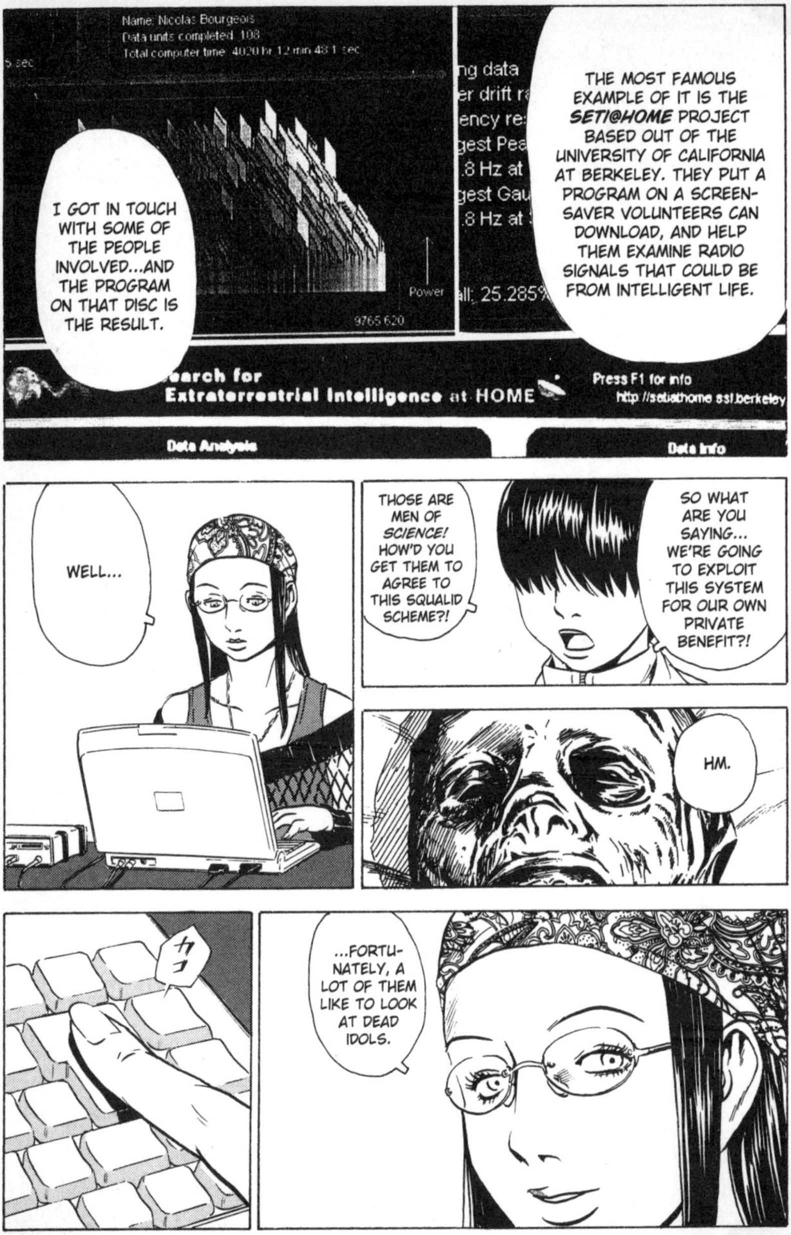
Name: Nicolas Bourgeois
Data units completed: 108
Total computer time: 4020 hr 12 min 43.1 sec
THE MOST FAMOUS EXAMPLE OF IT IS THE ***SETI@HOME*** PROJECT BASED OUT OF THE UNIVERSITY OF CALIFORNIA AT BERKELEY. THEY PUT A PROGRAM ON A SCREEN-SAVER VOLUNTEERS CAN DOWNLOAD, AND HELP THEM EXAMINE RADIO SIGNALS THAT COULD BE FROM INTELLIGENT LIFE.
I GOT IN TOUCH WITH SOME OF THE PEOPLE INVOLVED...AND THE PROGRAM ON THAT DISC IS THE RESULT.
Power
Extraterrestrial Intelligence at HOME
Press F1 for info
Data Analysis
Data Info
SO WHAT ARE YOU SAYING... WE'RE GOING TO EXPLOIT THIS SYSTEM FOR OUR OWN PRIVATE BENEFIT?!
THOSE ARE MEN OF *SCIENCE!* HOW'D YOU GET THEM TO AGREE TO THIS SQUALID SCHEME?!
HM.
WELL...
...FORTU-NATELY, A LOT OF THEM LIKE TO LOOK AT DEAD IDOLS.
カコ

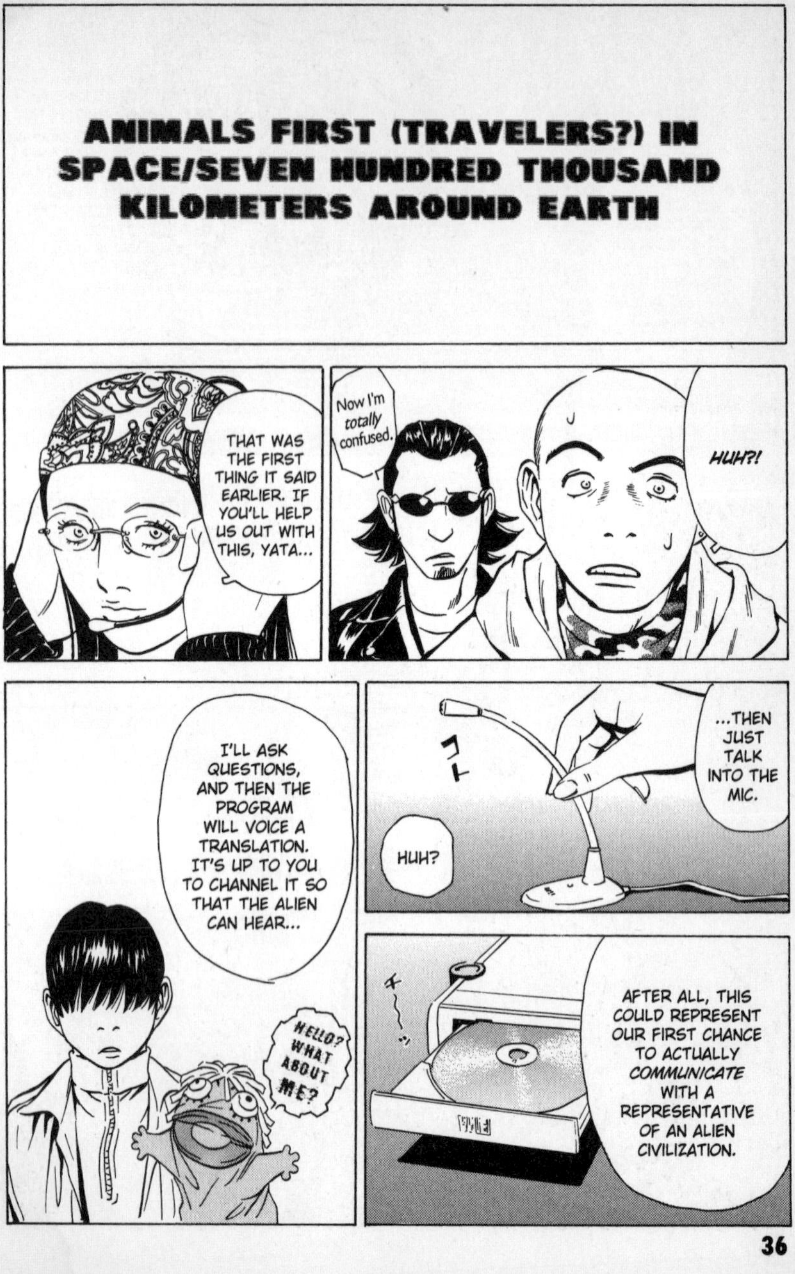
ANIMALS FIRST (TRAVELERS?) IN SPACE/SEVEN HUNDRED THOUSAND KILOMETERS AROUND EARTH
HUH?!
Now I'm *totally* confused.
THAT WAS THE FIRST THING IT SAID EARLIER. IF YOU'LL HELP US OUT WITH THIS, YATA...
...THEN JUST TALK INTO THE MIC.
HUH?
AFTER ALL, THIS COULD REPRESENT OUR FIRST CHANCE TO ACTUALLY *COMMUNICATE* WITH A REPRESENTATIVE OF AN ALIEN CIVILIZATION.
I'LL ASK QUESTIONS, AND THEN THE PROGRAM WILL VOICE A TRANSLATION. IT'S UP TO YOU TO CHANNEL IT SO THAT THE ALIEN CAN HEAR...
HELLO? WHAT ABOUT ME?

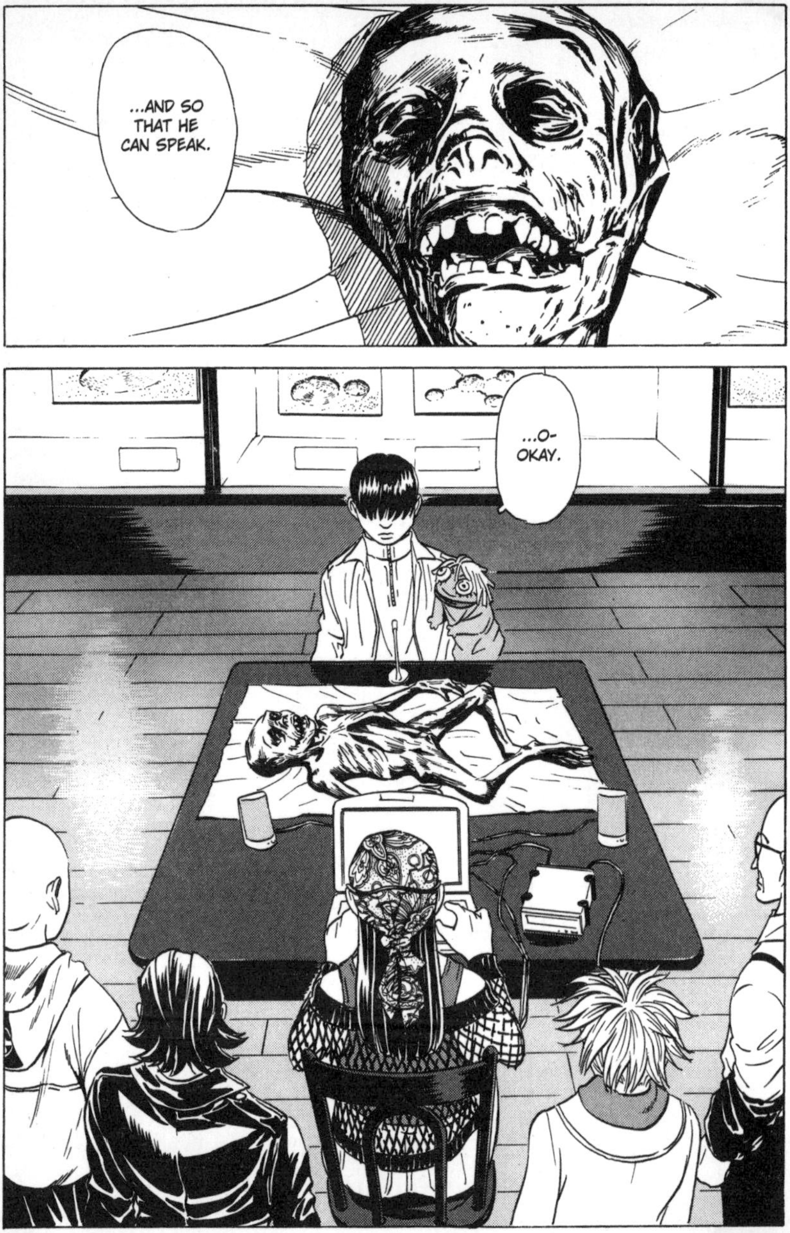
...AND SO THAT HE CAN SPEAK.
...O-OKAY.

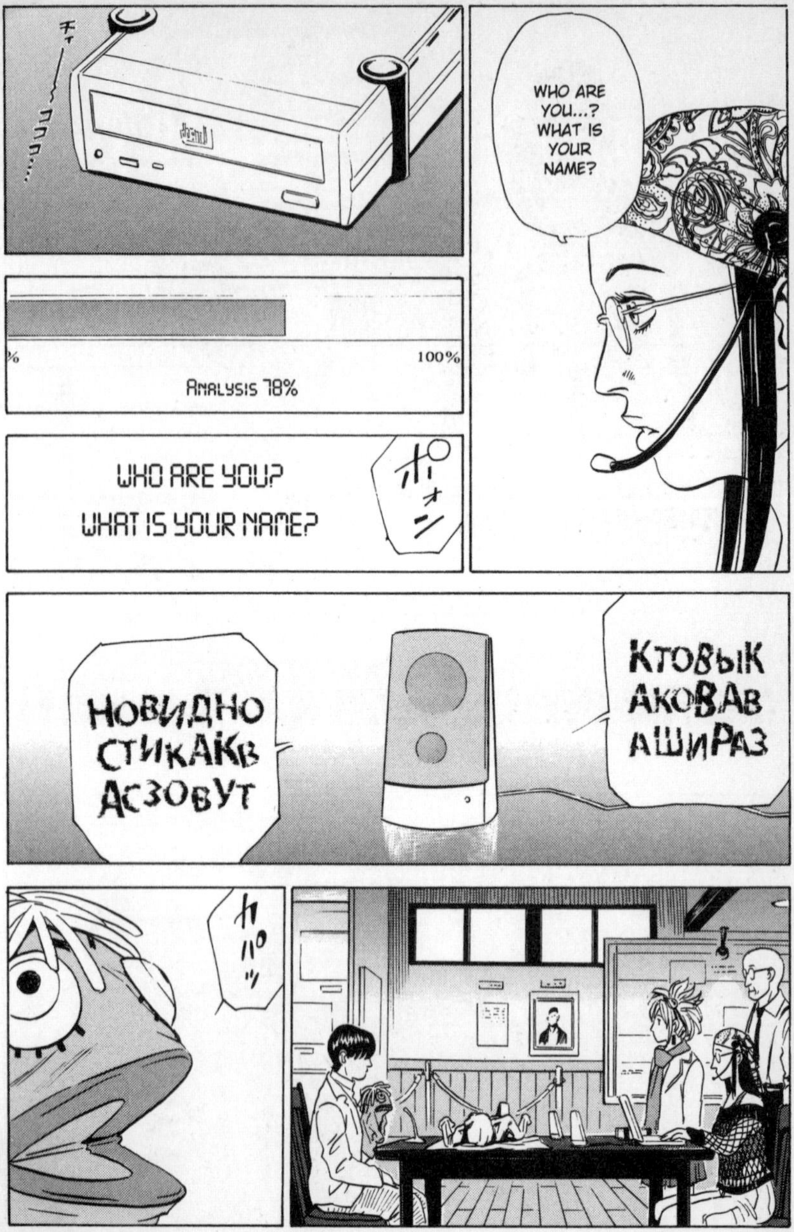
WHO ARE YOU...? WHAT IS YOUR NAME?
チィ〜コロロ…
%
100%
Analysis 78%
ポォン
WHO ARE YOU?
WHAT IS YOUR NAME?
КтоВыК АкоВАв АшиРаз
НоВидно СтиКаКв АсЗоВут
カパッ

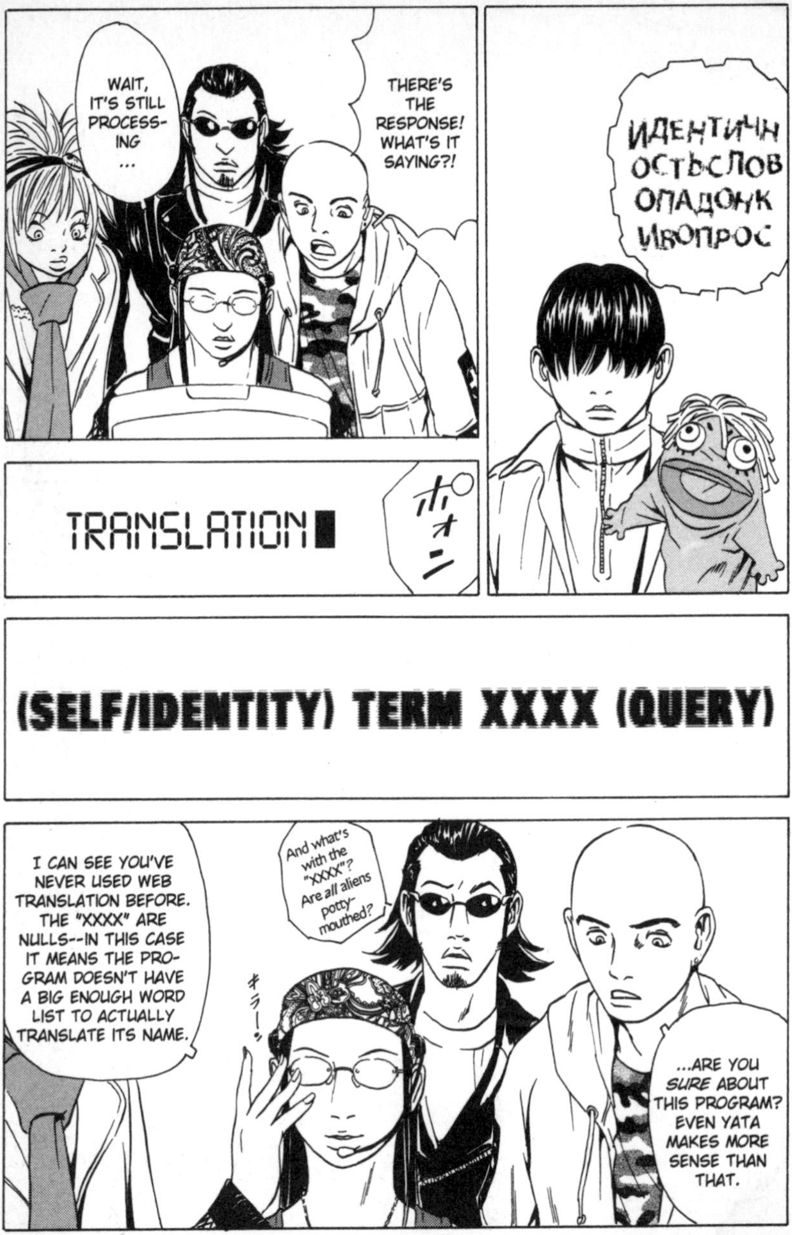
ИДЕНТИЧН
ОСТЬСЛОВ
ОПАДОНК
ИВОПРОС
THERE'S THE RESPONSE! WHAT'S IT SAYING?!
WAIT, IT'S STILL PROCESSING...
ホォン
TRANSLATION
(SELF/IDENTITY) TERM XXXX (QUERY)
And what's with the "XXXX"? Are *all* aliens potty-mouthed?
...ARE YOU *SURE* ABOUT THIS PROGRAM? EVEN YATA MAKES MORE SENSE THAN THAT.
キラーッ
I CAN SEE YOU'VE NEVER USED WEB TRANSLATION BEFORE. THE "XXXX" ARE NULLS--IN THIS CASE IT MEANS THE PROGRAM DOESN'T HAVE A BIG ENOUGH WORD LIST TO ACTUALLY TRANSLATE ITS NAME.

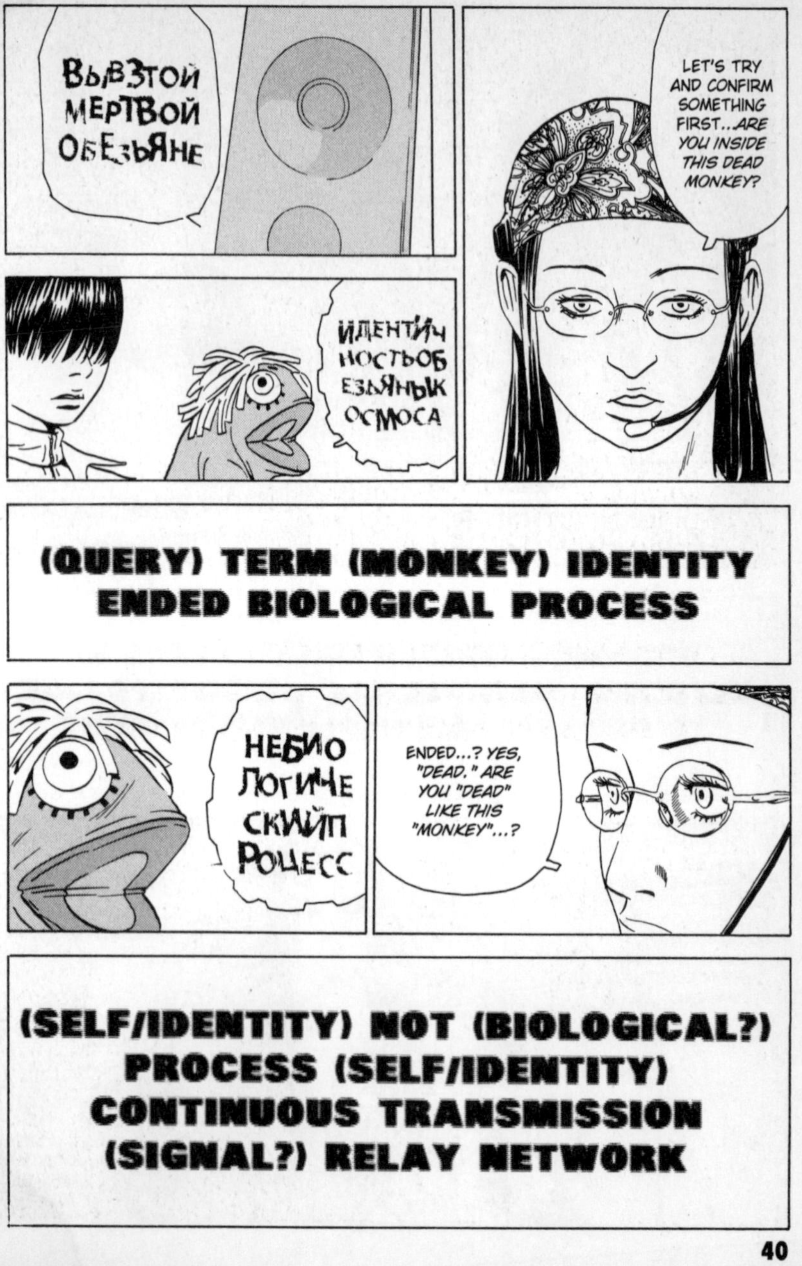
LET'S TRY AND CONFIRM SOMETHING FIRST...ARE YOU INSIDE THIS DEAD MONKEY?
ВыВЗТОЙ МЕРТВОЙ ОБЕЗЬЯНЕ
ИДЕНТИЧ НОСТЬОБ ЕЗЬЯНЫК ОСМОСА
(QUERY) TERM (MONKEY) IDENTITY ENDED BIOLOGICAL PROCESS
ENDED...? YES, "DEAD." ARE YOU "DEAD" LIKE THIS "MONKEY"...?
НЕБИО ЛОГИЧЕ СКИЙП РОЦЕСС
(SELF/IDENTITY) NOT (BIOLOGICAL?) PROCESS (SELF/IDENTITY) CONTINUOUS TRANSMISSION (SIGNAL?) RELAY NETWORK

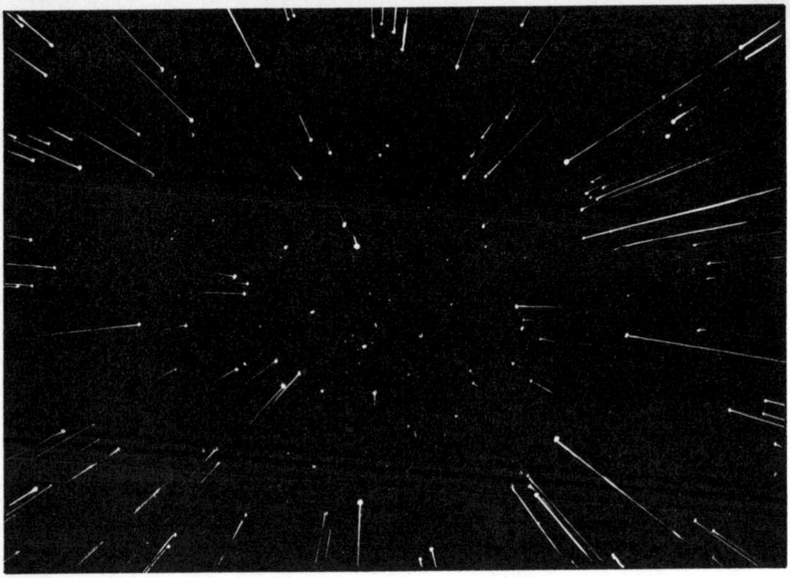

ORGANIC (MINDS/SPECIES?) NODES OF NETWORK (SELF/IDENTITY) ATTEMPTED LINK TO ORGANIC (MIND/SPECIES?) IN ORBIT

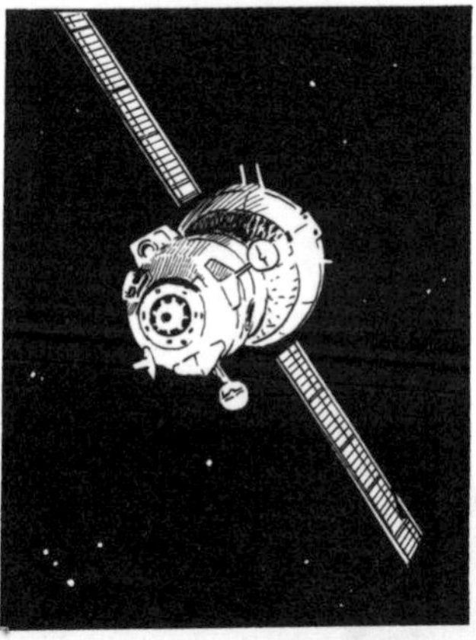

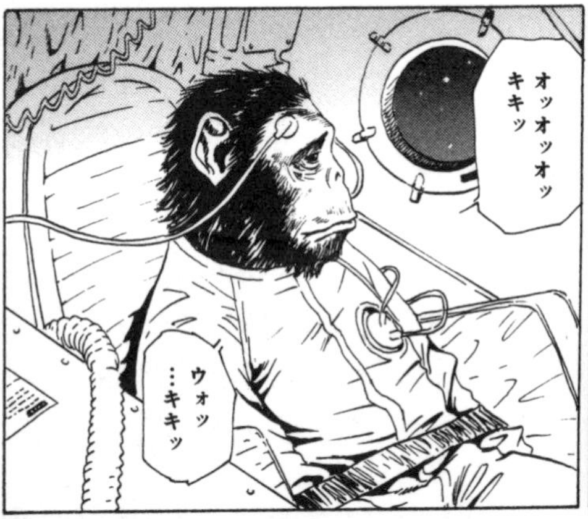
オッオッオッ
キキッ
ウォッ
…キキッ

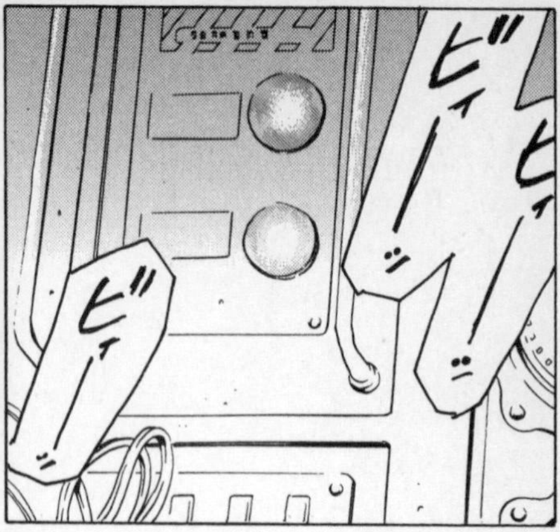
ビィーッ
ヒィーッ
ビィーッ
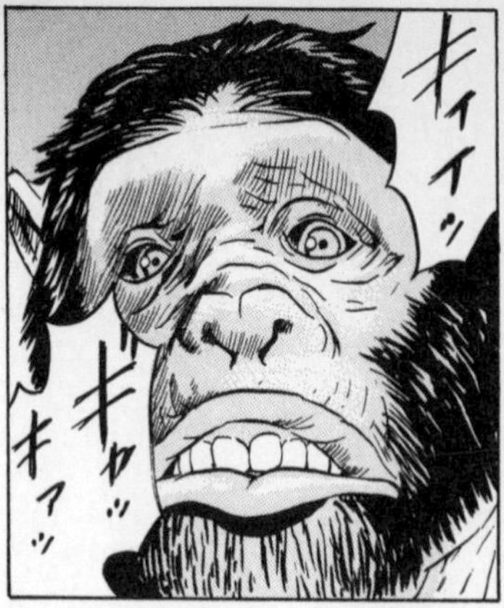
キイイッ
ギャッ
キァッ
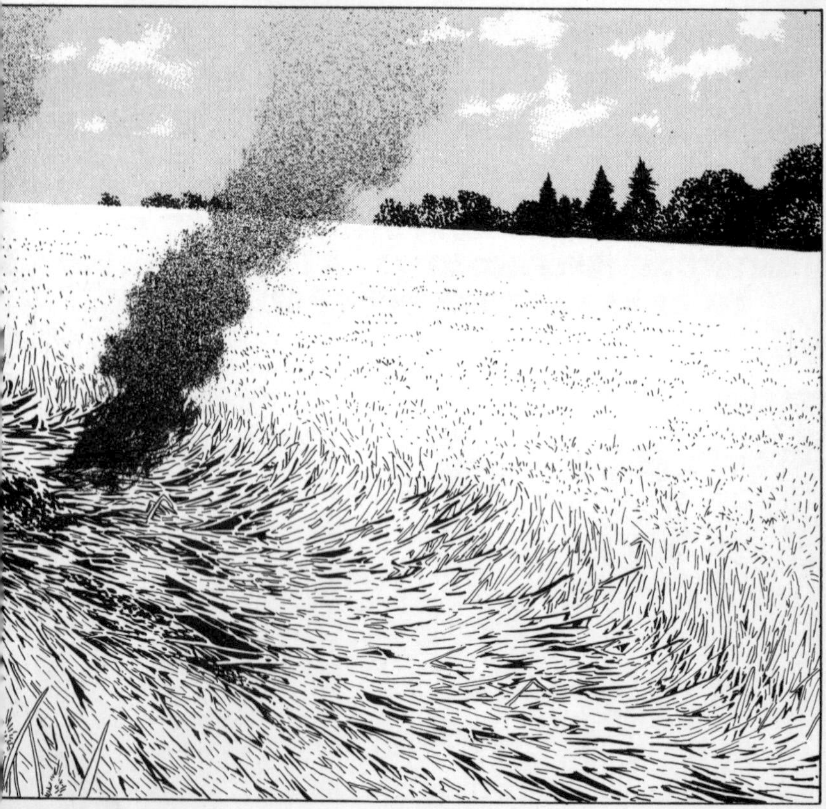

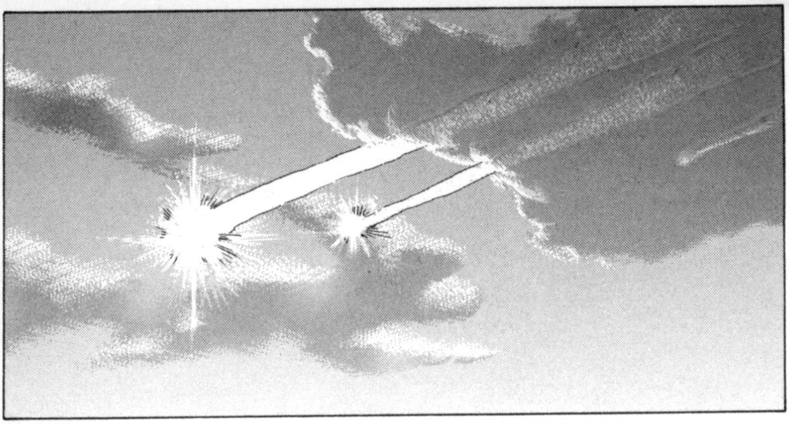

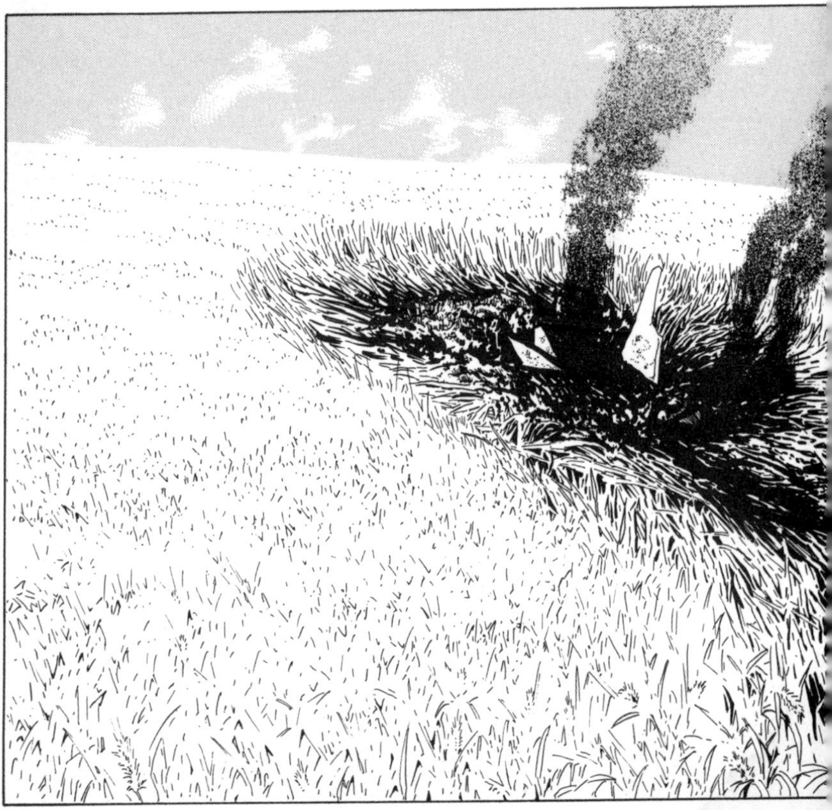

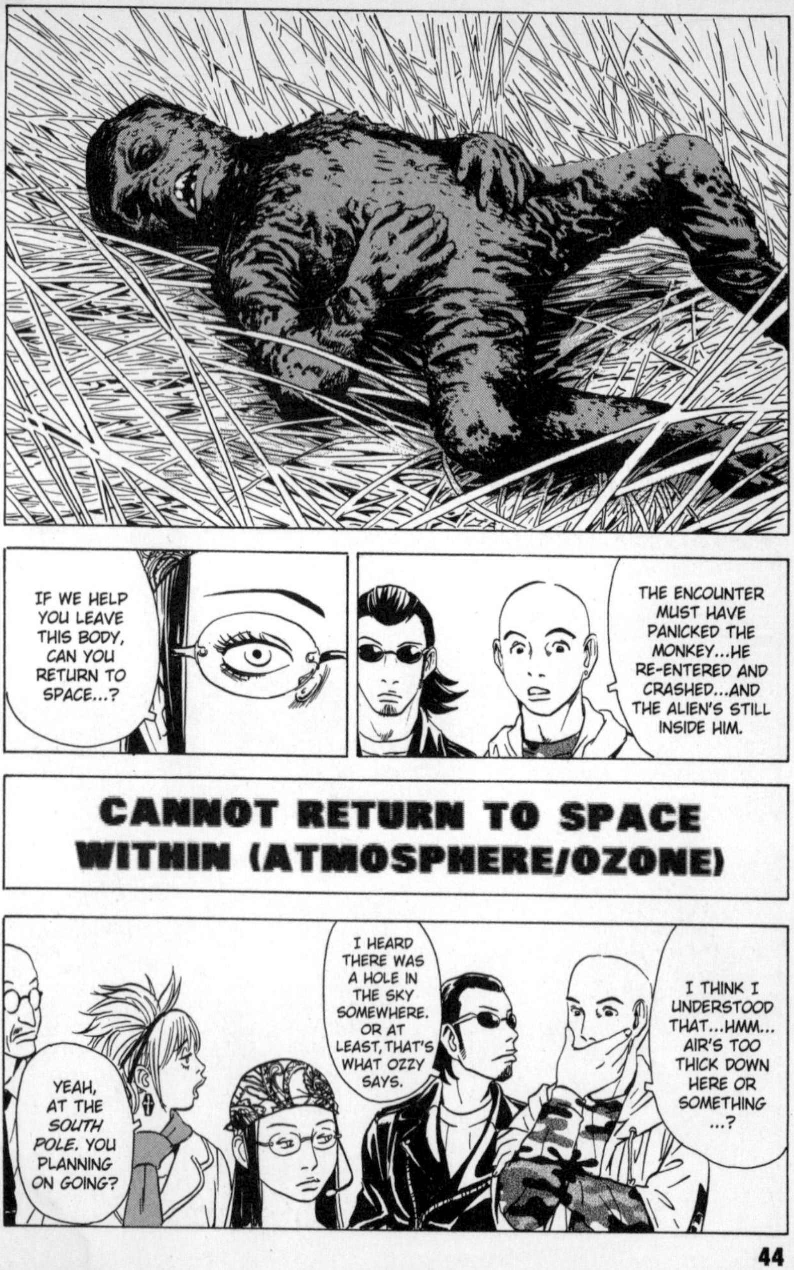
THE ENCOUNTER MUST HAVE PANICKED THE MONKEY...HE RE-ENTERED AND CRASHED...AND THE ALIEN'S STILL INSIDE HIM.
IF WE HELP YOU LEAVE THIS BODY, CAN YOU RETURN TO SPACE...?
CANNOT RETURN TO SPACE WITHIN (ATMOSPHERE/OZONE)
I THINK I UNDERSTOOD THAT...HMM... AIR'S TOO THICK DOWN HERE OR SOMETHING ...?
I HEARD THERE WAS A HOLE IN THE SKY SOMEWHERE. OR AT LEAST, THAT'S WHAT OZZY SAYS.
YEAH, AT THE *SOUTH POLE*. YOU PLANNING ON GOING?

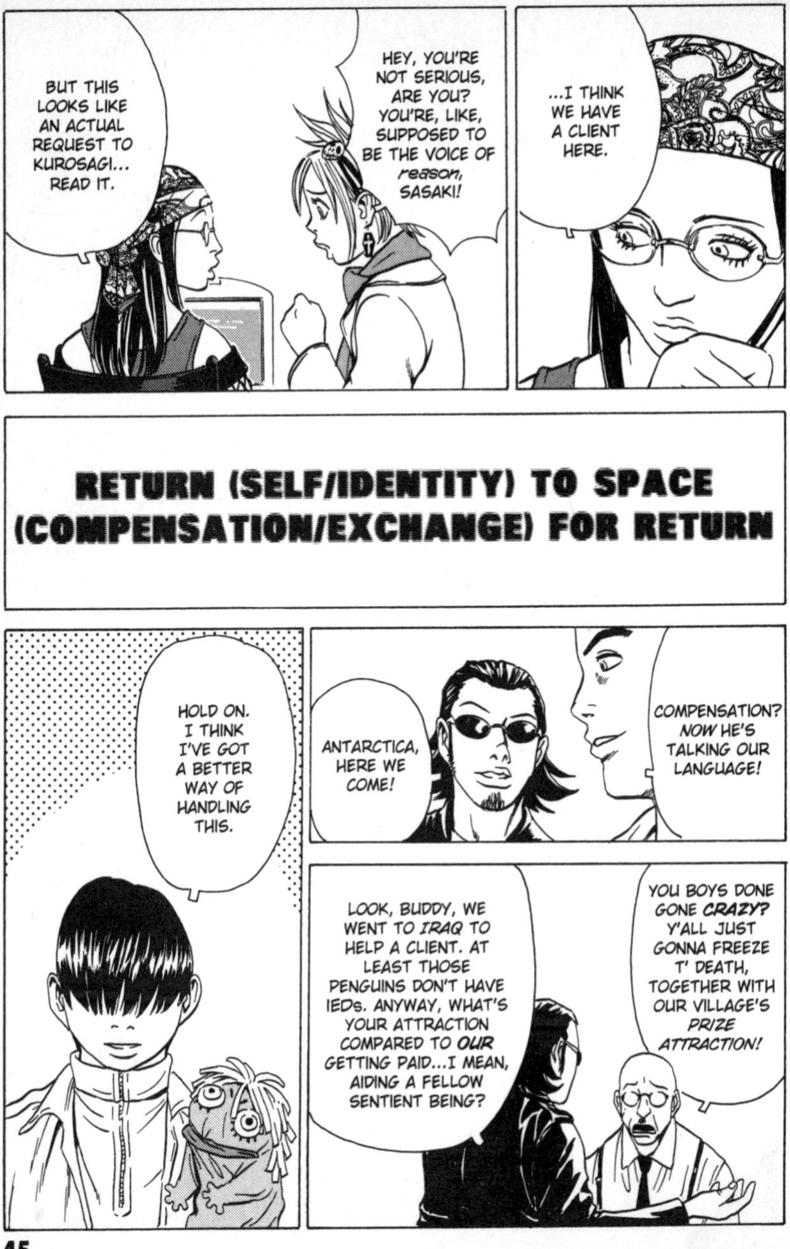
...I THINK WE HAVE A CLIENT HERE.
HEY, YOU'RE NOT SERIOUS, ARE YOU? YOU'RE, LIKE, SUPPOSED TO BE THE VOICE OF *reason*, SASAKI!
BUT THIS LOOKS LIKE AN ACTUAL REQUEST TO KUROSAGI... READ IT.
RETURN (SELF/IDENTITY) TO SPACE (COMPENSATION/EXCHANGE) FOR RETURN
COMPENSATION? *NOW* HE'S TALKING OUR LANGUAGE!
ANTARCTICA, HERE WE COME!
YOU BOYS DONE GONE ***CRAZY?*** Y'ALL JUST GONNA FREEZE T' DEATH, TOGETHER WITH OUR VILLAGE'S *PRIZE ATTRACTION!*
LOOK, BUDDY, WE WENT TO *IRAQ* TO HELP A CLIENT. AT LEAST THOSE PENGUINS DON'T HAVE IEDs. ANYWAY, WHAT'S YOUR ATTRACTION COMPARED TO ***OUR*** GETTING PAID...I MEAN, AIDING A FELLOW SENTIENT BEING?
HOLD ON. I THINK I'VE GOT A BETTER WAY OF HANDLING THIS.

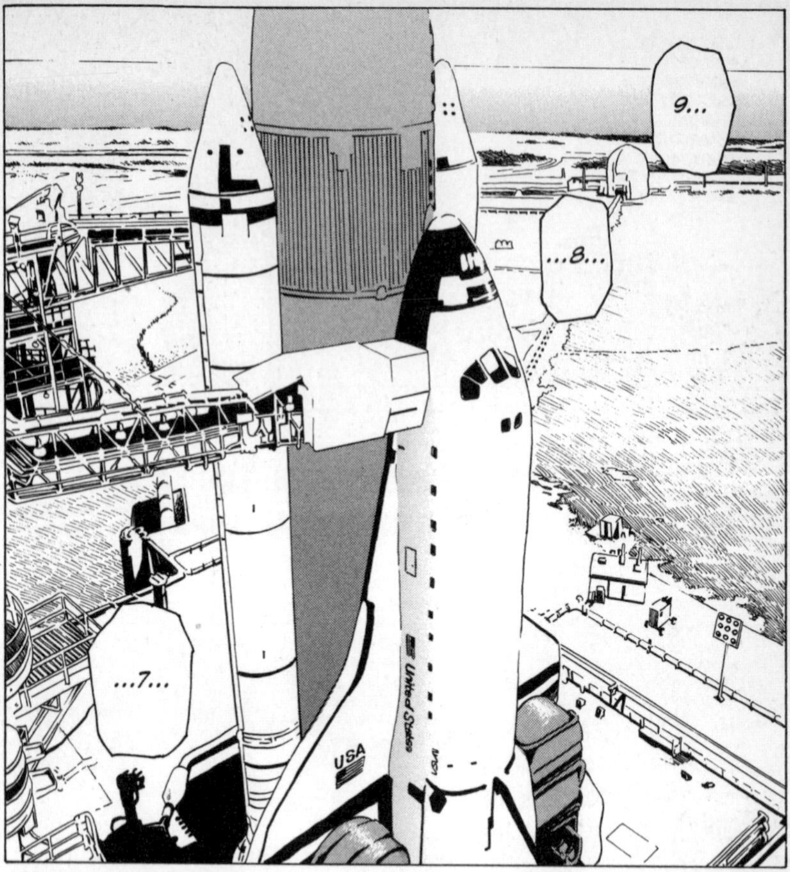
9...
...8...
USA
United States
...7...

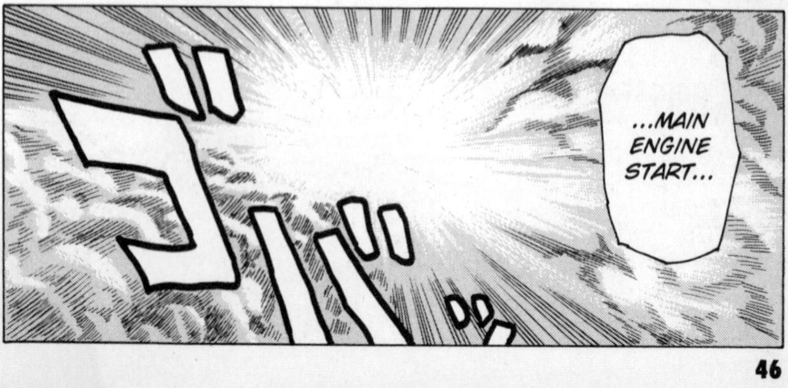
...MAIN ENGINE START...

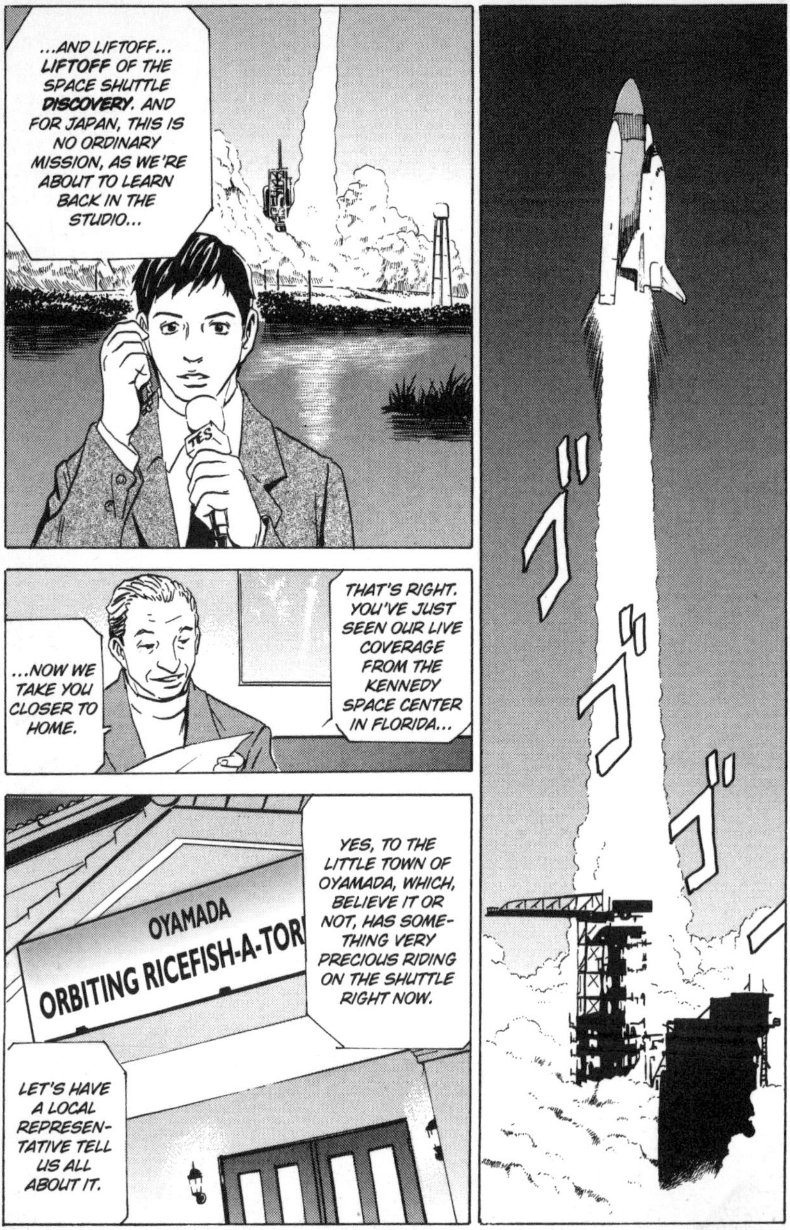
ゴゴゴ
...AND LIFTOFF... **LIFTOFF** OF THE SPACE SHUTTLE **DISCOVERY**. AND FOR JAPAN, THIS IS NO ORDINARY MISSION, AS WE'RE ABOUT TO LEARN BACK IN THE STUDIO...
TES
THAT'S RIGHT. YOU'VE JUST SEEN OUR LIVE COVERAGE FROM THE KENNEDY SPACE CENTER IN FLORIDA...
...NOW WE TAKE YOU CLOSER TO HOME.
YES, TO THE LITTLE TOWN OF OYAMADA, WHICH, BELIEVE IT OR NOT, HAS SOMETHING VERY PRECIOUS RIDING ON THE SHUTTLE RIGHT NOW.
OYAMADA
ORBITING RICEFISH-A-TOR
LET'S HAVE A LOCAL REPRESENTATIVE TELL US ALL ABOUT IT.

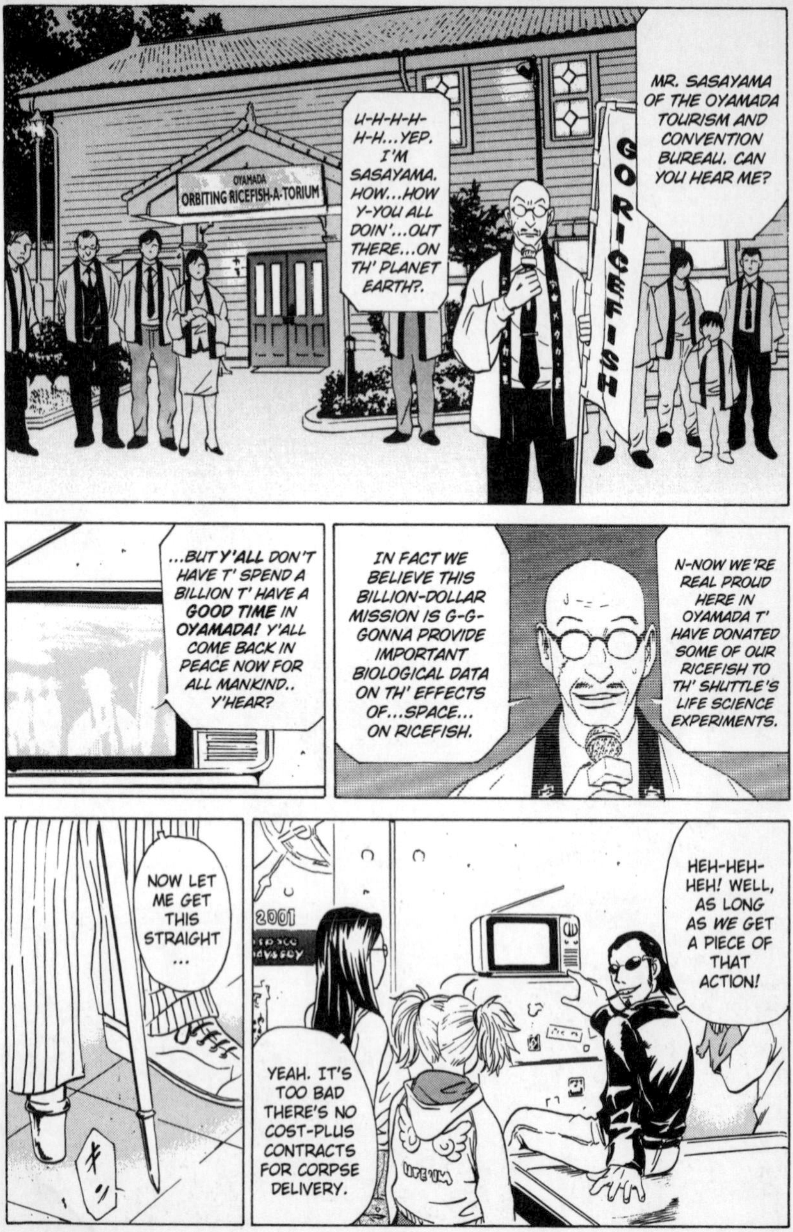
MR. SASAYAMA OF THE OYAMADA TOURISM AND CONVENTION BUREAU. CAN YOU HEAR ME?
U-H-H-H-H-H...YEP. I'M SASAYAMA. HOW...HOW Y-YOU ALL DOIN'...OUT THERE...ON TH' PLANET EARTH?.
OYAMADA ORBITING RICEFISH-A-TORIUM
GO RICEFISH
N-NOW WE'RE REAL PROUD HERE IN OYAMADA T' HAVE DONATED SOME OF OUR RICEFISH TO TH' SHUTTLE'S LIFE SCIENCE EXPERIMENTS.
IN FACT WE BELIEVE THIS BILLION-DOLLAR MISSION IS G-G-GONNA PROVIDE IMPORTANT BIOLOGICAL DATA ON TH' EFFECTS OF...SPACE... ON RICEFISH.
...BUT Y'ALL DON'T HAVE T' SPEND A BILLION T' HAVE A GOOD TIME IN OYAMADA! Y'ALL COME BACK IN PEACE NOW FOR ALL MANKIND.. Y'HEAR?
HEH-HEH-HEH! WELL, AS LONG AS WE GET A PIECE OF THAT ACTION!
2001
YEAH. IT'S TOO BAD THERE'S NO COST-PLUS CONTRACTS FOR CORPSE DELIVERY.
NOW LET ME GET THIS STRAIGHT ...

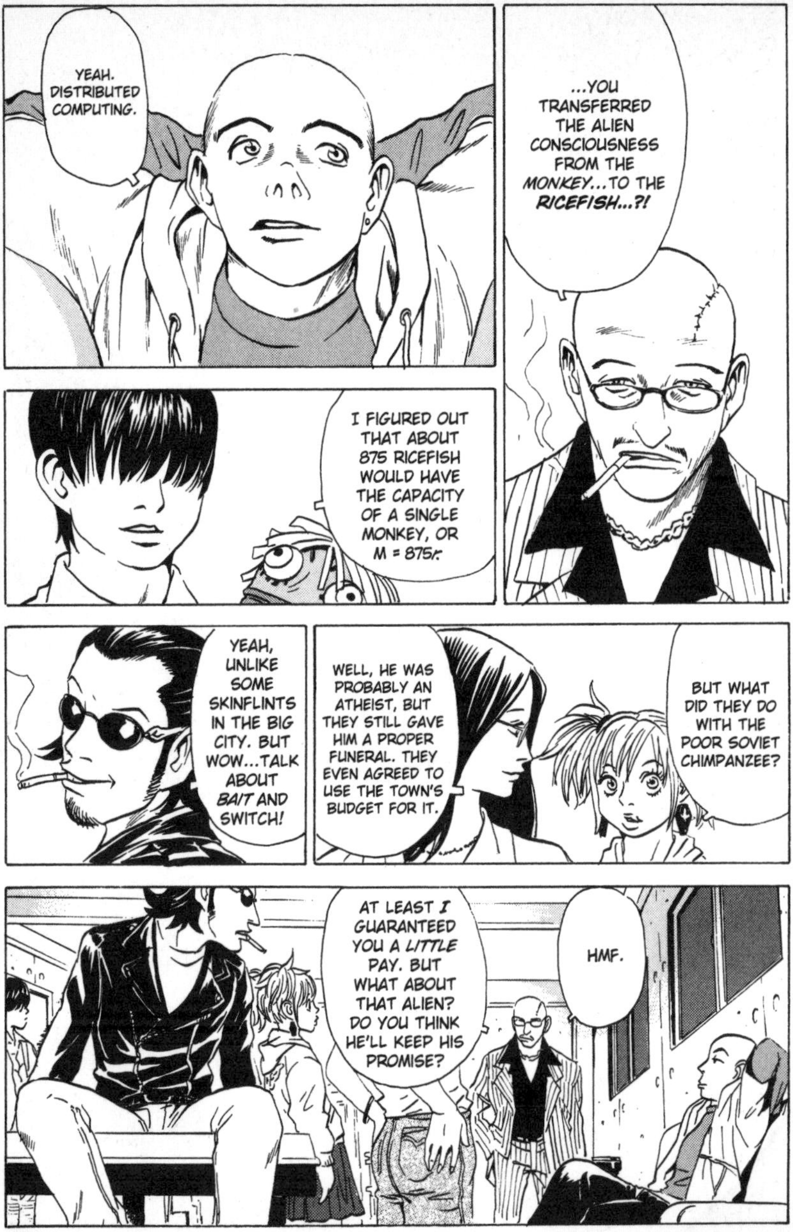
...YOU TRANSFERRED THE ALIEN CONSCIOUSNESS FROM THE *MONKEY*...TO THE ***RICEFISH***...?!
YEAH. DISTRIBUTED COMPUTING.
I FIGURED OUT THAT ABOUT 875 RICEFISH WOULD HAVE THE CAPACITY OF A SINGLE MONKEY, OR M = 875*r*.
BUT WHAT DID THEY DO WITH THE POOR SOVIET CHIMPANZEE?
WELL, HE WAS PROBABLY AN ATHEIST, BUT THEY STILL GAVE HIM A PROPER FUNERAL. THEY EVEN AGREED TO USE THE TOWN'S BUDGET FOR IT.
YEAH, UNLIKE SOME SKINFLINTS IN THE BIG CITY. BUT WOW...TALK ABOUT *BAIT* AND SWITCH!
HMF.
AT LEAST *I* GUARANTEED YOU A *LITTLE* PAY. BUT WHAT ABOUT THAT ALIEN? DO YOU THINK HE'LL KEEP HIS PROMISE?

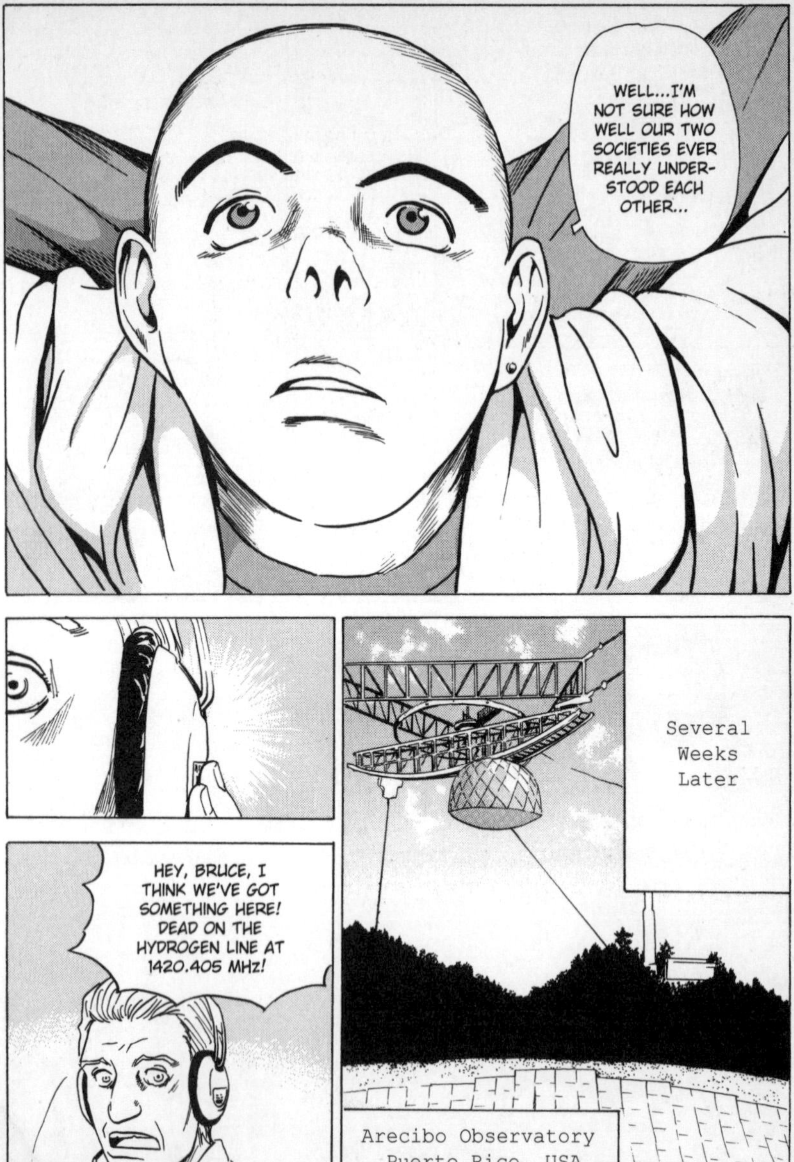
WELL...I'M NOT SURE HOW WELL OUR TWO SOCIETIES EVER REALLY UNDER-STOOD EACH OTHER...
Several Weeks Later
Arecibo Observatory Puerto Rico, USA
HEY, BRUCE, I THINK WE'VE GOT SOMETHING HERE! DEAD ON THE HYDROGEN LINE AT 1420.405 MHz!

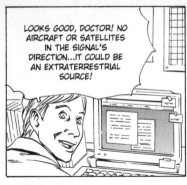

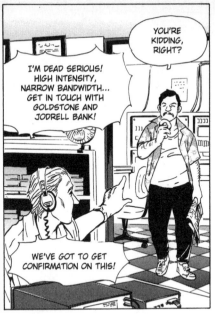

YOU'RE KIDDING, RIGHT?
I'M DEAD SERIOUS! HIGH INTENSITY, NARROW BANDWIDTH... GET IN TOUCH WITH GOLDSTONE AND JODRELL BANK!
WE'VE GOT TO GET CONFIRMATION ON THIS!
LOOKS GOOD, DOCTOR! NO AIRCRAFT OR SATELLITES IN THE SIGNAL'S DIRECTION...IT COULD BE AN EXTRATERRESTRIAL SOURCE!
WAIT...IT'S MODULATED...I THINK THERE'S A VIDEO COMPONENT!
VIDEO? ROUTE IT TO THE MONITOR!
BETTER MAKE SOME ROOM ON THE SHELF FOR A *NOBEL PRIZE!* WE'VE BEEN WAITING ALL THESE YEARS TO SEE THIS!
QUICK, TURN IT *ON!*
...AND DELETE THIS CRAP IMMEDIATELY.

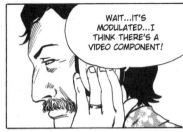

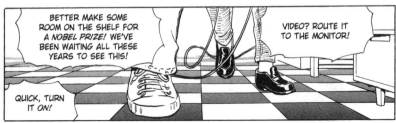

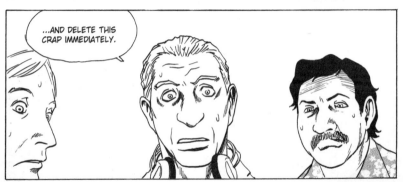

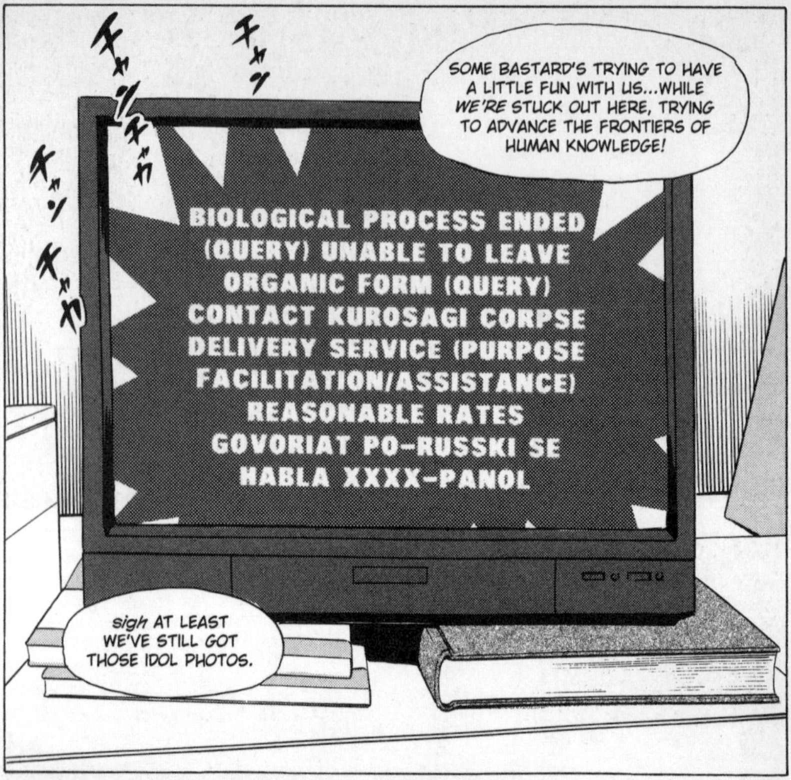
SOME BASTARD'S TRYING TO HAVE A LITTLE FUN WITH US...WHILE *WE'RE* STUCK OUT HERE, TRYING TO ADVANCE THE FRONTIERS OF HUMAN KNOWLEDGE!
BIOLOGICAL PROCESS ENDED (QUERY) UNABLE TO LEAVE ORGANIC FORM (QUERY) CONTACT KUROSAGI CORPSE DELIVERY SERVICE (PURPOSE FACILITATION/ASSISTANCE) REASONABLE RATES GOVORIAT PO-RUSSKI SE HABLA XXXX-PANOL
sigh AT LEAST WE'VE STILL GOT THOSE IDOL PHOTOS.

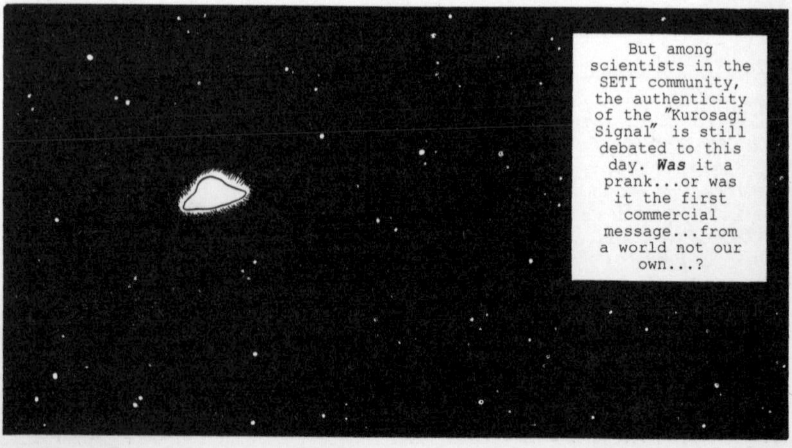
But among scientists in the SETI community, the authenticity of the "Kurosagi Signal" is still debated to this day. ***Was*** it a prank...or was it the first commercial message...from a world not our own...?

1st delivery: thank you, dear—the end

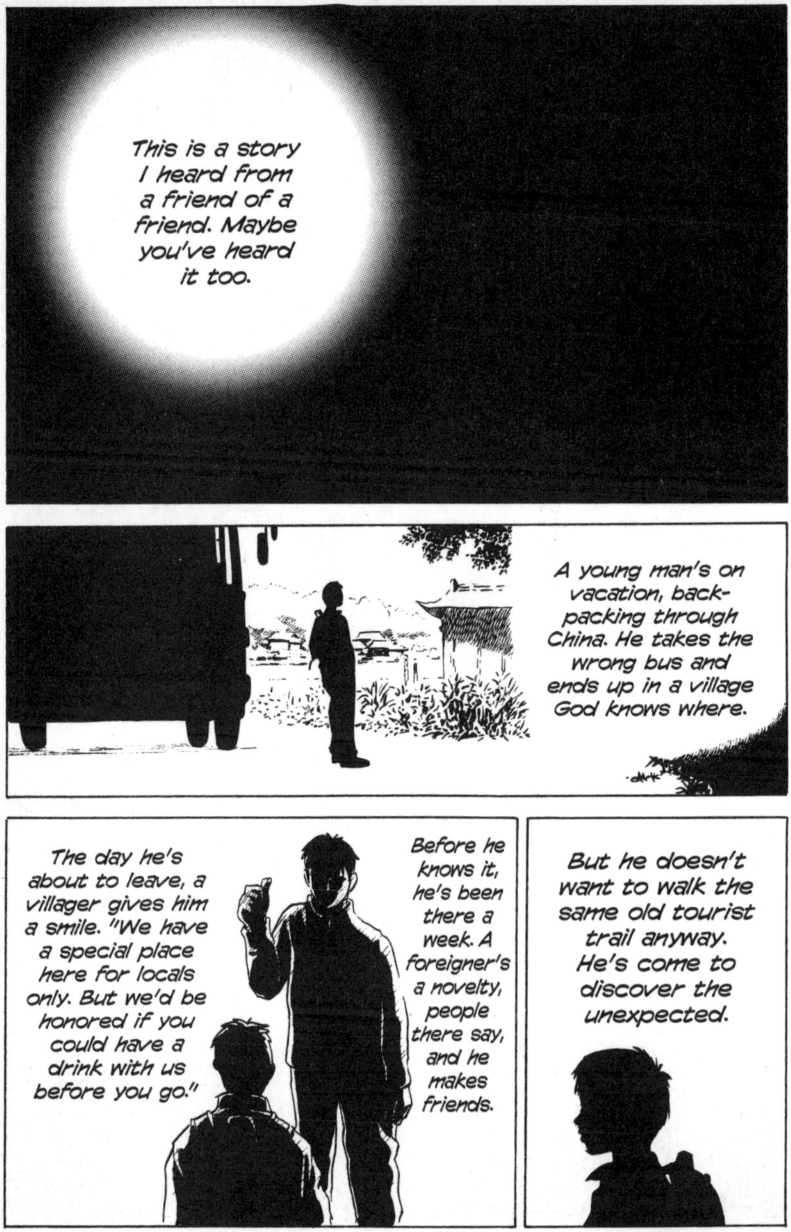
This is a story I heard from a friend of a friend. Maybe you've heard it too.
A young man's on vacation, back-packing through China. He takes the wrong bus and ends up in a village God knows where.
But he doesn't want to walk the same old tourist trail anyway. He's come to discover the unexpected.
Before he knows it, he's been there a week. A foreigner's a novelty, people there say, and he makes friends.
The day he's about to leave, a villager gives him a smile. "We have a special place here for locals only. But we'd be honored if you could have a drink with us before you go."

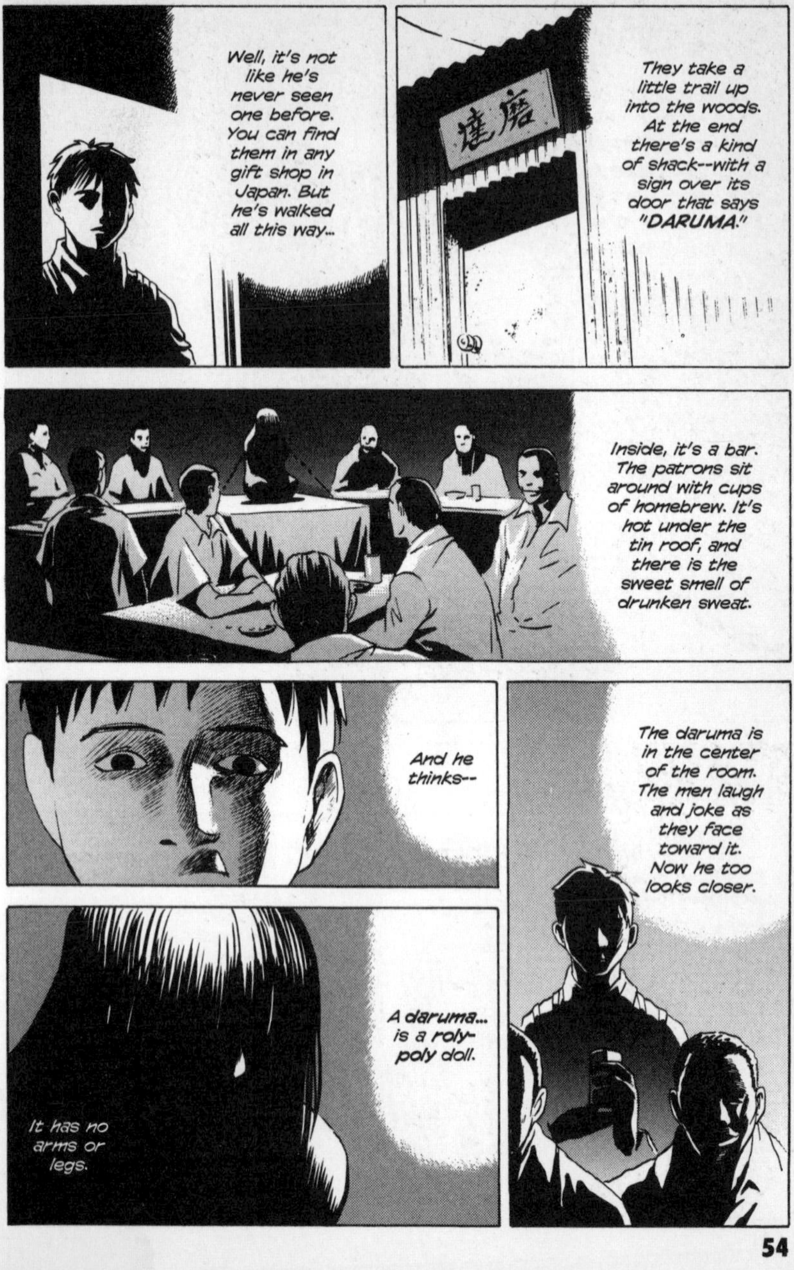

They take a little trail up into the woods. At the end there's a kind of shack--with a sign over its door that says "DARUMA."
達磨
Well, it's not like he's never seen one before. You can find them in any gift shop in Japan. But he's walked all this way...
Inside, it's a bar. The patrons sit around with cups of homebrew. It's hot under the tin roof, and there is the sweet smell of drunken sweat.
The daruma is in the center of the room. The men laugh and joke as they face toward it. Now he too looks closer.
And he thinks--
A daruma... is a roly-poly doll.
It has no arms or legs.

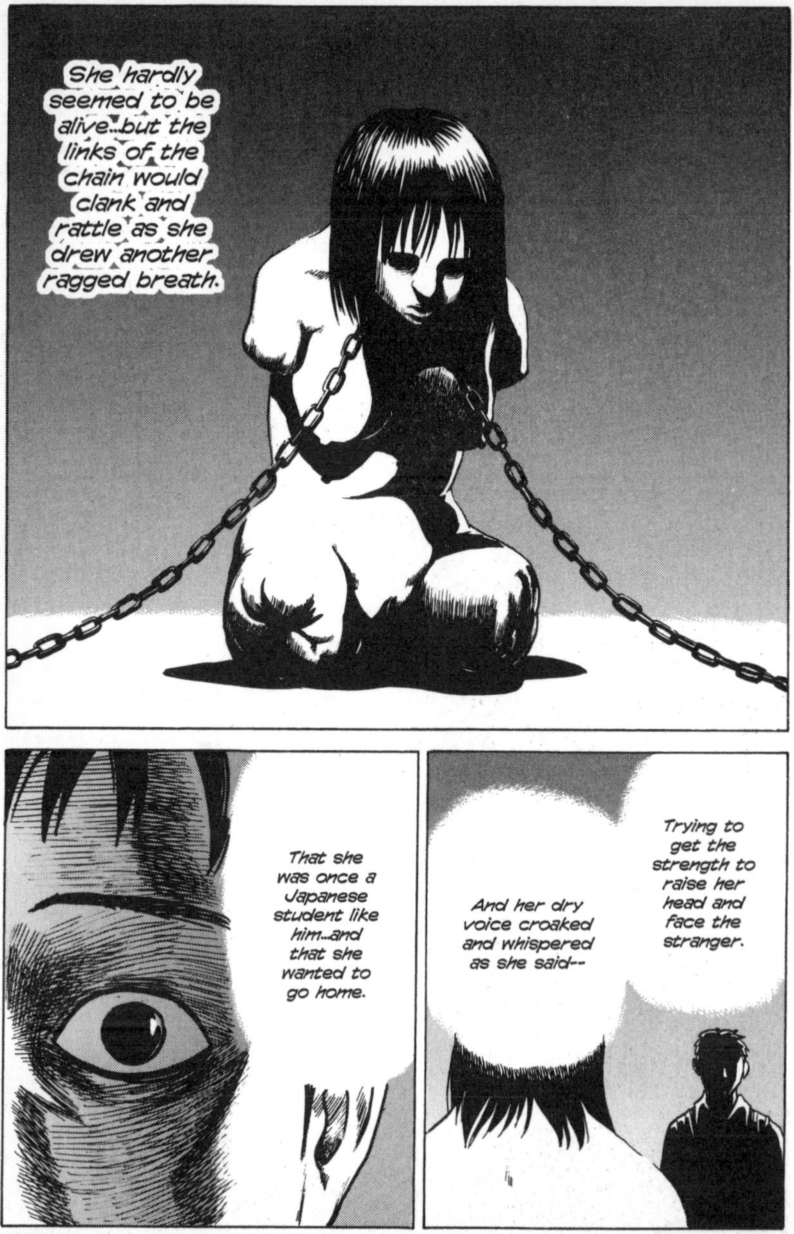
She hardly seemed to be alive...but the links of the chain would clank and rattle as she drew another ragged breath.
Trying to get the strength to raise her head and face the stranger.
And her dry voice croaked and whispered as she said--
That she was once a Japanese student like him...and that she wanted to go home.

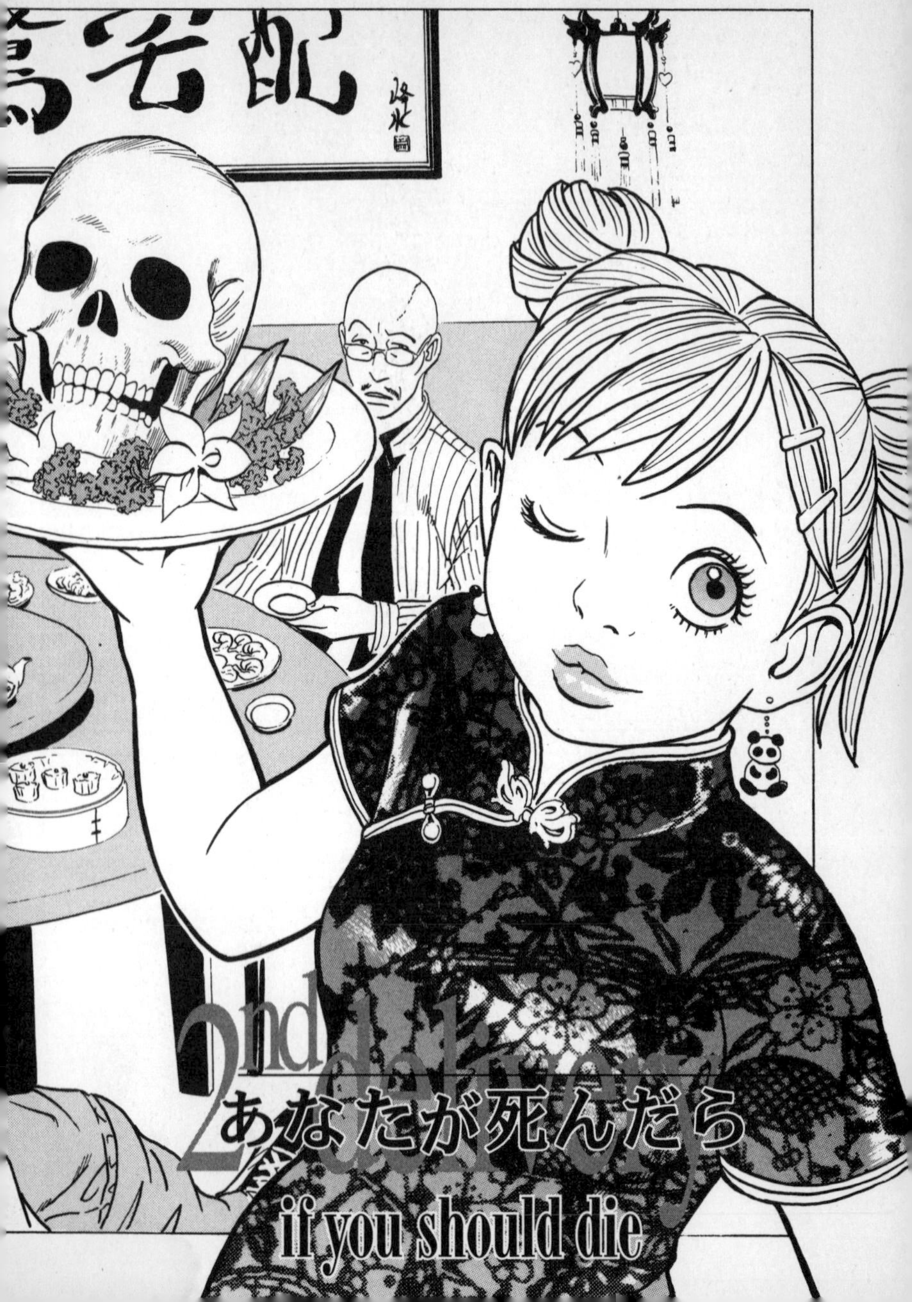
2nd delivery
あなたが死んだら
if you should die

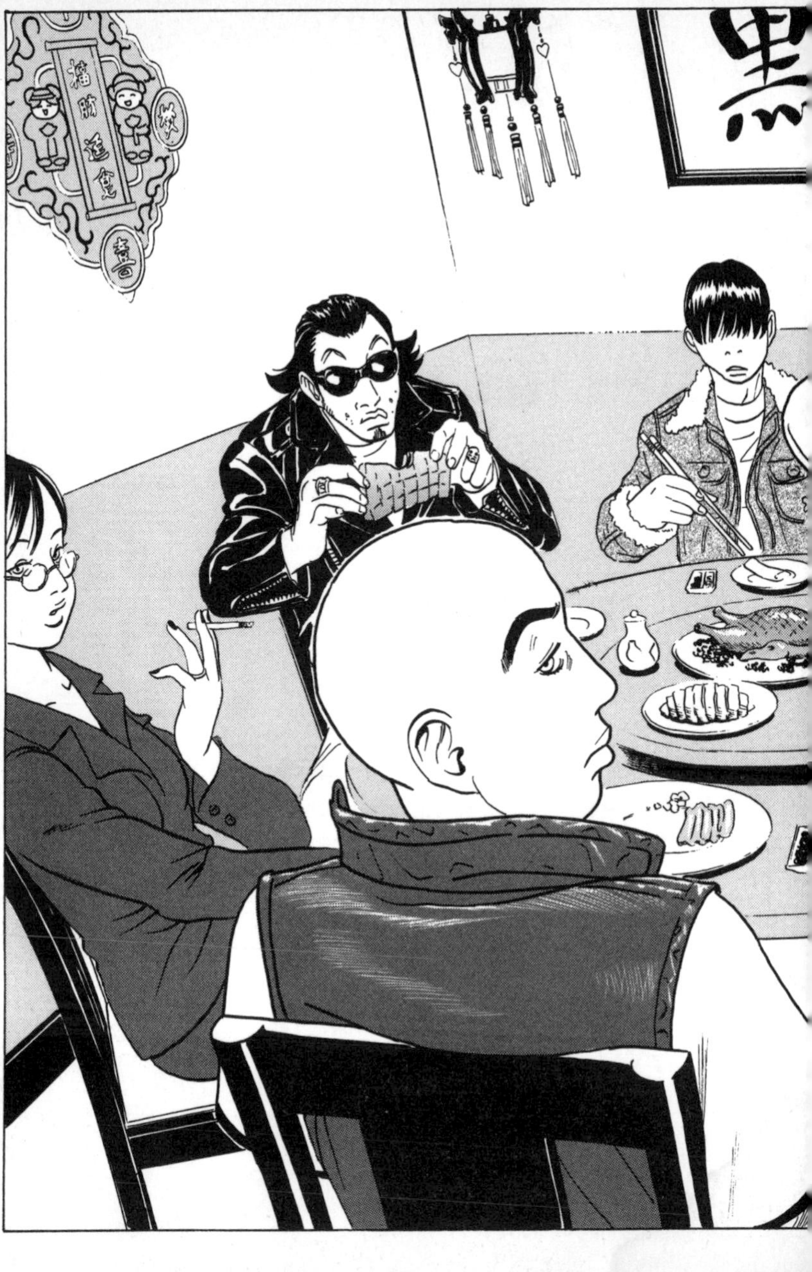

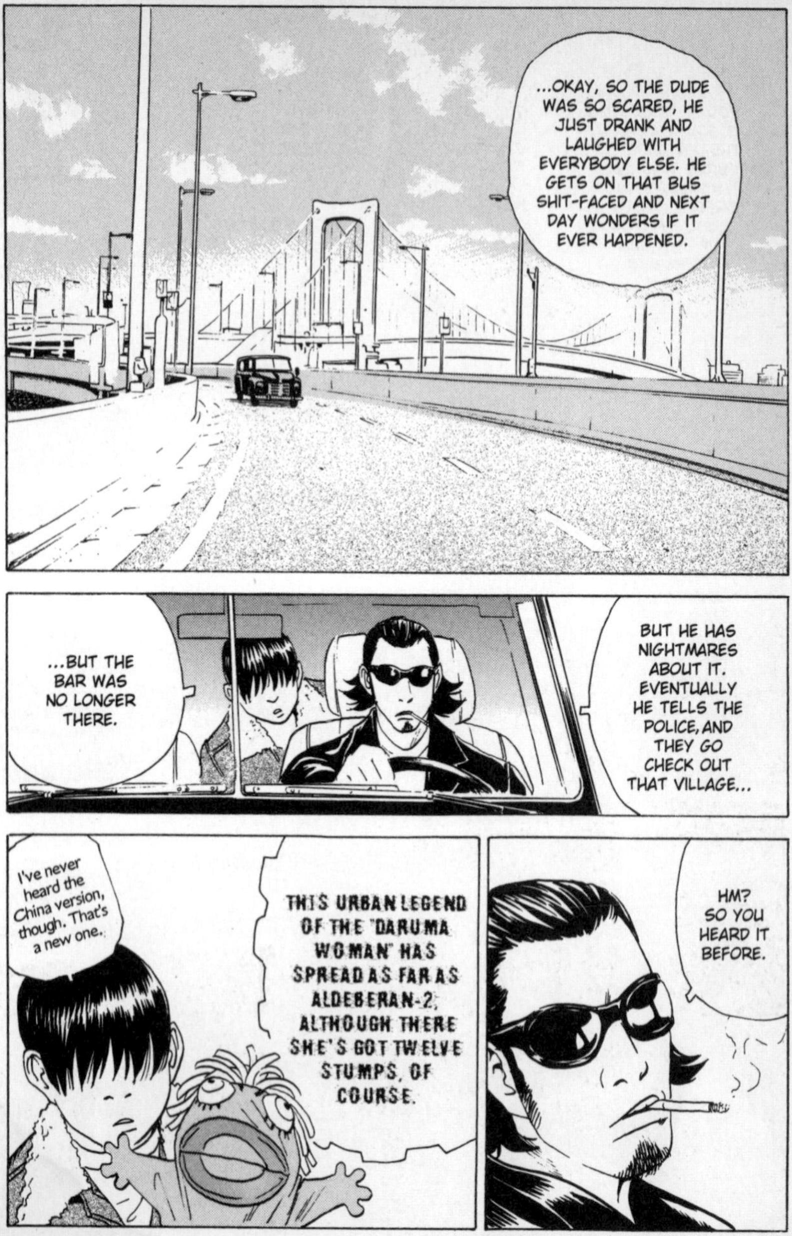
...OKAY, SO THE DUDE WAS SO SCARED, HE JUST DRANK AND LAUGHED WITH EVERYBODY ELSE. HE GETS ON THAT BUS SHIT-FACED AND NEXT DAY WONDERS IF IT EVER HAPPENED.
BUT HE HAS NIGHTMARES ABOUT IT. EVENTUALLY HE TELLS THE POLICE, AND THEY GO CHECK OUT THAT VILLAGE...
...BUT THE BAR WAS NO LONGER THERE.
HM? SO YOU HEARD IT BEFORE.
I've never heard the China version, though. That's a new one.
THIS URBAN LEGEND OF THE "DARUMA WOMAN" HAS SPREAD AS FAR AS ALDEBERAN-2; ALTHOUGH THERE SHE'S GOT TWELVE STUMPS, OF COURSE.

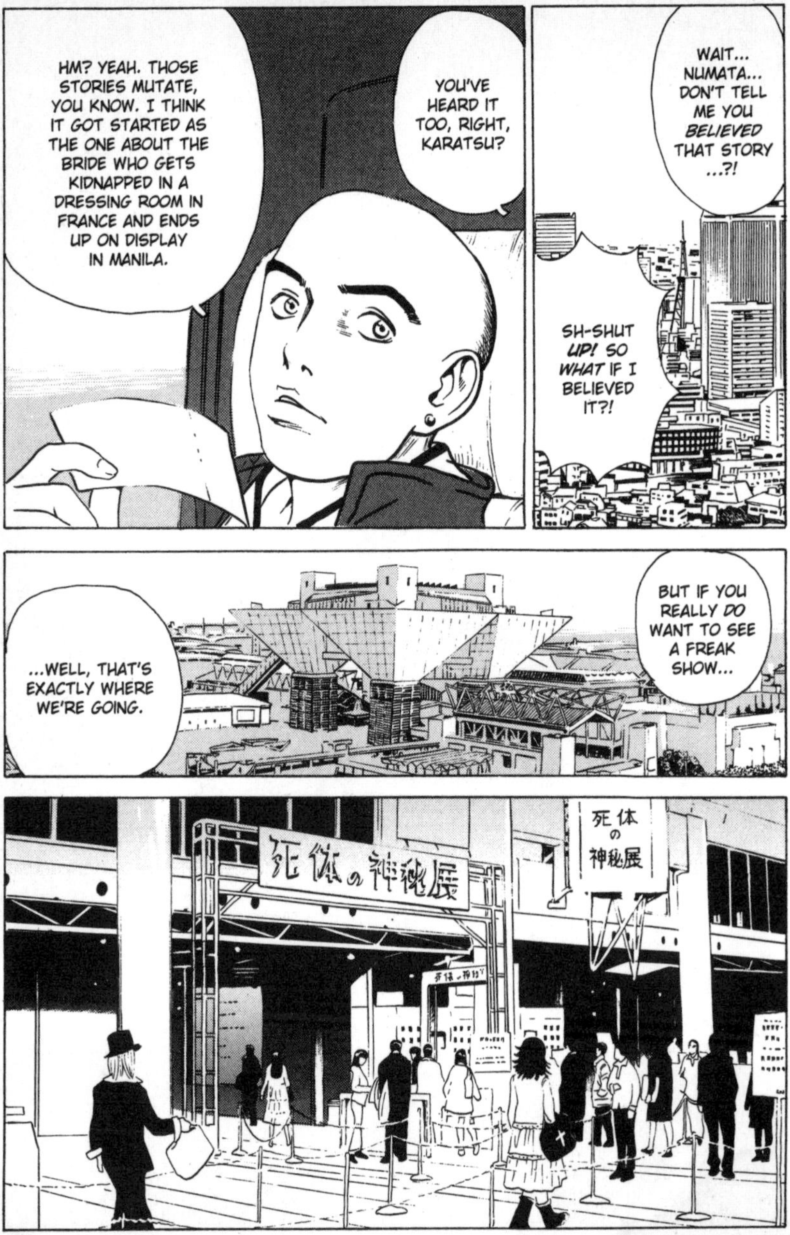
WAIT... NUMATA... DON'T TELL ME YOU *BELIEVED* THAT STORY ...?!
SH-SHUT *UP!* SO *WHAT* IF I BELIEVED IT?!
YOU'VE HEARD IT TOO, RIGHT, KARATSU?
HM? YEAH. THOSE STORIES MUTATE, YOU KNOW. I THINK IT GOT STARTED AS THE ONE ABOUT THE BRIDE WHO GETS KIDNAPPED IN A DRESSING ROOM IN FRANCE AND ENDS UP ON DISPLAY IN MANILA.
BUT IF YOU REALLY *DO* WANT TO SEE A FREAK SHOW...
...WELL, THAT'S EXACTLY WHERE WE'RE GOING.
死体の神秘展
死体の神秘展

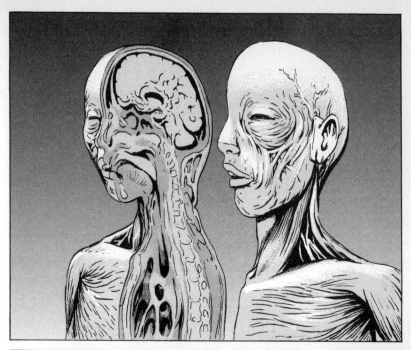

EWW... THIS WHOLE THING IS GROSS.

I DUNNO... I THINK IT'S MORE FUNNY THAN SCARY.

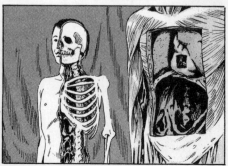

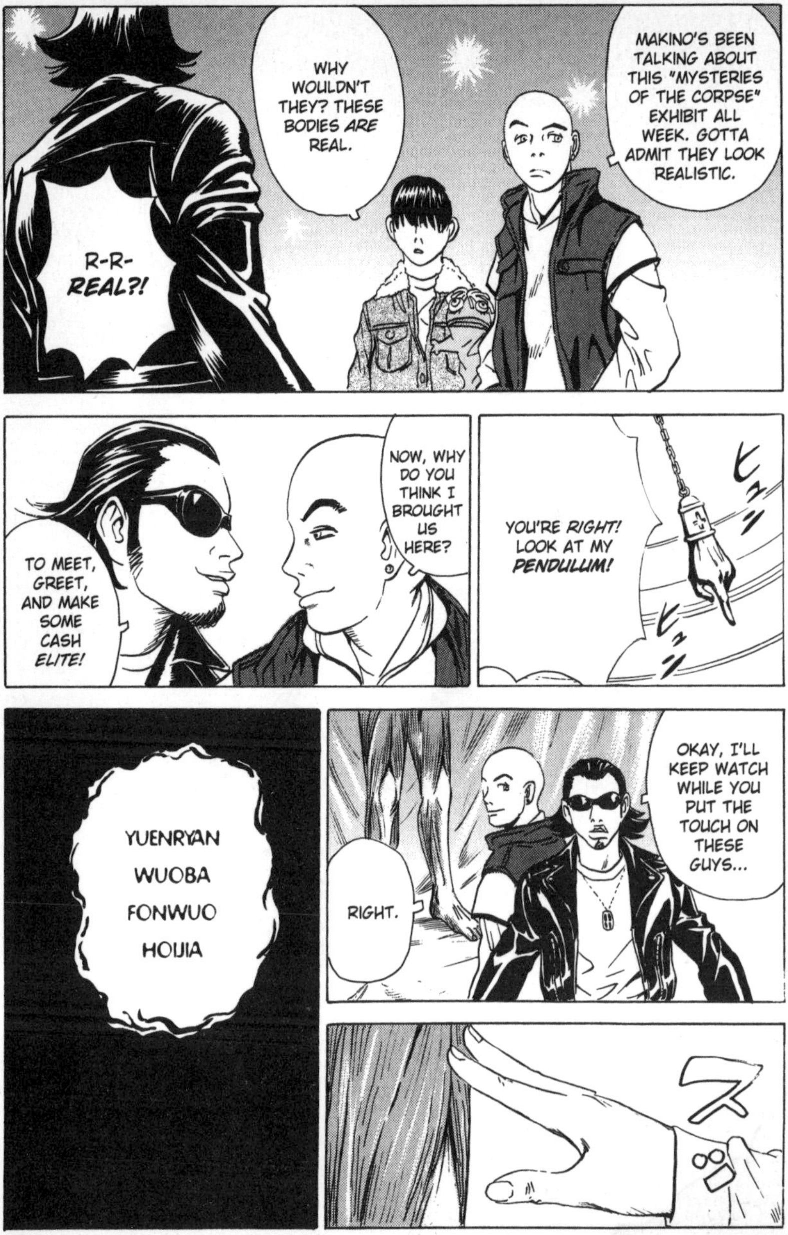
MAKINO'S BEEN TALKING ABOUT THIS "MYSTERIES OF THE CORPSE" EXHIBIT ALL WEEK. GOTTA ADMIT THEY LOOK REALISTIC.
WHY WOULDN'T THEY? THESE BODIES *ARE* REAL.
R-R- *REAL?!*
YOU'RE *RIGHT!* LOOK AT MY ***PENDULUM!***
NOW, WHY DO YOU THINK I BROUGHT US HERE?
TO MEET, GREET, AND MAKE SOME CASH *ELITE!*
OKAY, I'LL KEEP WATCH WHILE YOU PUT THE TOUCH ON THESE GUYS...
RIGHT.
ス
YUENRYAN WUOBA FONWUO HOIJIA

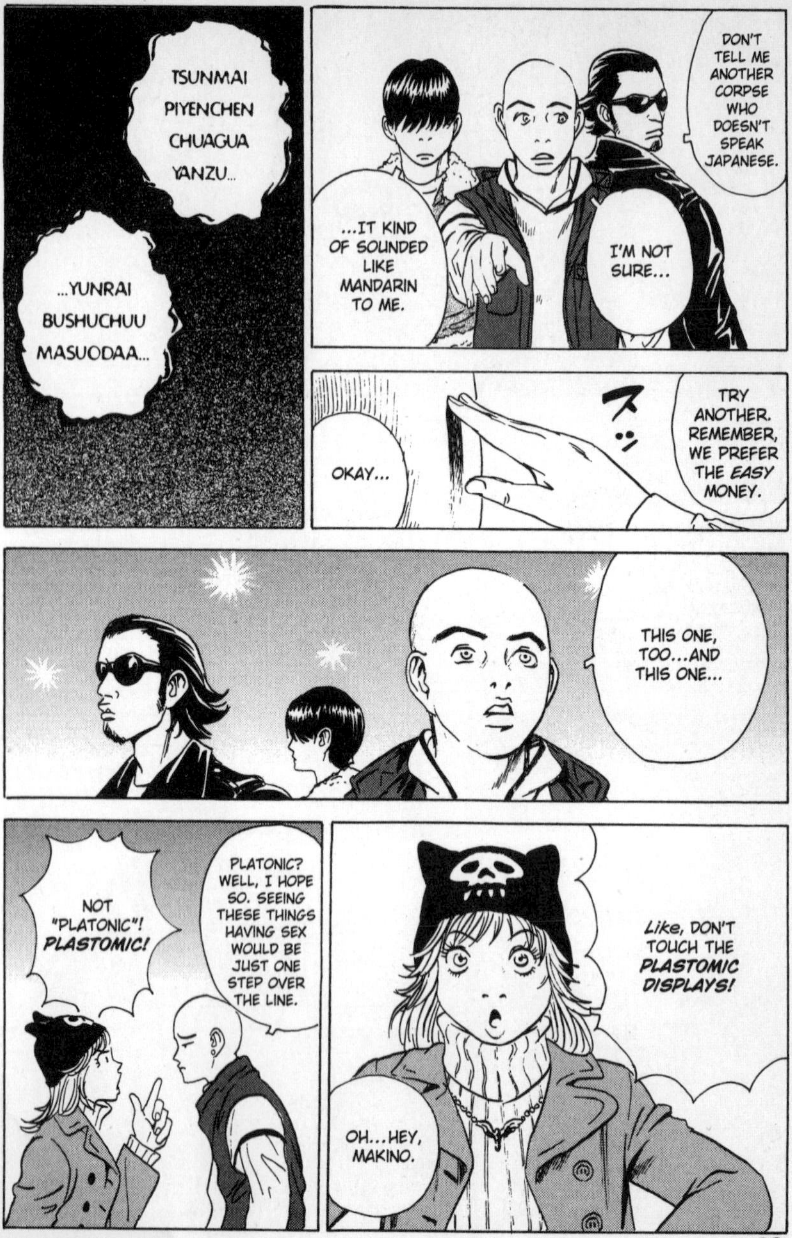
DON'T TELL ME ANOTHER CORPSE WHO DOESN'T SPEAK JAPANESE.
I'M NOT SURE...
...IT KIND OF SOUNDED LIKE MANDARIN TO ME.
TRY ANOTHER. REMEMBER, WE PREFER THE *EASY* MONEY.
スッ
OKAY...
TSUNMAI PIYENCHEN CHUAGUA YANZU...
...YUNRAI BUSHUCHUU MASUODAA...
THIS ONE, TOO...AND THIS ONE...
Like, DON'T TOUCH THE ***PLASTOMIC DISPLAYS!***
OH...HEY, MAKINO.
PLATONIC? WELL, I HOPE SO. SEEING THESE THINGS HAVING SEX WOULD BE JUST ONE STEP OVER THE LINE.
NOT "PLATONIC"! ***PLASTOMIC!***

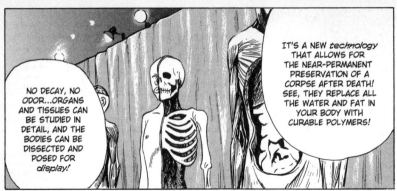

IT'S A NEW *technology* THAT ALLOWS FOR THE NEAR-PERMANENT PRESERVATION OF A CORPSE AFTER DEATH! SEE, THEY REPLACE ALL THE WATER AND FAT IN YOUR BODY WITH CURABLE POLYMERS!

NO DECAY, NO ODOR...ORGANS AND TISSUES CAN BE STUDIED IN DETAIL, AND THE BODIES CAN BE DISSECTED AND POSED FOR *display!*

huh?

WHO'S THIS?

...WHERE ALL THE SIGNS SAY, "DO NOT TOUCH"...IF ANYONE BOTHERS TO READ THEM.

OH! I GOT THE TICKETS FROM THIS GUY. *Um,* THIS IS TAKASHI NUNOKUSA, DIRECTOR OF THE NUNOKUSA BIOLOGICAL PRESERVATION & RESEARCH FACILITY. THEY SPONSORED THIS EXHIBITION.

HELLO. NICE TO MEET YOU ALL.

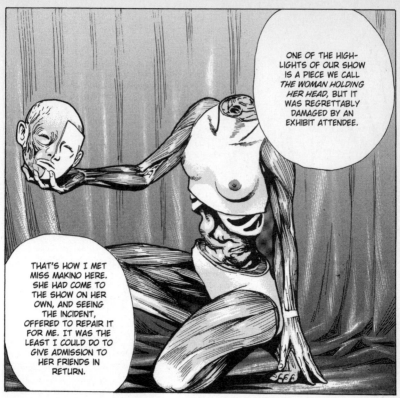

ONE OF THE HIGH-LIGHTS OF OUR SHOW IS A PIECE WE CALL *THE WOMAN HOLDING HER HEAD*, BUT IT WAS REGRETTABLY DAMAGED BY AN EXHIBIT ATTENDEE.

THAT'S HOW I MET MISS MAKINO HERE. SHE HAD COME TO THE SHOW ON HER OWN, AND SEEING THE INCIDENT, OFFERED TO REPAIR IT FOR ME. IT WAS THE LEAST I COULD DO TO GIVE ADMISSION TO HER FRIENDS IN RETURN.

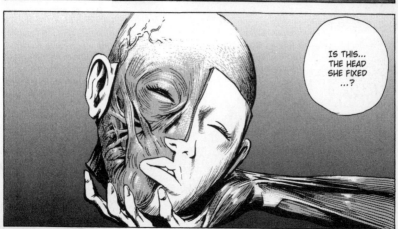

IS THIS... THE HEAD SHE FIXED ...?

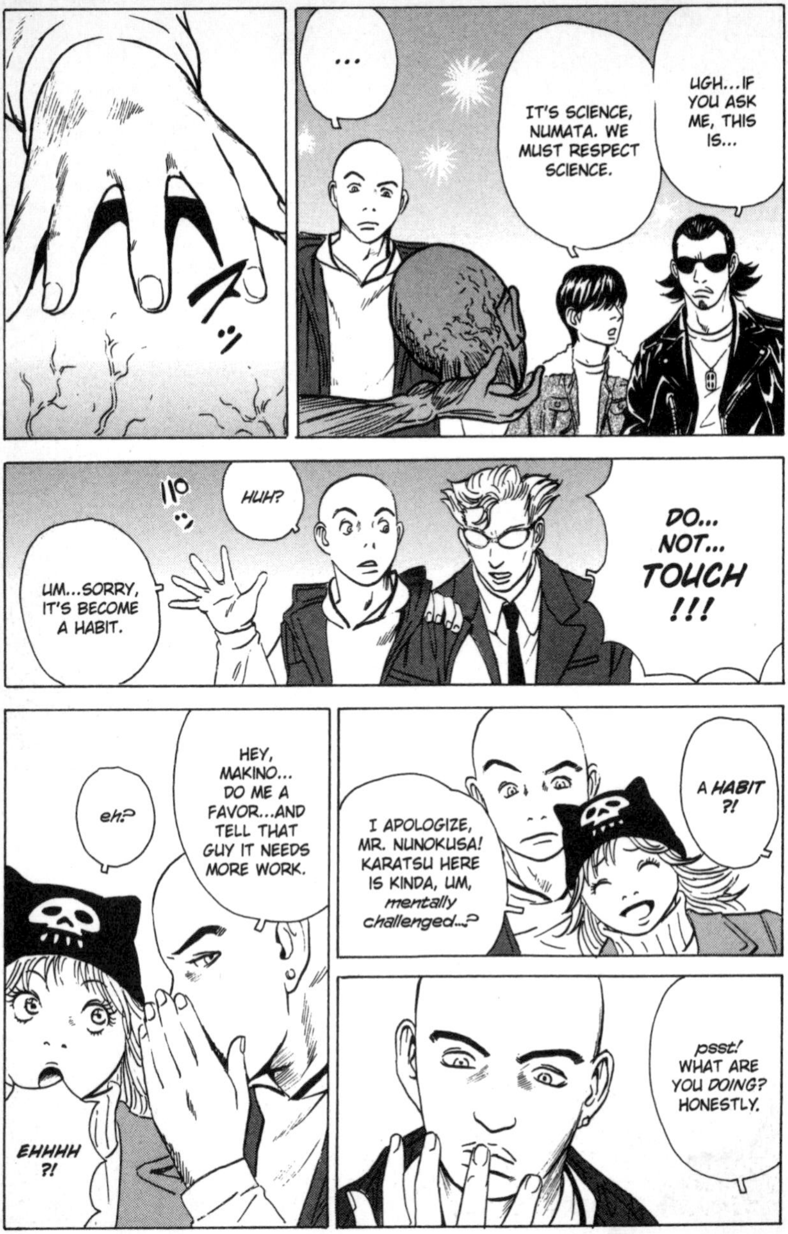
UGH...IF YOU ASK ME, THIS IS...
IT'S SCIENCE, NUMATA. WE MUST RESPECT SCIENCE.
...
DO... NOT... TOUCH !!!
HUH?
UM...SORRY, IT'S BECOME A HABIT.
A HABIT ?!
I APOLOGIZE, MR. NUNOKUSA! KARATSU HERE IS KINDA, UM, mentally challenged...?
psst! WHAT ARE YOU DOING? HONESTLY.
HEY, MAKINO... DO ME A FAVOR...AND TELL THAT GUY IT NEEDS MORE WORK.
eh?
EHHHH ?!

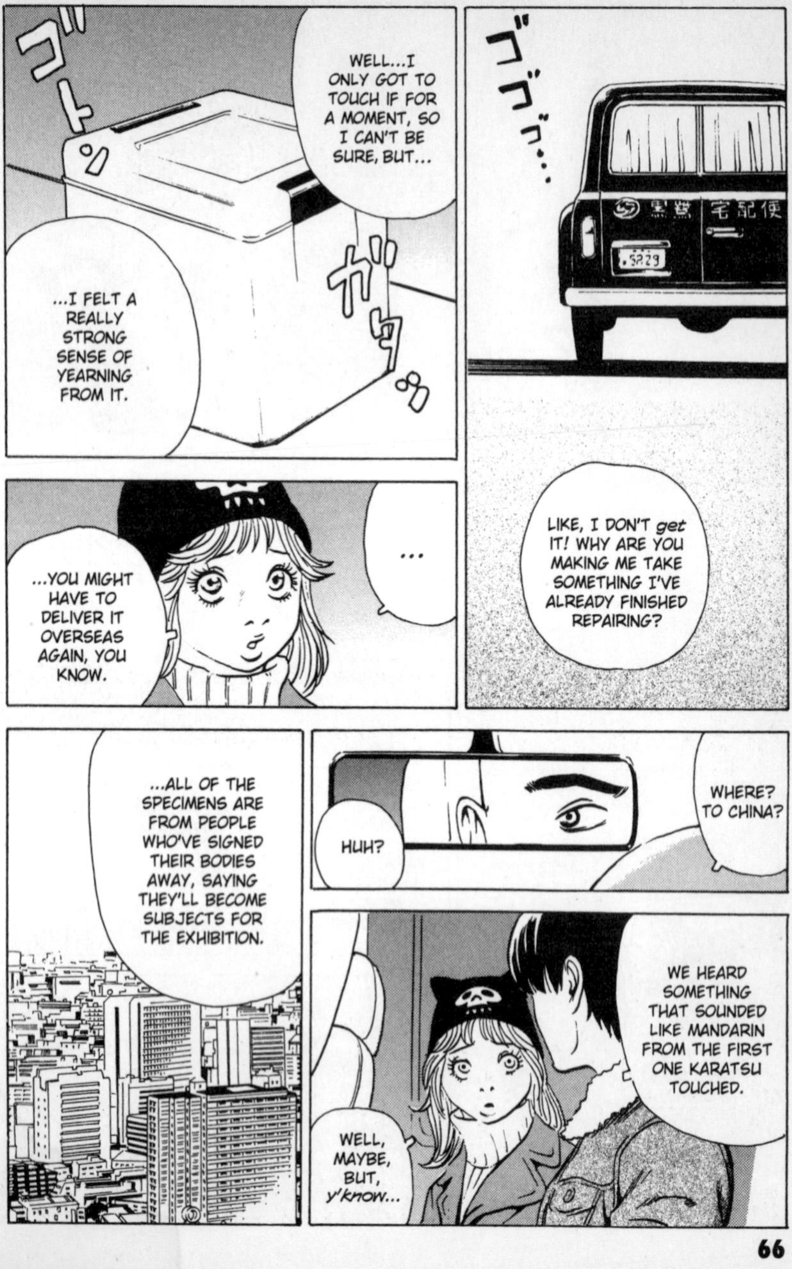
ゴゴゴ…
宅配便
LIKE, I DON'T *get* IT! WHY ARE YOU MAKING ME TAKE SOMETHING I'VE ALREADY FINISHED REPAIRING?
ゴトッ
WELL...I ONLY GOT TO TOUCH IF FOR A MOMENT, SO I CAN'T BE SURE, BUT...
ガタッ
...I FELT A REALLY STRONG SENSE OF YEARNING FROM IT.
...
...YOU MIGHT HAVE TO DELIVER IT OVERSEAS AGAIN, YOU KNOW.
WHERE? TO CHINA?
HUH?
WE HEARD SOMETHING THAT SOUNDED LIKE MANDARIN FROM THE FIRST ONE KARATSU TOUCHED.
WELL, MAYBE, BUT, *y'know*...
...ALL OF THE SPECIMENS ARE FROM PEOPLE WHO'VE SIGNED THEIR BODIES AWAY, SAYING THEY'LL BECOME SUBJECTS FOR THE EXHIBITION.

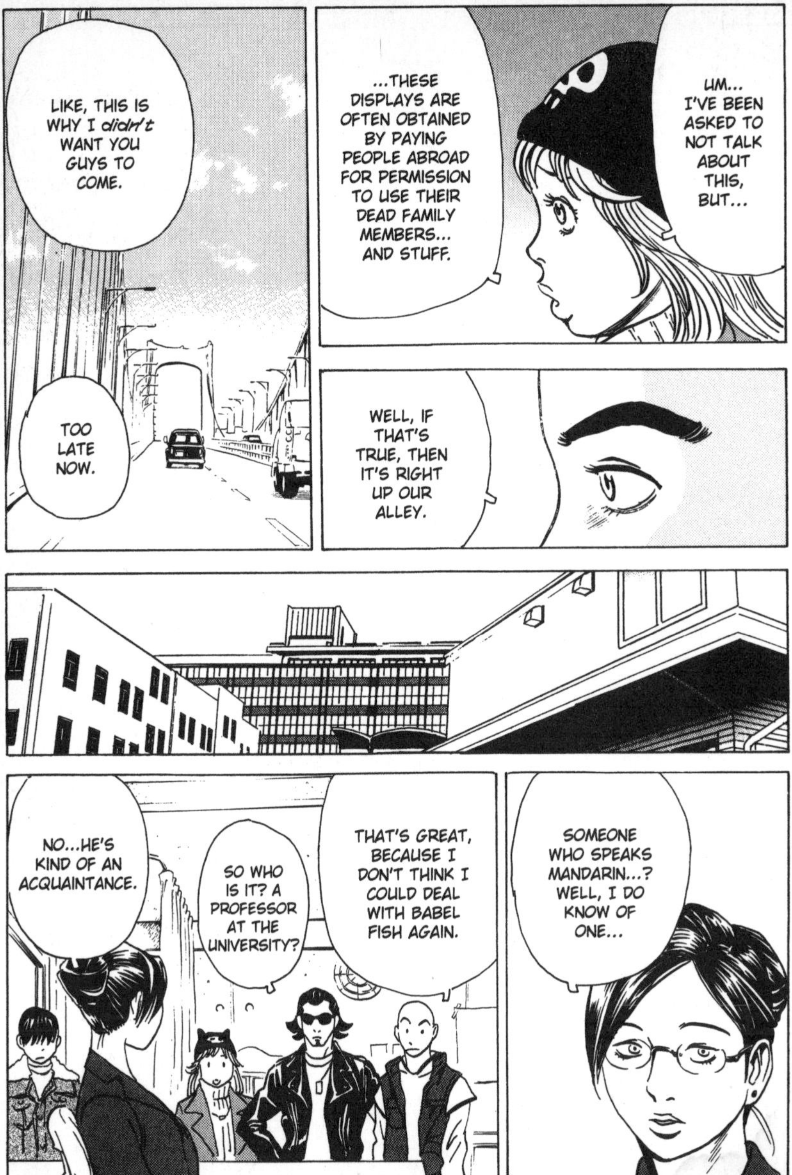
UM... I'VE BEEN ASKED TO NOT TALK ABOUT THIS, BUT...
...THESE DISPLAYS ARE OFTEN OBTAINED BY PAYING PEOPLE ABROAD FOR PERMISSION TO USE THEIR DEAD FAMILY MEMBERS... AND STUFF.
WELL, IF THAT'S TRUE, THEN IT'S RIGHT UP OUR ALLEY.
LIKE, THIS IS WHY I *didn't* WANT YOU GUYS TO COME.
TOO LATE NOW.
SOMEONE WHO SPEAKS MANDARIN...? WELL, I DO KNOW OF ONE...
THAT'S GREAT, BECAUSE I DON'T THINK I COULD DEAL WITH BABEL FISH AGAIN.
SO WHO IS IT? A PROFESSOR AT THE UNIVERSITY?
NO...HE'S KIND OF AN ACQUAINTANCE.

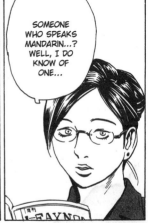

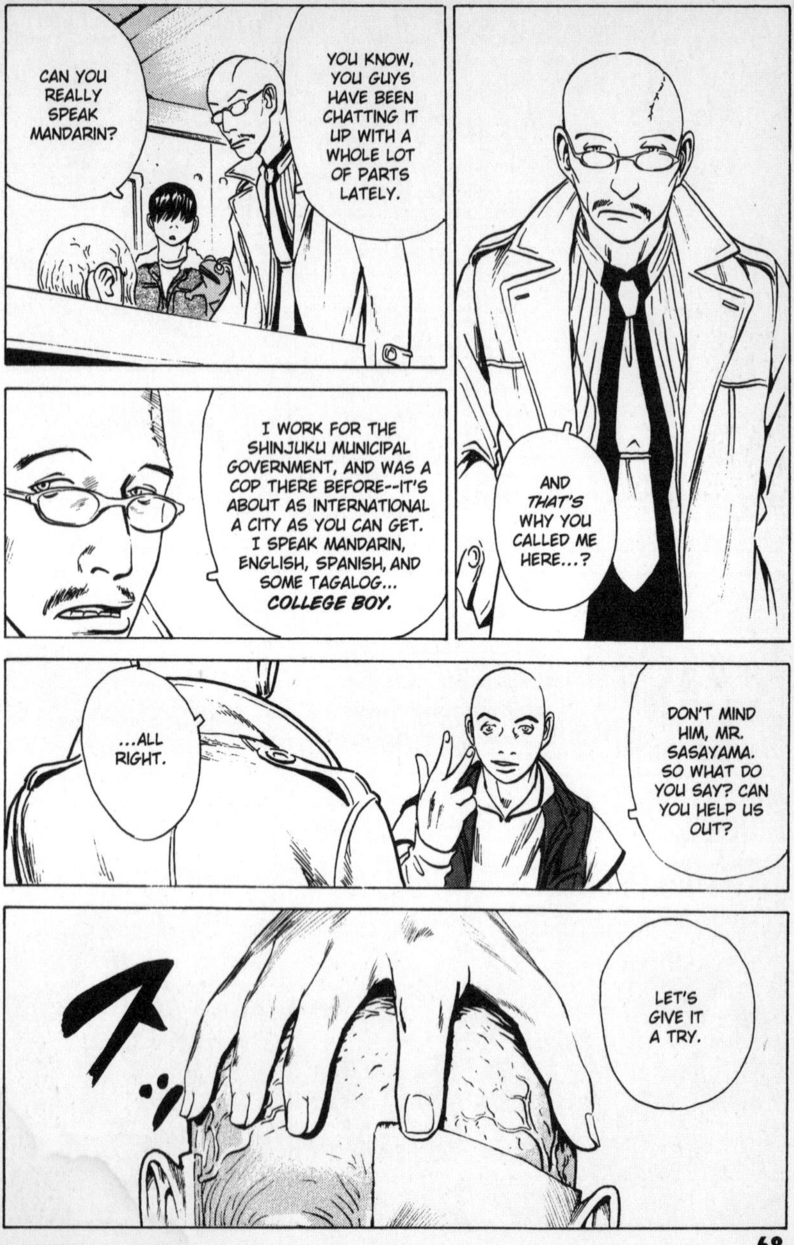
AND *THAT'S* WHY YOU CALLED ME HERE...?
YOU KNOW, YOU GUYS HAVE BEEN CHATTING IT UP WITH A WHOLE LOT OF PARTS LATELY.
CAN YOU REALLY SPEAK MANDARIN?
I WORK FOR THE SHINJUKU MUNICIPAL GOVERNMENT, AND WAS A COP THERE BEFORE--IT'S ABOUT AS INTERNATIONAL A CITY AS YOU CAN GET. I SPEAK MANDARIN, ENGLISH, SPANISH, AND SOME TAGALOG... ***COLLEGE BOY.***
DON'T MIND HIM, MR. SASAYAMA. SO WHAT DO YOU SAY? CAN YOU HELP US OUT?
...ALL RIGHT.
LET'S GIVE IT A TRY.

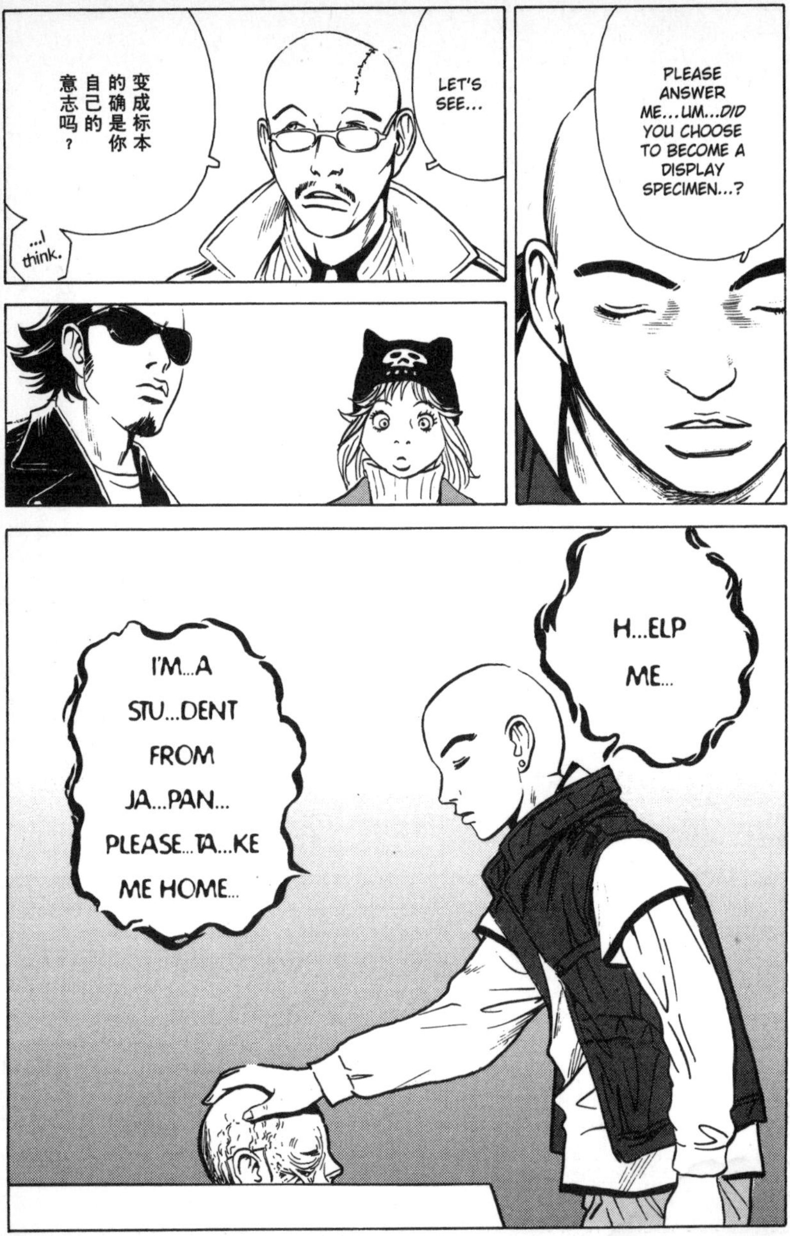
PLEASE ANSWER ME...UM...*DID* YOU CHOOSE TO BECOME A DISPLAY SPECIMEN...?
LET'S SEE...
变成标本的确是你自己的意志吗？
...I think.
H...ELP ME...
I'M...A STU...DENT FROM JA...PAN... PLEASE...TA...KE ME HOME...

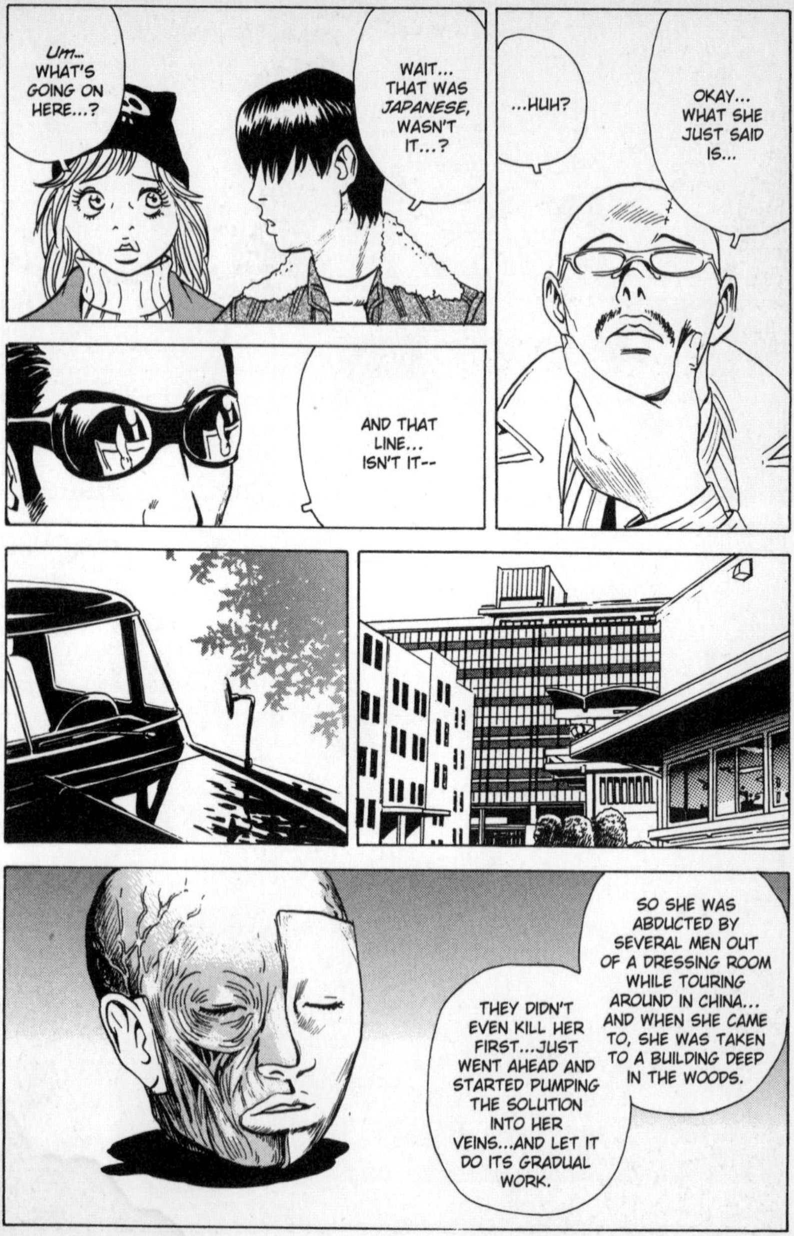
OKAY... WHAT SHE JUST SAID IS...
...HUH?
WAIT... THAT WAS *JAPANESE,* WASN'T IT...?
Um... WHAT'S GOING ON HERE...?
AND THAT LINE... ISN'T IT--
SO SHE WAS ABDUCTED BY SEVERAL MEN OUT OF A DRESSING ROOM WHILE TOURING AROUND IN CHINA... AND WHEN SHE CAME TO, SHE WAS TAKEN TO A BUILDING DEEP IN THE WOODS.
THEY DIDN'T EVEN KILL HER FIRST...JUST WENT AHEAD AND STARTED PUMPING THE SOLUTION INTO HER VEINS...AND LET IT DO ITS GRADUAL WORK.

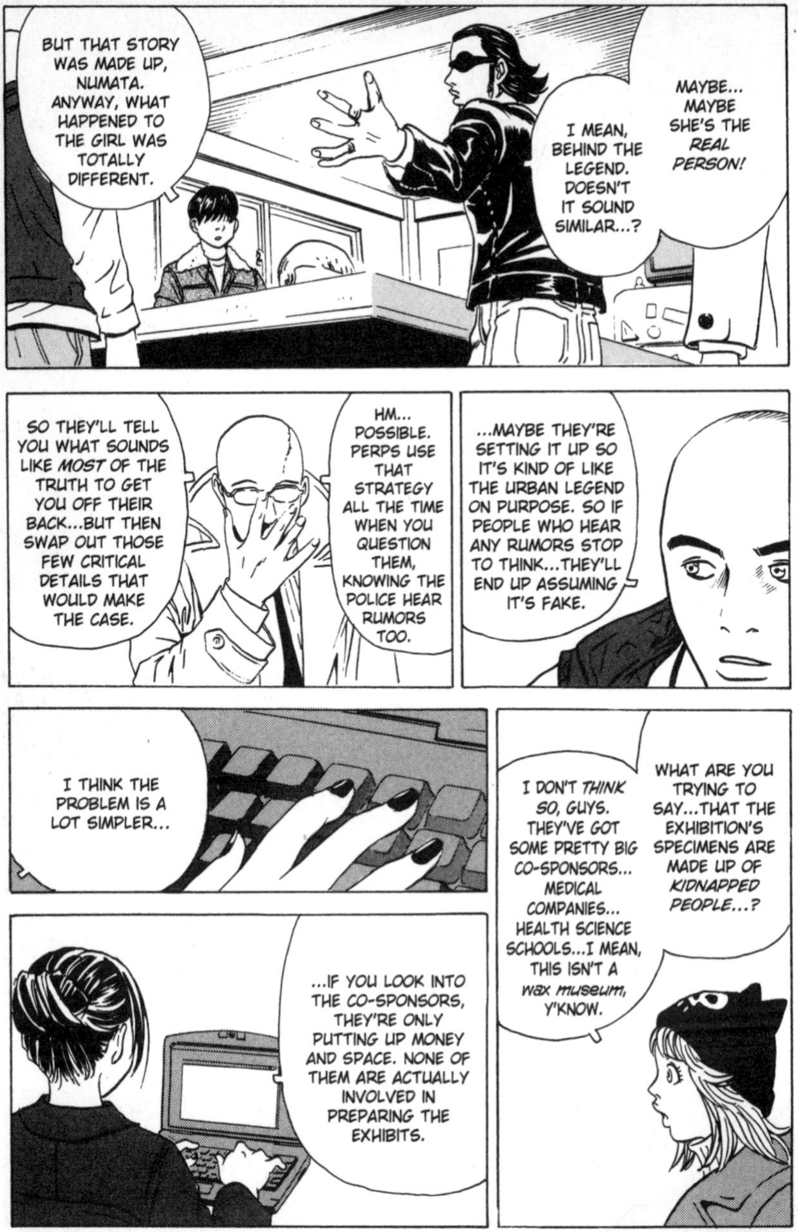
MAYBE... MAYBE SHE'S THE *REAL PERSON!*
I MEAN, BEHIND THE LEGEND. DOESN'T IT SOUND SIMILAR...?
BUT THAT STORY WAS MADE UP, NUMATA. ANYWAY, WHAT HAPPENED TO THE GIRL WAS TOTALLY DIFFERENT.
...MAYBE THEY'RE SETTING IT UP SO IT'S KIND OF LIKE THE URBAN LEGEND ON PURPOSE. SO IF PEOPLE WHO HEAR ANY RUMORS STOP TO THINK...THEY'LL END UP ASSUMING IT'S FAKE.
HM... POSSIBLE. PERPS USE THAT STRATEGY ALL THE TIME WHEN YOU QUESTION THEM, KNOWING THE POLICE HEAR RUMORS TOO.
SO THEY'LL TELL YOU WHAT SOUNDS LIKE *MOST* OF THE TRUTH TO GET YOU OFF THEIR BACK...BUT THEN SWAP OUT THOSE FEW CRITICAL DETAILS THAT WOULD MAKE THE CASE.
WHAT ARE YOU TRYING TO SAY...THAT THE EXHIBITION'S SPECIMENS ARE MADE UP OF *KIDNAPPED PEOPLE...?*
I DON'T *THINK SO*, GUYS. THEY'VE GOT SOME PRETTY BIG CO-SPONSORS... MEDICAL COMPANIES... HEALTH SCIENCE SCHOOLS...I MEAN, THIS ISN'T A *wax museum*, Y'KNOW.
I THINK THE PROBLEM IS A LOT SIMPLER...
...IF YOU LOOK INTO THE CO-SPONSORS, THEY'RE ONLY PUTTING UP MONEY AND SPACE. NONE OF THEM ARE ACTUALLY INVOLVED IN PREPARING THE EXHIBITS.

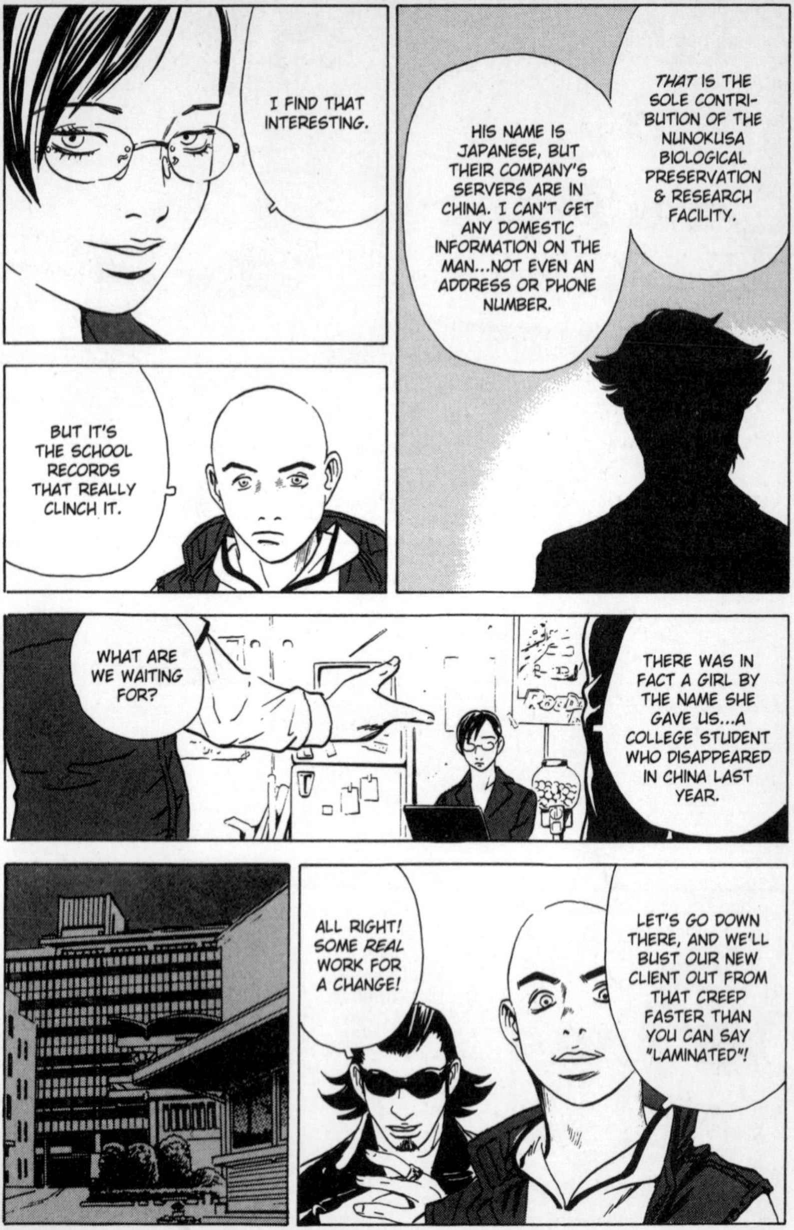

THAT IS THE SOLE CONTRIBUTION OF THE NUNOKUSA BIOLOGICAL PRESERVATION & RESEARCH FACILITY.
HIS NAME IS JAPANESE, BUT THEIR COMPANY'S SERVERS ARE IN CHINA. I CAN'T GET ANY DOMESTIC INFORMATION ON THE MAN...NOT EVEN AN ADDRESS OR PHONE NUMBER.
I FIND THAT INTERESTING.
BUT IT'S THE SCHOOL RECORDS THAT REALLY CLINCH IT.
THERE WAS IN FACT A GIRL BY THE NAME SHE GAVE US...A COLLEGE STUDENT WHO DISAPPEARED IN CHINA LAST YEAR.
WHAT ARE WE WAITING FOR?
LET'S GO DOWN THERE, AND WE'LL BUST OUR NEW CLIENT OUT FROM THAT CREEP FASTER THAN YOU CAN SAY "LAMINATED"!
ALL RIGHT! SOME *REAL* WORK FOR A CHANGE!

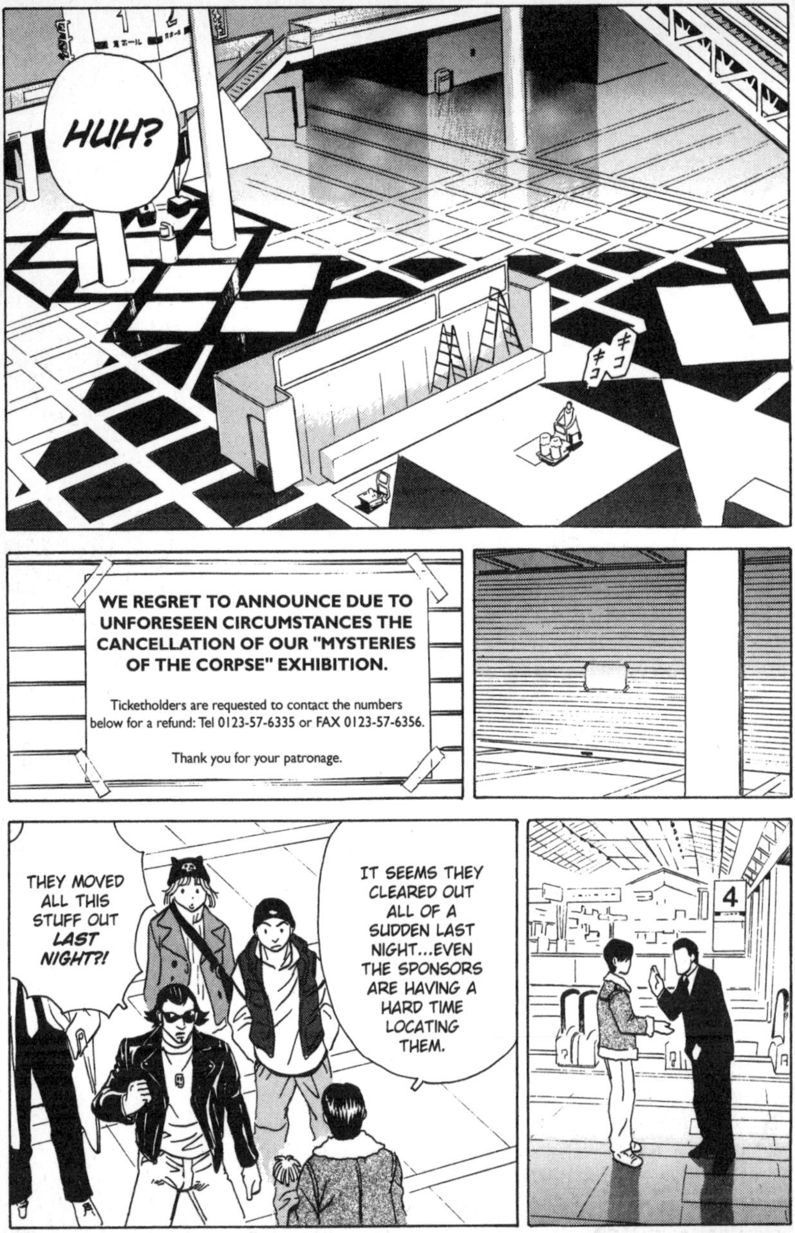
HUH?
キコ キコ
WE REGRET TO ANNOUNCE DUE TO UNFORESEEN CIRCUMSTANCES THE CANCELLATION OF OUR "MYSTERIES OF THE CORPSE" EXHIBITION.
Ticketholders are requested to contact the numbers below for a refund: Tel 0123-57-6335 or FAX 0123-57-6356.
Thank you for your patronage.
IT SEEMS THEY CLEARED OUT ALL OF A SUDDEN LAST NIGHT...EVEN THE SPONSORS ARE HAVING A HARD TIME LOCATING THEM.
THEY MOVED ALL THIS STUFF OUT LAST NIGHT?!
4

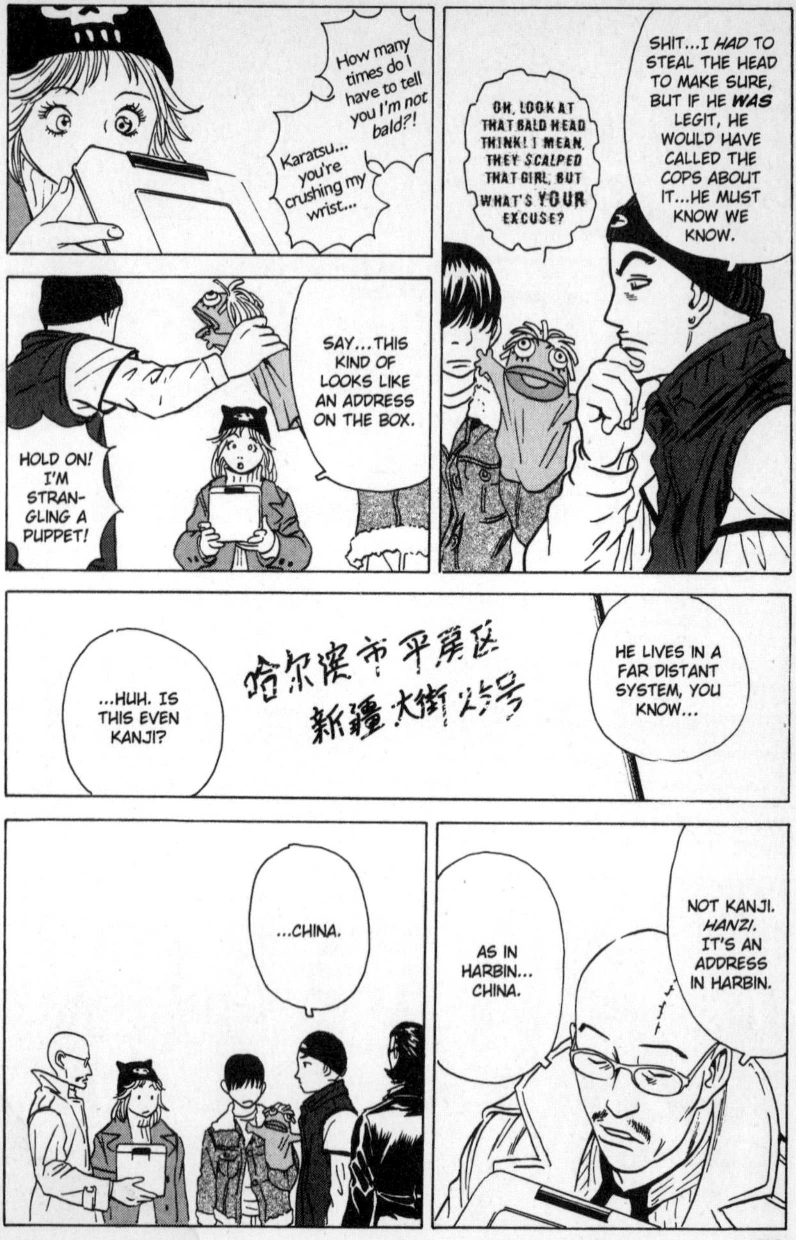
SHIT...I *HAD* TO STEAL THE HEAD TO MAKE SURE, BUT IF HE *WAS* LEGIT, HE WOULD HAVE CALLED THE COPS ABOUT IT...HE MUST KNOW WE KNOW.
OH, LOOK AT THAT BALD HEAD THINK! I MEAN, THEY *SCALPED* THAT GIRL, BUT WHAT'S **YOUR** EXCUSE?
How many times do I have to tell you I'm not bald?!
Karatsu... you're crushing my wrist...
SAY...THIS KIND OF LOOKS LIKE AN ADDRESS ON THE BOX.
HOLD ON! I'M STRAN-GLING A PUPPET!
HE LIVES IN A FAR DISTANT SYSTEM, YOU KNOW...
哈尔滨市平房区
...HUH. IS THIS EVEN KANJI?
NOT KANJI. *HANZI.* IT'S AN ADDRESS IN HARBIN.
AS IN HARBIN... CHINA.
...CHINA.

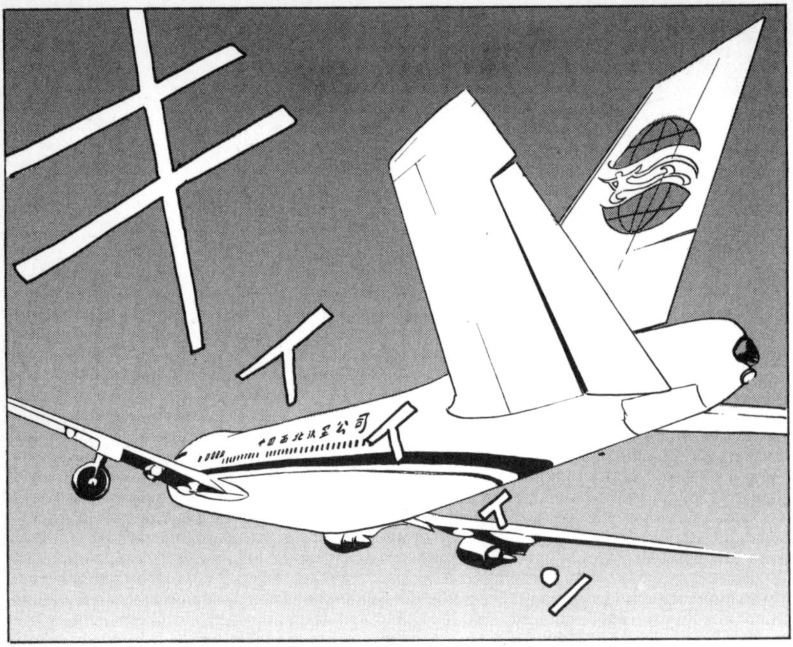
キィィィン

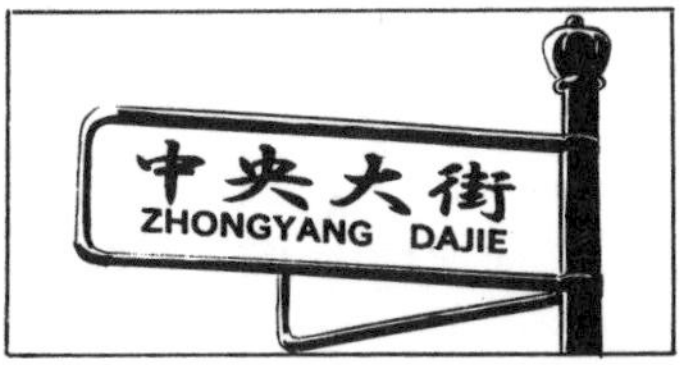
中央大街
ZHONGYANG DAJIE

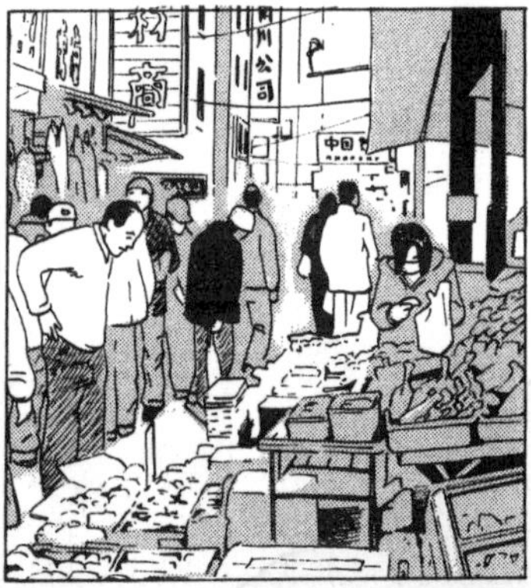

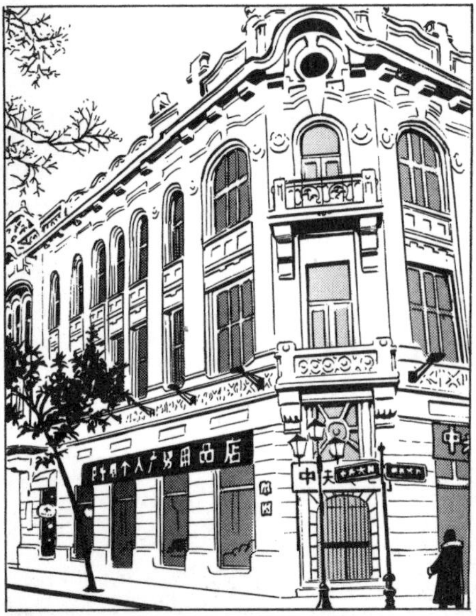

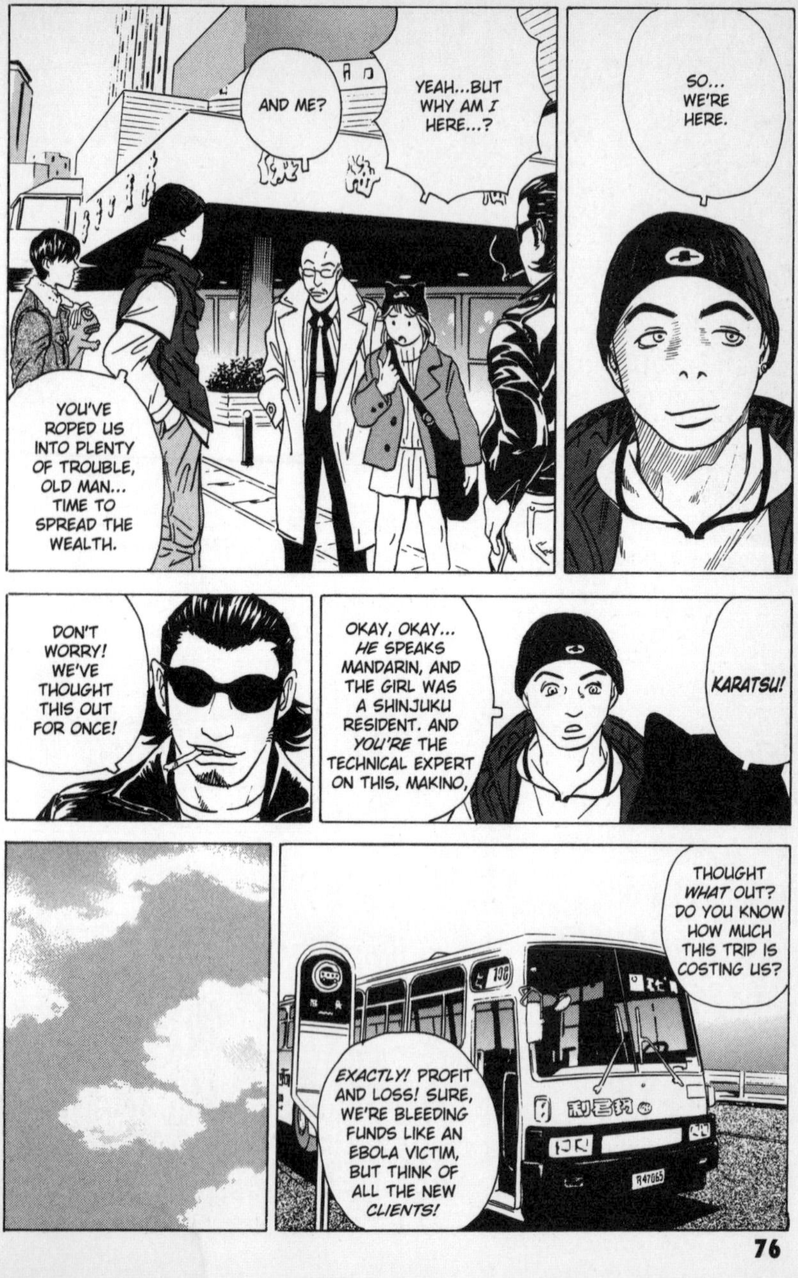
SO... WE'RE HERE.
YEAH...BUT WHY AM *I* HERE...?
AND ME?
YOU'VE ROPED US INTO PLENTY OF TROUBLE, OLD MAN... TIME TO SPREAD THE WEALTH.
KARATSU!
OKAY, OKAY... *HE* SPEAKS MANDARIN, AND THE GIRL WAS A SHINJUKU RESIDENT. AND *YOU'RE* THE TECHNICAL EXPERT ON THIS, MAKINO,
DON'T WORRY! WE'VE THOUGHT THIS OUT FOR ONCE!
THOUGHT *WHAT* OUT? DO YOU KNOW HOW MUCH THIS TRIP IS COSTING US?
EXACTLY! PROFIT AND LOSS! SURE, WE'RE BLEEDING FUNDS LIKE AN EBOLA VICTIM, BUT THINK OF ALL THE NEW *CLIENTS!*

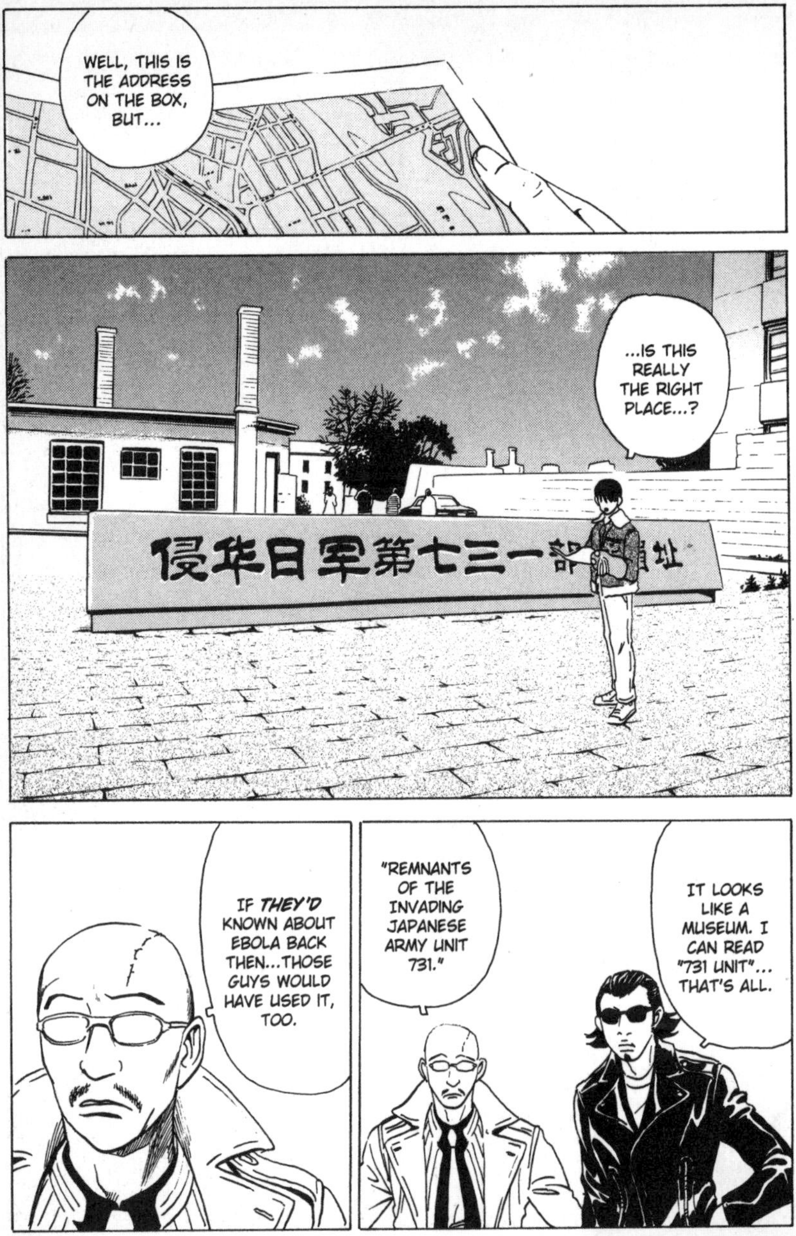
WELL, THIS IS THE ADDRESS ON THE BOX, BUT...
...IS THIS REALLY THE RIGHT PLACE...?
侵华日军第七三一部
址
IT LOOKS LIKE A MUSEUM. I CAN READ "731 UNIT"... THAT'S ALL.
"REMNANTS OF THE INVADING JAPANESE ARMY UNIT 731."
IF *THEY'D* KNOWN ABOUT EBOLA BACK THEN...THOSE GUYS WOULD HAVE USED IT, TOO.

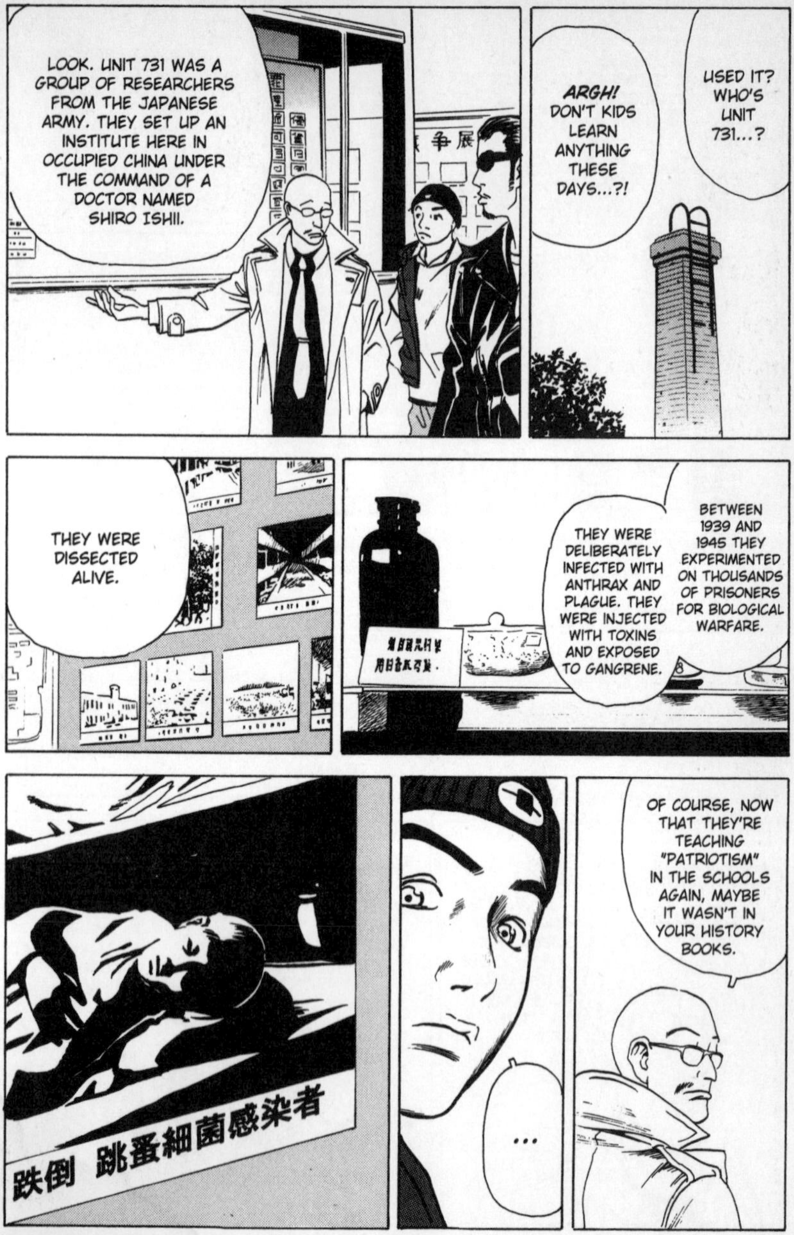
USED IT? WHO'S UNIT 731...?
ARGH! DON'T KIDS LEARN ANYTHING THESE DAYS...?!
LOOK. UNIT 731 WAS A GROUP OF RESEARCHERS FROM THE JAPANESE ARMY. THEY SET UP AN INSTITUTE HERE IN OCCUPIED CHINA UNDER THE COMMAND OF A DOCTOR NAMED SHIRO ISHII.
BETWEEN 1939 AND 1945 THEY EXPERIMENTED ON THOUSANDS OF PRISONERS FOR BIOLOGICAL WARFARE.
THEY WERE DELIBERATELY INFECTED WITH ANTHRAX AND PLAGUE. THEY WERE INJECTED WITH TOXINS AND EXPOSED TO GANGRENE.
THEY WERE DISSECTED ALIVE.
OF COURSE, NOW THAT THEY'RE TEACHING "PATRIOTISM" IN THE SCHOOLS AGAIN, MAYBE IT WASN'T IN YOUR HISTORY BOOKS.
...
跌倒 跳蚤細菌感染者

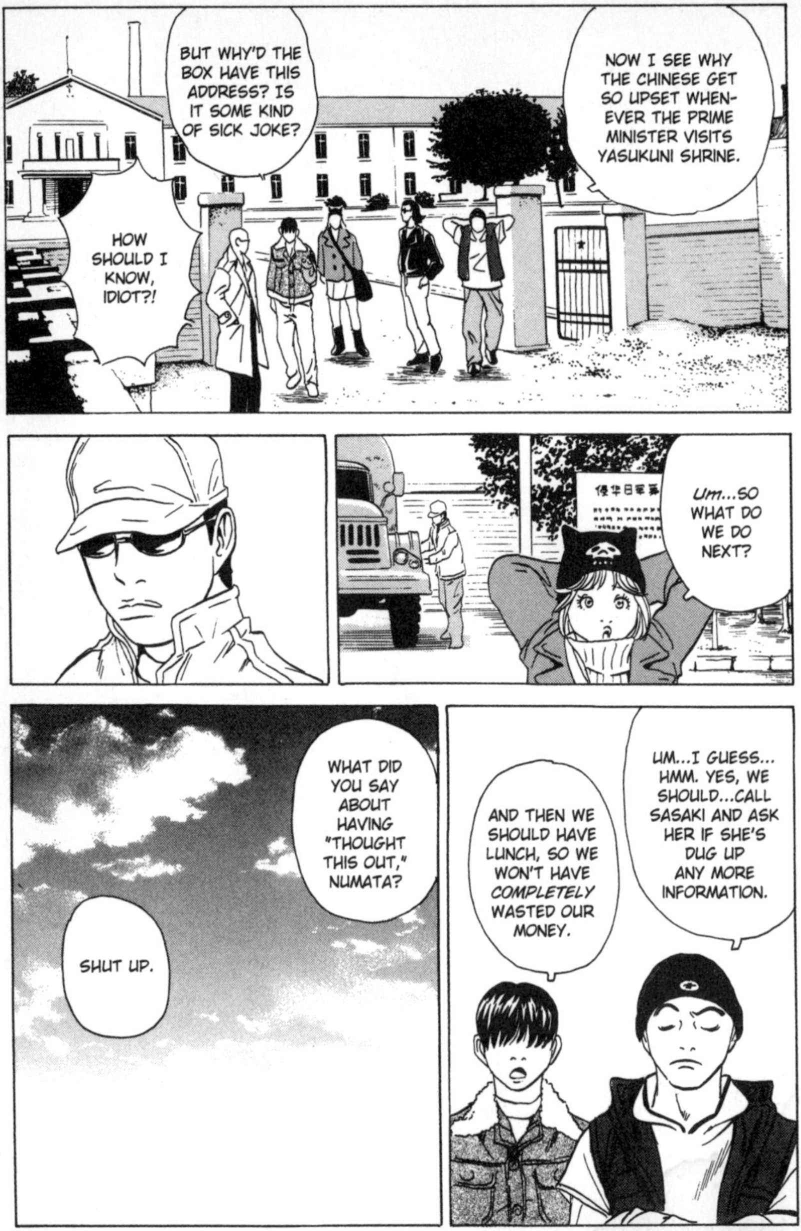
NOW I SEE WHY THE CHINESE GET SO UPSET WHENEVER THE PRIME MINISTER VISITS YASUKUNI SHRINE.
BUT WHY'D THE BOX HAVE THIS ADDRESS? IS IT SOME KIND OF SICK JOKE?
HOW SHOULD I KNOW, IDIOT?!
Um...SO WHAT DO WE DO NEXT?
UM...I GUESS... HMM. YES, WE SHOULD...CALL SASAKI AND ASK HER IF SHE'S DUG UP ANY MORE INFORMATION.
AND THEN WE SHOULD HAVE LUNCH, SO WE WON'T HAVE *COMPLETELY* WASTED OUR MONEY.
WHAT DID YOU SAY ABOUT HAVING "THOUGHT THIS OUT," NUMATA?
SHUT UP.

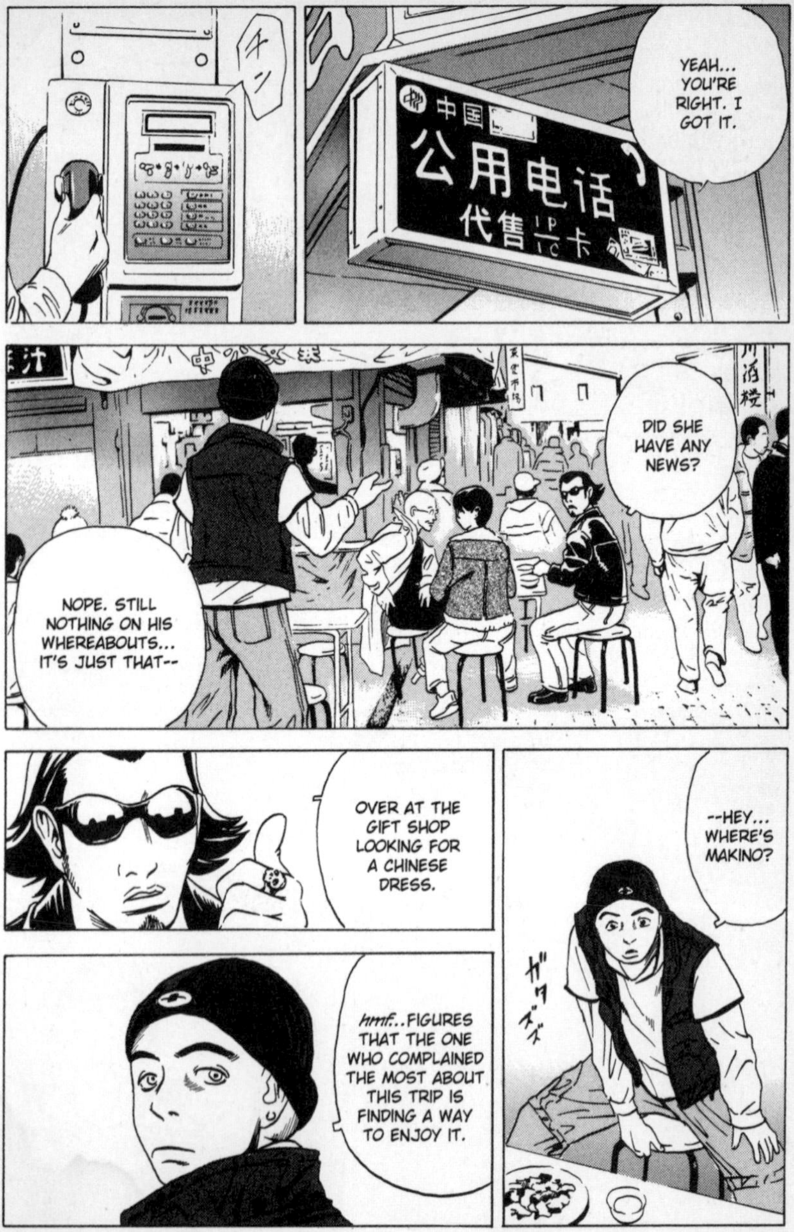
中国
公用电话
YEAH... YOU'RE RIGHT. I GOT IT.
DID SHE HAVE ANY NEWS?
NOPE. STILL NOTHING ON HIS WHEREABOUTS... IT'S JUST THAT--
--HEY... WHERE'S MAKINO?
OVER AT THE GIFT SHOP LOOKING FOR A CHINESE DRESS.
hmf...FIGURES THAT THE ONE WHO COMPLAINED THE MOST ABOUT THIS TRIP IS FINDING A WAY TO ENJOY IT.

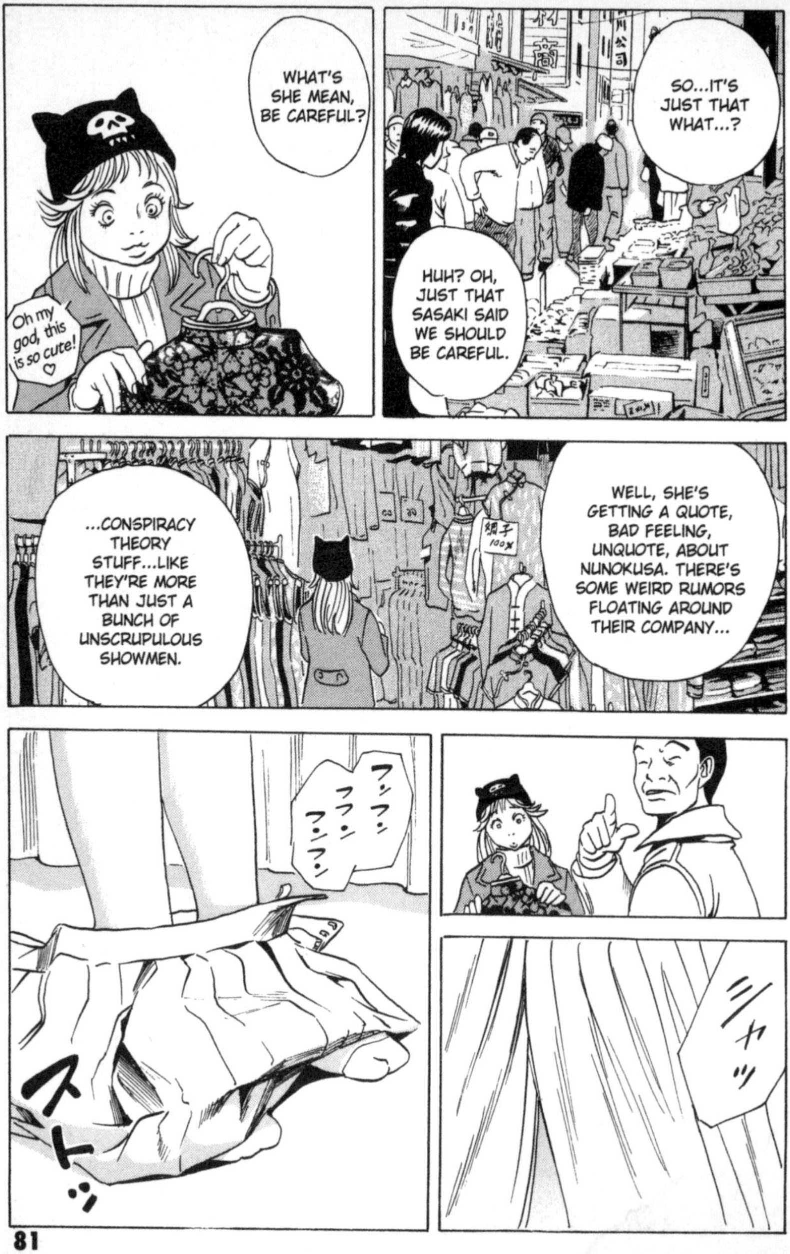
SO...IT'S JUST THAT WHAT...?
HUH? OH, JUST THAT SASAKI SAID WE SHOULD BE CAREFUL.
WHAT'S SHE MEAN, BE CAREFUL?
Oh my god, this is so cute! ♡
WELL, SHE'S GETTING A QUOTE, BAD FEELING, UNQUOTE, ABOUT NUNOKUSA. THERE'S SOME WEIRD RUMORS FLOATING AROUND THEIR COMPANY...
...CONSPIRACY THEORY STUFF...LIKE THEY'RE MORE THAN JUST A BUNCH OF UNSCRUPULOUS SHOWMEN.
シャッ
フンフン
フフン
フンフン
ストッ

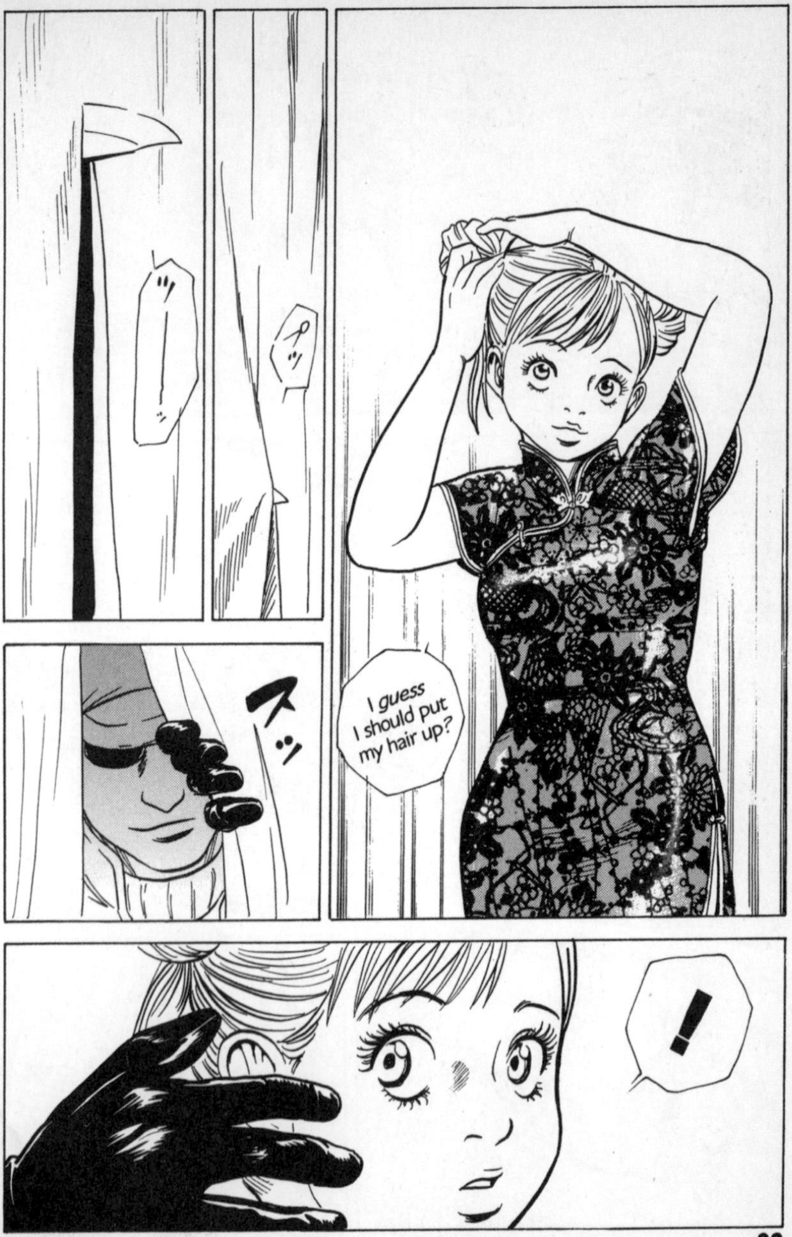
I *guess*
I should put
my hair up?
スッ
!

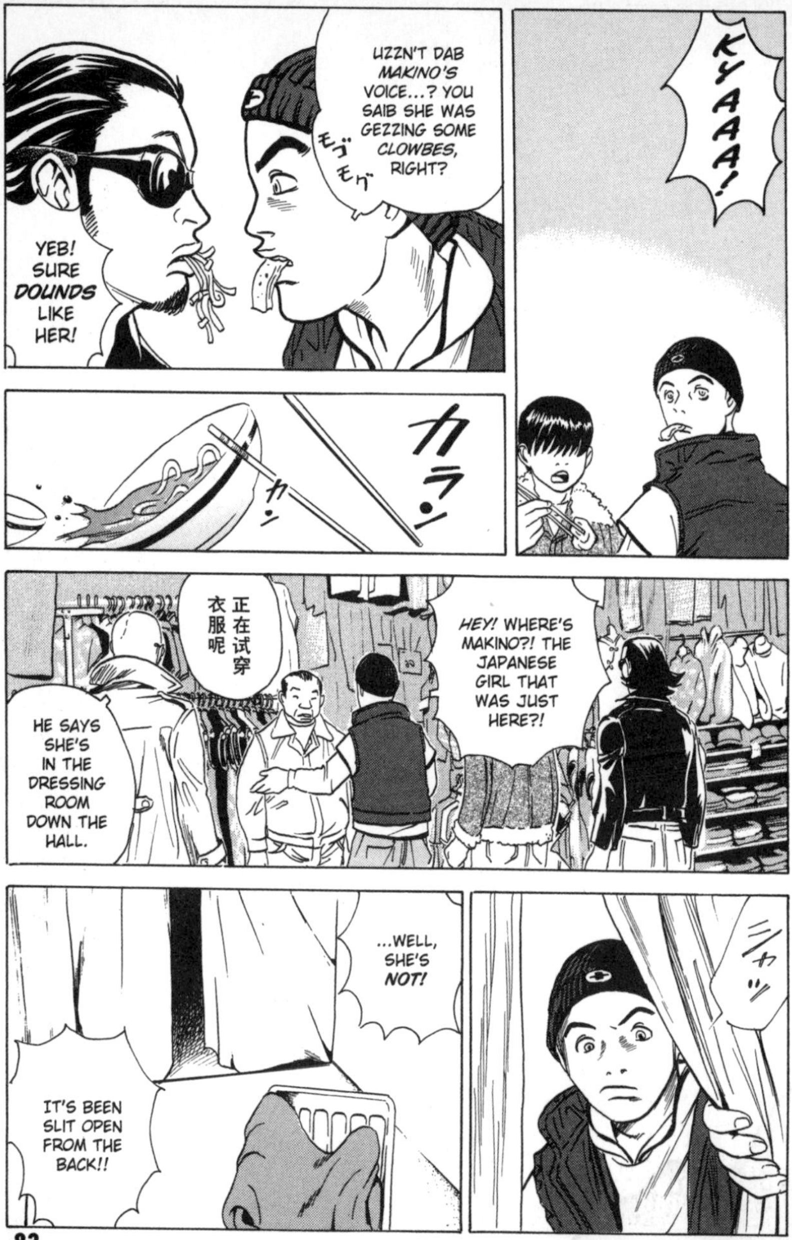
KYAAAA!
UZZN'T DAB *MAKINO'S* VOICE...? YOU SAIB SHE WAS GEZZING SOME *CLOWBES*, RIGHT?
モゴモグ
YEB! SURE ***DOUNDS*** LIKE HER!
カラン
カン
HEY! WHERE'S MAKINO?! THE JAPANESE GIRL THAT WAS JUST HERE?!
正在试穿衣服呢
HE SAYS SHE'S IN THE DRESSING ROOM DOWN THE HALL.
シャッ
...WELL, SHE'S ***NOT!***
IT'S BEEN SLIT OPEN FROM THE BACK!!

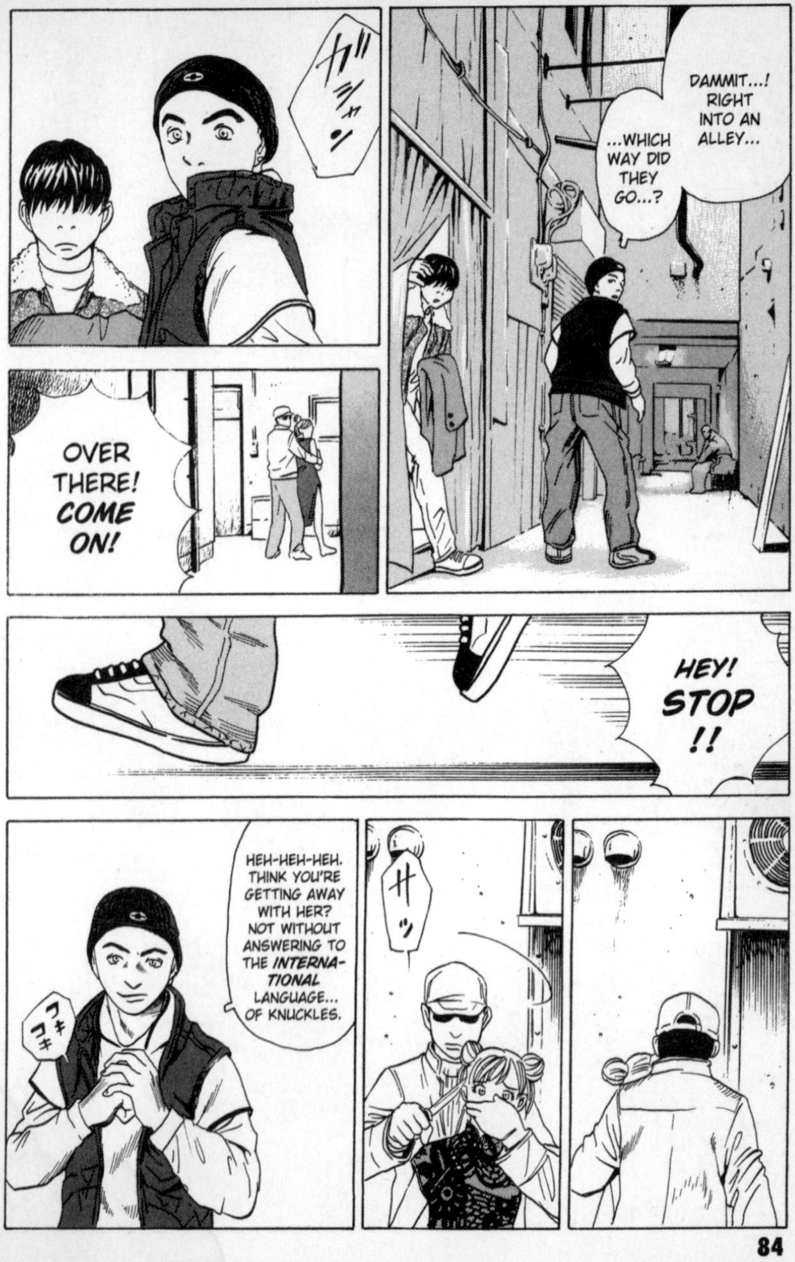
DAMMIT...! RIGHT INTO AN ALLEY...
...WHICH WAY DID THEY GO...?
ガシャン
OVER THERE! COME ON!
HEY! STOP!!
ハッ
HEH-HEH-HEH. THINK YOU'RE GETTING AWAY WITH HER? NOT WITHOUT ANSWERING TO THE INTERNATIONAL LANGUAGE... OF KNUCKLES.
コキ コキ

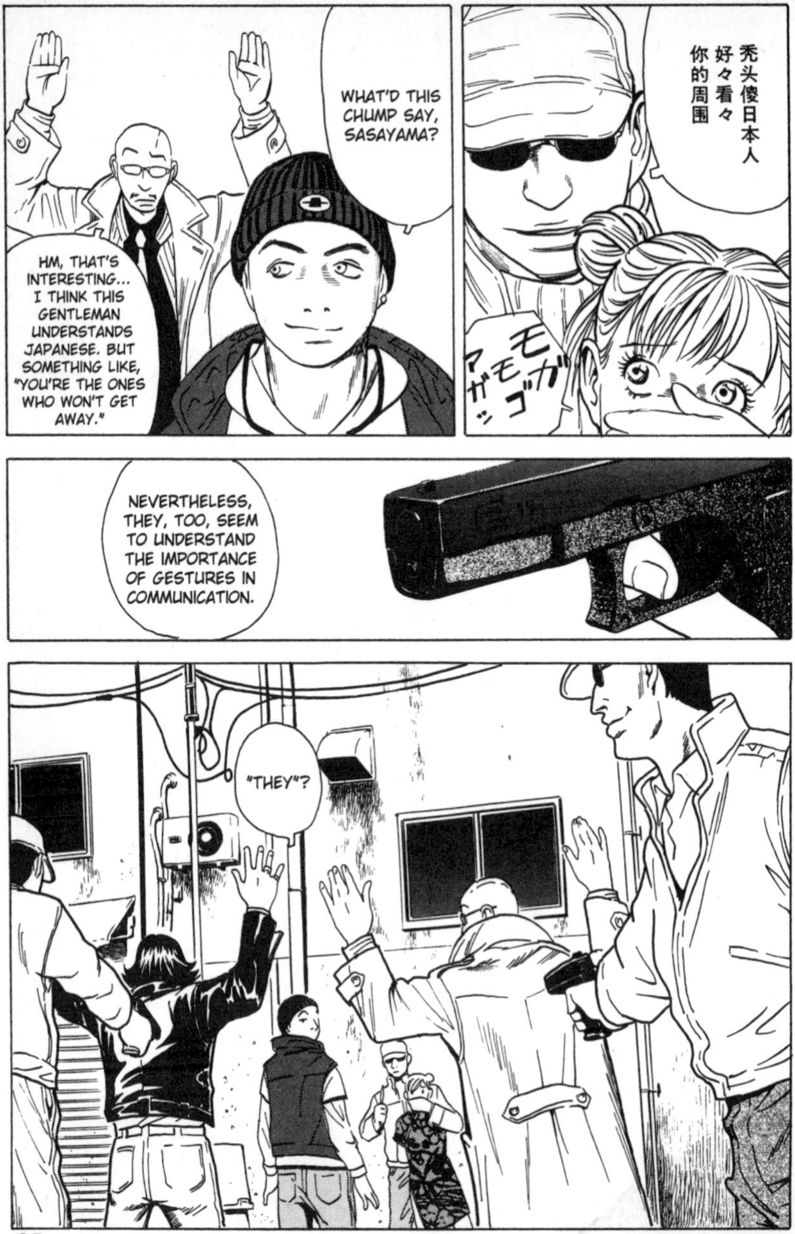
秃头傻日本人好々看々你的周围
モガモゴマガッ
WHAT'D THIS CHUMP SAY, SASAYAMA?
HM, THAT'S INTERESTING... I THINK THIS GENTLEMAN UNDERSTANDS JAPANESE. BUT SOMETHING LIKE, "YOU'RE THE ONES WHO WON'T GET AWAY."
NEVERTHELESS, THEY, TOO, SEEM TO UNDERSTAND THE IMPORTANCE OF GESTURES IN COMMUNICATION.
"THEY"?

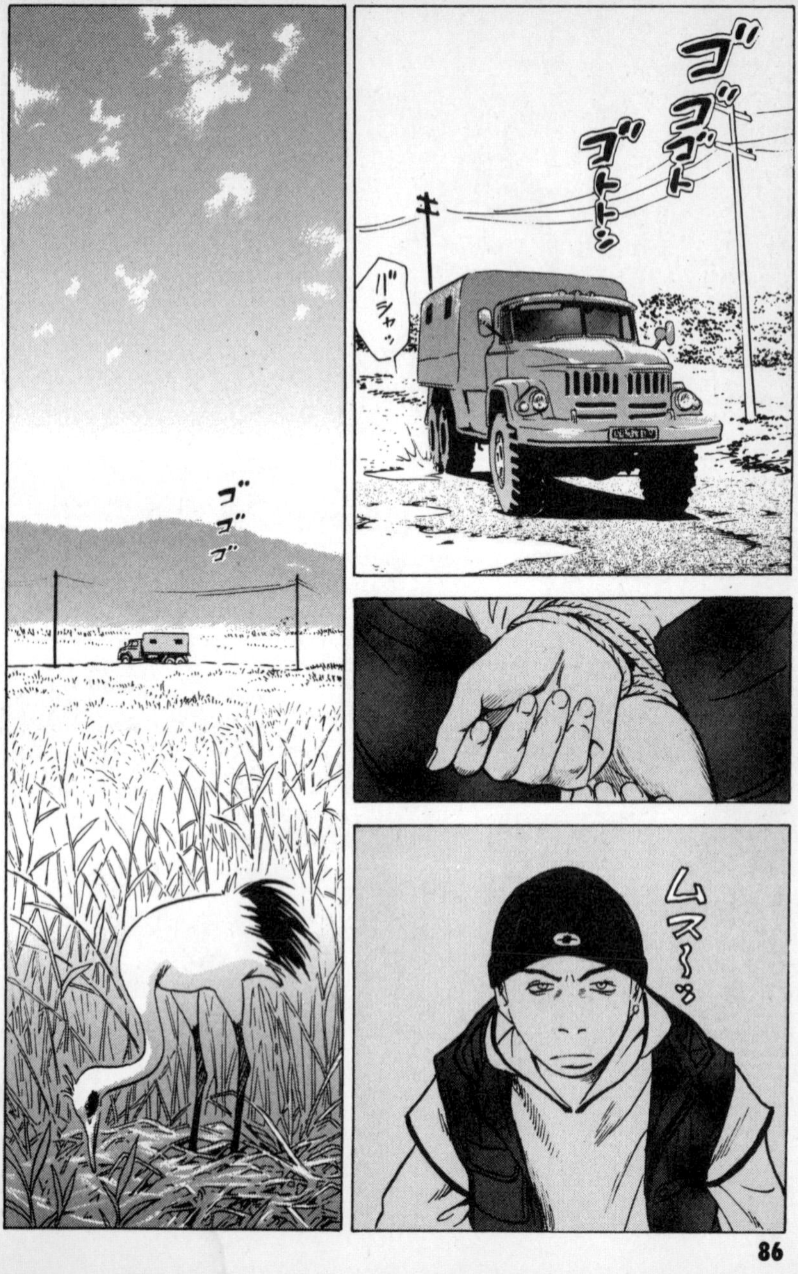
ゴゴゴト
ゴトトン
バシャッ
ムス～ッ
ゴゴゴ

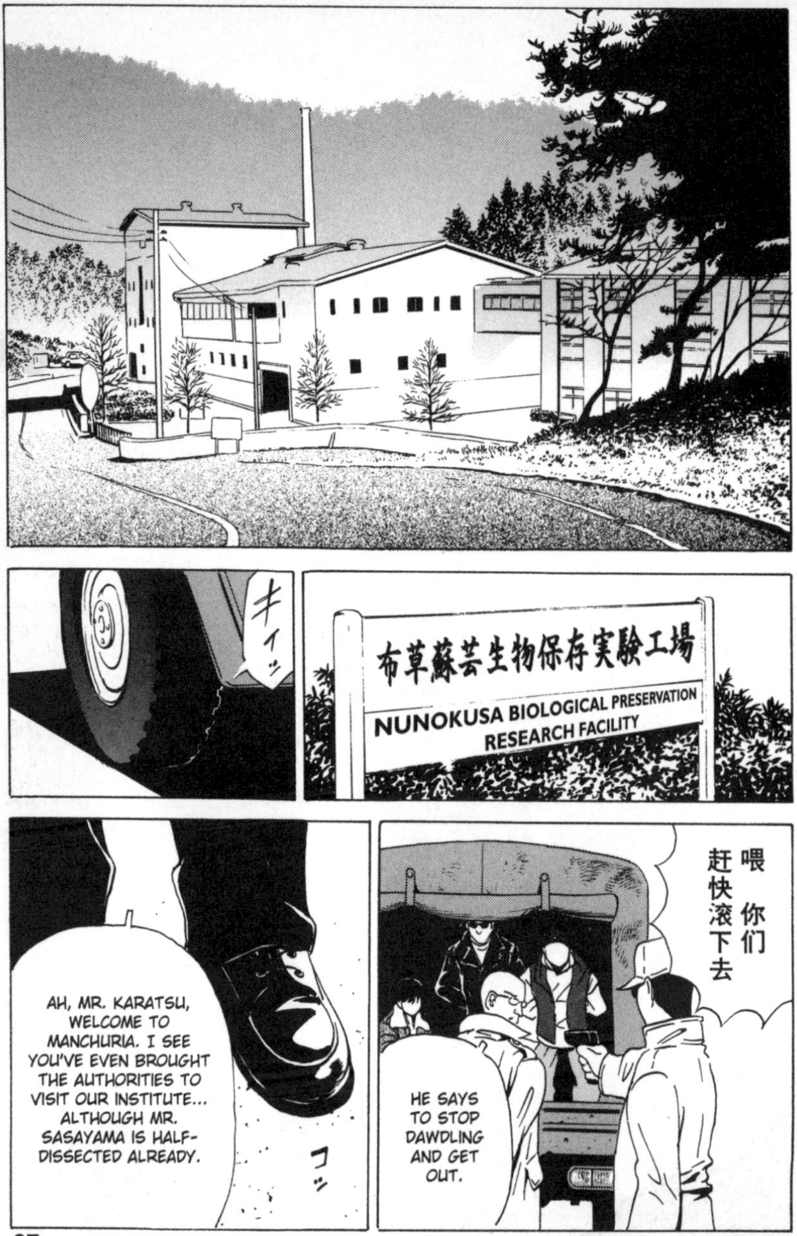
布草蘇芸生物保存実験工場
NUNOKUSA BIOLOGICAL PRESERVATION RESEARCH FACILITY
キイッ
喂 你们
赶快滚下去
HE SAYS TO STOP DAWDLING AND GET OUT.
AH, MR. KARATSU, WELCOME TO MANCHURIA. I SEE YOU'VE EVEN BROUGHT THE AUTHORITIES TO VISIT OUR INSTITUTE... ALTHOUGH MR. SASAYAMA IS HALF-DISSECTED ALREADY.
コツ

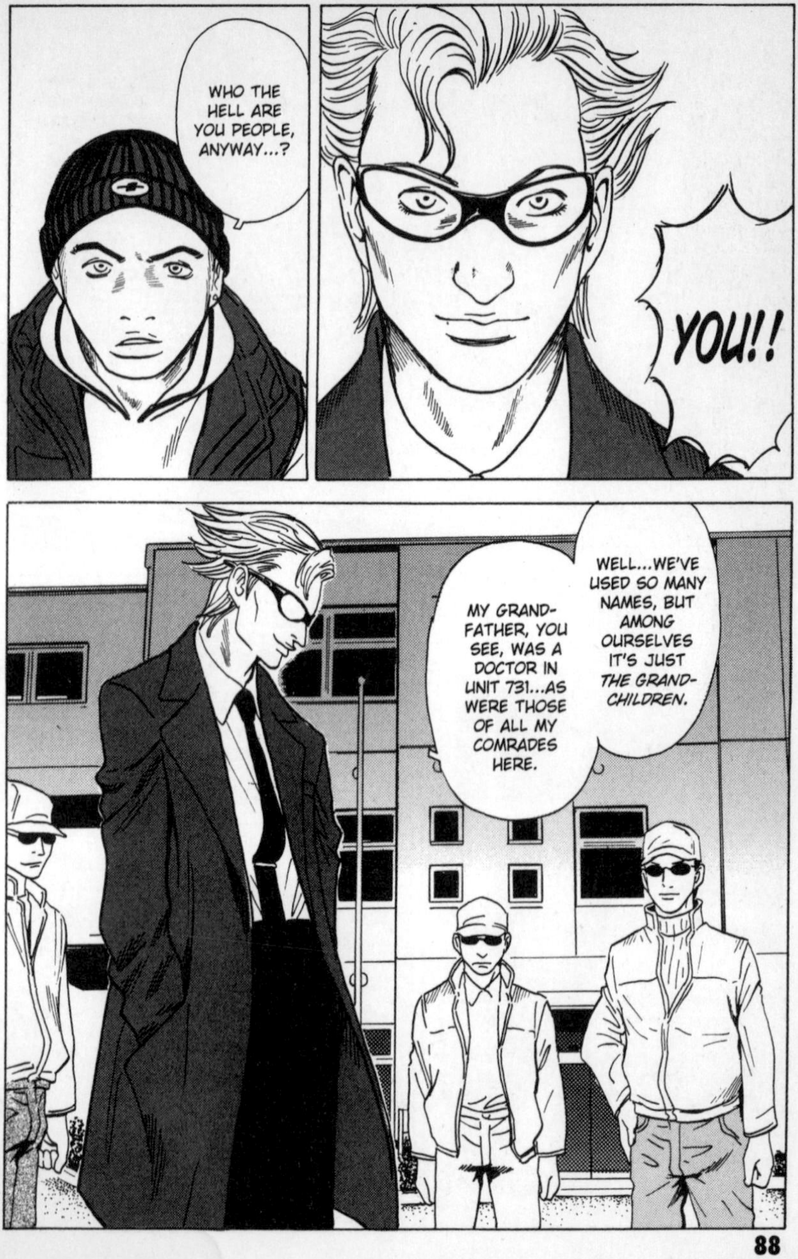
YOU!!
WHO THE HELL ARE YOU PEOPLE, ANYWAY...?
WELL...WE'VE USED SO MANY NAMES, BUT AMONG OURSELVES IT'S JUST *THE GRAND-CHILDREN.*
MY GRAND-FATHER, YOU SEE, WAS A DOCTOR IN UNIT 731...AS WERE THOSE OF ALL MY COMRADES HERE.

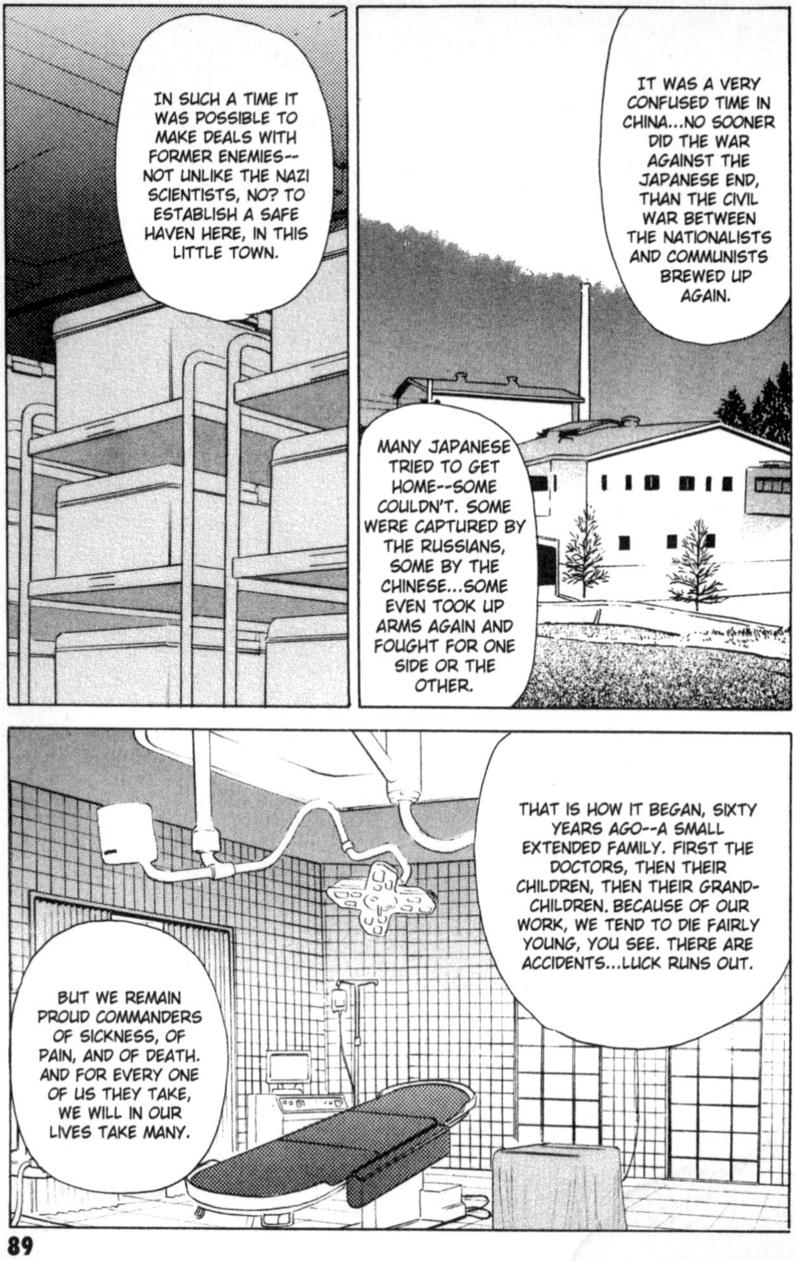
IT WAS A VERY CONFUSED TIME IN CHINA...NO SOONER DID THE WAR AGAINST THE JAPANESE END, THAN THE CIVIL WAR BETWEEN THE NATIONALISTS AND COMMUNISTS BREWED UP AGAIN.
MANY JAPANESE TRIED TO GET HOME--SOME COULDN'T. SOME WERE CAPTURED BY THE RUSSIANS, SOME BY THE CHINESE...SOME EVEN TOOK UP ARMS AGAIN AND FOUGHT FOR ONE SIDE OR THE OTHER.
IN SUCH A TIME IT WAS POSSIBLE TO MAKE DEALS WITH FORMER ENEMIES-- NOT UNLIKE THE NAZI SCIENTISTS, NO? TO ESTABLISH A SAFE HAVEN HERE, IN THIS LITTLE TOWN.
THAT IS HOW IT BEGAN, SIXTY YEARS AGO--A SMALL EXTENDED FAMILY. FIRST THE DOCTORS, THEN THEIR CHILDREN, THEN THEIR GRAND-CHILDREN. BECAUSE OF OUR WORK, WE TEND TO DIE FAIRLY YOUNG, YOU SEE. THERE ARE ACCIDENTS...LUCK RUNS OUT.
BUT WE REMAIN PROUD COMMANDERS OF SICKNESS, OF PAIN, AND OF DEATH. AND FOR EVERY ONE OF US THEY TAKE, WE WILL IN OUR LIVES TAKE MANY.

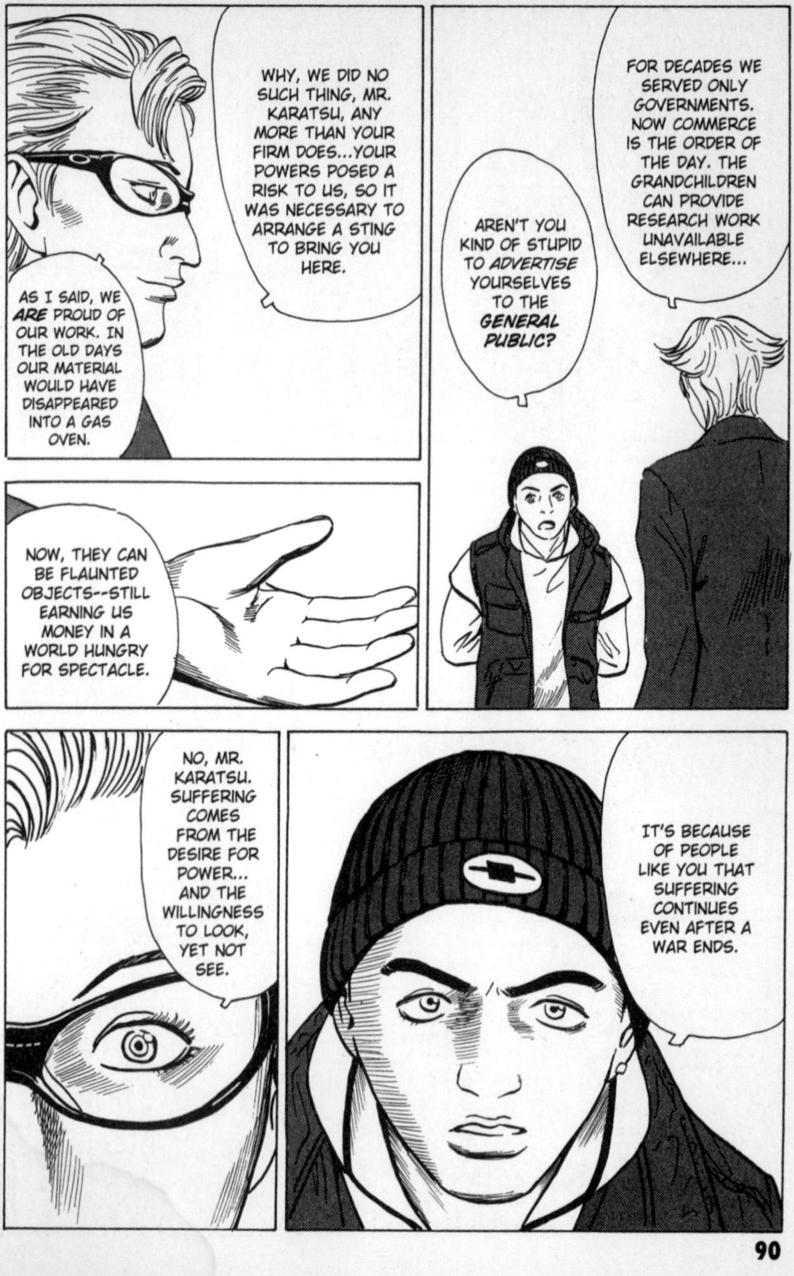
FOR DECADES WE SERVED ONLY GOVERNMENTS. NOW COMMERCE IS THE ORDER OF THE DAY. THE GRANDCHILDREN CAN PROVIDE RESEARCH WORK UNAVAILABLE ELSEWHERE...
AREN'T YOU KIND OF STUPID TO *ADVERTISE* YOURSELVES TO THE ***GENERAL PUBLIC?***
WHY, WE DID NO SUCH THING, MR. KARATSU, ANY MORE THAN YOUR FIRM DOES...YOUR POWERS POSED A RISK TO US, SO IT WAS NECESSARY TO ARRANGE A STING TO BRING YOU HERE.
AS I SAID, WE ***ARE*** PROUD OF OUR WORK. IN THE OLD DAYS OUR MATERIAL WOULD HAVE DISAPPEARED INTO A GAS OVEN.
NOW, THEY CAN BE FLAUNTED OBJECTS--STILL EARNING US MONEY IN A WORLD HUNGRY FOR SPECTACLE.
IT'S BECAUSE OF PEOPLE LIKE YOU THAT SUFFERING CONTINUES EVEN AFTER A WAR ENDS.
NO, MR. KARATSU. SUFFERING COMES FROM THE DESIRE FOR POWER... AND THE WILLINGNESS TO LOOK, YET NOT SEE.

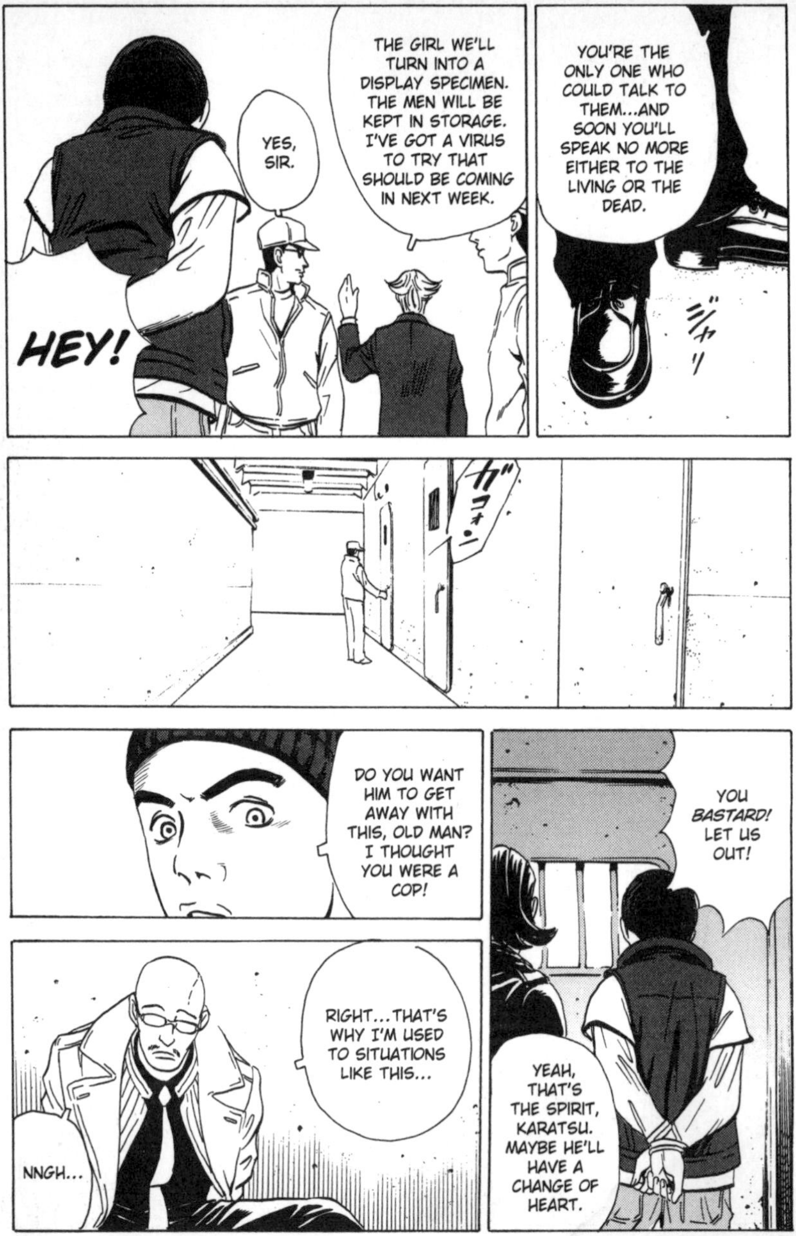
YOU'RE THE ONLY ONE WHO COULD TALK TO THEM...AND SOON YOU'LL SPEAK NO MORE EITHER TO THE LIVING OR THE DEAD.
ジャリ
THE GIRL WE'LL TURN INTO A DISPLAY SPECIMEN. THE MEN WILL BE KEPT IN STORAGE. I'VE GOT A VIRUS TO TRY THAT SHOULD BE COMING IN NEXT WEEK.
YES, SIR.
HEY!
ガコォン
YOU BASTARD! LET US OUT!
YEAH, THAT'S THE SPIRIT, KARATSU. MAYBE HE'LL HAVE A CHANGE OF HEART.
DO YOU WANT HIM TO GET AWAY WITH THIS, OLD MAN? I THOUGHT YOU WERE A COP!
RIGHT...THAT'S WHY I'M USED TO SITUATIONS LIKE THIS...
NNGH...

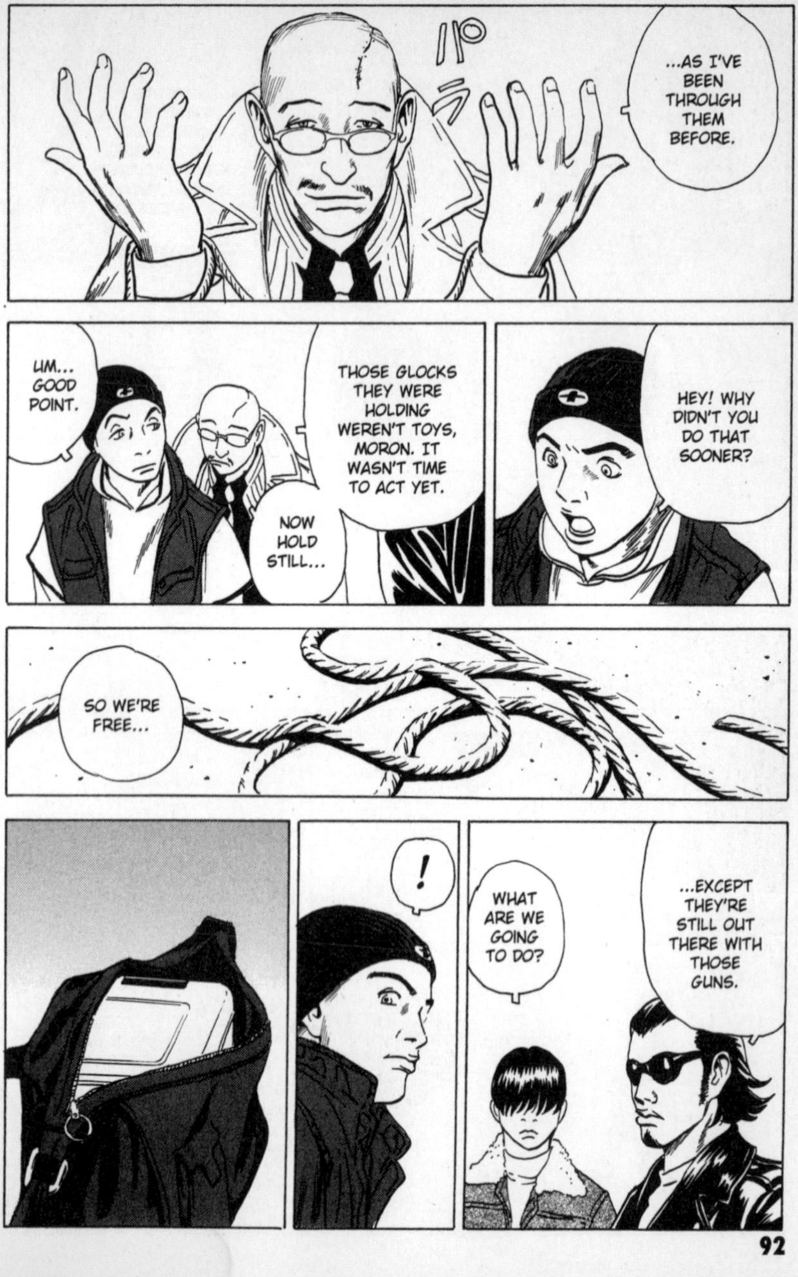
パラ
...AS I'VE BEEN THROUGH THEM BEFORE.
HEY! WHY DIDN'T YOU DO THAT SOONER?
THOSE GLOCKS THEY WERE HOLDING WEREN'T TOYS, MORON. IT WASN'T TIME TO ACT YET.
NOW HOLD STILL...
UM... GOOD POINT.
SO WE'RE FREE...
...EXCEPT THEY'RE STILL OUT THERE WITH THOSE GUNS.
WHAT ARE WE GOING TO DO?
!

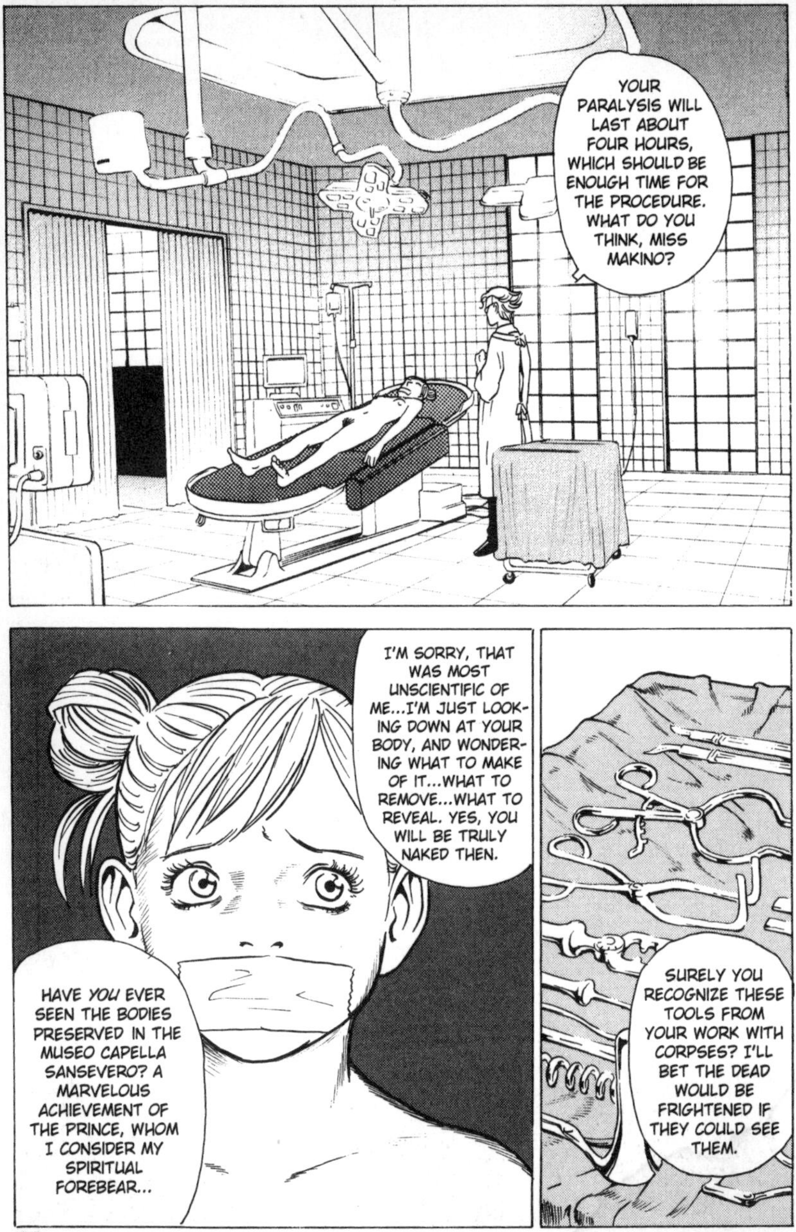
YOUR PARALYSIS WILL LAST ABOUT FOUR HOURS, WHICH SHOULD BE ENOUGH TIME FOR THE PROCEDURE. WHAT DO YOU THINK, MISS MAKINO?
SURELY YOU RECOGNIZE THESE TOOLS FROM YOUR WORK WITH CORPSES? I'LL BET THE DEAD WOULD BE FRIGHTENED IF THEY COULD SEE THEM.
I'M SORRY, THAT WAS MOST UNSCIENTIFIC OF ME...I'M JUST LOOKING DOWN AT YOUR BODY, AND WONDERING WHAT TO MAKE OF IT...WHAT TO REMOVE...WHAT TO REVEAL. YES, YOU WILL BE TRULY NAKED THEN.
HAVE *YOU* EVER SEEN THE BODIES PRESERVED IN THE MUSEO CAPELLA SANSEVERO? A MARVELOUS ACHIEVEMENT OF THE PRINCE, WHOM I CONSIDER MY SPIRITUAL FOREBEAR...

...NOW, MISS MAKINO. YOU'RE NOT THE FIRST PERSON I'VE DONE THIS TO. NO, NOT THE TENTH, OR EVEN THE TWENTIETH.
LET ME BEGIN TO REMOVE YOUR BLOOD. THEN I'LL FLUSH OUT YOUR INTESTINES. WOULD YOU LIKE TO SEE ALL THE FILTHY THINGS THAT ARE INSIDE YOU? YOU WILL, YOU KNOW. YOU'LL LIVE THAT LONG.
I HAVE A CONFESSION TO MAKE.
THE TRUTH IS, I SO ENJOY SEEING THAT EXPRESSION OF FEAR AND SHAME UPON YOUR FACE.

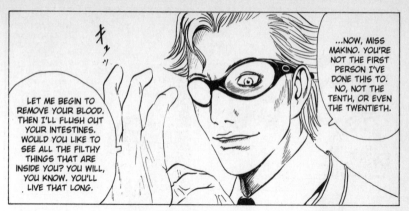

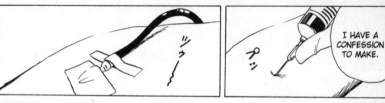

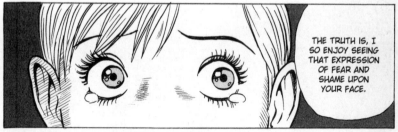

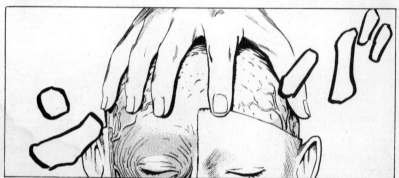

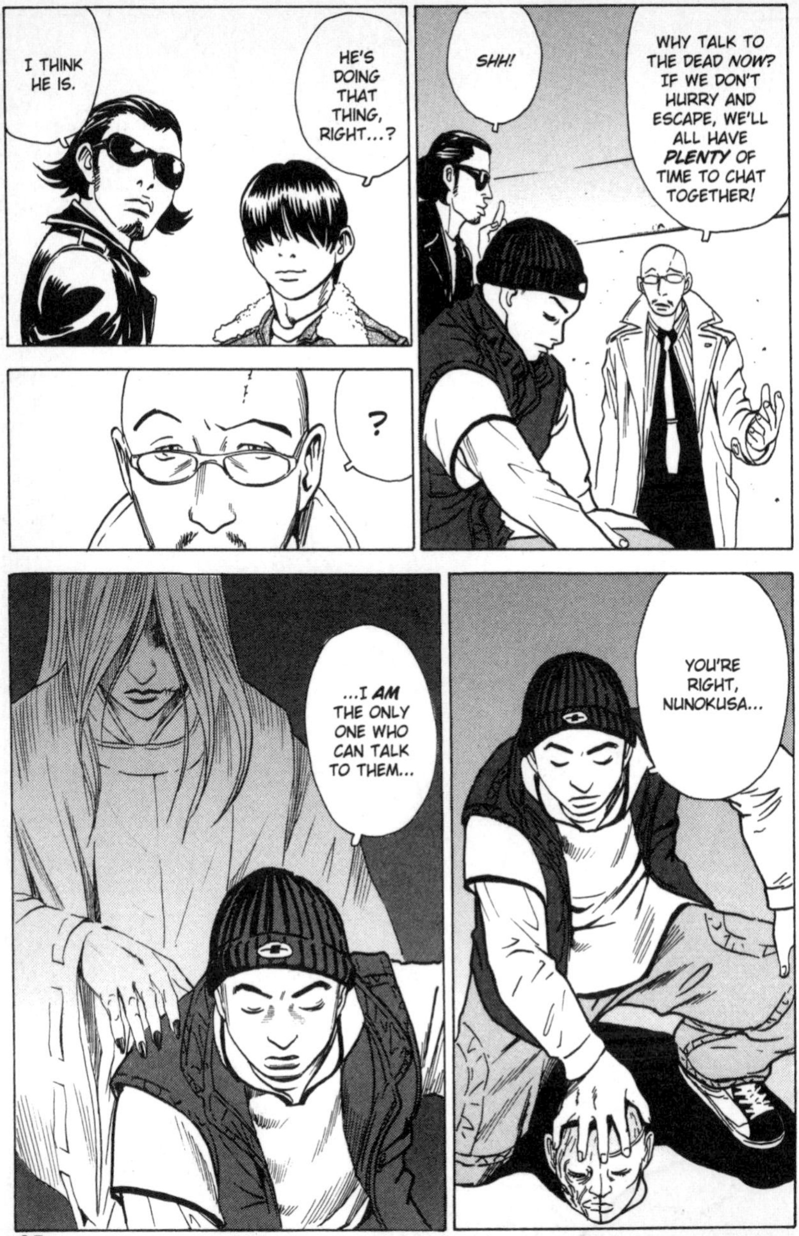
WHY TALK TO THE DEAD *NOW*? IF WE DON'T HURRY AND ESCAPE, WE'LL ALL HAVE ***PLENTY*** OF TIME TO CHAT TOGETHER!
SHH!
HE'S DOING THAT THING, RIGHT...?
I THINK HE IS.
?
YOU'RE RIGHT, NUNOKUSA...
...I ***AM*** THE ONLY ONE WHO CAN TALK TO THEM...

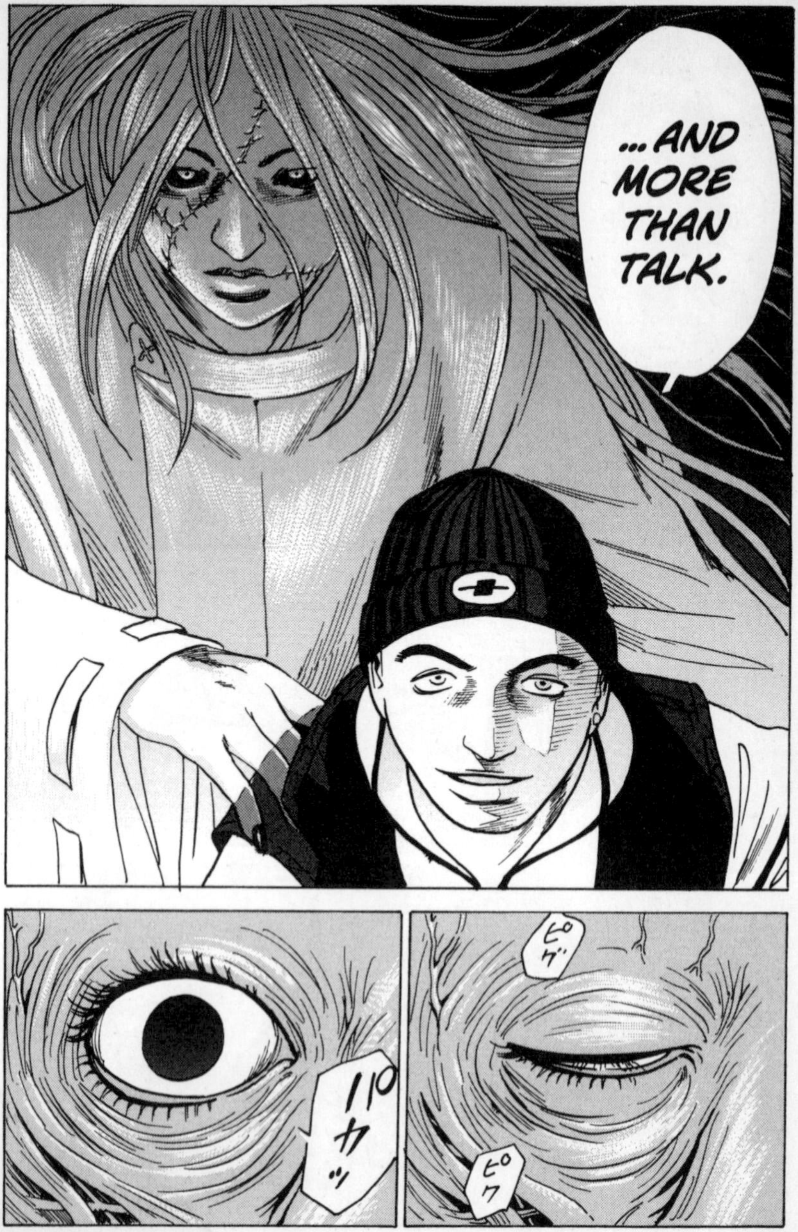
...AND MORE THAN TALK.
ピク
ピク
パカッ

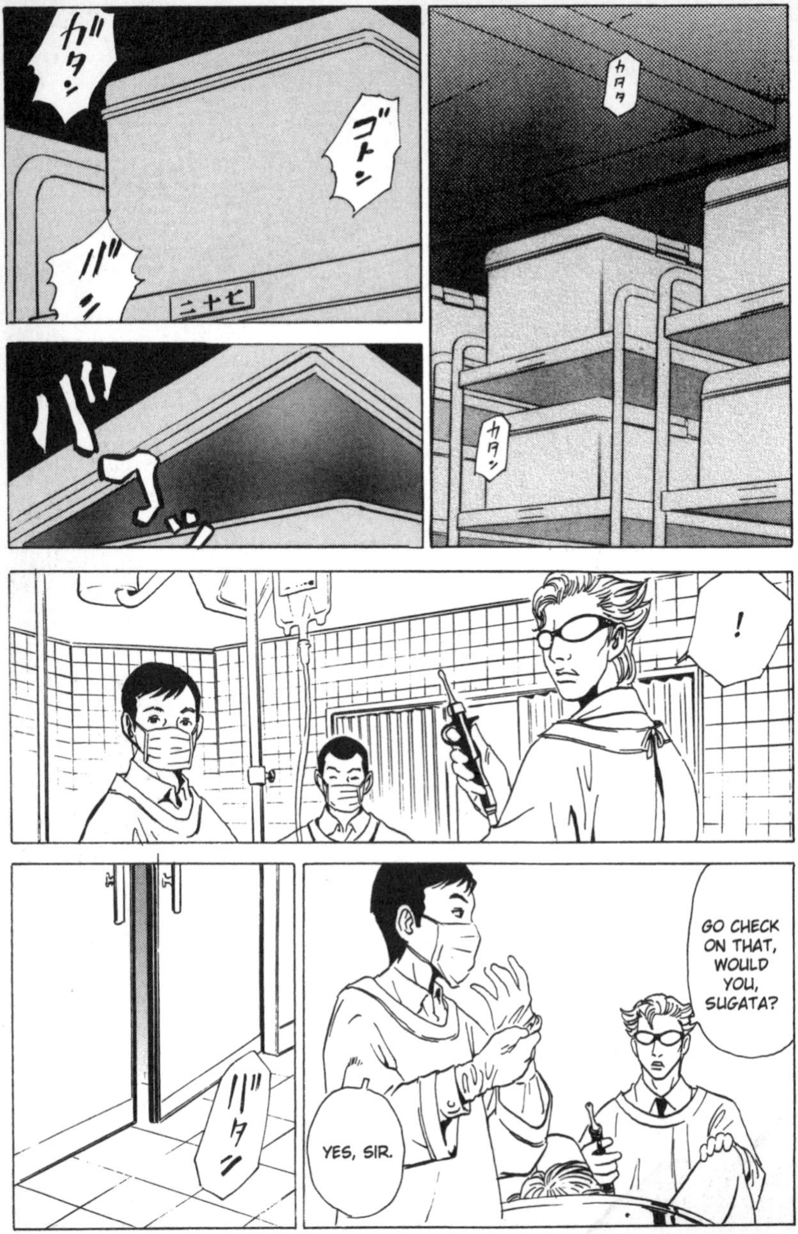
カタタ
カタン
ガタン
ゴトン
バン
二十七
バッ
!
GO CHECK ON THAT, WOULD YOU, SUGATA?
YES, SIR.
バタン

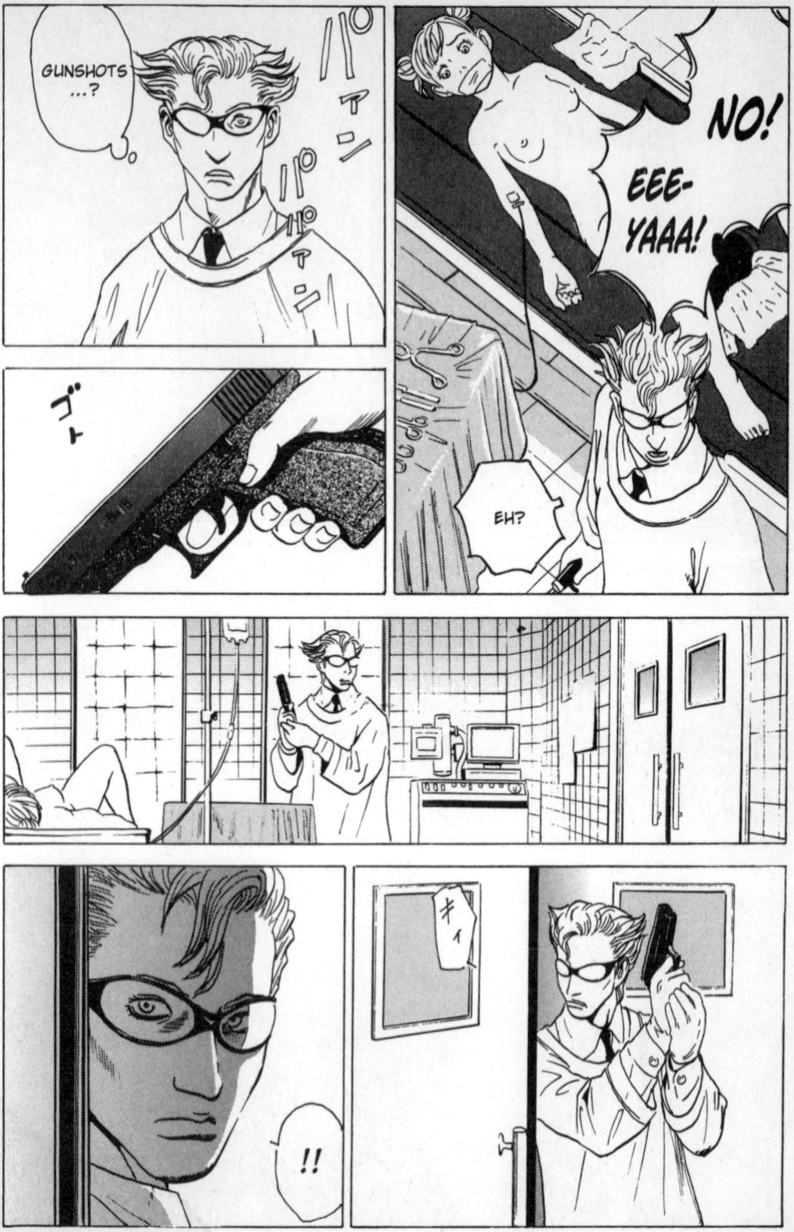
NO!
EEE-YAAA!
EH?
GUNSHOTS ...?
パァン
パパァン
ゴト
キィ
...!!

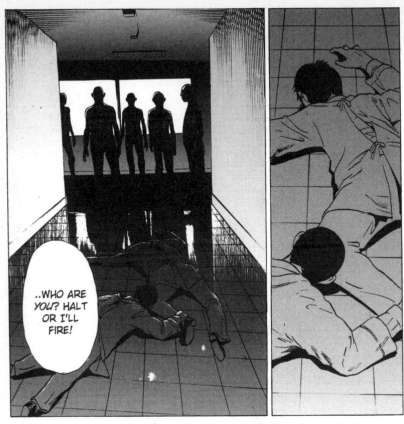

..WHO ARE *YOU?* HALT OR I'LL FIRE!

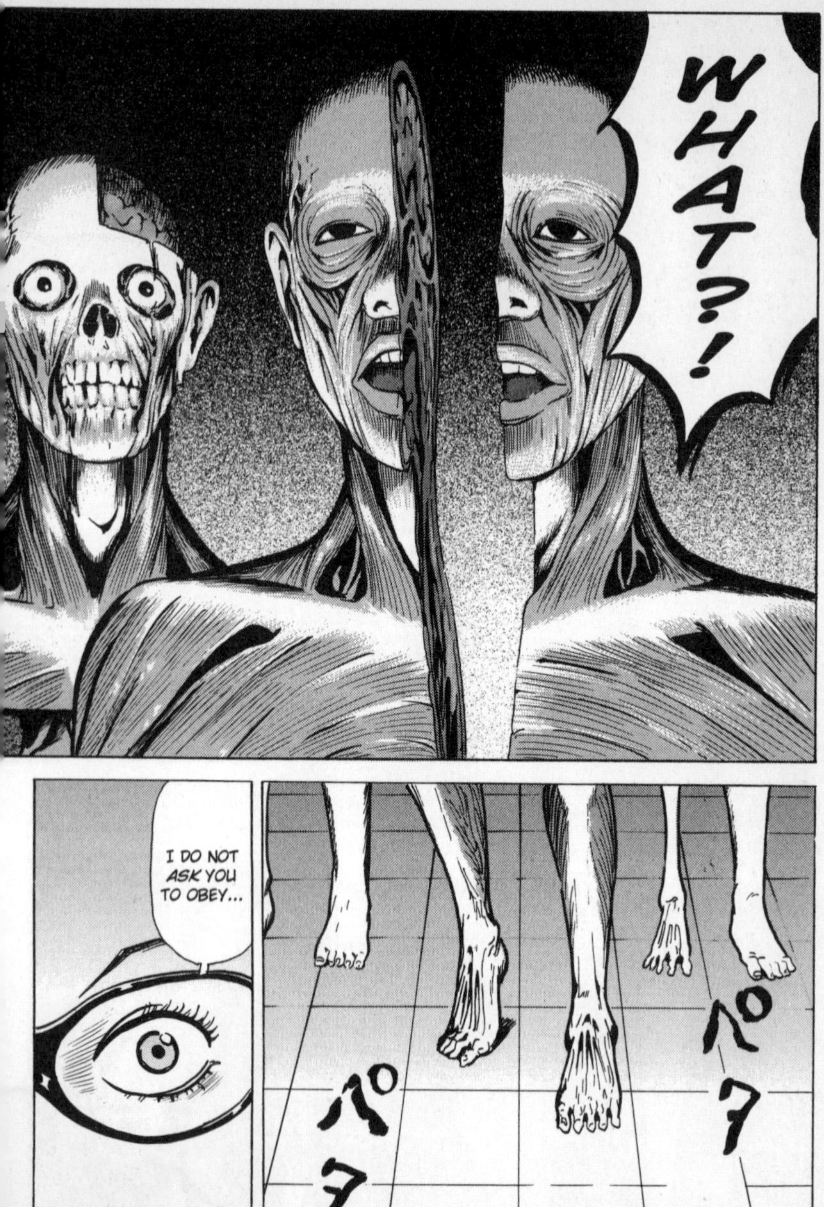
WHAT?!
ペタ
ペタ
I DO NOT ASK YOU TO OBEY...

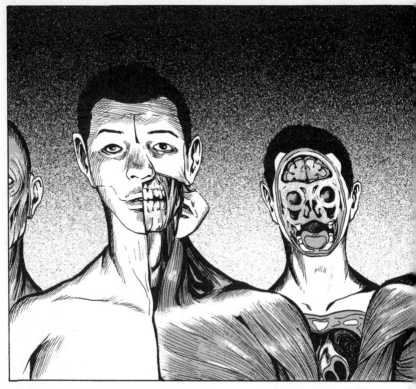

...I HAVE POWER OVER YOU.

YOUR LIVES, YOUR DEATHS... BELONG TO ME.

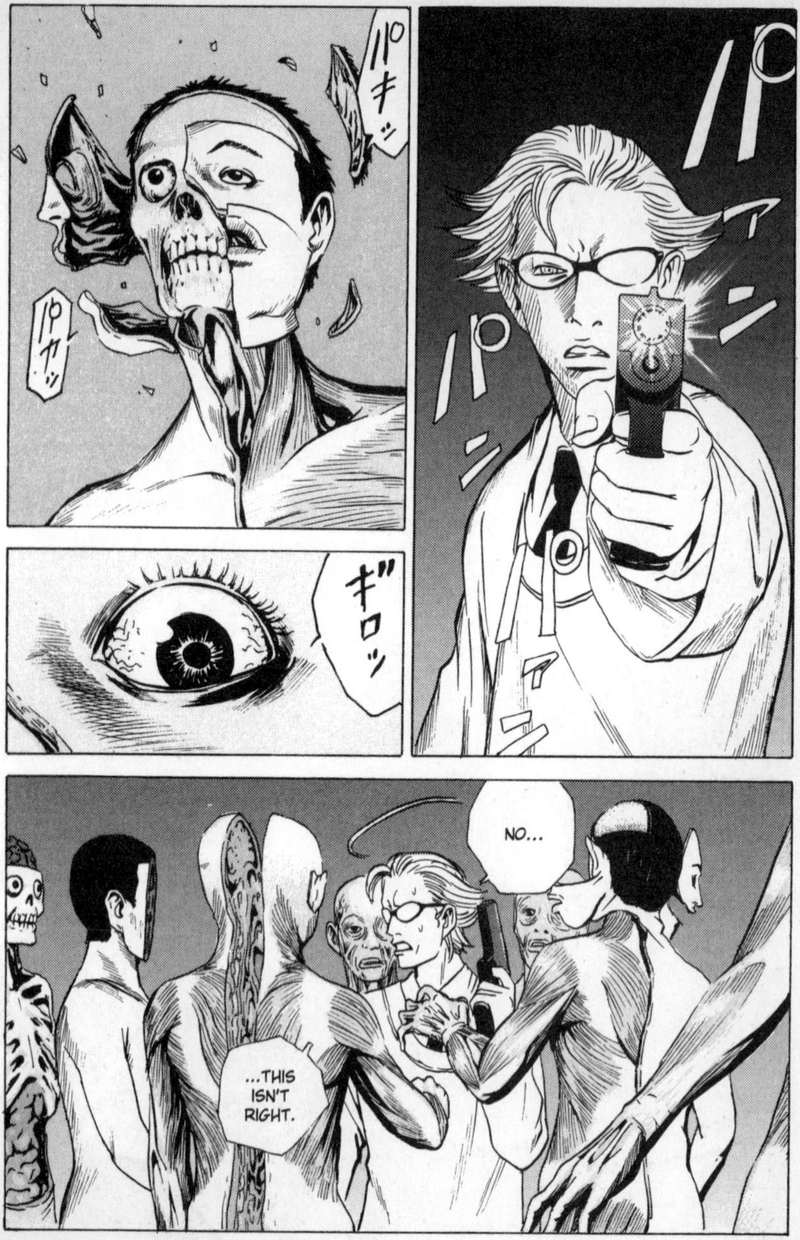
パァン
パン
ァン
パキッ
パカッ
ギロッ
NO...
...THIS ISN'T RIGHT.

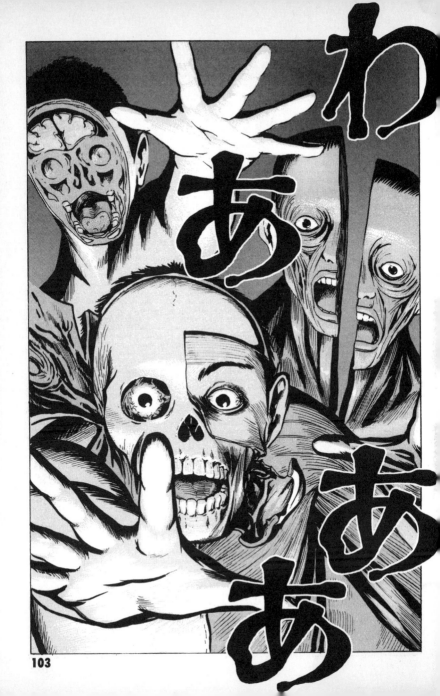

わ

ああ

あ

あ

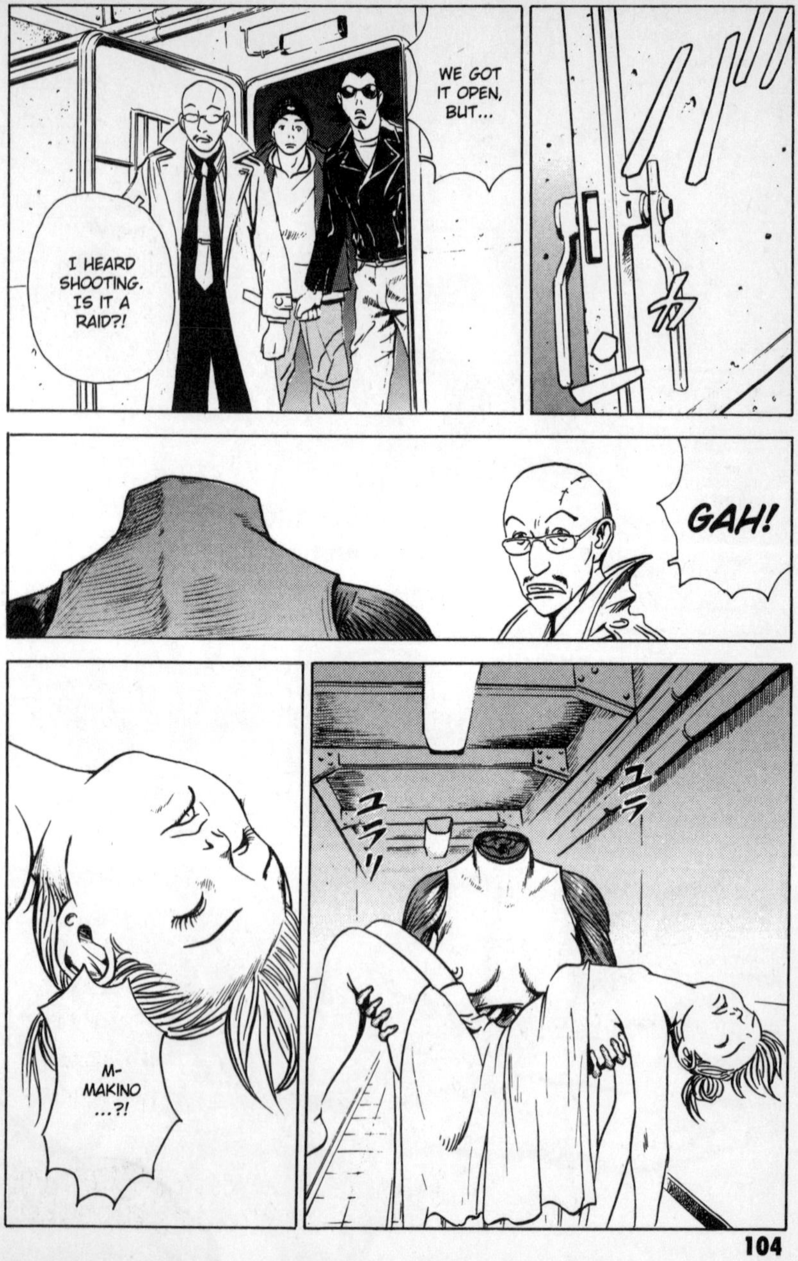
WE GOT IT OPEN, BUT...
I HEARD SHOOTING. IS IT A RAID?!
GAH!
ユラ
ユラッ
M-MAKINO ...?!

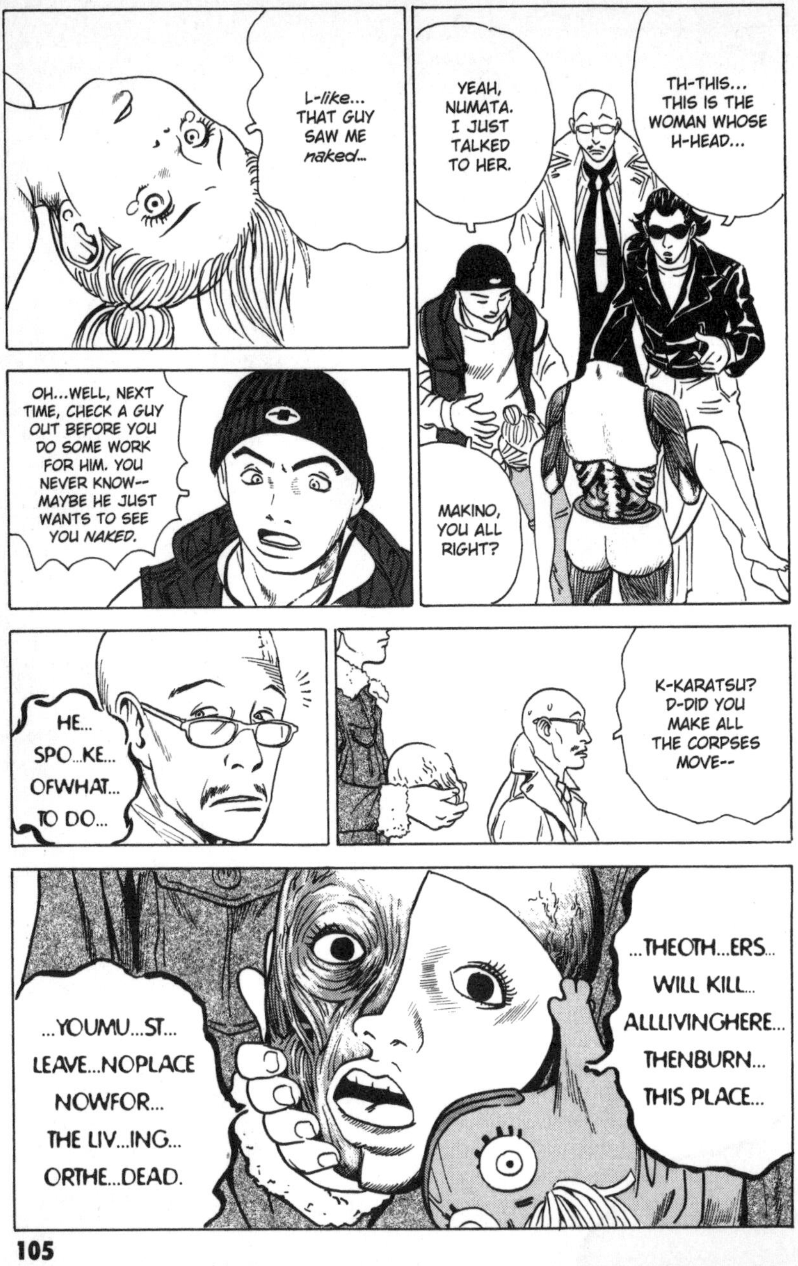
TH-THIS... THIS IS THE WOMAN WHOSE H-HEAD...
YEAH, NUMATA. I JUST TALKED TO HER.
MAKINO, YOU ALL RIGHT?
L-*like*... THAT GUY SAW ME *naked*...
OH...WELL, NEXT TIME, CHECK A GUY OUT BEFORE YOU DO SOME WORK FOR HIM. YOU NEVER KNOW--MAYBE HE JUST WANTS TO SEE YOU *NAKED*.
K-KARATSU? D-DID YOU MAKE ALL THE CORPSES MOVE--
HE... SPO...KE... OFWHAT... TO DO...
...THEOTH...ERS... WILL KILL... ALLLIVINGHERE... THENBURN... THIS PLACE...
...YOUMU...ST... LEAVE...NOPLACE NOWFOR... THE LIV...ING... ORTHE...DEAD.

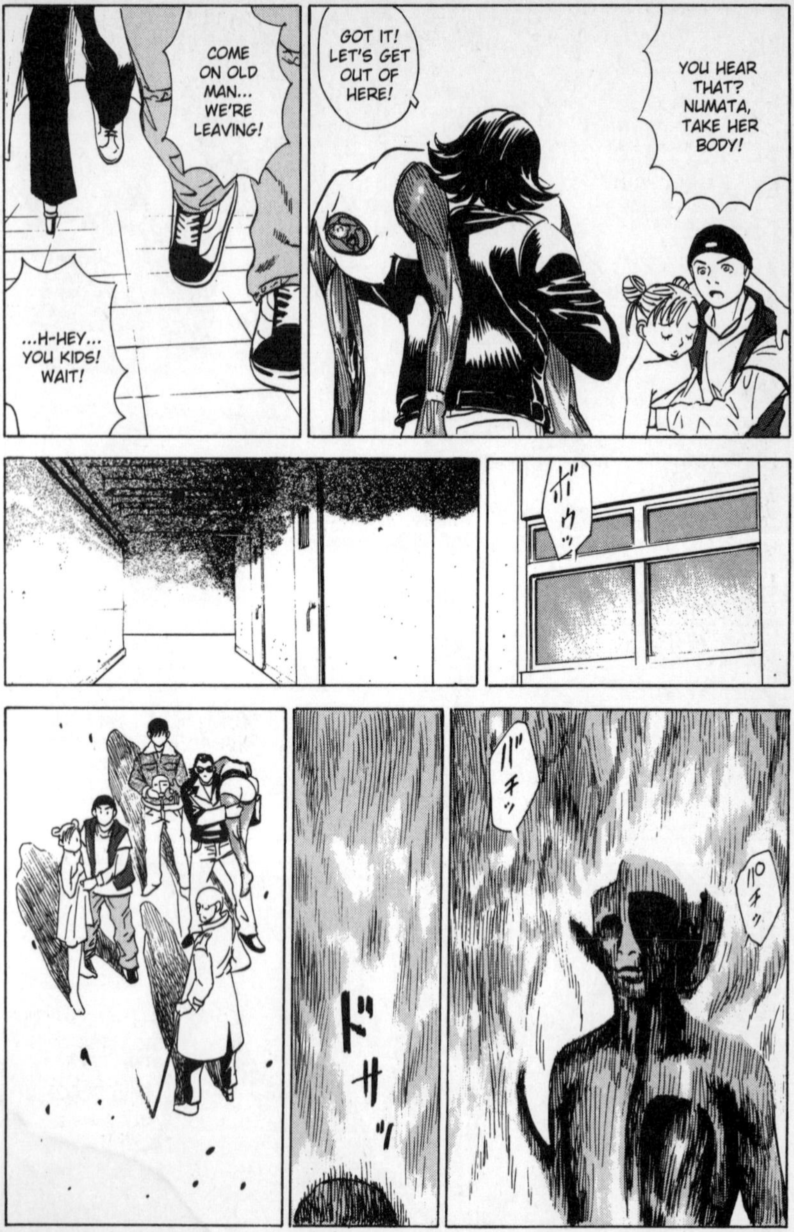
YOU HEAR THAT? NUMATA, TAKE HER BODY!
GOT IT! LET'S GET OUT OF HERE!
COME ON OLD MAN... WE'RE LEAVING!
...H-HEY... YOU KIDS! WAIT!
ボウッ
バチッ
パチッ
ドサッ

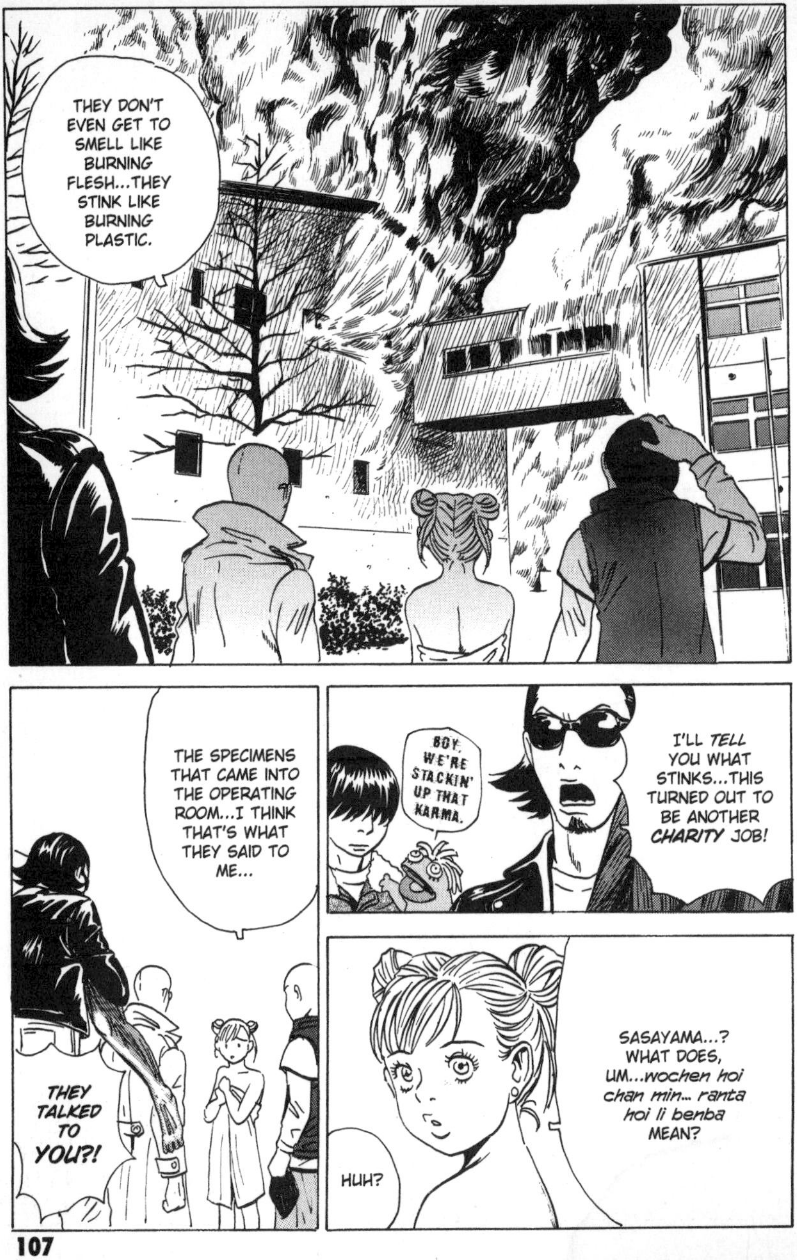
THEY DON'T EVEN GET TO SMELL LIKE BURNING FLESH...THEY STINK LIKE BURNING PLASTIC.
I'LL *TELL* YOU WHAT STINKS...THIS TURNED OUT TO BE ANOTHER ***CHARITY*** JOB!
BOY, WE'RE STACKIN' UP THAT KARMA.
SASAYAMA...? WHAT DOES, UM...*wochen hoi chan min... ranta hoi li benba* MEAN?
HUH?
THE SPECIMENS THAT CAME INTO THE OPERATING ROOM...I THINK THAT'S WHAT THEY SAID TO ME...
THEY TALKED TO YOU?!

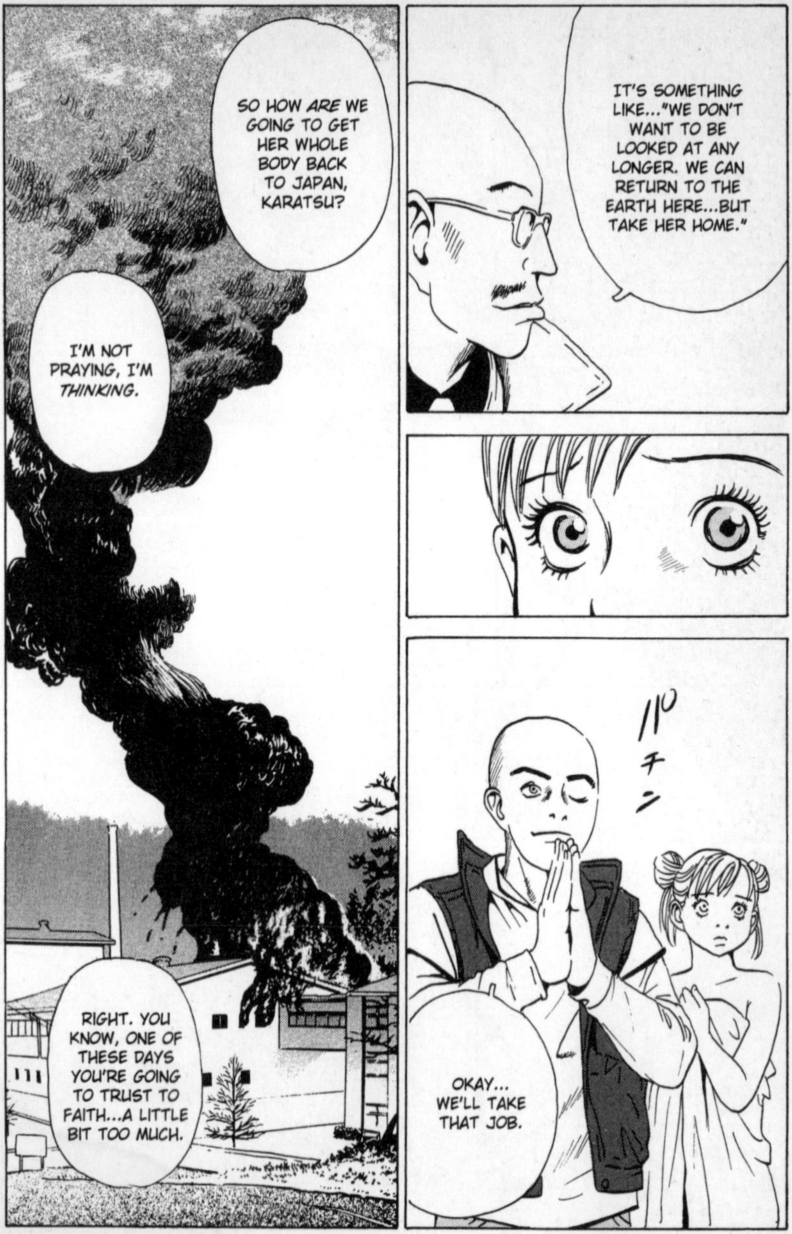
IT'S SOMETHING LIKE..."WE DON'T WANT TO BE LOOKED AT ANY LONGER. WE CAN RETURN TO THE EARTH HERE...BUT TAKE HER HOME."
パチン
OKAY... WE'LL TAKE THAT JOB.
SO HOW *ARE* WE GOING TO GET HER WHOLE BODY BACK TO JAPAN, KARATSU?
I'M NOT PRAYING, I'M *THINKING*.
RIGHT. YOU KNOW, ONE OF THESE DAYS YOU'RE GOING TO TRUST TO FAITH...A LITTLE BIT TOO MUCH.

2nd delivery: if you should die—the end

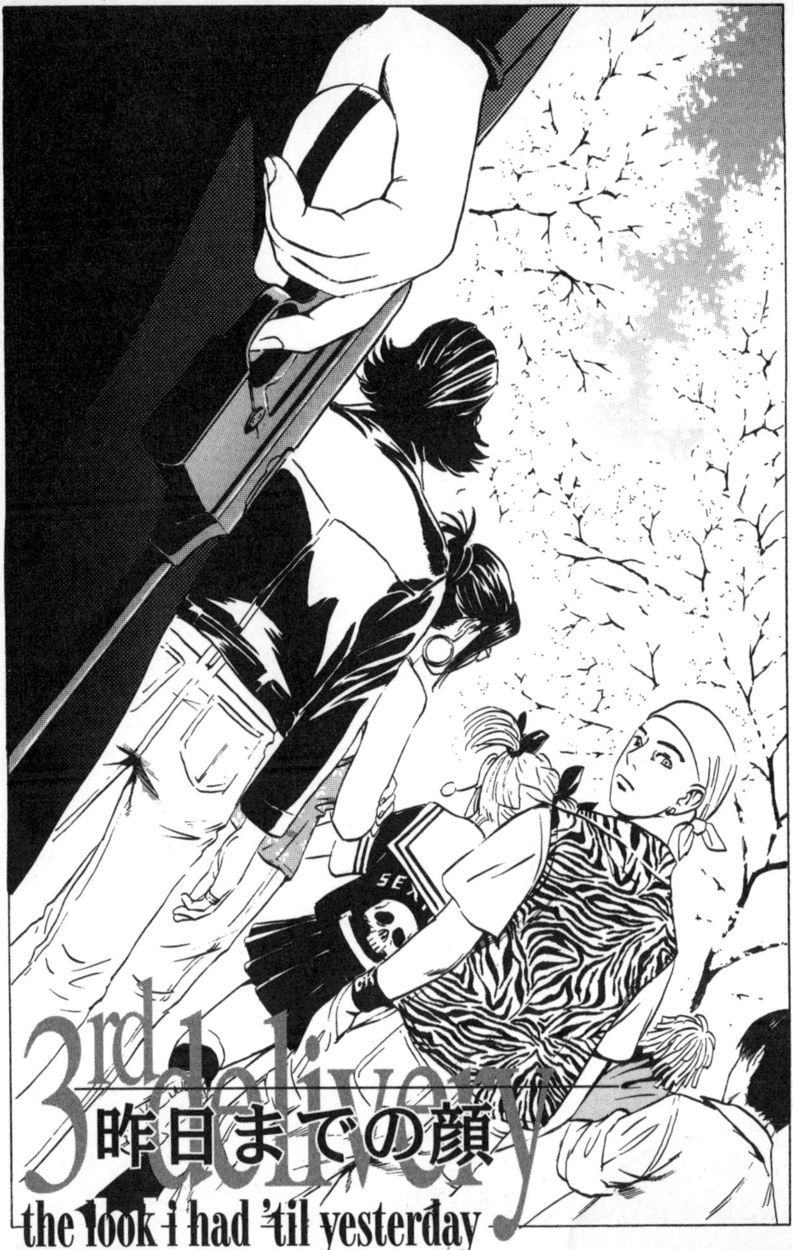

3rd delivery
昨日までの顔
the look i had 'til yesterday

WH-WHERE
...

...WHERE DID SHE HIDE MY BABY...?!

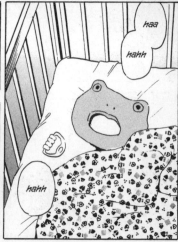

haa

hahh

hahh

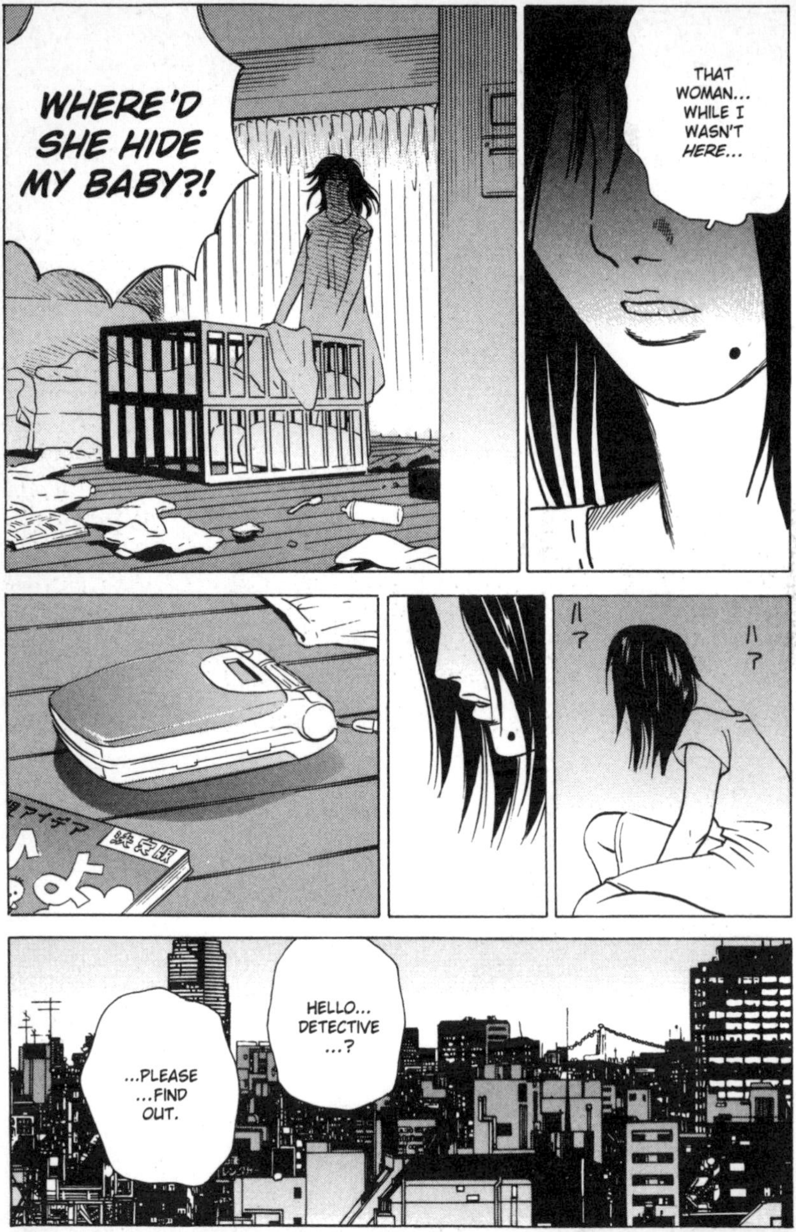
THAT WOMAN... WHILE I WASN'T *HERE*...
WHERE'D SHE HIDE MY BABY?!
ハァ
ハァ
HELLO... DETECTIVE ...?
...PLEASE ...FIND OUT.

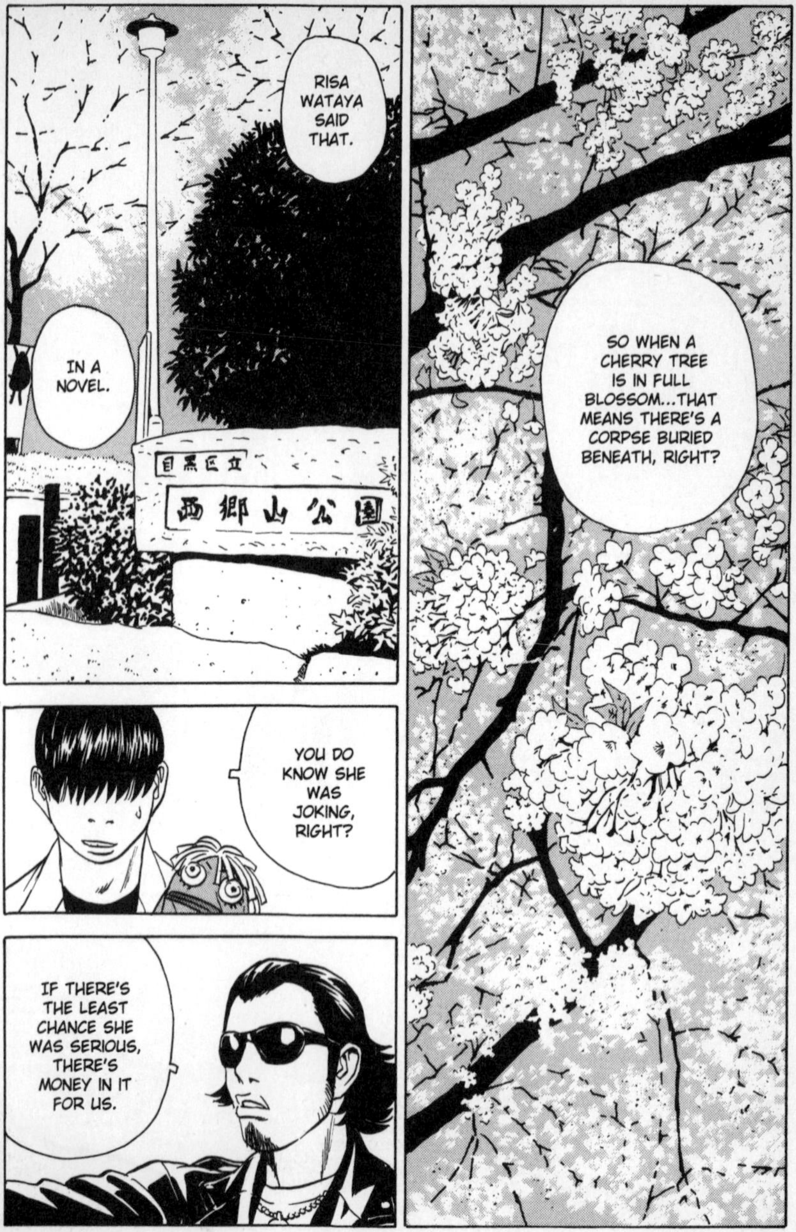
SO WHEN A CHERRY TREE IS IN FULL BLOSSOM...THAT MEANS THERE'S A CORPSE BURIED BENEATH, RIGHT?
RISA WATAYA SAID THAT.
IN A NOVEL.
目黒区立
西郷山公園
YOU DO KNOW SHE WAS JOKING, RIGHT?
IF THERE'S THE LEAST CHANCE SHE WAS SERIOUS, THERE'S MONEY IN IT FOR US.

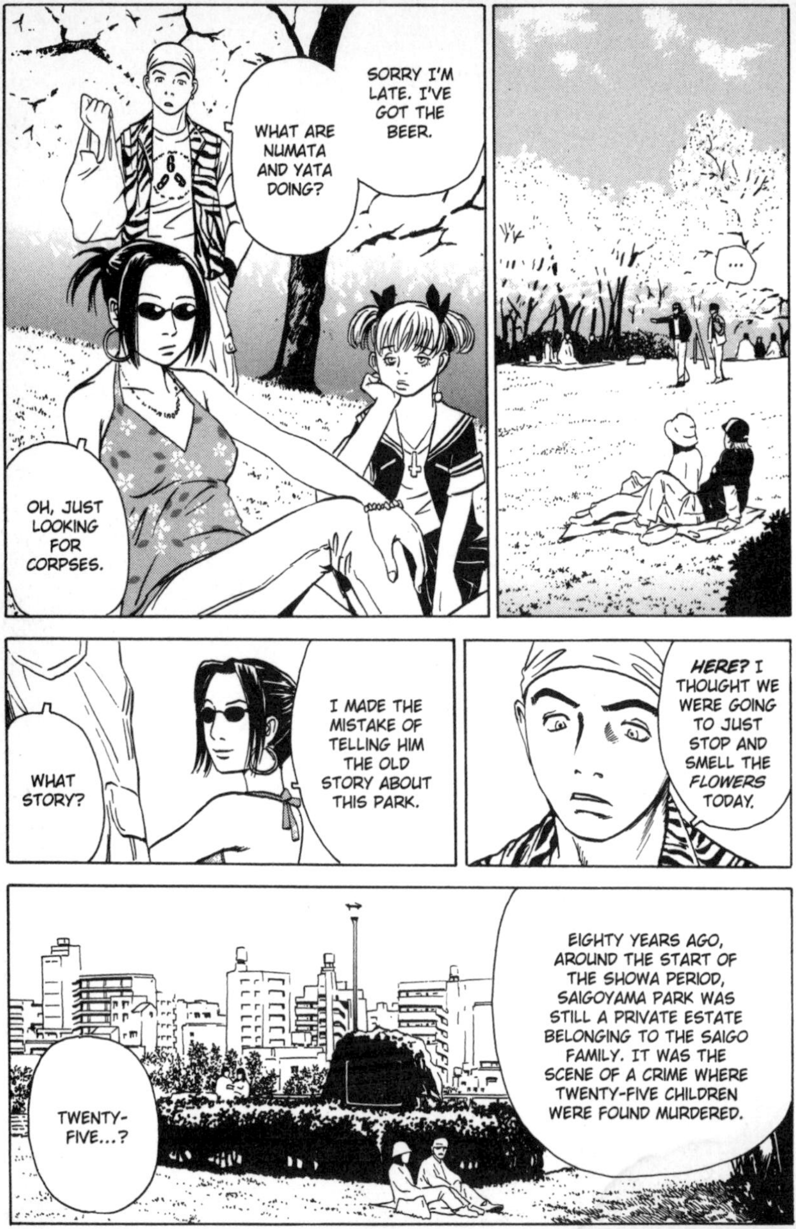
...
SORRY I'M LATE. I'VE GOT THE BEER.
WHAT ARE NUMATA AND YATA DOING?
OH, JUST LOOKING FOR CORPSES.
HERE? I THOUGHT WE WERE GOING TO JUST STOP AND SMELL THE *FLOWERS* TODAY.
I MADE THE MISTAKE OF TELLING HIM THE OLD STORY ABOUT THIS PARK.
WHAT STORY?
EIGHTY YEARS AGO, AROUND THE START OF THE SHOWA PERIOD, SAIGOYAMA PARK WAS STILL A PRIVATE ESTATE BELONGING TO THE SAIGO FAMILY. IT WAS THE SCENE OF A CRIME WHERE TWENTY-FIVE CHILDREN WERE FOUND MURDERED.
TWENTY-FIVE...?

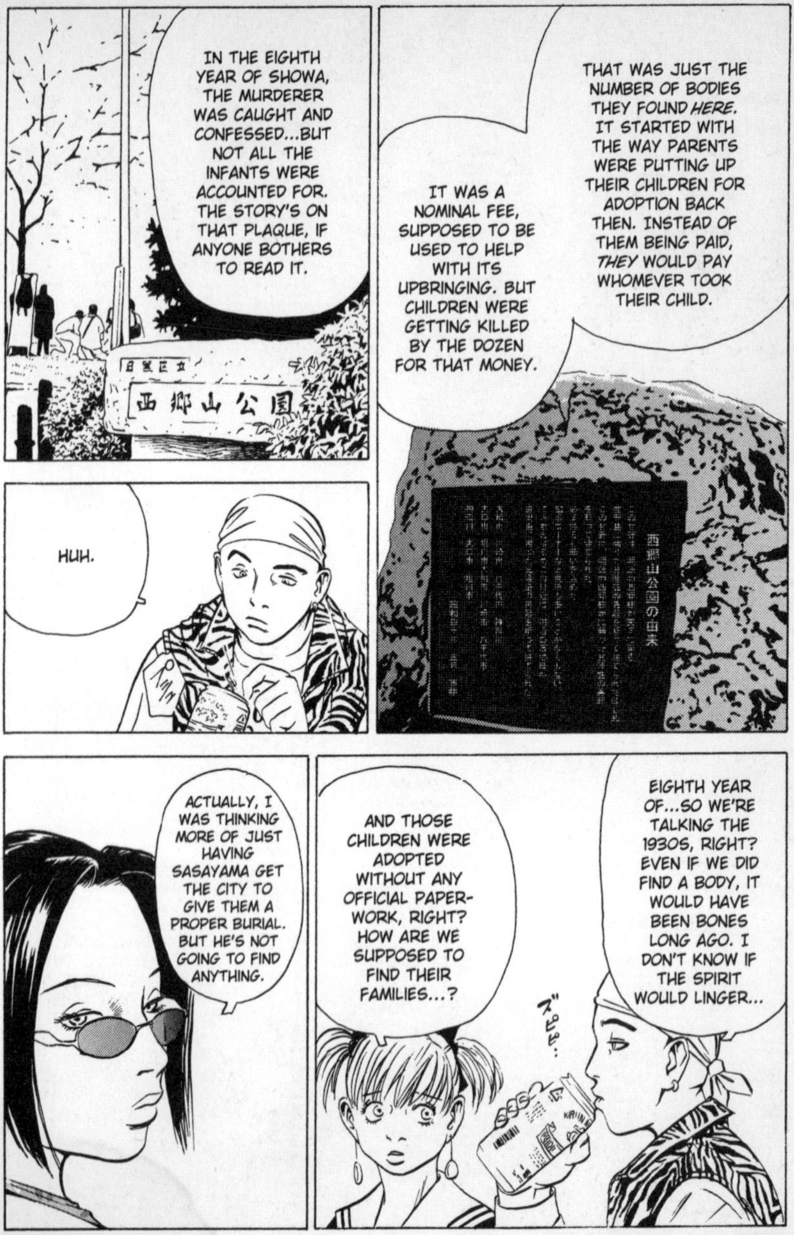
THAT WAS JUST THE NUMBER OF BODIES THEY FOUND *HERE*. IT STARTED WITH THE WAY PARENTS WERE PUTTING UP THEIR CHILDREN FOR ADOPTION BACK THEN. INSTEAD OF THEM BEING PAID, *THEY* WOULD PAY WHOMEVER TOOK THEIR CHILD.
IT WAS A NOMINAL FEE, SUPPOSED TO BE USED TO HELP WITH ITS UPBRINGING. BUT CHILDREN WERE GETTING KILLED BY THE DOZEN FOR THAT MONEY.
西郷山公園の由来
IN THE EIGHTH YEAR OF SHOWA, THE MURDERER WAS CAUGHT AND CONFESSED...BUT NOT ALL THE INFANTS WERE ACCOUNTED FOR. THE STORY'S ON THAT PLAQUE, IF ANYONE BOTHERS TO READ IT.
西郷山公園
HUH.
EIGHTH YEAR OF...SO WE'RE TALKING THE 1930S, RIGHT? EVEN IF WE DID FIND A BODY, IT WOULD HAVE BEEN BONES LONG AGO. I DON'T KNOW IF THE SPIRIT WOULD LINGER...
AND THOSE CHILDREN WERE ADOPTED WITHOUT ANY OFFICIAL PAPER-WORK, RIGHT? HOW ARE WE SUPPOSED TO FIND THEIR FAMILIES...?
ACTUALLY, I WAS THINKING MORE OF JUST HAVING SASAYAMA GET THE CITY TO GIVE THEM A PROPER BURIAL. BUT HE'S NOT GOING TO FIND ANYTHING.

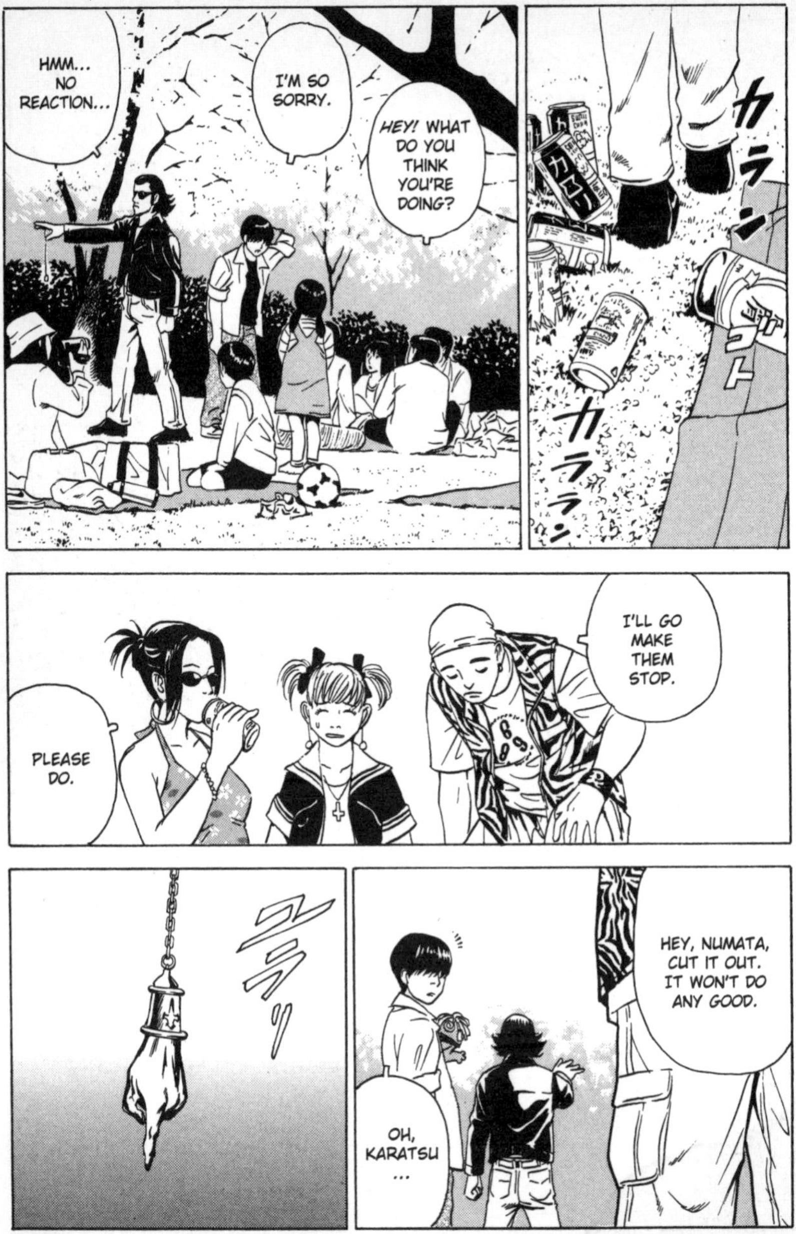

カラン
カララン
HEY! WHAT DO YOU THINK YOU'RE DOING?
I'M SO SORRY.
HMM... NO REACTION...
I'LL GO MAKE THEM STOP.
PLEASE DO.
HEY, NUMATA, CUT IT OUT. IT WON'T DO ANY GOOD.
OH, KARATSU ...

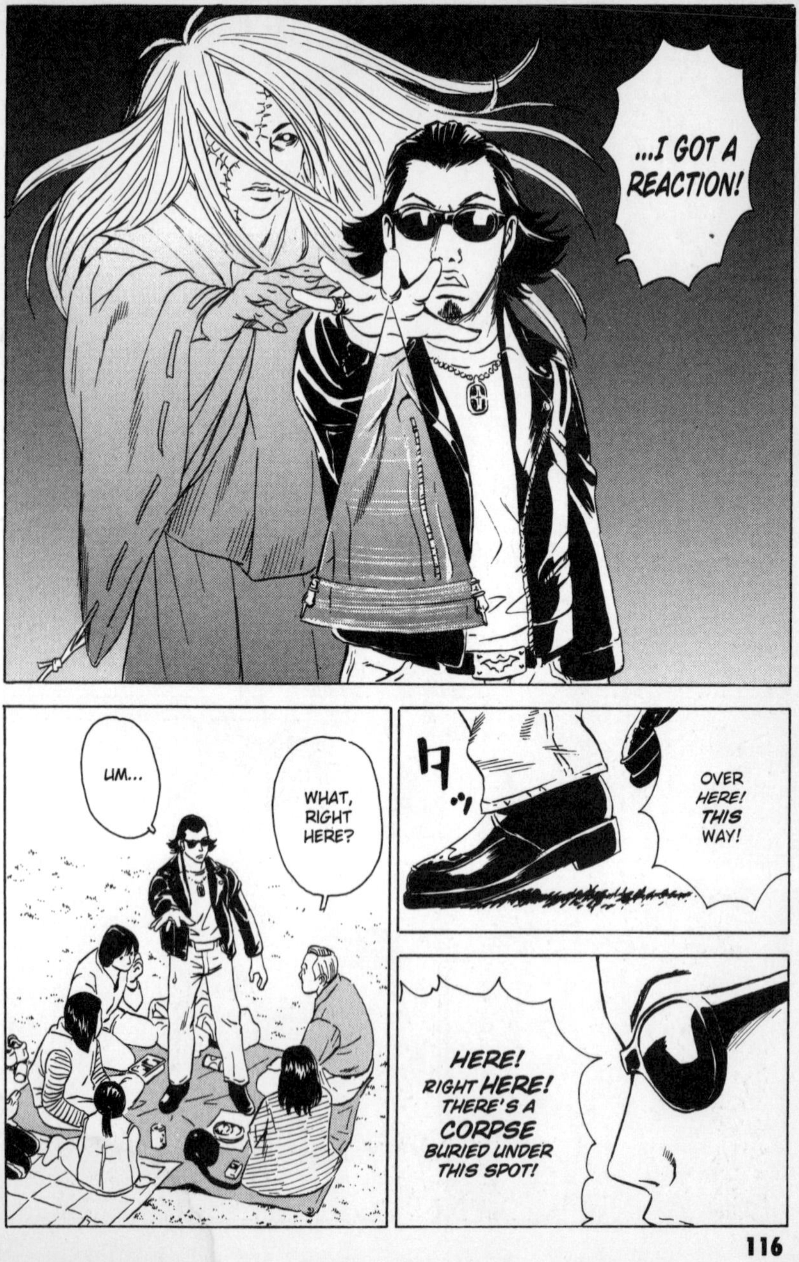
...I GOT A REACTION!
タッ
OVER HERE! THIS WAY!
HERE! RIGHT HERE! THERE'S A CORPSE BURIED UNDER THIS SPOT!
WHAT, RIGHT HERE?
UM...

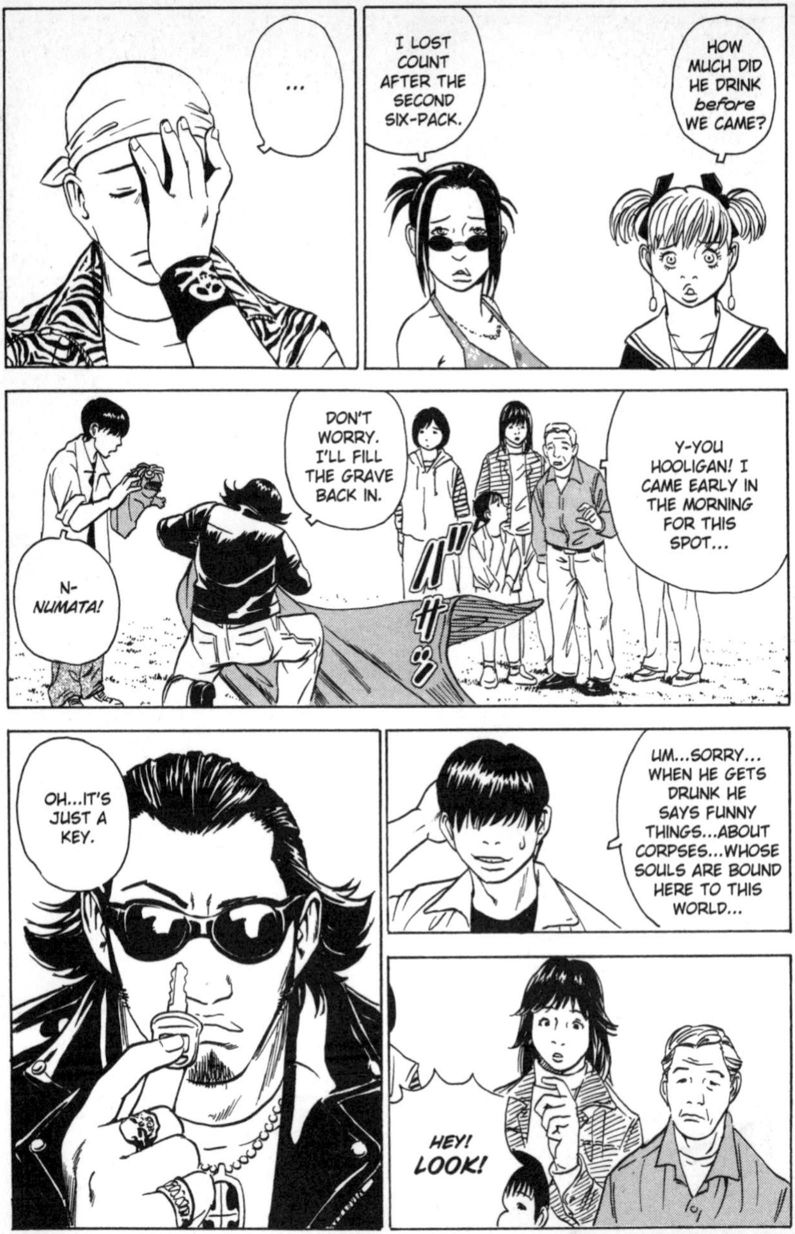
HOW MUCH DID HE DRINK *before* WE CAME?
I LOST COUNT AFTER THE SECOND SIX-PACK.
...
Y-YOU HOOLIGAN! I CAME EARLY IN THE MORNING FOR THIS SPOT...
DON'T WORRY. I'LL FILL THE GRAVE BACK IN.
N-NUMATA!
UM...SORRY... WHEN HE GETS DRUNK HE SAYS FUNNY THINGS...ABOUT CORPSES...WHOSE SOULS ARE BOUND HERE TO THIS WORLD...
HEY! LOOK!
OH...IT'S JUST A KEY.

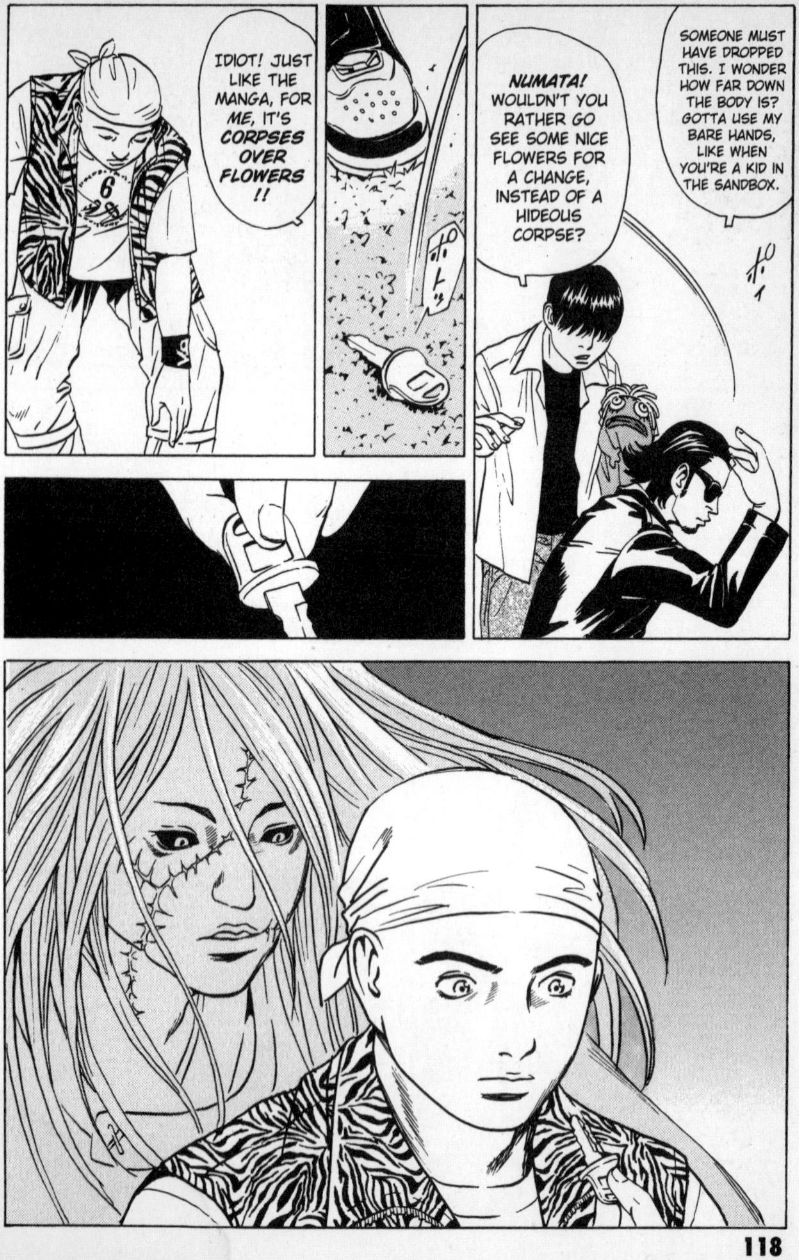
SOMEONE MUST HAVE DROPPED THIS. I WONDER HOW FAR DOWN THE BODY IS? GOTTA USE MY BARE HANDS, LIKE WHEN YOU'RE A KID IN THE SANDBOX.
NUMATA! WOULDN'T YOU RATHER GO SEE SOME NICE FLOWERS FOR A CHANGE, INSTEAD OF A HIDEOUS CORPSE?
IDIOT! JUST LIKE THE MANGA, FOR ME, IT'S CORPSES OVER FLOWERS !!

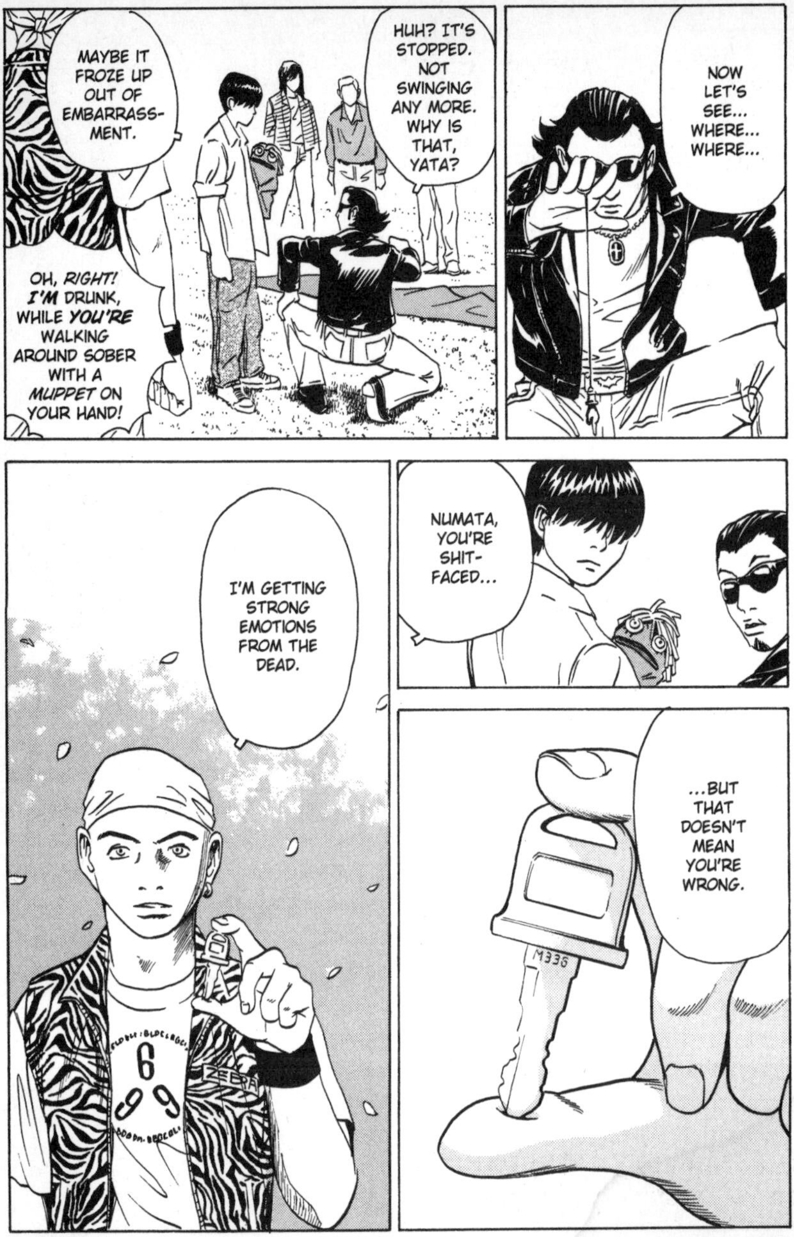
NOW LET'S SEE... WHERE... WHERE...
HUH? IT'S STOPPED. NOT SWINGING ANY MORE. WHY IS THAT, YATA?
MAYBE IT FROZE UP OUT OF EMBARRASS-MENT.
OH, *RIGHT!* ***I'M*** DRUNK, WHILE ***YOU'RE*** WALKING AROUND SOBER WITH A *MUPPET* ON YOUR HAND!
NUMATA, YOU'RE SHIT-FACED...
...BUT THAT DOESN'T MEAN YOU'RE WRONG.
I'M GETTING STRONG EMOTIONS FROM THE DEAD.

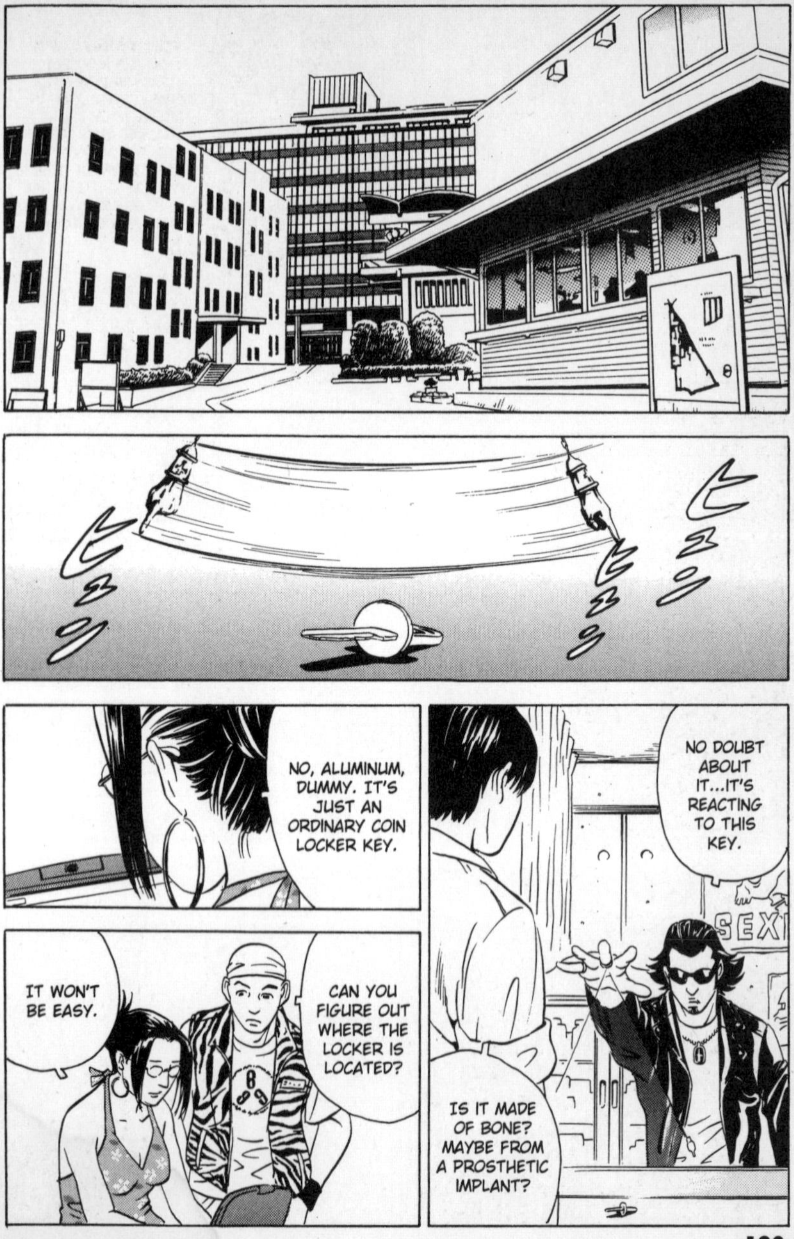
NO DOUBT ABOUT IT...IT'S REACTING TO THIS KEY.
IS IT MADE OF BONE? MAYBE FROM A PROSTHETIC IMPLANT?
NO, ALUMINUM, DUMMY. IT'S JUST AN ORDINARY COIN LOCKER KEY.
CAN YOU FIGURE OUT WHERE THE LOCKER IS LOCATED?
IT WON'T BE EASY.

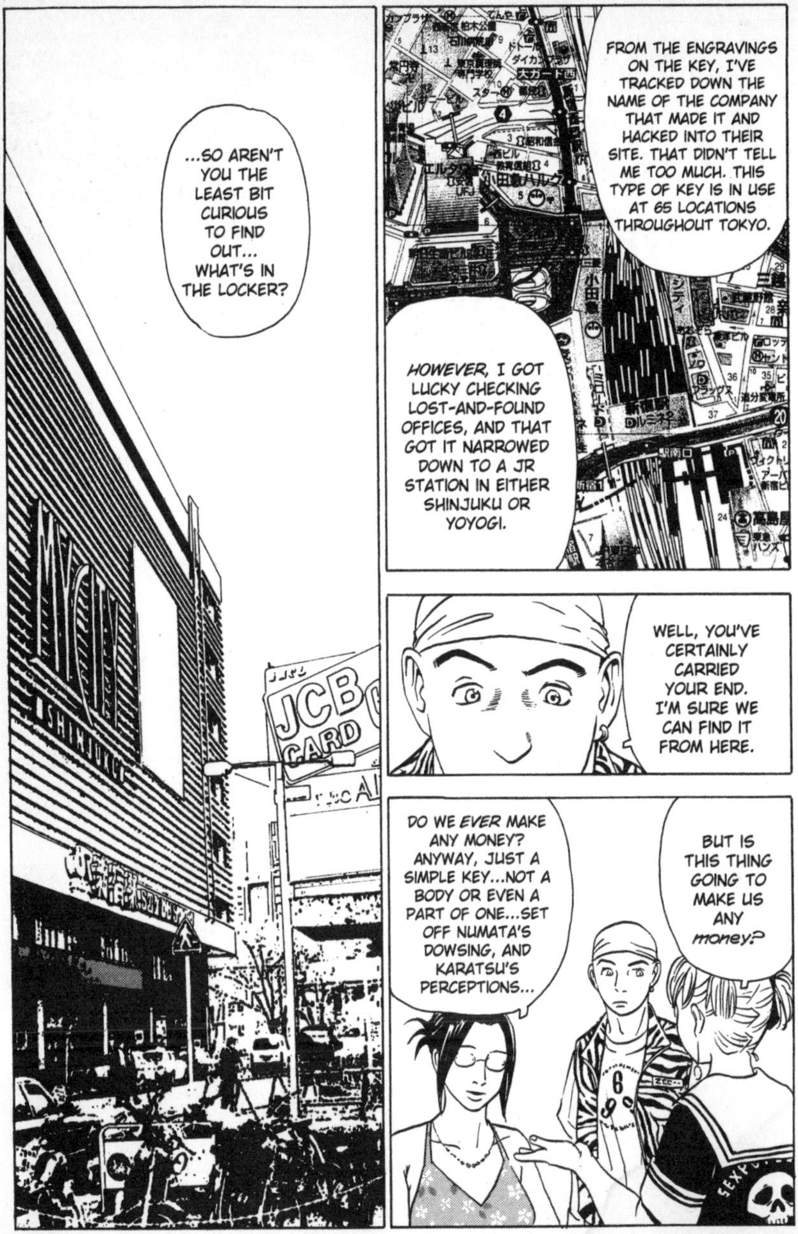
FROM THE ENGRAVINGS ON THE KEY, I'VE TRACKED DOWN THE NAME OF THE COMPANY THAT MADE IT AND HACKED INTO THEIR SITE. THAT DIDN'T TELL ME TOO MUCH. THIS TYPE OF KEY IS IN USE AT 65 LOCATIONS THROUGHOUT TOKYO.
HOWEVER, I GOT LUCKY CHECKING LOST-AND-FOUND OFFICES, AND THAT GOT IT NARROWED DOWN TO A JR STATION IN EITHER SHINJUKU OR YOYOGI.
WELL, YOU'VE CERTAINLY CARRIED YOUR END. I'M SURE WE CAN FIND IT FROM HERE.
BUT IS THIS THING GOING TO MAKE US ANY *money?*
DO WE *EVER* MAKE ANY MONEY? ANYWAY, JUST A SIMPLE KEY...NOT A BODY OR EVEN A PART OF ONE...SET OFF NUMATA'S DOWSING, AND KARATSU'S PERCEPTIONS...
...SO AREN'T YOU THE LEAST BIT CURIOUS TO FIND OUT... WHAT'S IN THE LOCKER?
MY CITY
SHINJUKU
JCB
CARD

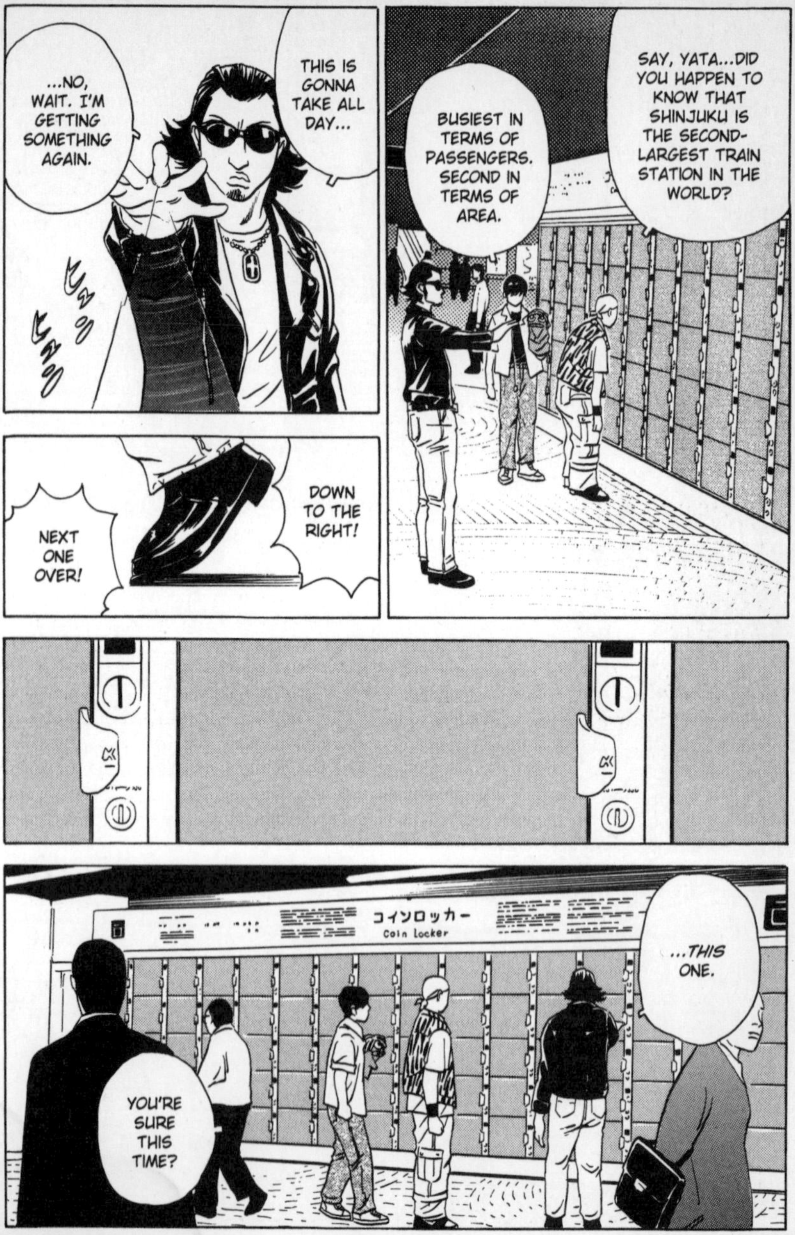
SAY, YATA...DID YOU HAPPEN TO KNOW THAT SHINJUKU IS THE SECOND-LARGEST TRAIN STATION IN THE WORLD?
BUSIEST IN TERMS OF PASSENGERS. SECOND IN TERMS OF AREA.
THIS IS GONNA TAKE ALL DAY...
...NO, WAIT. I'M GETTING SOMETHING AGAIN.
DOWN TO THE RIGHT!
NEXT ONE OVER!
コインロッカー
Coin Locker
...THIS ONE.
YOU'RE SURE THIS TIME?

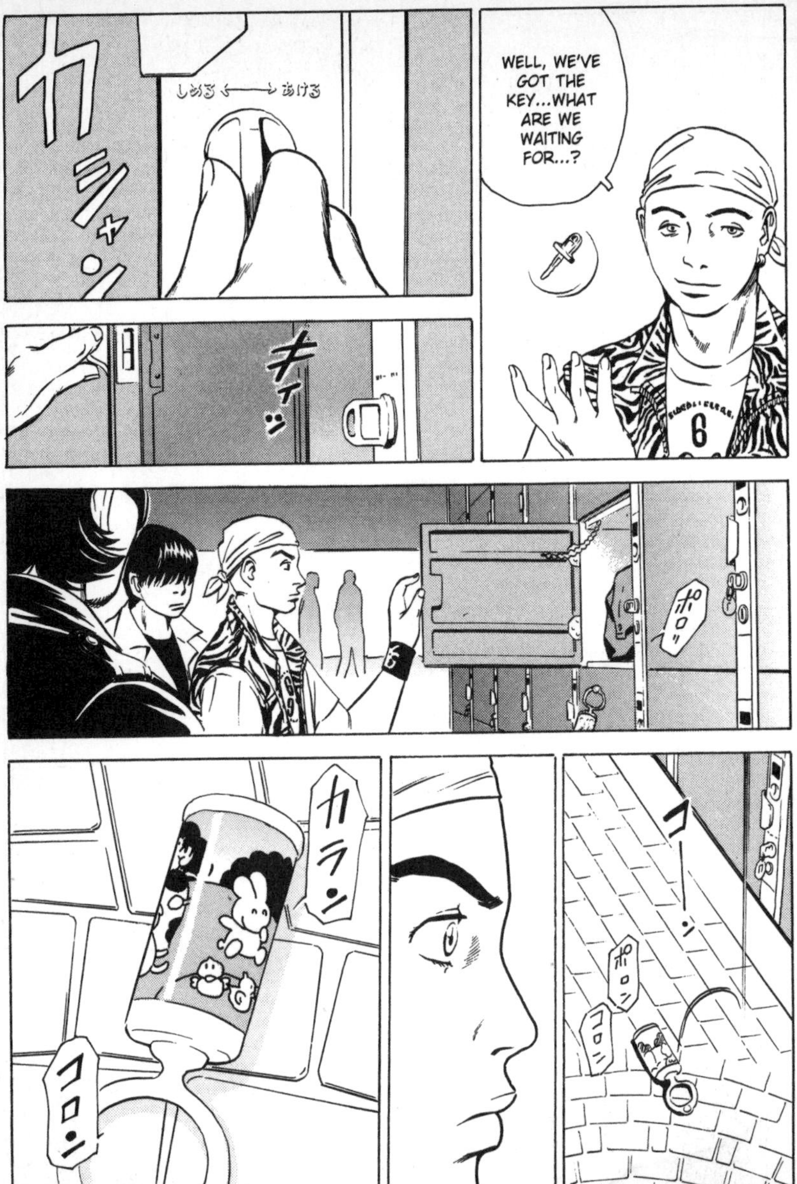
WELL, WE'VE GOT THE KEY...WHAT ARE WE WAITING FOR...?
カシャン
しめる ←→ あける
キィッ
ポロッ
コーン
ポロン
コロン
カラン
コロン

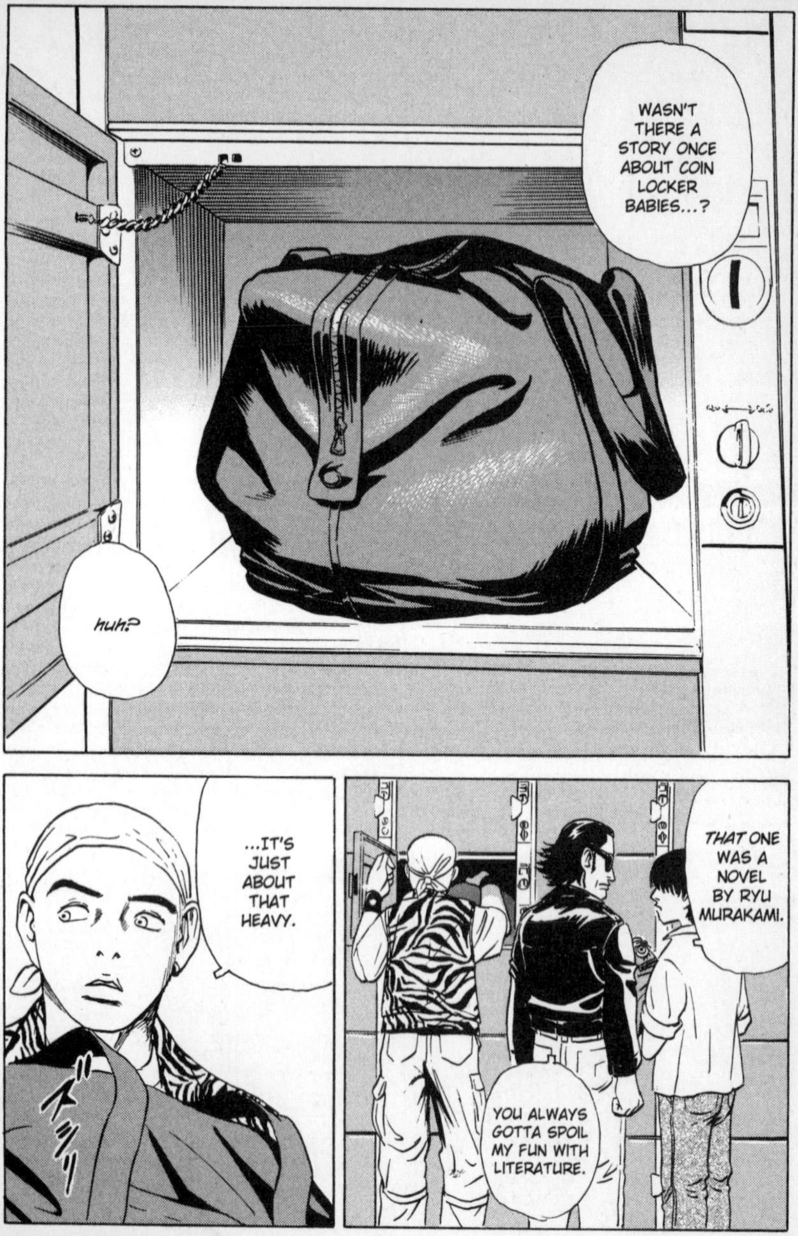
WASN'T THERE A STORY ONCE ABOUT COIN LOCKER BABIES...?
huh?
THAT ONE WAS A NOVEL BY RYU MURAKAMI.
YOU ALWAYS GOTTA SPOIL MY FUN WITH LITERATURE.
...IT'S JUST ABOUT THAT HEAVY.

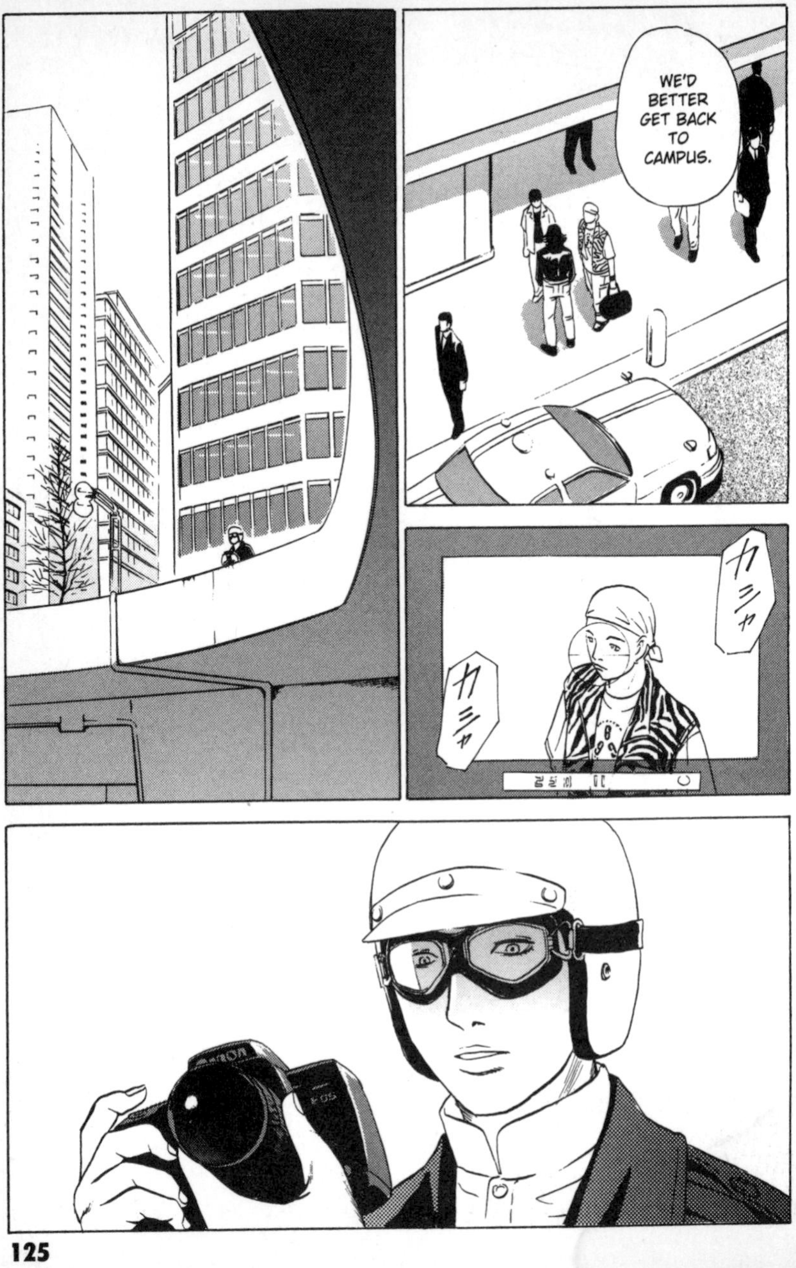
WE'D BETTER GET BACK TO CAMPUS.
カシャ
カシャ

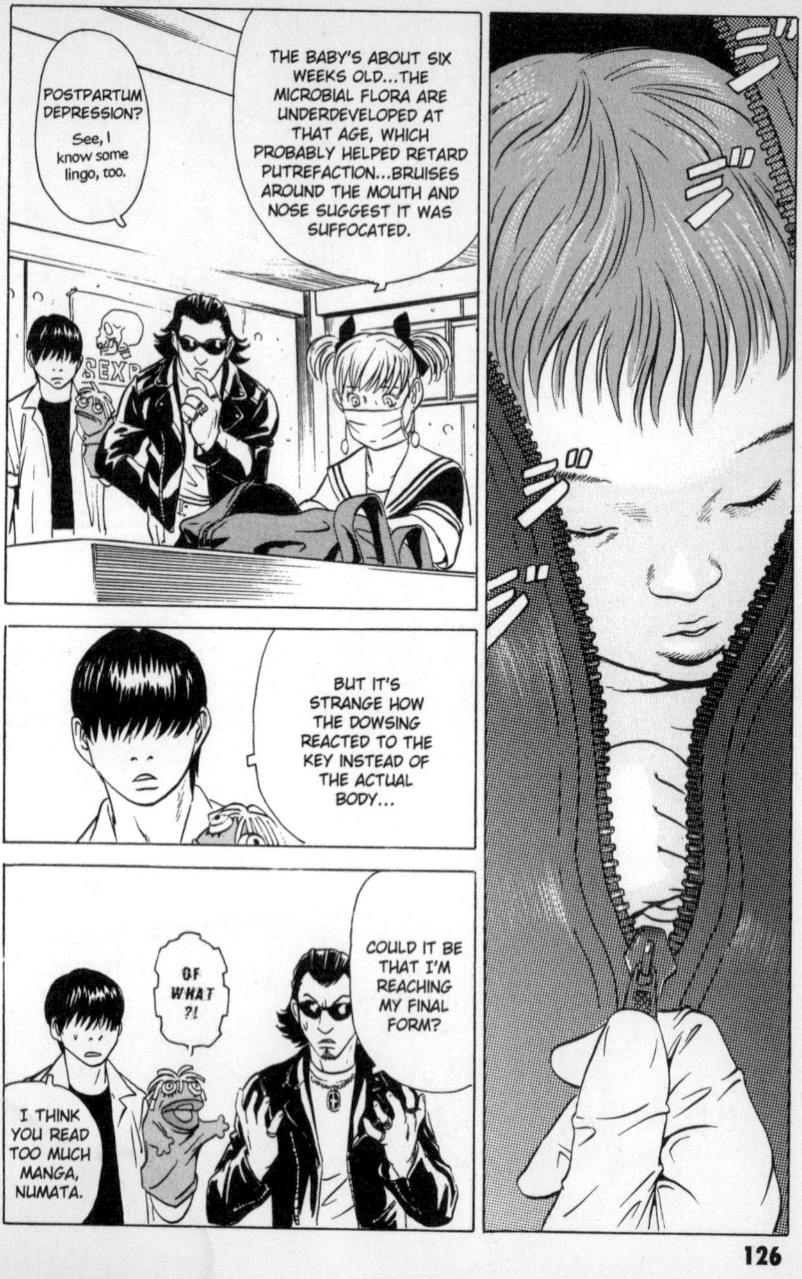

THE BABY'S ABOUT SIX WEEKS OLD...THE MICROBIAL FLORA ARE UNDERDEVELOPED AT THAT AGE, WHICH PROBABLY HELPED RETARD PUTREFACTION...BRUISES AROUND THE MOUTH AND NOSE SUGGEST IT WAS SUFFOCATED.
POSTPARTUM DEPRESSION? See, I know some lingo, too.
SEXP
BUT IT'S STRANGE HOW THE DOWSING REACTED TO THE KEY INSTEAD OF THE ACTUAL BODY...
COULD IT BE THAT I'M REACHING MY FINAL FORM?
OF WHAT ?!
I THINK YOU READ TOO MUCH MANGA, NUMATA.

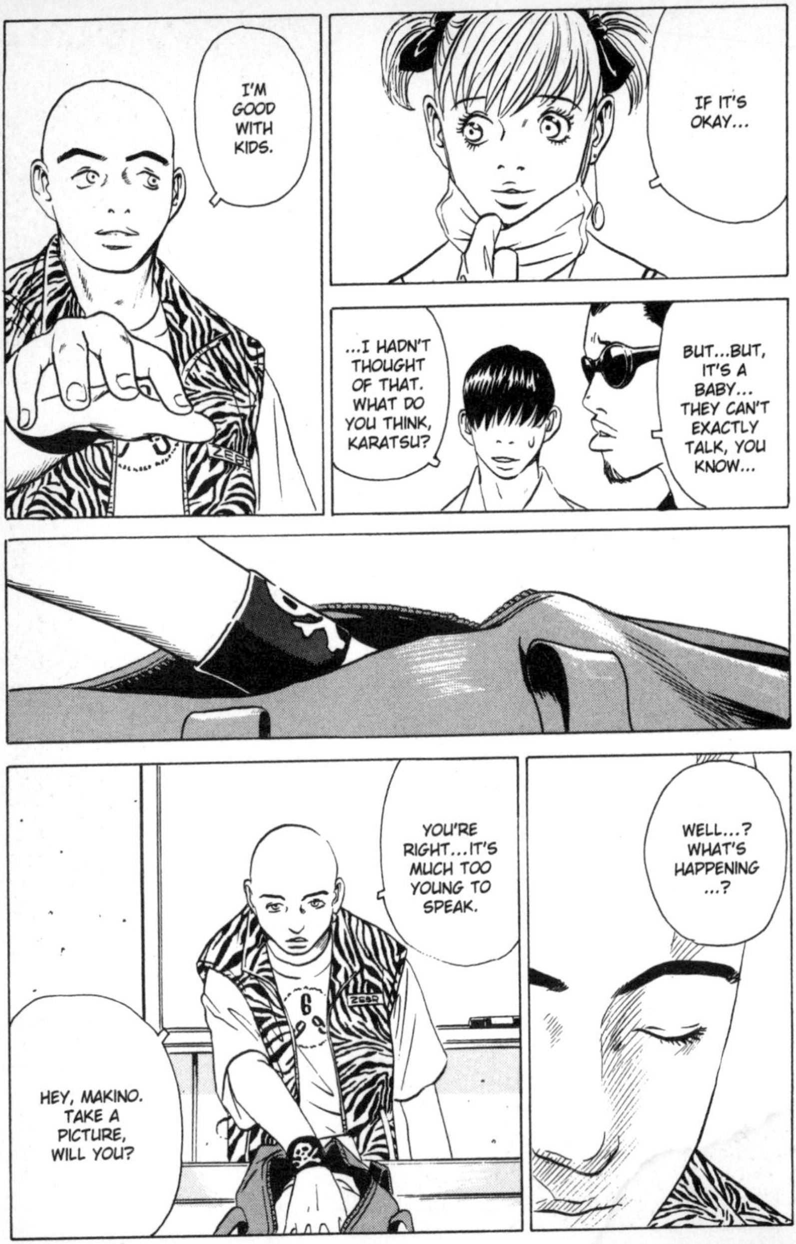
IF IT'S OKAY...
BUT...BUT, IT'S A BABY... THEY CAN'T EXACTLY TALK, YOU KNOW...
...I HADN'T THOUGHT OF THAT. WHAT DO YOU THINK, KARATSU?
I'M GOOD WITH KIDS.
WELL...? WHAT'S HAPPENING ...?
YOU'RE RIGHT...IT'S MUCH TOO YOUNG TO SPEAK.
HEY, MAKINO. TAKE A PICTURE, WILL YOU?

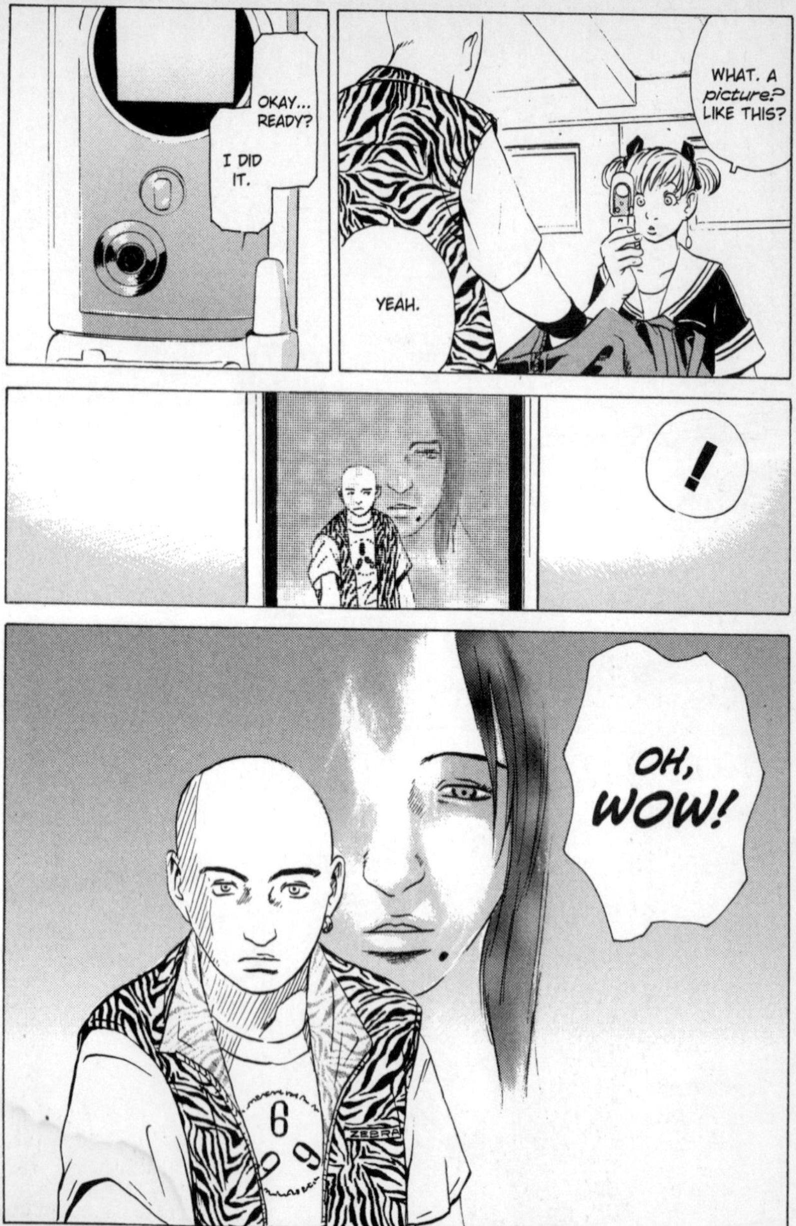

WHAT. A *picture?* LIKE THIS?
YEAH.
OKAY... READY?
I DID IT.
!
OH, WOW!
ZEBRA

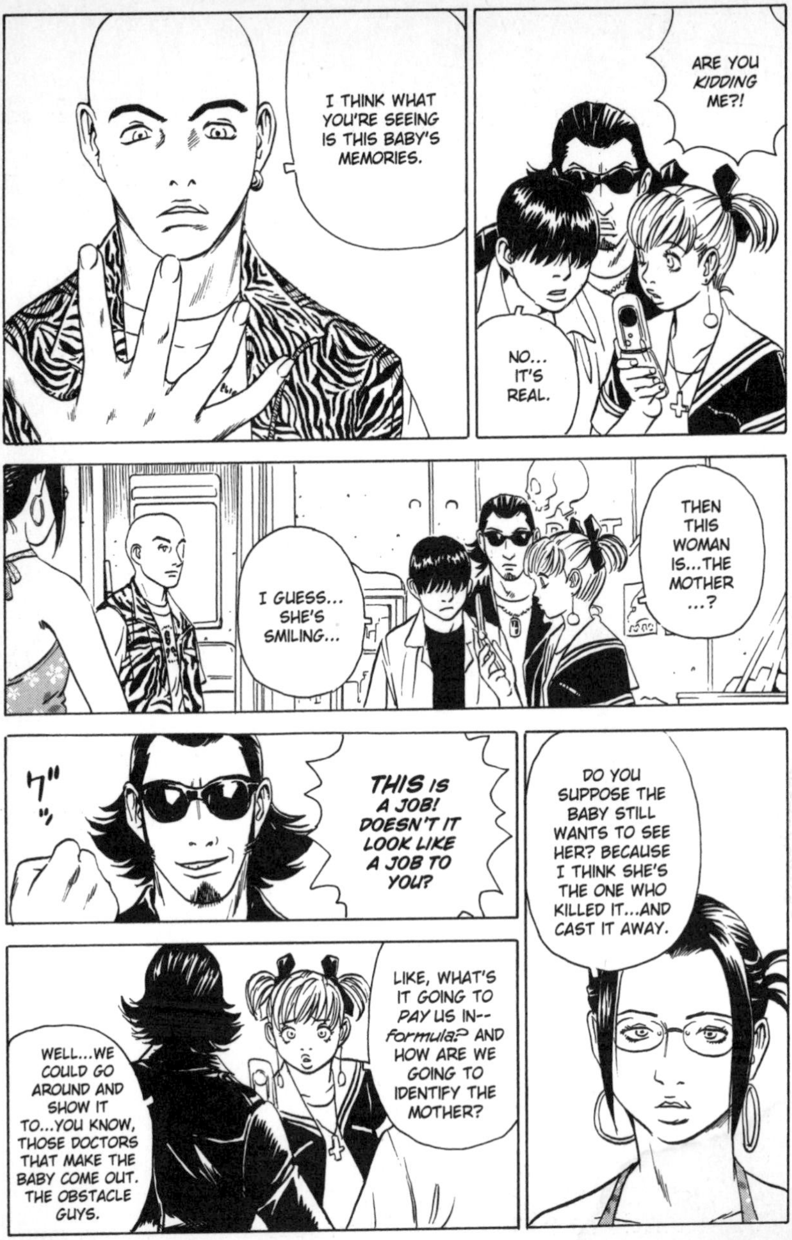
ARE YOU *KIDDING* ME?!
NO... IT'S REAL.
I THINK WHAT YOU'RE SEEING IS THIS BABY'S MEMORIES.
THEN THIS WOMAN IS...THE MOTHER ...?
I GUESS... SHE'S SMILING...
DO YOU SUPPOSE THE BABY STILL WANTS TO SEE HER? BECAUSE I THINK SHE'S THE ONE WHO KILLED IT...AND CAST IT AWAY.
***THIS** IS A JOB! DOESN'T IT LOOK LIKE A JOB TO YOU?*
グッ
LIKE, WHAT'S IT GOING TO *PAY* US IN--*formula?* AND HOW ARE WE GOING TO IDENTIFY THE MOTHER?
WELL...WE COULD GO AROUND AND SHOW IT TO...YOU KNOW, THOSE DOCTORS THAT MAKE THE BABY COME OUT. THE OBSTACLE GUYS.

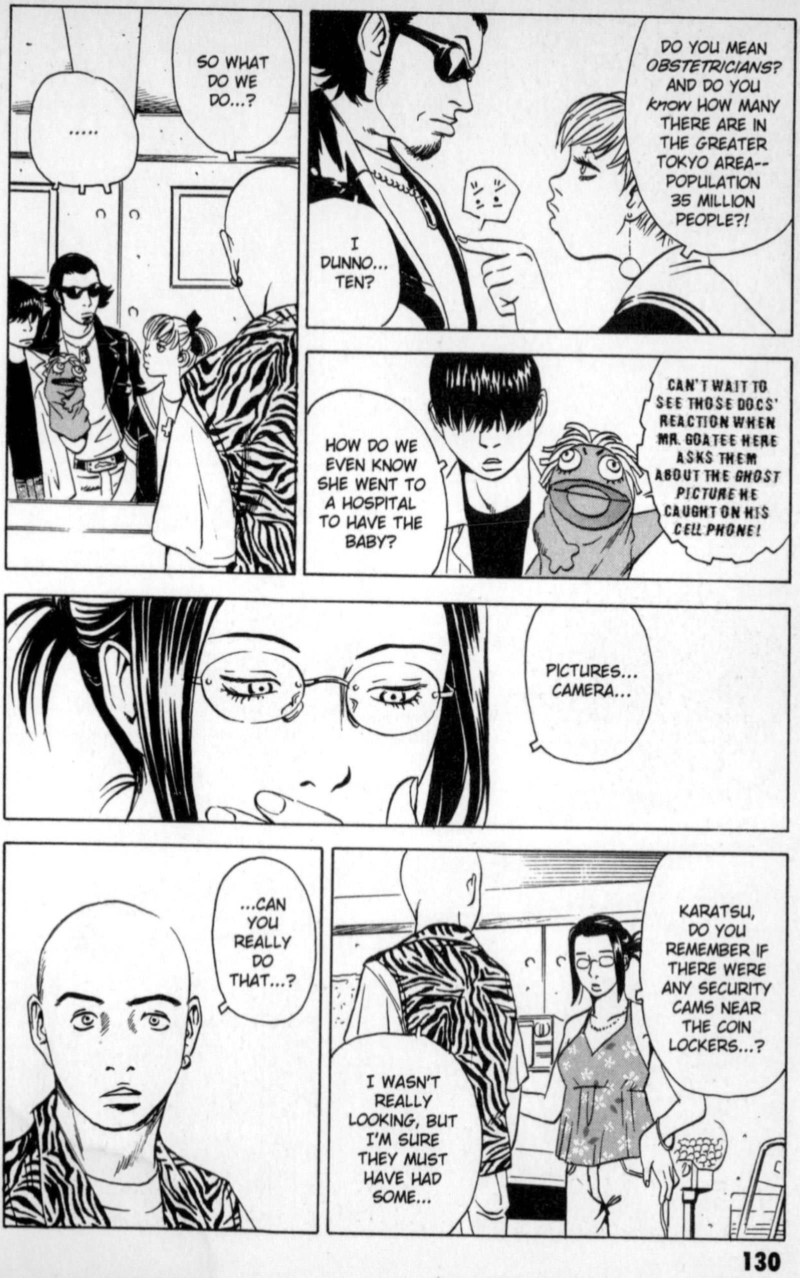
DO YOU MEAN *OBSTETRICIANS?* AND DO YOU *know* HOW MANY THERE ARE IN THE GREATER TOKYO AREA-- POPULATION 35 MILLION PEOPLE?!
I DUNNO... TEN?
CAN'T WAIT TO SEE THOSE DOCS' REACTION WHEN MR. GOATEE HERE ASKS THEM ABOUT THE *GHOST PICTURE* HE CAUGHT ON HIS *CELL PHONE!*
HOW DO WE EVEN KNOW SHE WENT TO A HOSPITAL TO HAVE THE BABY?
SO WHAT DO WE DO...?
.....
PICTURES... CAMERA...
KARATSU, DO YOU REMEMBER IF THERE WERE ANY SECURITY CAMS NEAR THE COIN LOCKERS...?
I WASN'T REALLY LOOKING, BUT I'M SURE THEY MUST HAVE HAD SOME...
...CAN YOU REALLY DO THAT...?

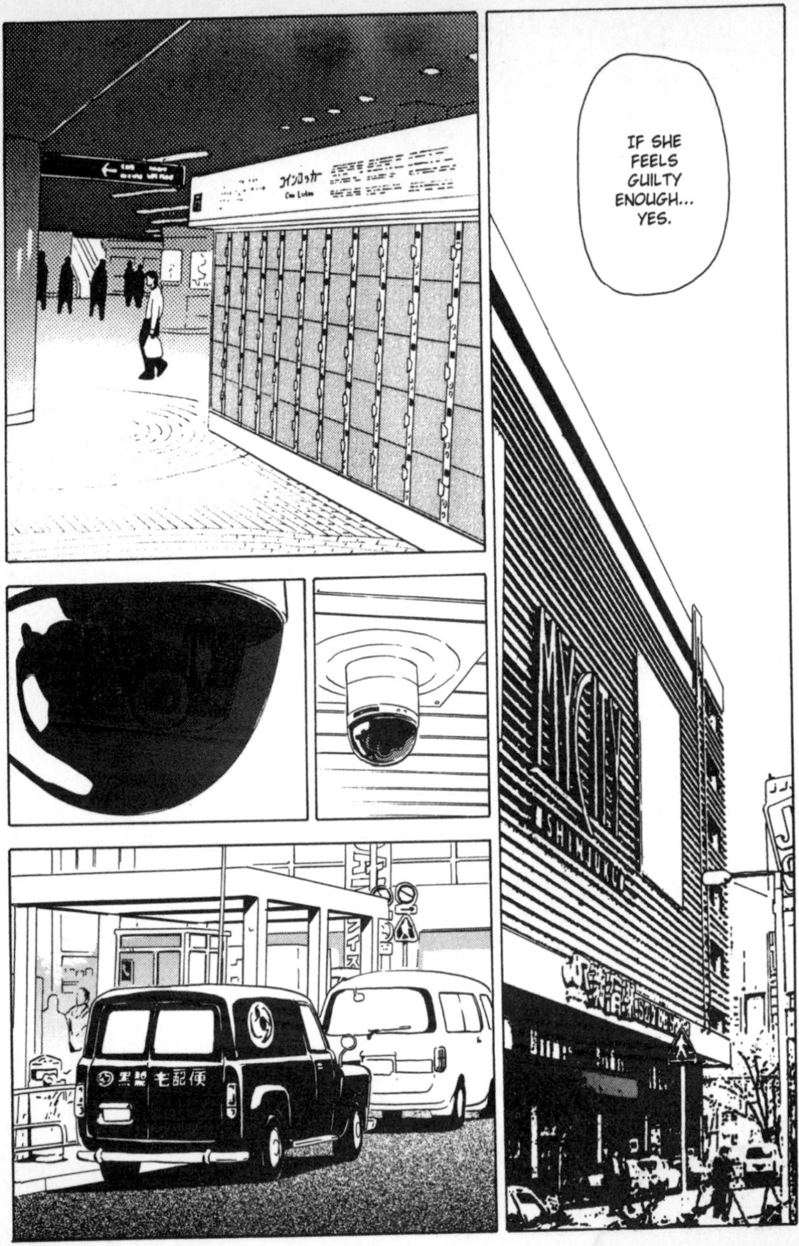
IF SHE FEELS GUILTY ENOUGH... YES.
MY CITY
SHINJUKU
コインロッカー
宅配便

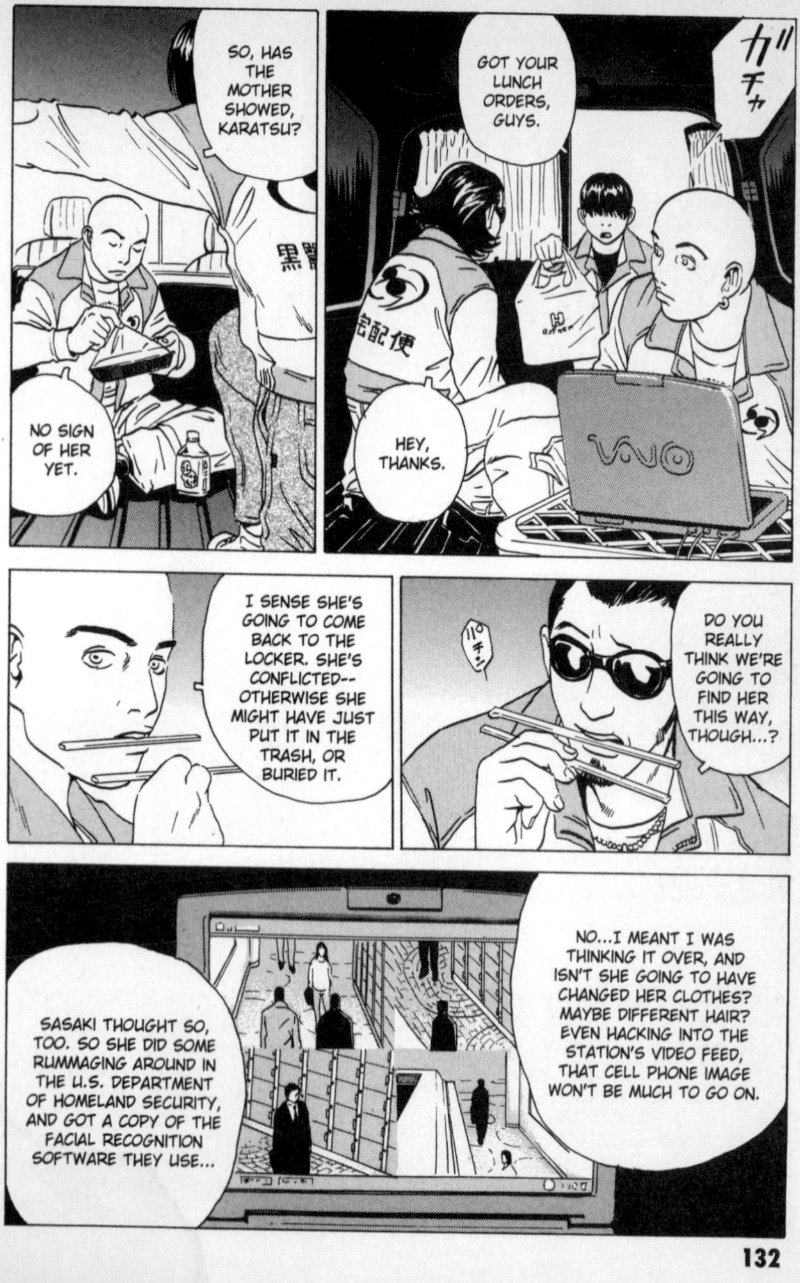
ガチャ
GOT YOUR LUNCH ORDERS, GUYS.
HEY, THANKS.
SO, HAS THE MOTHER SHOWED, KARATSU?
NO SIGN OF HER YET.
パチン
DO YOU REALLY THINK WE'RE GOING TO FIND HER THIS WAY, THOUGH...?
I SENSE SHE'S GOING TO COME BACK TO THE LOCKER. SHE'S CONFLICTED--OTHERWISE SHE MIGHT HAVE JUST PUT IT IN THE TRASH, OR BURIED IT.
NO...I MEANT I WAS THINKING IT OVER, AND ISN'T SHE GOING TO HAVE CHANGED HER CLOTHES? MAYBE DIFFERENT HAIR? EVEN HACKING INTO THE STATION'S VIDEO FEED, THAT CELL PHONE IMAGE WON'T BE MUCH TO GO ON.
SASAKI THOUGHT SO, TOO. SO SHE DID SOME RUMMAGING AROUND IN THE U.S. DEPARTMENT OF HOMELAND SECURITY, AND GOT A COPY OF THE FACIAL RECOGNITION SOFTWARE THEY USE...

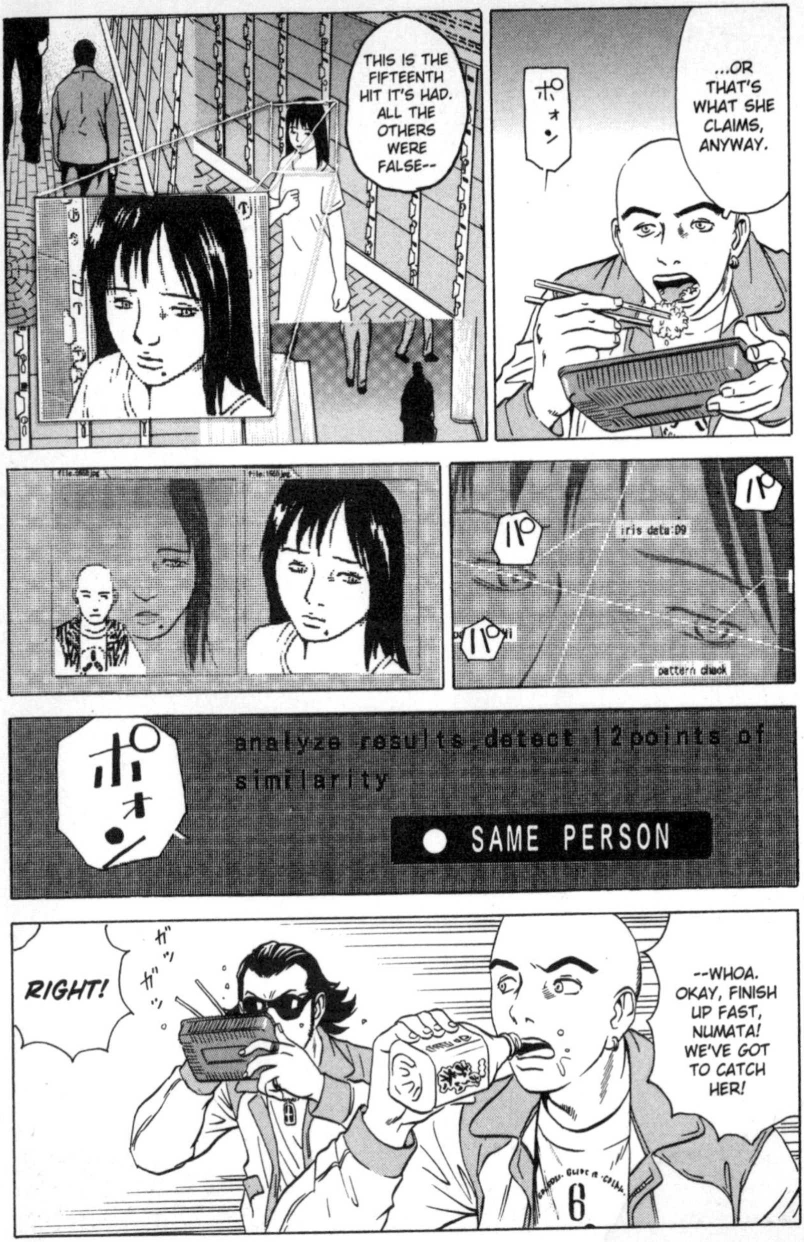
...OR THAT'S WHAT SHE CLAIMS, ANYWAY.
ポォン
THIS IS THE FIFTEENTH HIT IT'S HAD. ALL THE OTHERS WERE FALSE--
パ
iris data:09
パ
パ
pattern check
analyze results,detect 12points of similarity
SAME PERSON
ポォン
--WHOA. OKAY, FINISH UP FAST, NUMATA! WE'VE GOT TO CATCH HER!
ガツガツ
RIGHT!

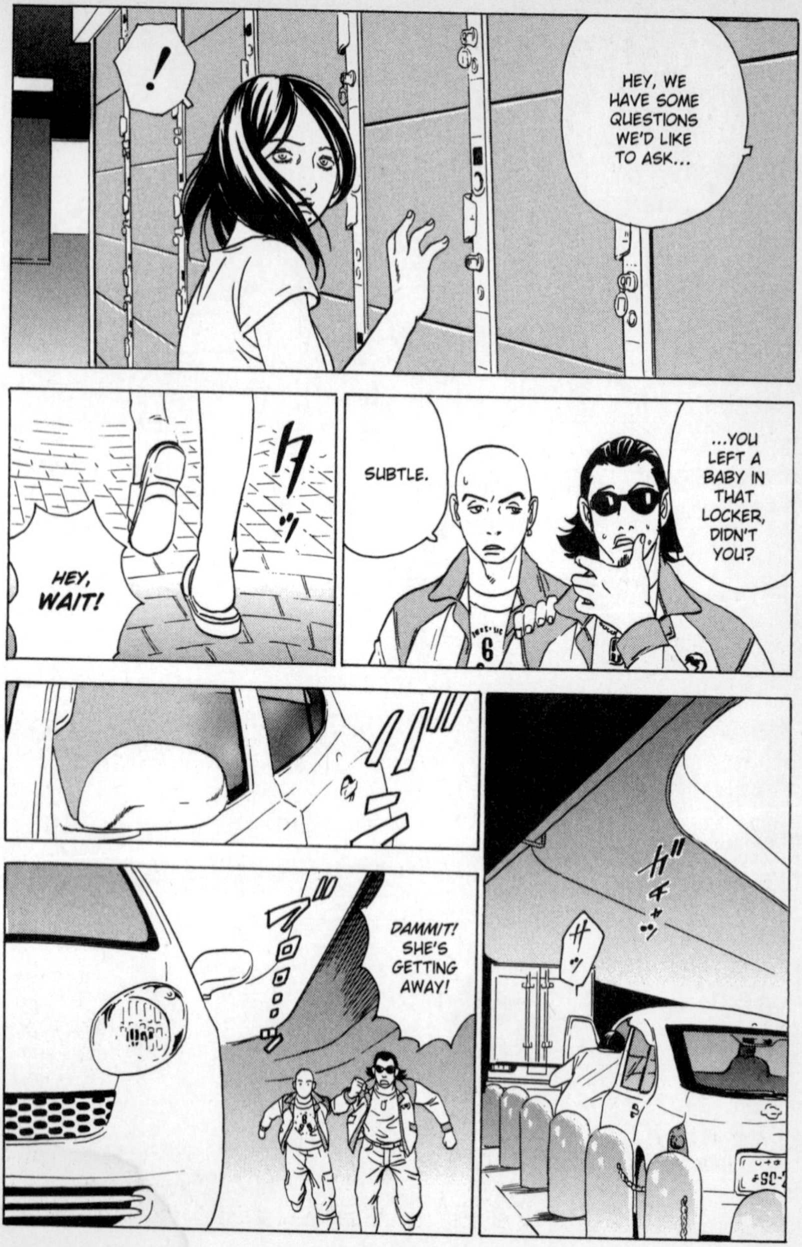
HEY, WE HAVE SOME QUESTIONS WE'D LIKE TO ASK...
!
...YOU LEFT A BABY IN THAT LOCKER, DIDN'T YOU?
SUBTLE.
HEY, WAIT!
DAMMIT! SHE'S GETTING AWAY!

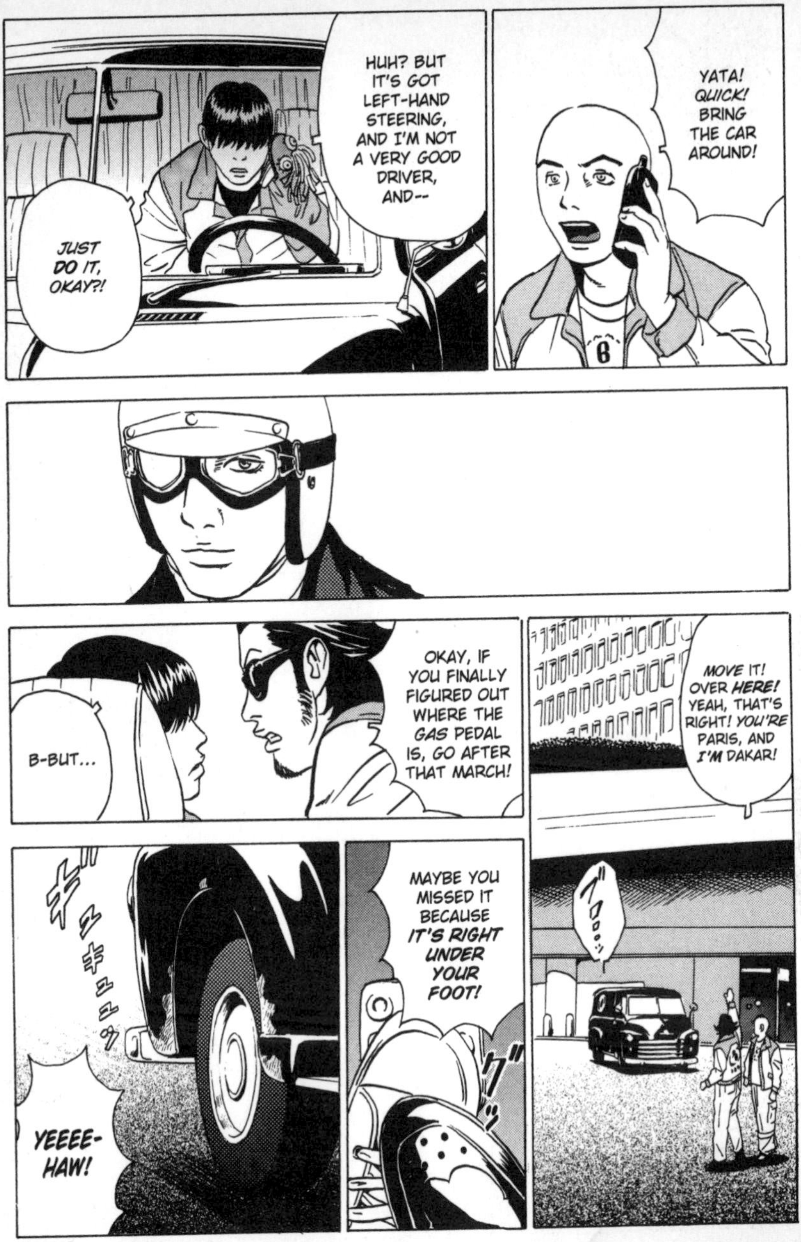
YATA! QUICK! BRING THE CAR AROUND!
HUH? BUT IT'S GOT LEFT-HAND STEERING, AND I'M NOT A VERY GOOD DRIVER, AND--
JUST DO IT, OKAY?!
MOVE IT! OVER HERE! YEAH, THAT'S RIGHT! YOU'RE PARIS, AND I'M DAKAR!
OKAY, IF YOU FINALLY FIGURED OUT WHERE THE GAS PEDAL IS, GO AFTER THAT MARCH!
B-BUT...
MAYBE YOU MISSED IT BECAUSE IT'S RIGHT UNDER YOUR FOOT!
YEEEE-HAW!

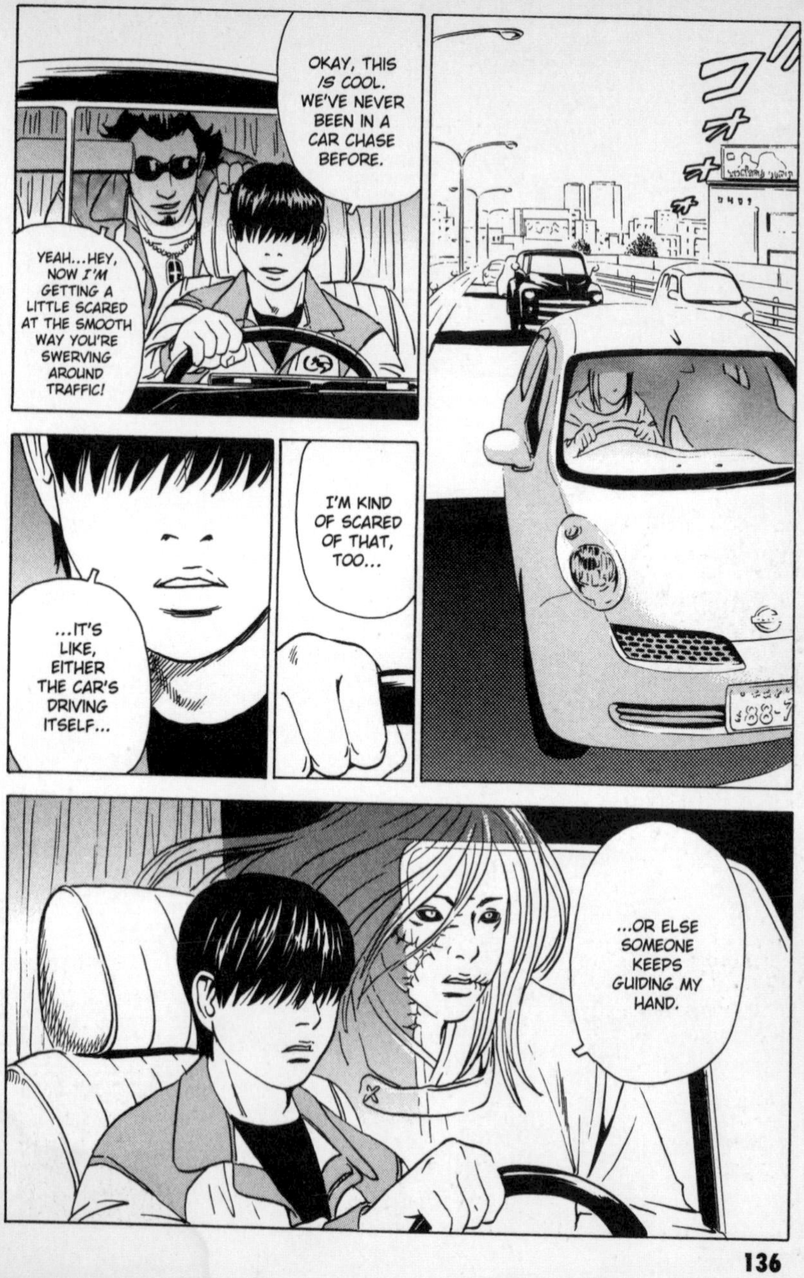
OKAY, THIS IS COOL. WE'VE NEVER BEEN IN A CAR CHASE BEFORE.
YEAH...HEY, NOW I'M GETTING A LITTLE SCARED AT THE SMOOTH WAY YOU'RE SWERVING AROUND TRAFFIC!
I'M KIND OF SCARED OF THAT, TOO...
...IT'S LIKE, EITHER THE CAR'S DRIVING ITSELF...
...OR ELSE SOMEONE KEEPS GUIDING MY HAND.

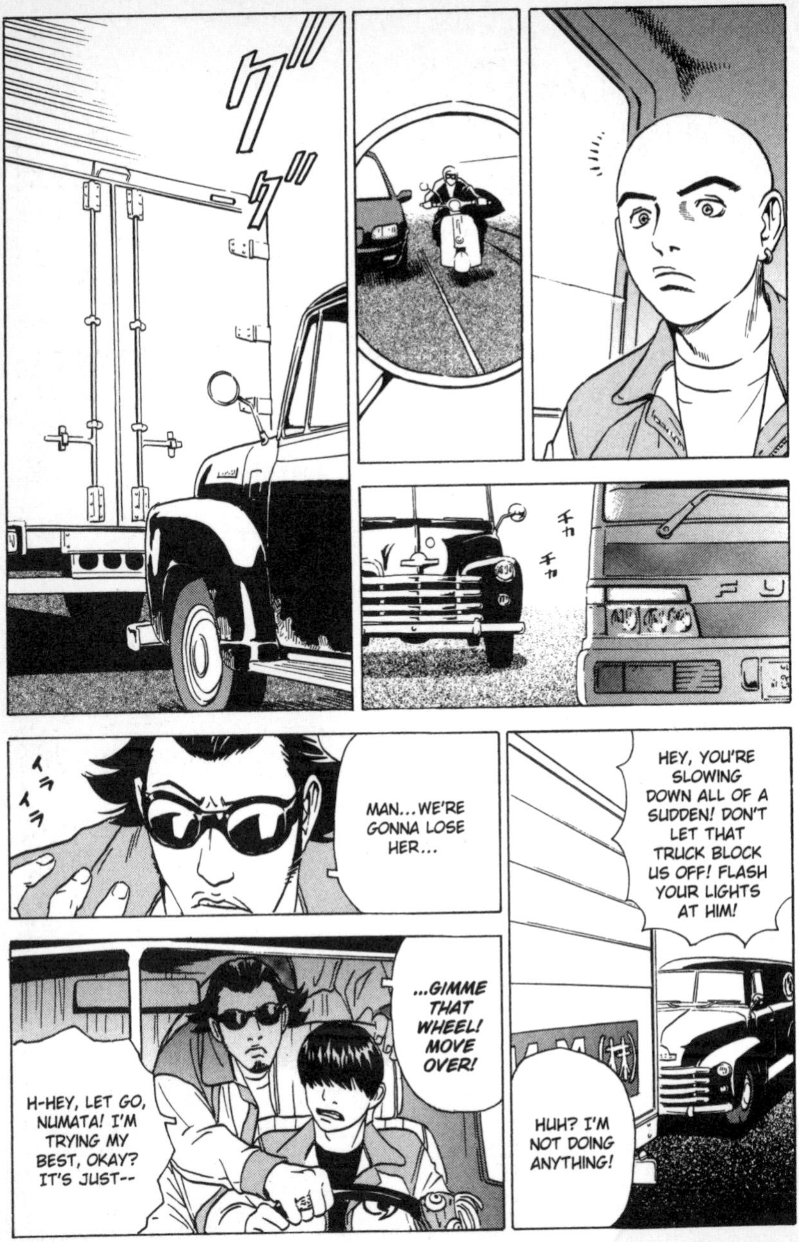
チカ
チカ
HEY, YOU'RE SLOWING DOWN ALL OF A SUDDEN! DON'T LET THAT TRUCK BLOCK US OFF! FLASH YOUR LIGHTS AT HIM!
HUH? I'M NOT DOING ANYTHING!
イラ
イラ
MAN...WE'RE GONNA LOSE HER...
...GIMME THAT WHEEL! MOVE OVER!
H-HEY, LET GO, NUMATA! I'M TRYING MY BEST, OKAY? IT'S JUST--

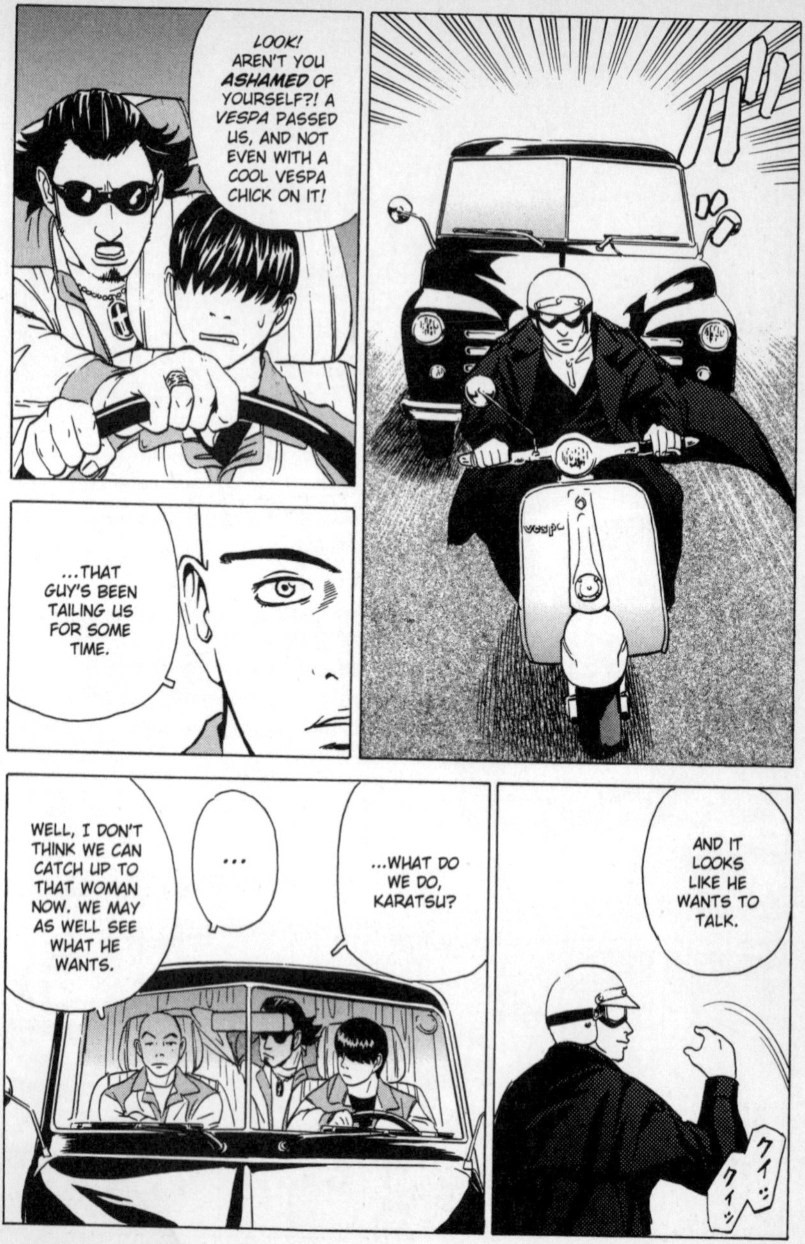
LOOK! AREN'T YOU ***ASHAMED*** OF YOURSELF?! A *VESPA* PASSED US, AND NOT EVEN WITH A COOL VESPA CHICK ON IT!
...THAT GUY'S BEEN TAILING US FOR SOME TIME.
AND IT LOOKS LIKE HE WANTS TO TALK.
クイッ クイッ
...WHAT DO WE DO, KARATSU?
...
WELL, I DON'T THINK WE CAN CATCH UP TO THAT WOMAN NOW. WE MAY AS WELL SEE WHAT HE WANTS.

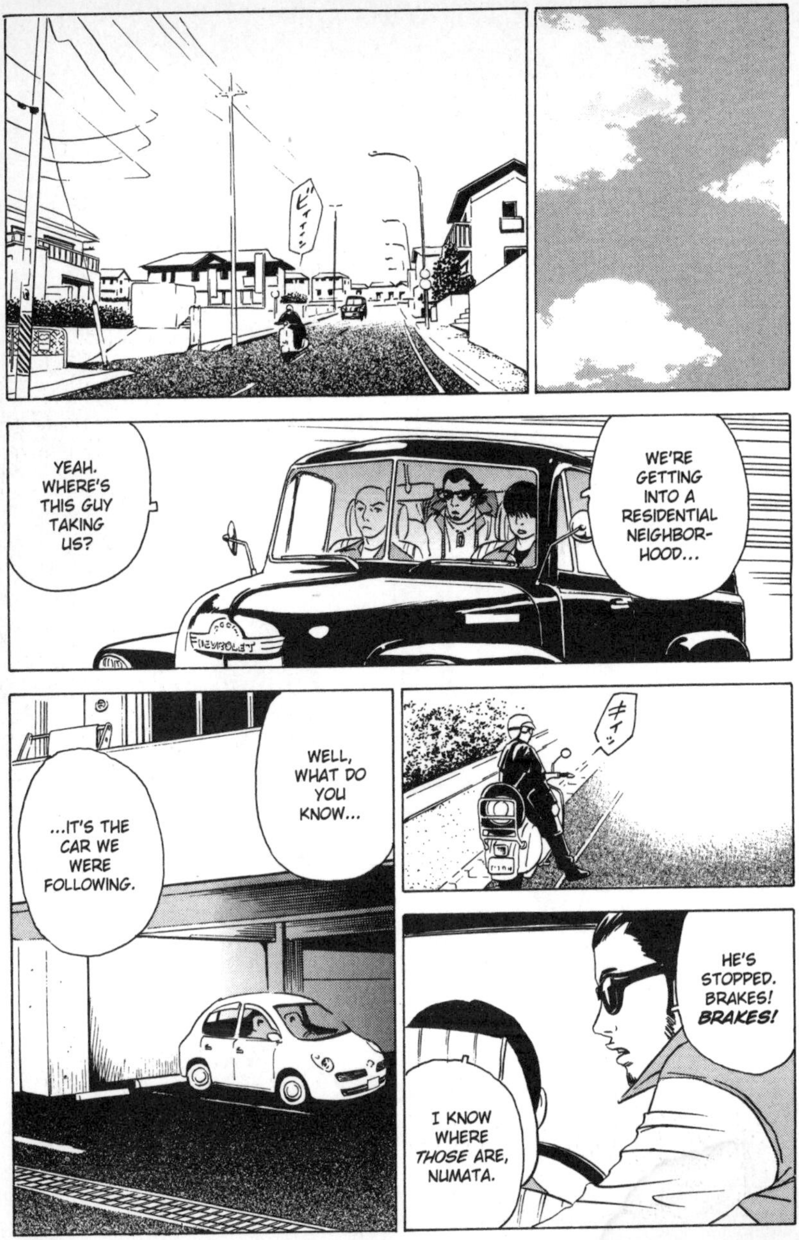
ビィィィン
WE'RE GETTING INTO A RESIDENTIAL NEIGHBOR-HOOD...
YEAH. WHERE'S THIS GUY TAKING US?
キィッ
HE'S STOPPED. BRAKES! *BRAKES!*
I KNOW WHERE *THOSE* ARE, NUMATA.
WELL, WHAT DO YOU KNOW...
...IT'S THE CAR WE WERE FOLLOWING.

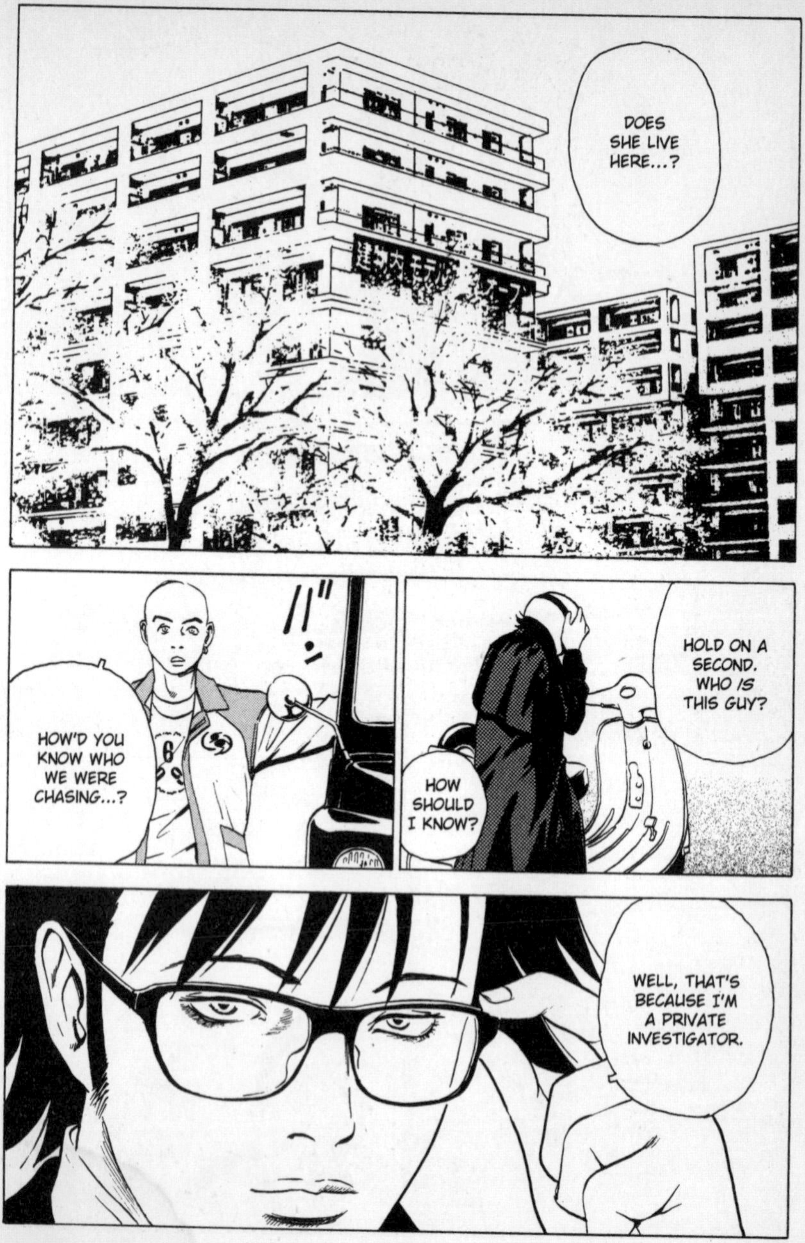
DOES SHE LIVE HERE...?
HOLD ON A SECOND. WHO *IS* THIS GUY?
HOW SHOULD I KNOW?
HOW'D YOU KNOW WHO WE WERE CHASING...?
WELL, THAT'S BECAUSE I'M A PRIVATE INVESTIGATOR.

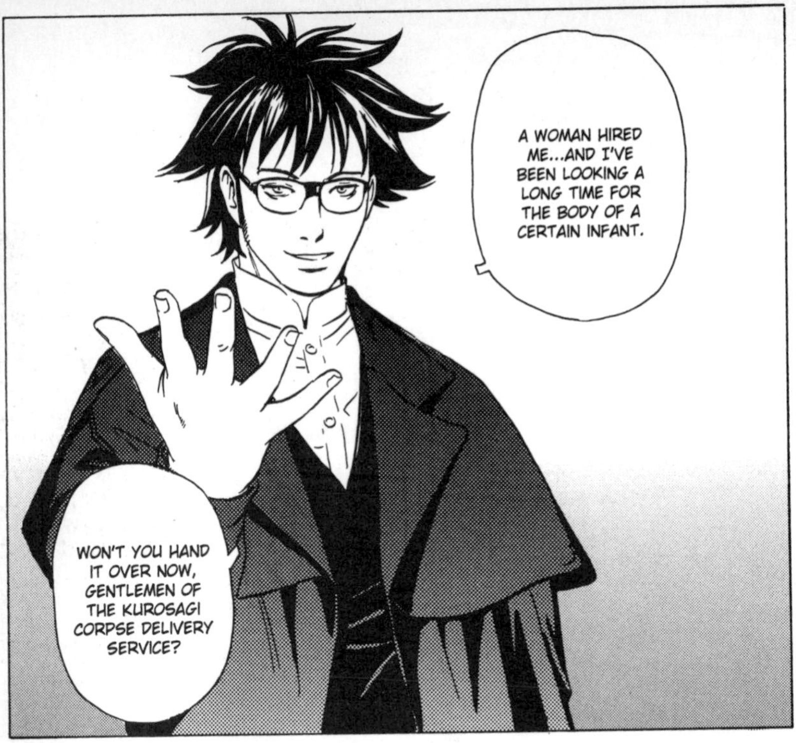
A WOMAN HIRED ME...AND I'VE BEEN LOOKING A LONG TIME FOR THE BODY OF A CERTAIN INFANT.
WON'T YOU HAND IT OVER NOW, GENTLEMEN OF THE KUROSAGI CORPSE DELIVERY SERVICE?

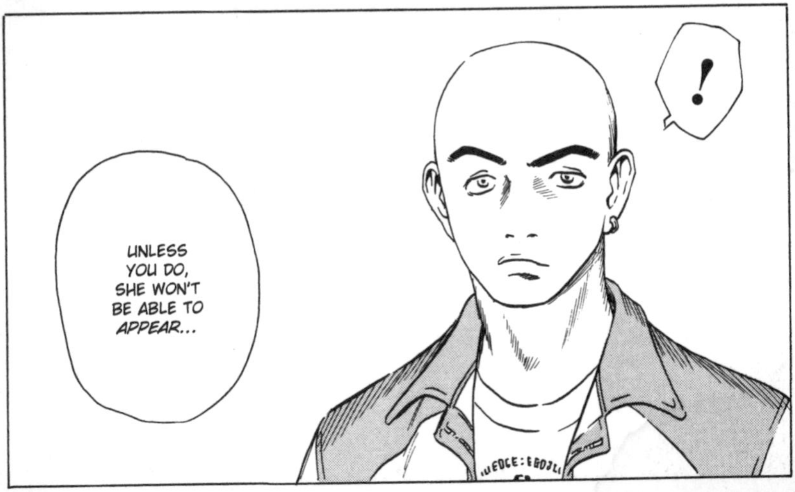
!
UNLESS YOU DO, SHE WON'T BE ABLE TO *APPEAR*...

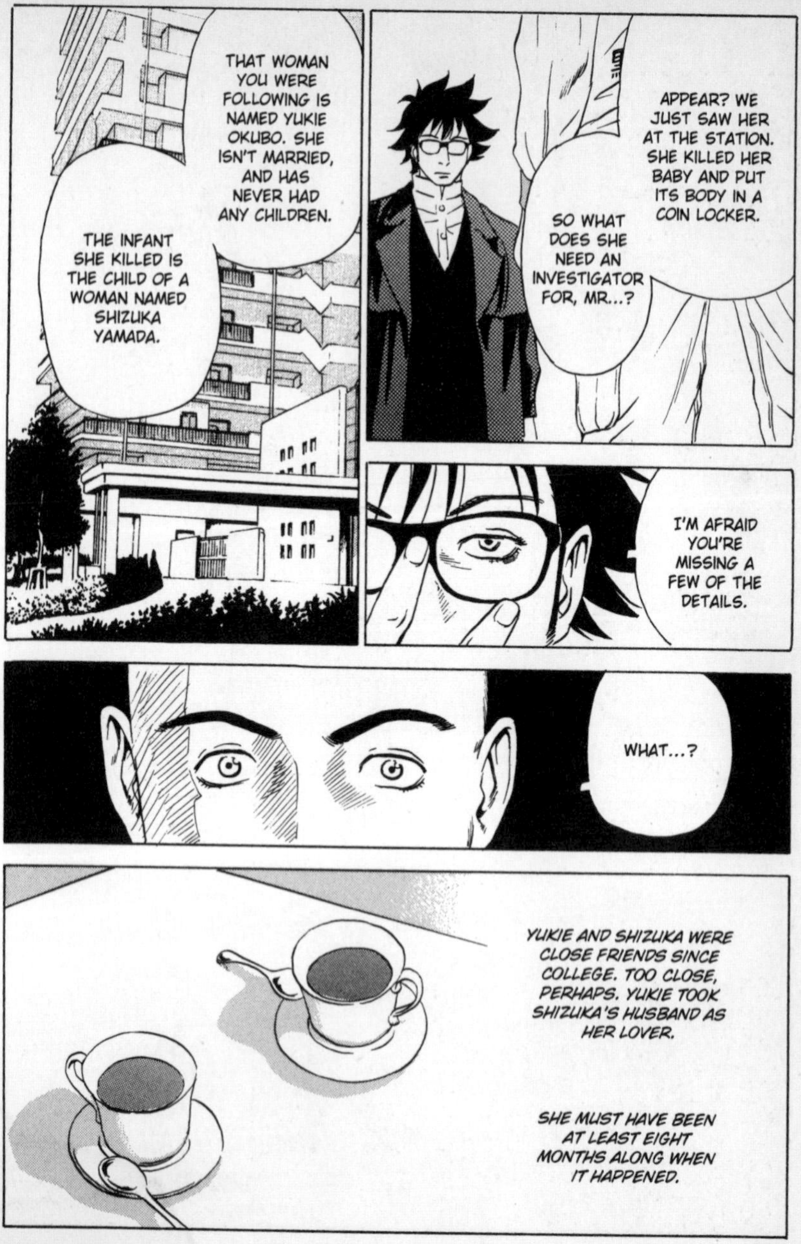
APPEAR? WE JUST SAW HER AT THE STATION. SHE KILLED HER BABY AND PUT ITS BODY IN A COIN LOCKER.
SO WHAT DOES SHE NEED AN INVESTIGATOR FOR, MR...?
I'M AFRAID YOU'RE MISSING A FEW OF THE DETAILS.
THAT WOMAN YOU WERE FOLLOWING IS NAMED YUKIE OKUBO. SHE ISN'T MARRIED, AND HAS NEVER HAD ANY CHILDREN.
THE INFANT SHE KILLED IS THE CHILD OF A WOMAN NAMED SHIZUKA YAMADA.
WHAT...?
YUKIE AND SHIZUKA WERE CLOSE FRIENDS SINCE COLLEGE. TOO CLOSE, PERHAPS. YUKIE TOOK SHIZUKA'S HUSBAND AS HER LOVER.
SHE MUST HAVE BEEN AT LEAST EIGHT MONTHS ALONG WHEN IT HAPPENED.

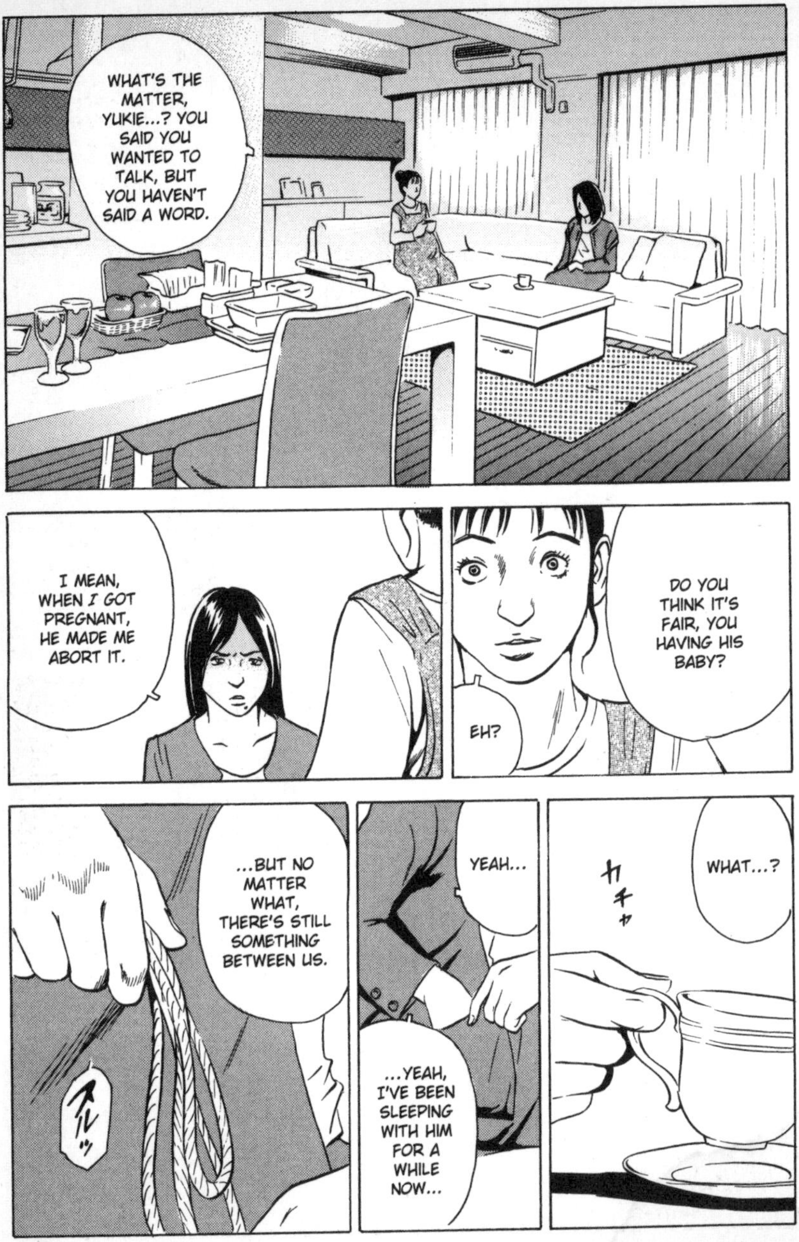

WHAT'S THE MATTER, YUKIE...? YOU SAID YOU WANTED TO TALK, BUT YOU HAVEN'T SAID A WORD.
DO YOU THINK IT'S FAIR, YOU HAVING HIS BABY?
EH?
I MEAN, WHEN *I* GOT PREGNANT, HE MADE ME ABORT IT.
WHAT...?
カチャ
YEAH...
...YEAH, I'VE BEEN SLEEPING WITH HIM FOR A WHILE NOW...
...BUT NO MATTER WHAT, THERE'S STILL SOMETHING BETWEEN US.
スルッ

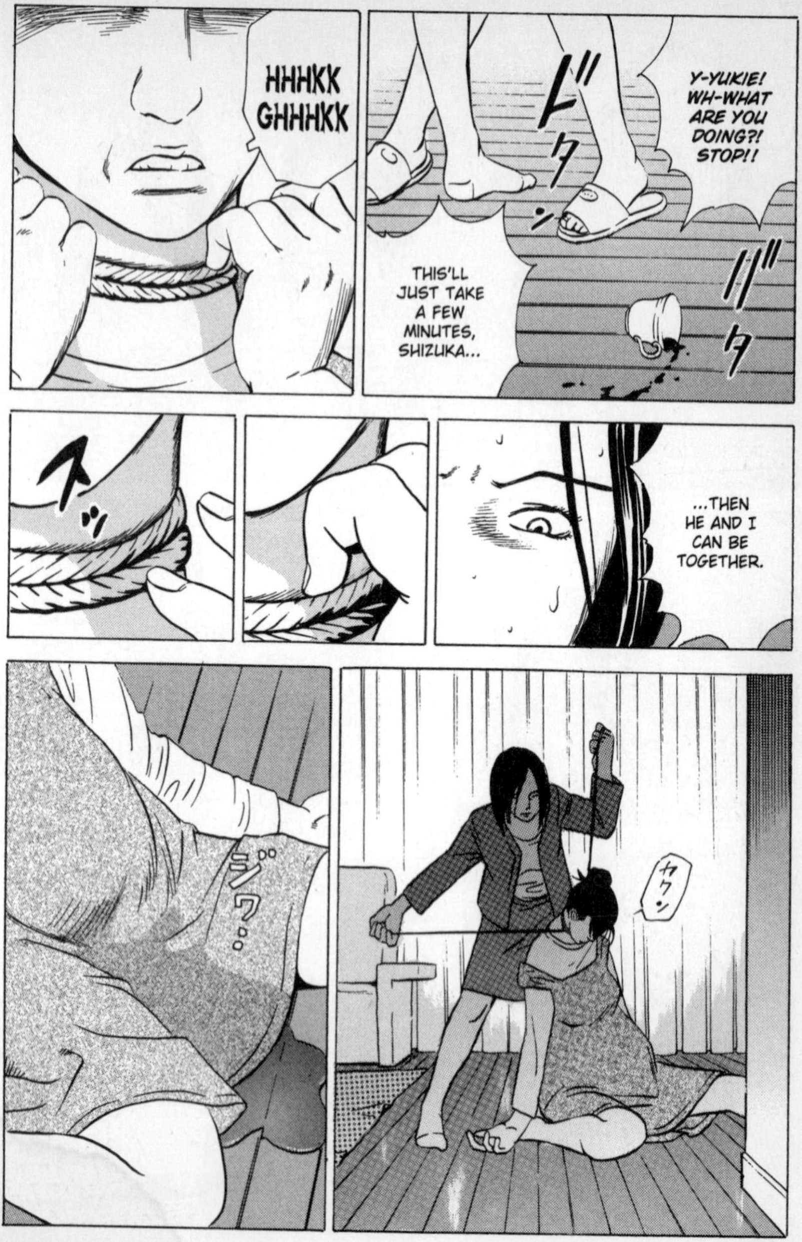
Y-YUKIE! WH-WHAT ARE YOU DOING?! STOP!!
THIS'LL JUST TAKE A FEW MINUTES, SHIZUKA...
HHHKK GHHHKK
...THEN HE AND I CAN BE TOGETHER.

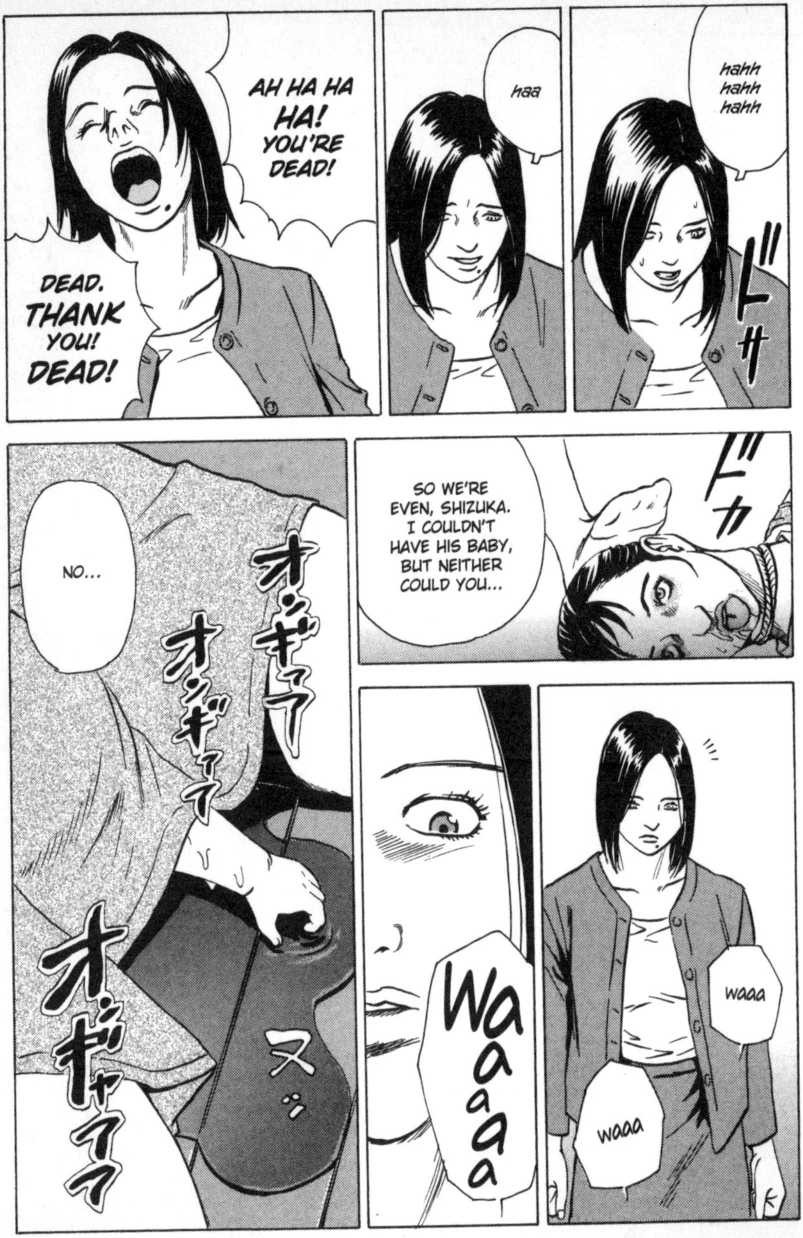
hahh hahh hahh
haa
AH HA HA HA! YOU'RE DEAD!
DEAD. THANK YOU! DEAD!
SO WE'RE EVEN, SHIZUKA. I COULDN'T HAVE HIS BABY, BUT NEITHER COULD YOU...
waaa
waaa
Waaaaa
NO...

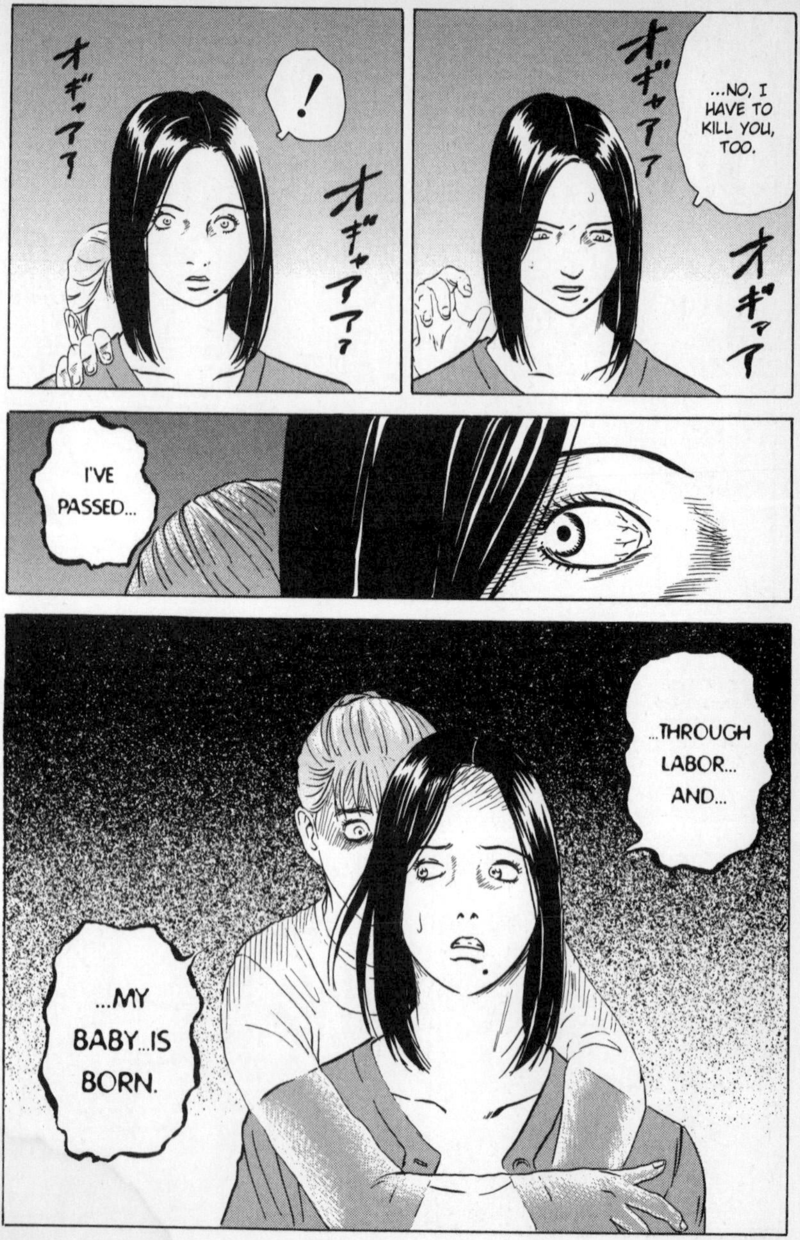
オギャアア
...NO, I HAVE TO KILL YOU, TOO.
オギャアア
オギャアァ
!
オギャアアァ
I'VE PASSED...
...THROUGH LABOR... AND...
...MY BABY...IS BORN.

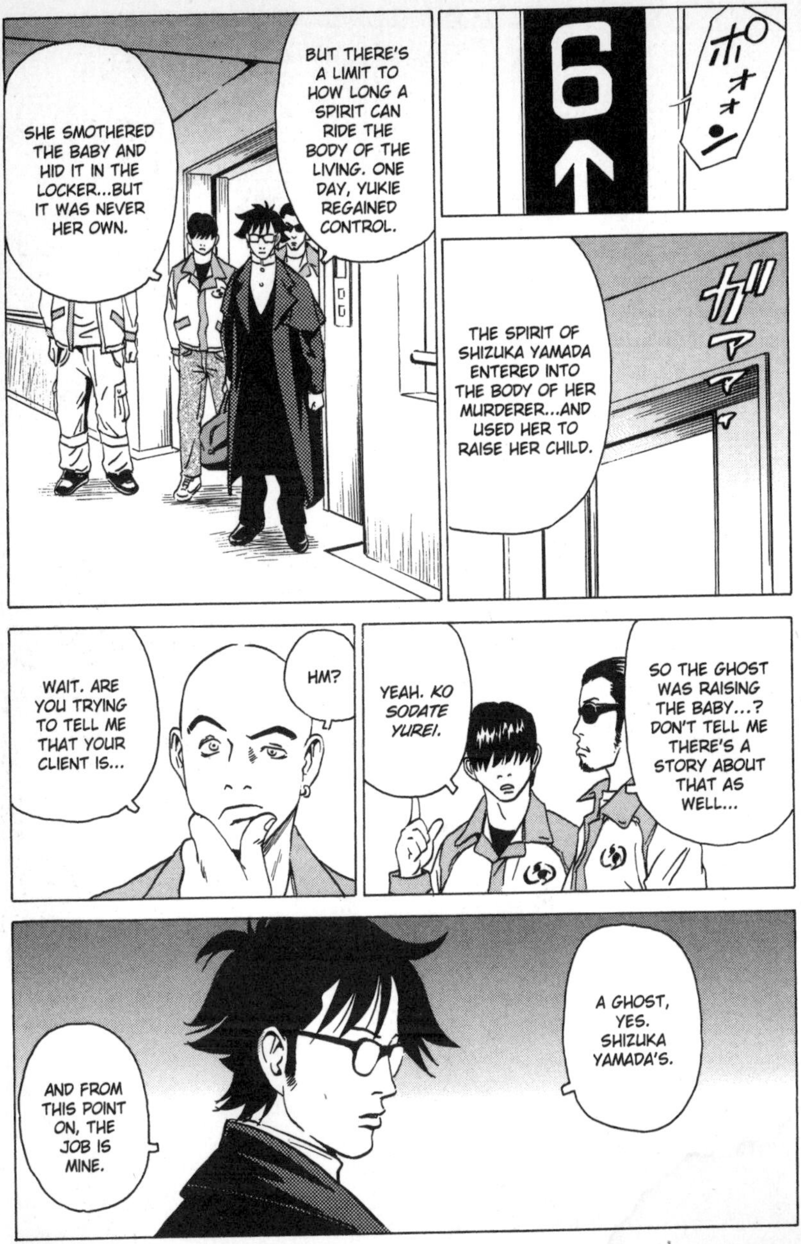

ポォオォン
ガアァァ
THE SPIRIT OF SHIZUKA YAMADA ENTERED INTO THE BODY OF HER MURDERER...AND USED HER TO RAISE HER CHILD.
BUT THERE'S A LIMIT TO HOW LONG A SPIRIT CAN RIDE THE BODY OF THE LIVING. ONE DAY, YUKIE REGAINED CONTROL.
SHE SMOTHERED THE BABY AND HID IT IN THE LOCKER...BUT IT WAS NEVER HER OWN.
SO THE GHOST WAS RAISING THE BABY...? DON'T TELL ME THERE'S A STORY ABOUT THAT AS WELL...
YEAH. *KO SODATE YUREI.*
HM?
WAIT. ARE YOU TRYING TO TELL ME THAT YOUR CLIENT IS...
A GHOST, YES. SHIZUKA YAMADA'S.
AND FROM THIS POINT ON, THE JOB IS MINE.

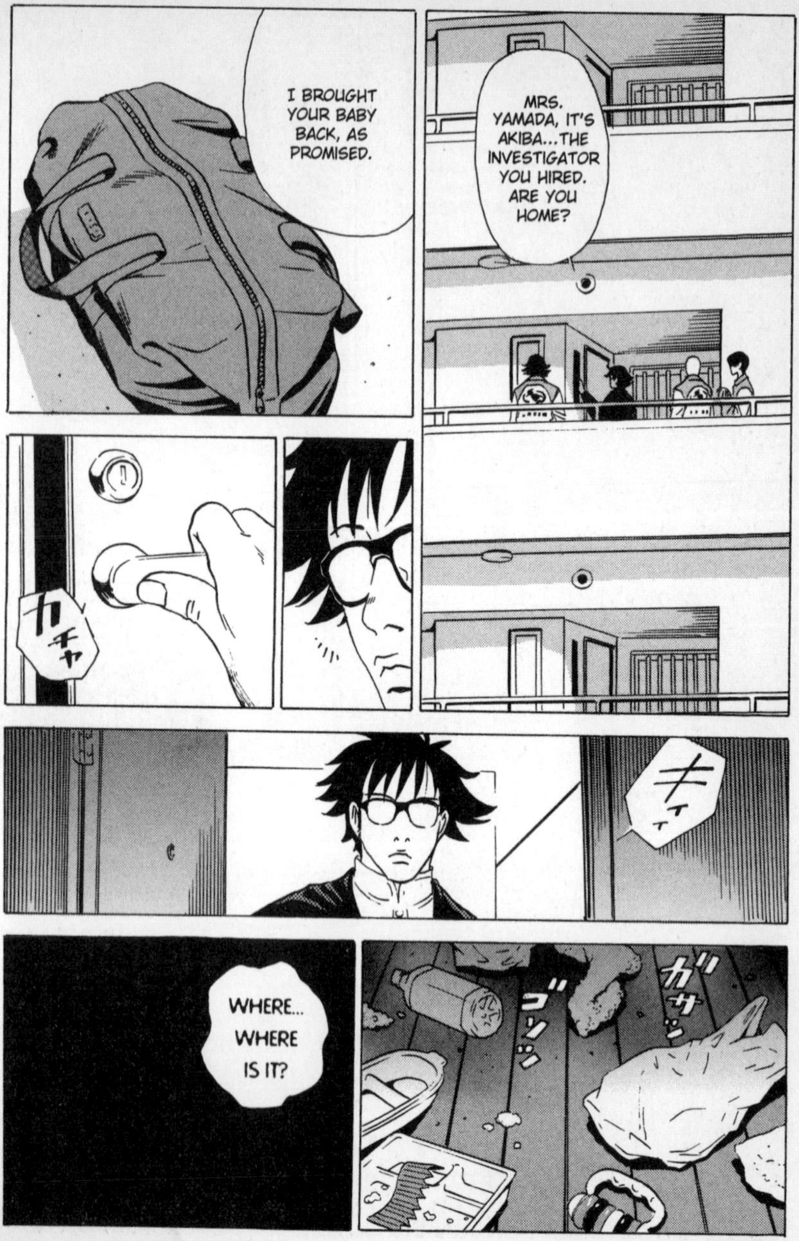
MRS. YAMADA, IT'S AKIBA...THE INVESTIGATOR YOU HIRED. ARE YOU HOME?
I BROUGHT YOUR BABY BACK, AS PROMISED.
カチャ
キィ
ガサ
ゴソ
WHERE... WHERE IS IT?

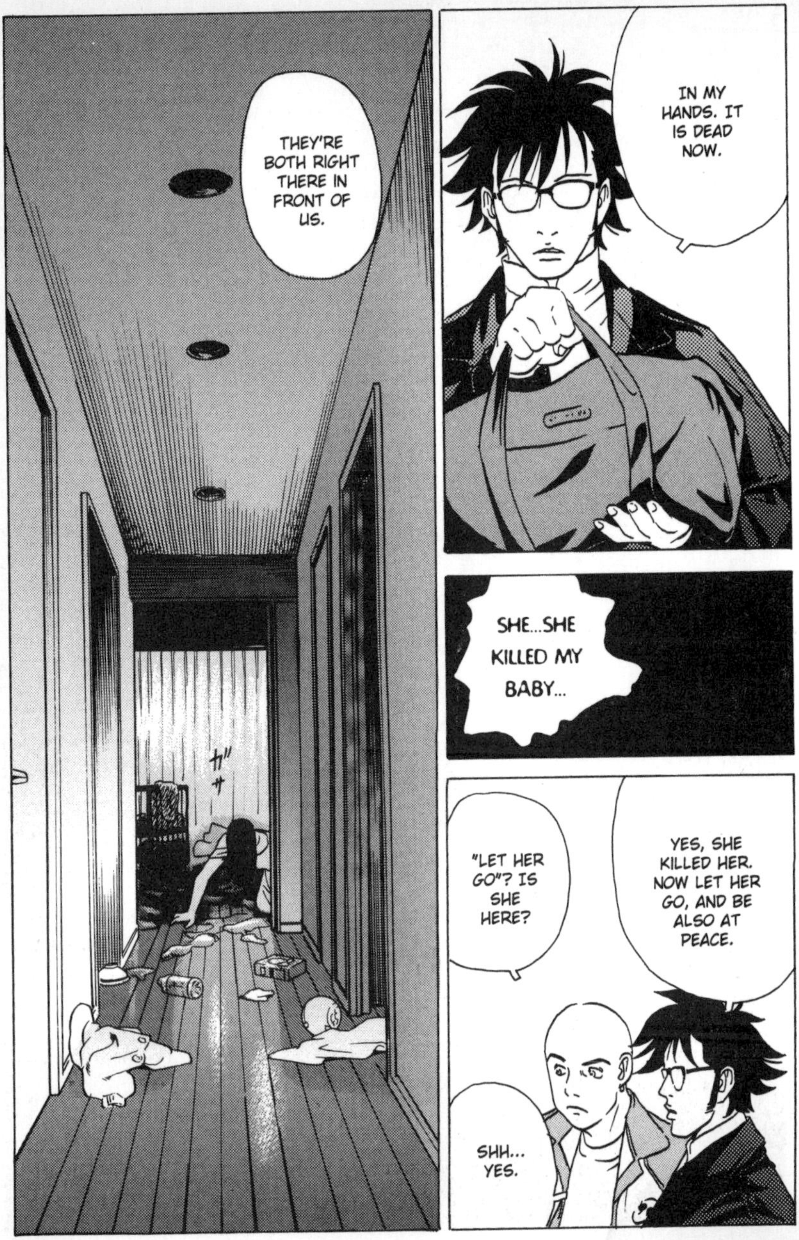
IN MY HANDS. IT IS DEAD NOW.
SHE...SHE KILLED MY BABY...
YES, SHE KILLED HER. NOW LET HER GO, AND BE ALSO AT PEACE.
"LET HER GO"? IS SHE HERE?
SHH... YES.
THEY'RE BOTH RIGHT THERE IN FRONT OF US.
ガサ

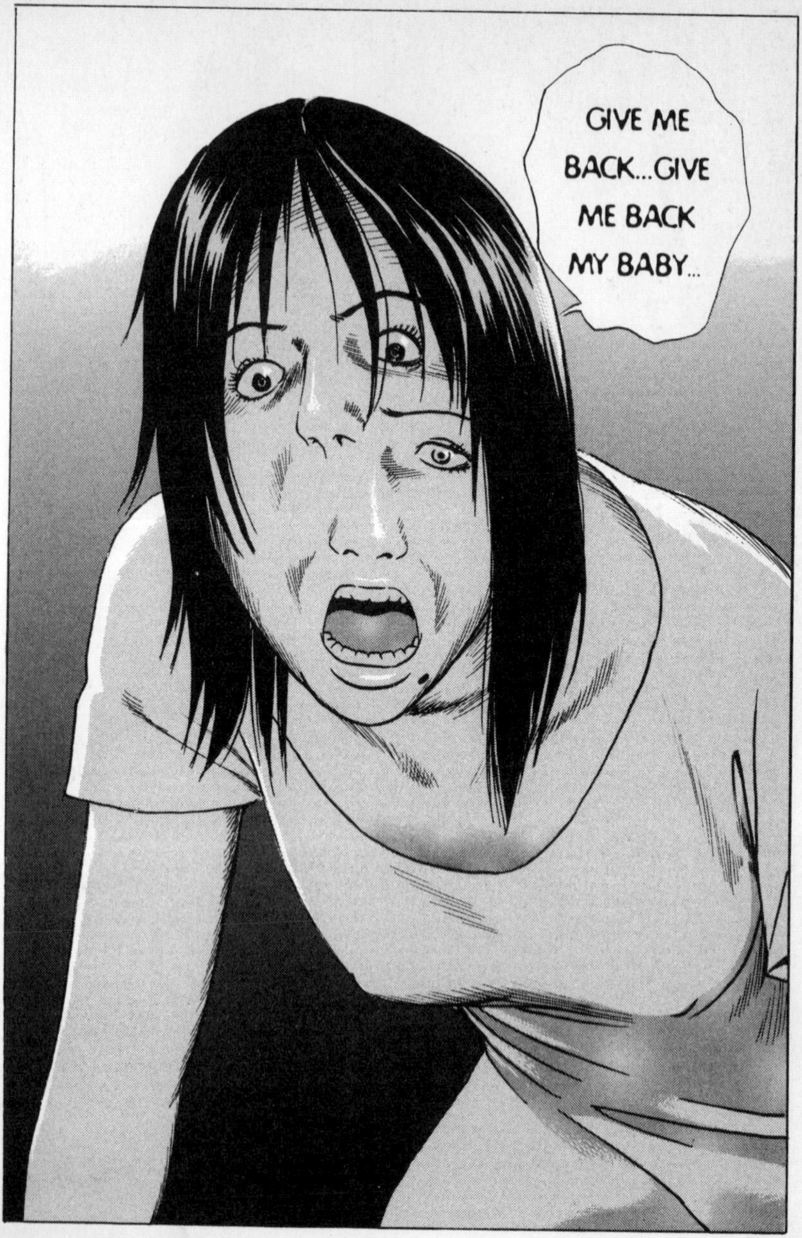
GIVE ME BACK...GIVE ME BACK MY BABY...

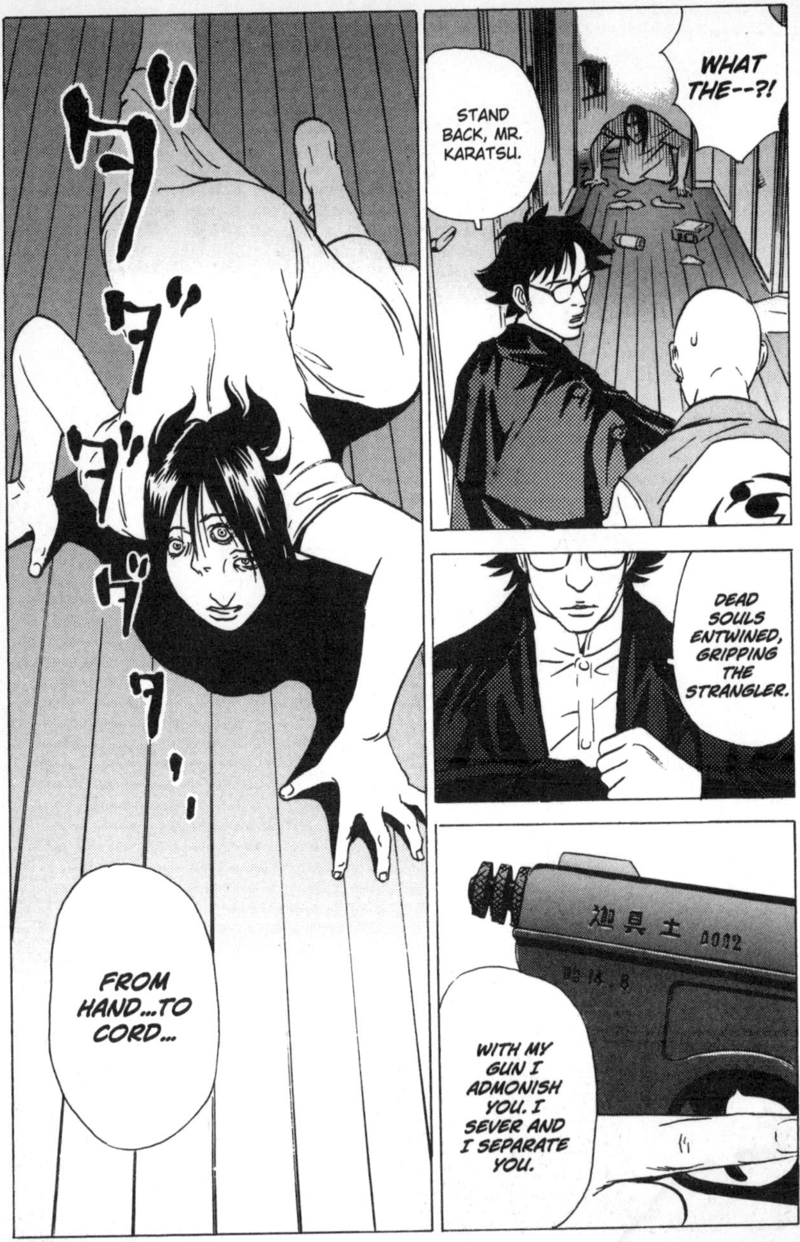
WHAT THE--?!
STAND BACK, MR. KARATSU.
DEAD SOULS ENTWINED, GRIPPING THE STRANGLER.
迦具土 0012
WITH MY GUN I ADMONISH YOU. I SEVER AND I SEPARATE YOU.
FROM HAND...TO CORD...

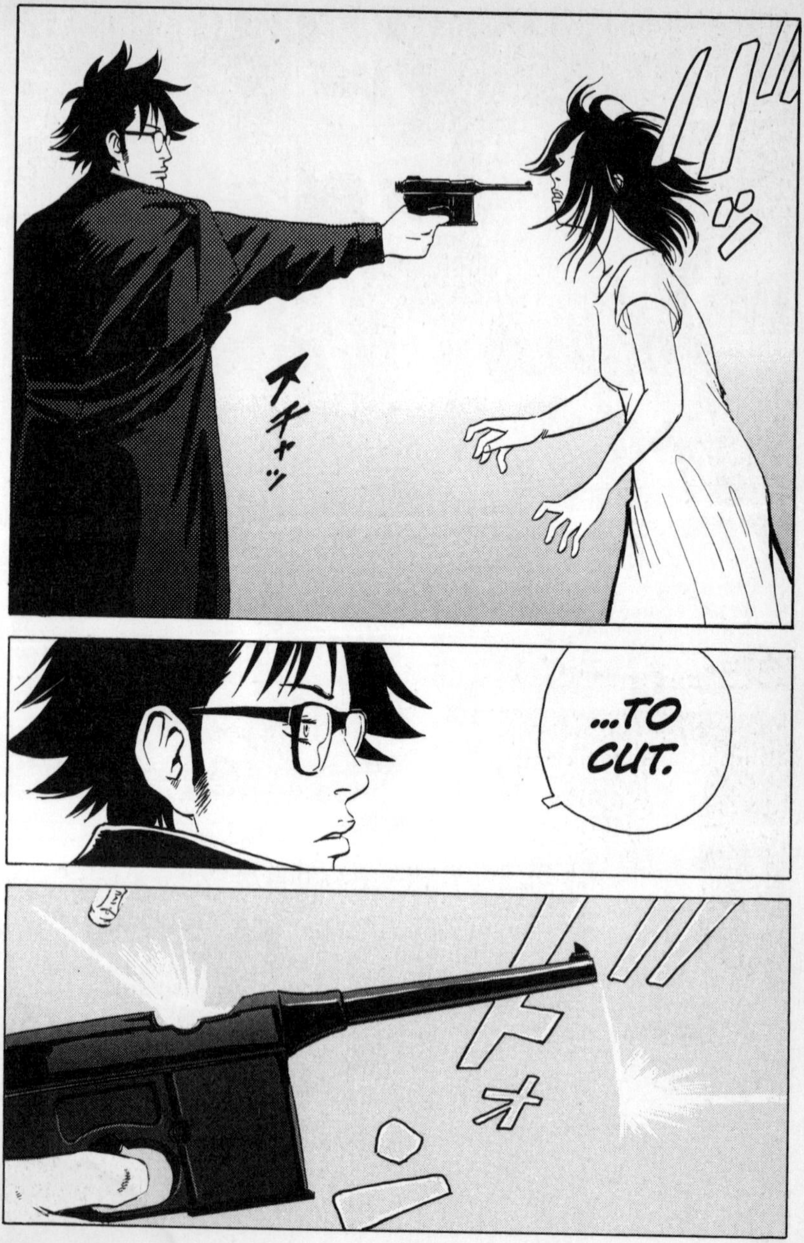
スチャッ
...TO CUT.

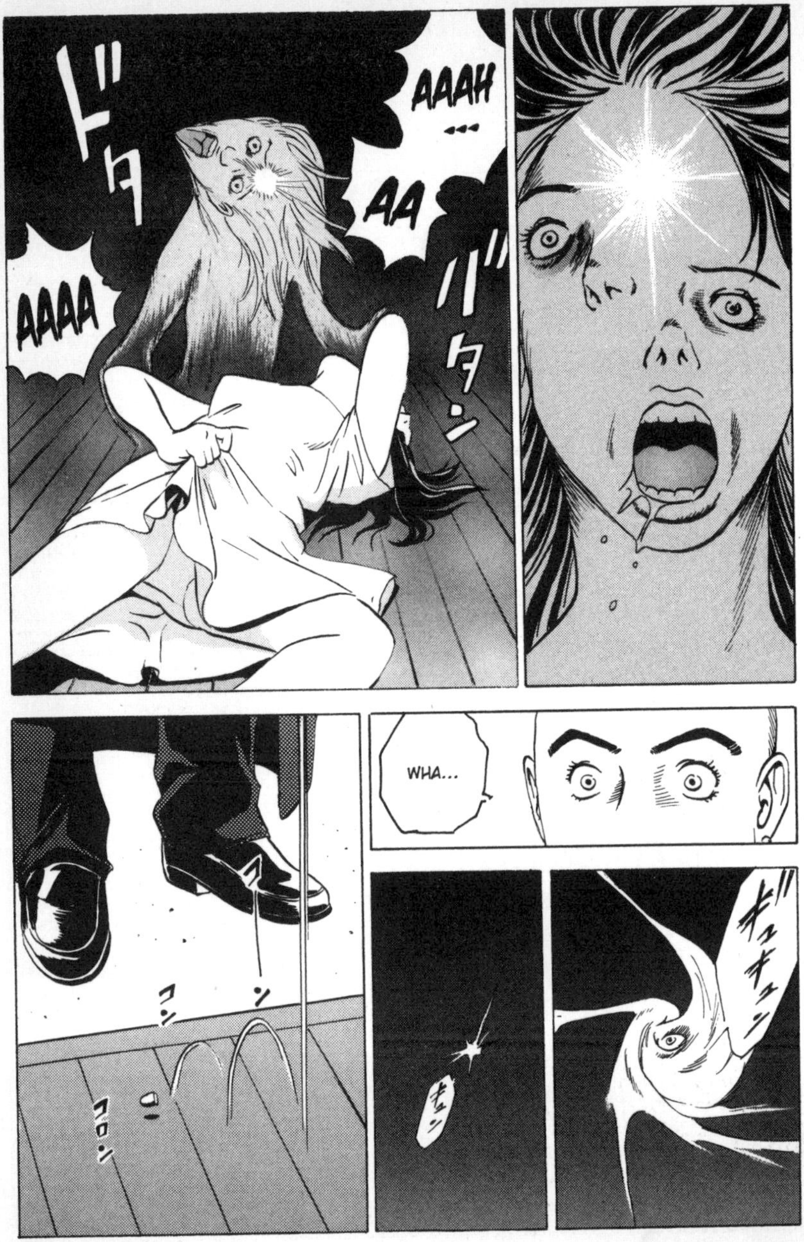
AAAH...
AA
AAAA
ドタ
バタン
WHA...
ギュギュン
キュン
コン
ン
コロン

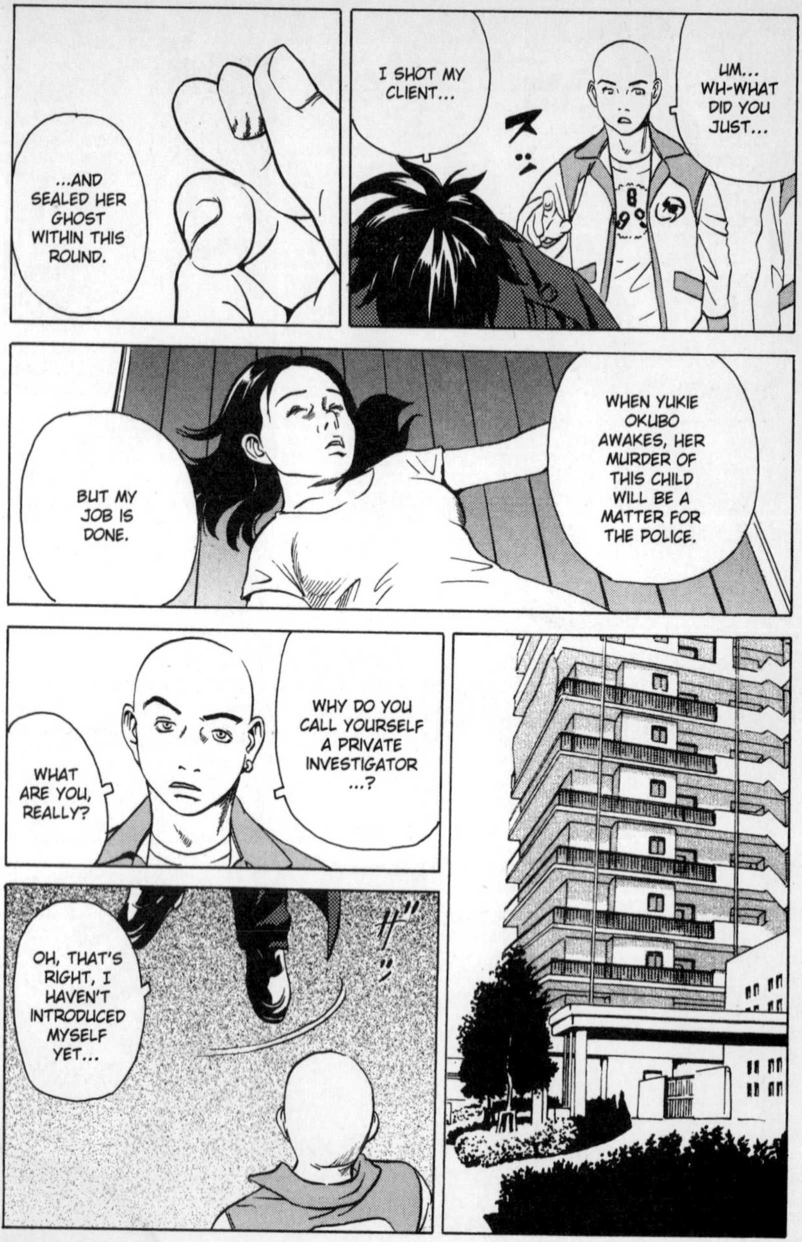
UM... WH-WHAT DID YOU JUST...
スッ
I SHOT MY CLIENT...
...AND SEALED HER GHOST WITHIN THIS ROUND.
WHEN YUKIE OKUBO AWAKES, HER MURDER OF THIS CHILD WILL BE A MATTER FOR THE POLICE.
BUT MY JOB IS DONE.
WHY DO YOU CALL YOURSELF A PRIVATE INVESTIGATOR ...?
WHAT ARE YOU, REALLY?
ザッ
OH, THAT'S RIGHT, I HAVEN'T INTRODUCED MYSELF YET...

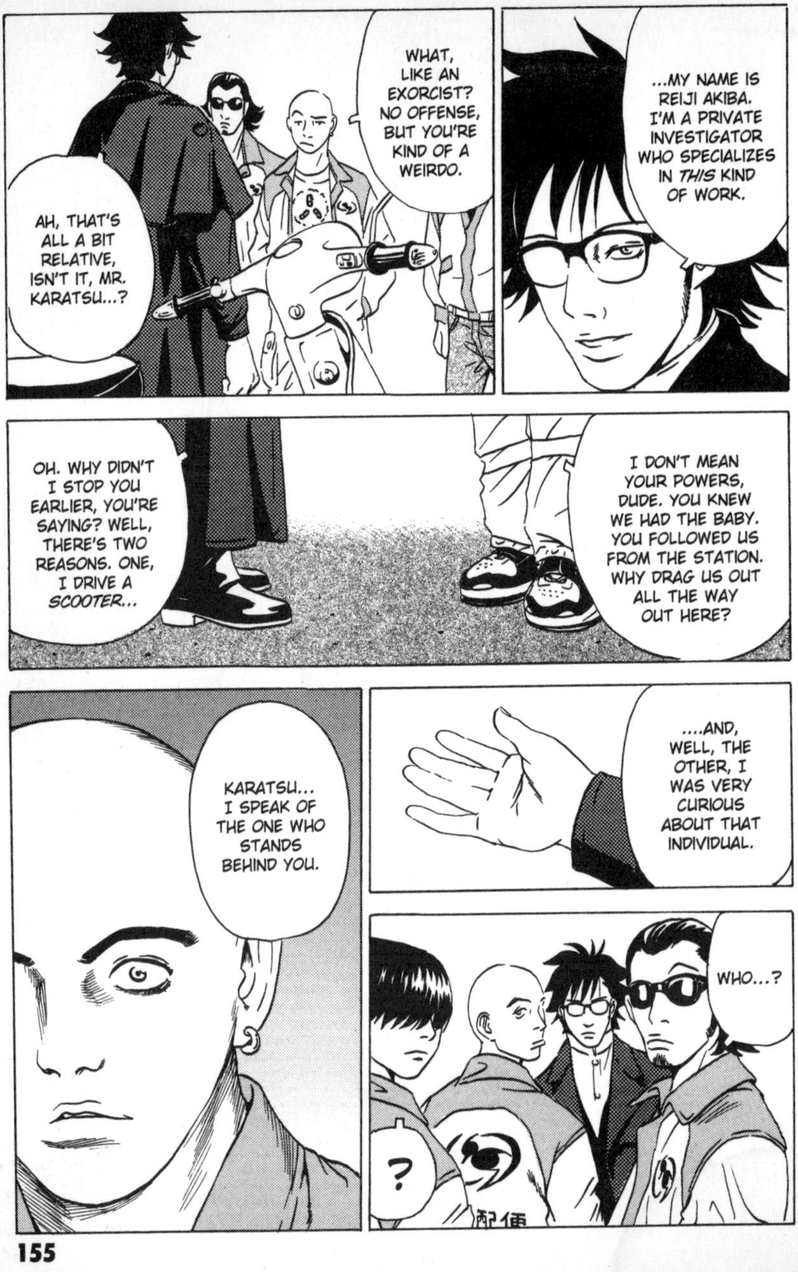

...MY NAME IS REIJI AKIBA. I'M A PRIVATE INVESTIGATOR WHO SPECIALIZES IN *THIS* KIND OF WORK.
WHAT, LIKE AN EXORCIST? NO OFFENSE, BUT YOU'RE KIND OF A WEIRDO.
AH, THAT'S ALL A BIT RELATIVE, ISN'T IT, MR. KARATSU...?
I DON'T MEAN YOUR POWERS, DUDE. YOU KNEW WE HAD THE BABY. YOU FOLLOWED US FROM THE STATION. WHY DRAG US OUT ALL THE WAY OUT HERE?
OH. WHY DIDN'T I STOP YOU EARLIER, YOU'RE SAYING? WELL, THERE'S TWO REASONS. ONE, I DRIVE A *SCOOTER*...
....AND, WELL, THE OTHER, I WAS VERY CURIOUS ABOUT THAT INDIVIDUAL.
WHO...?
?
KARATSU... I SPEAK OF THE ONE WHO STANDS BEHIND YOU.

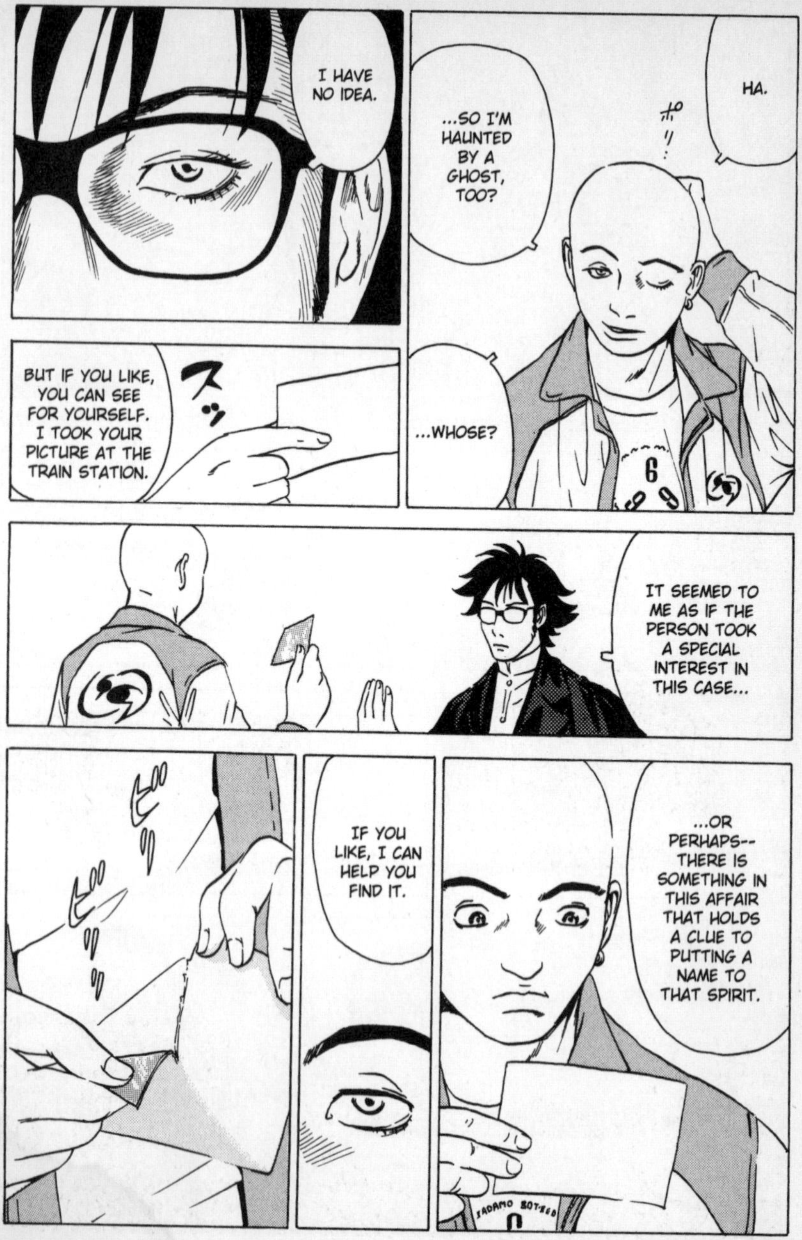
HA.
ポリ
...SO I'M HAUNTED BY A GHOST, TOO?
...WHOSE?
I HAVE NO IDEA.
BUT IF YOU LIKE, YOU CAN SEE FOR YOURSELF. I TOOK YOUR PICTURE AT THE TRAIN STATION.
スッ
IT SEEMED TO ME AS IF THE PERSON TOOK A SPECIAL INTEREST IN THIS CASE...
...OR PERHAPS-- THERE IS SOMETHING IN THIS AFFAIR THAT HOLDS A CLUE TO PUTTING A NAME TO THAT SPIRIT.
IF YOU LIKE, I CAN HELP YOU FIND IT.

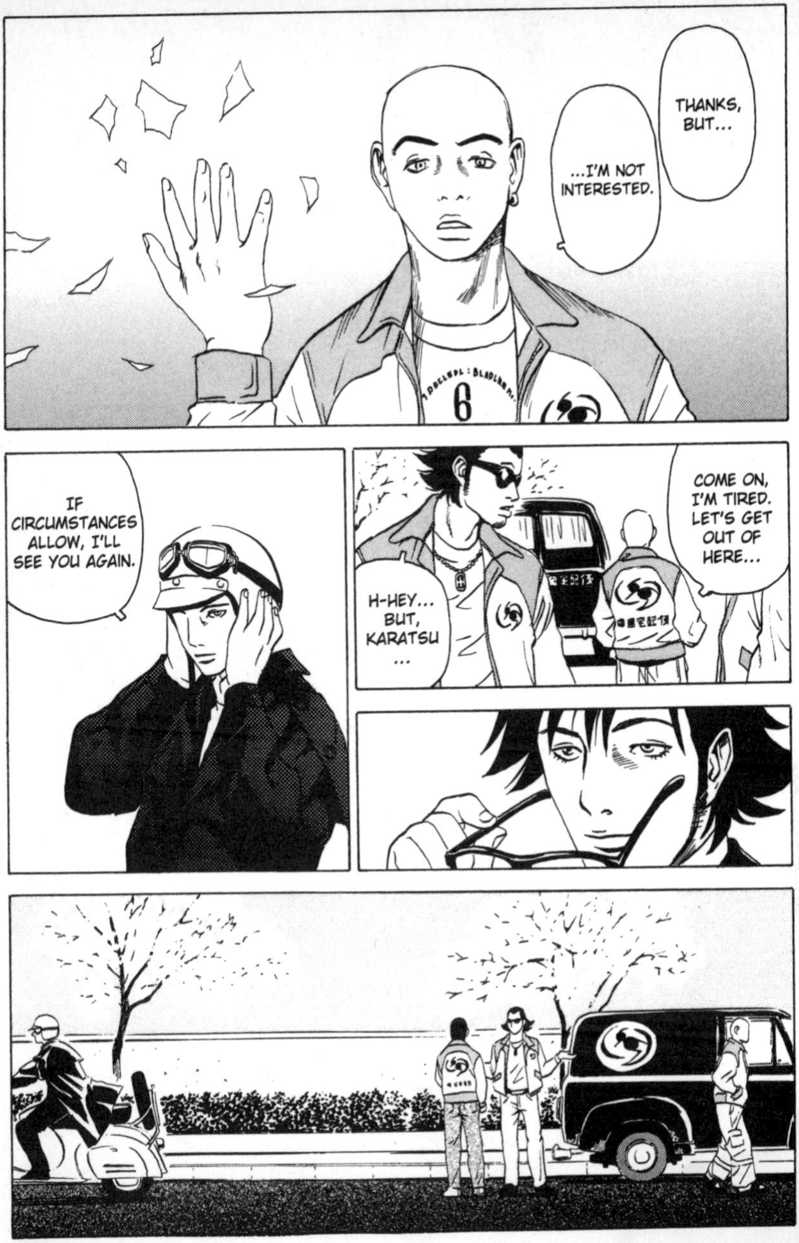
THANKS, BUT...
...I'M NOT INTERESTED.
COME ON, I'M TIRED. LET'S GET OUT OF HERE...
H-HEY... BUT, KARATSU ...
IF CIRCUMSTANCES ALLOW, I'LL SEE YOU AGAIN.

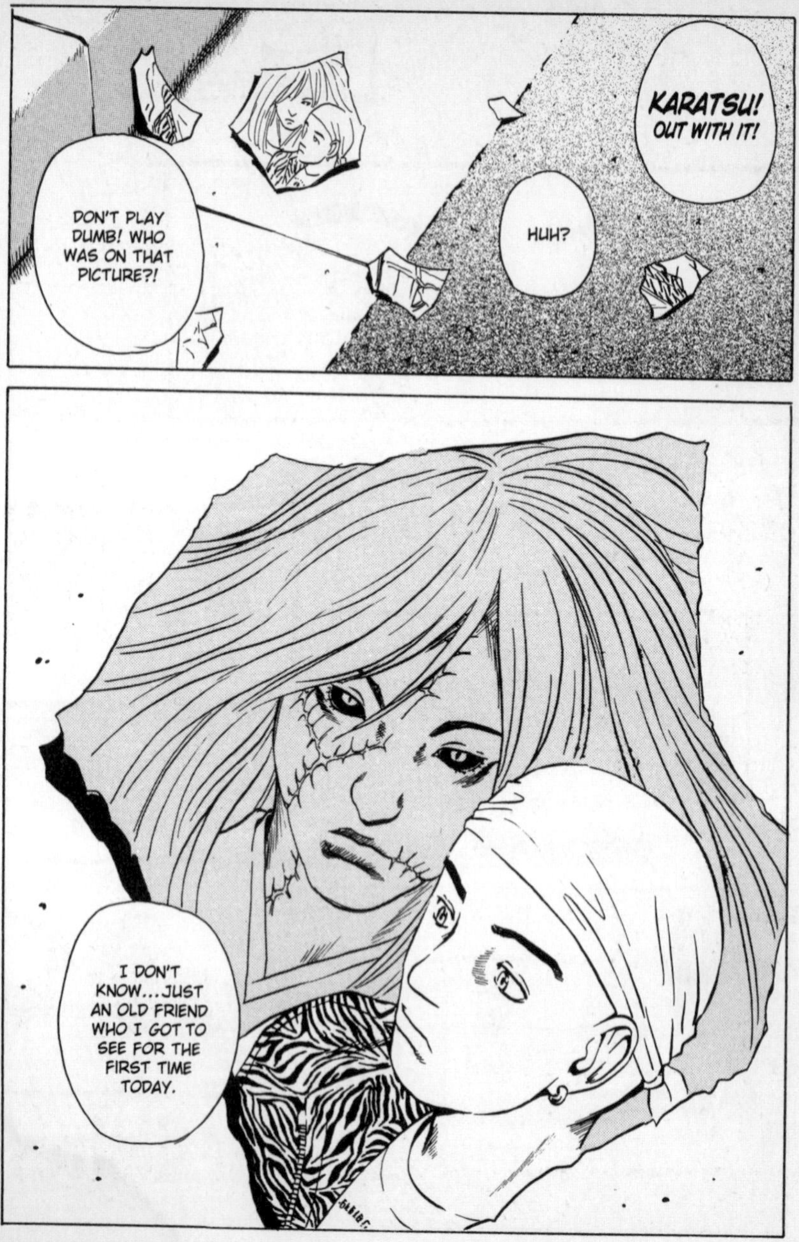
KARATSU! OUT WITH IT!
HUH?
DON'T PLAY DUMB! WHO WAS ON THAT PICTURE?!
I DON'T KNOW...JUST AN OLD FRIEND WHO I GOT TO SEE FOR THE FIRST TIME TODAY.

3rd delivery: the look i had 'til yesterday—the end

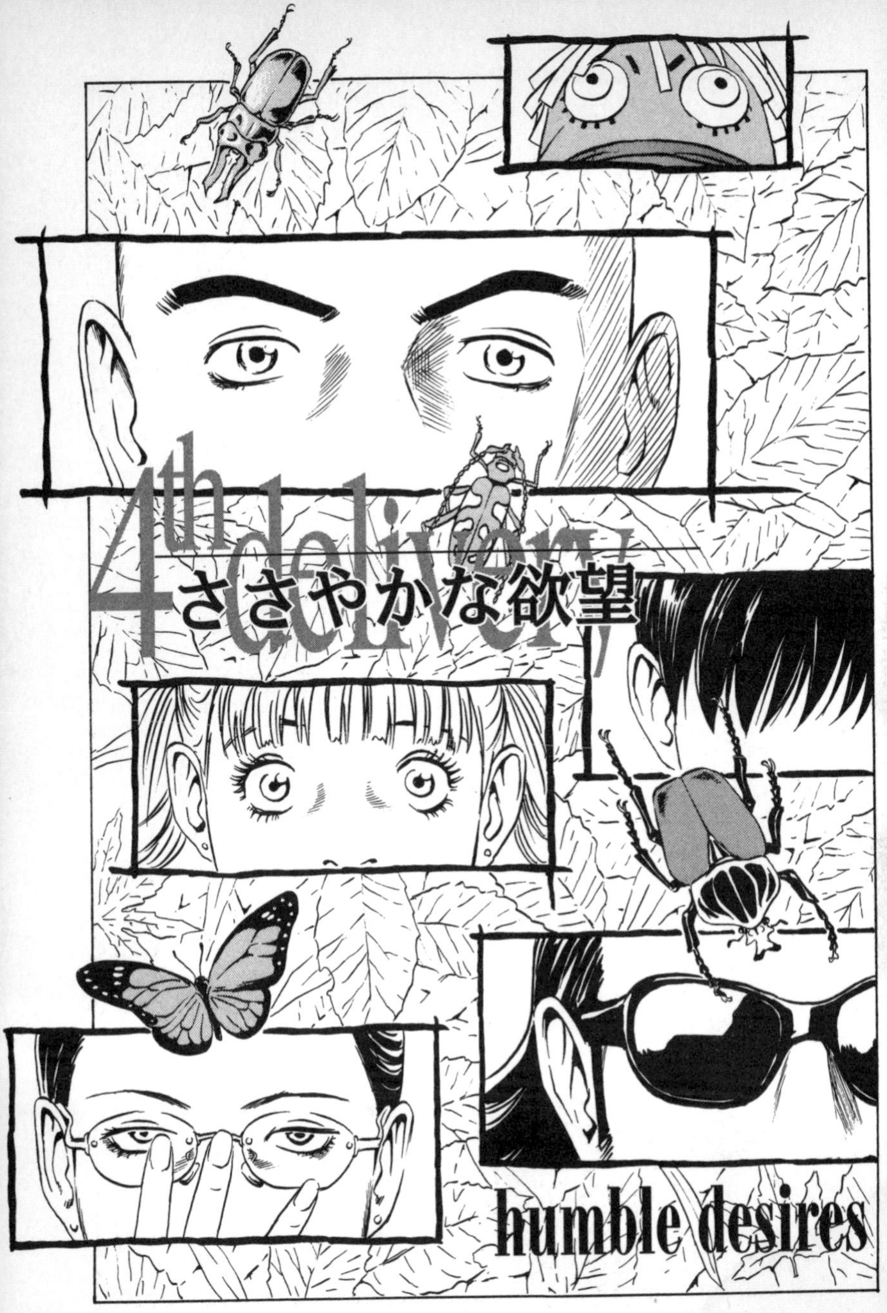
4th delivery
ささやかな欲望
humble desires

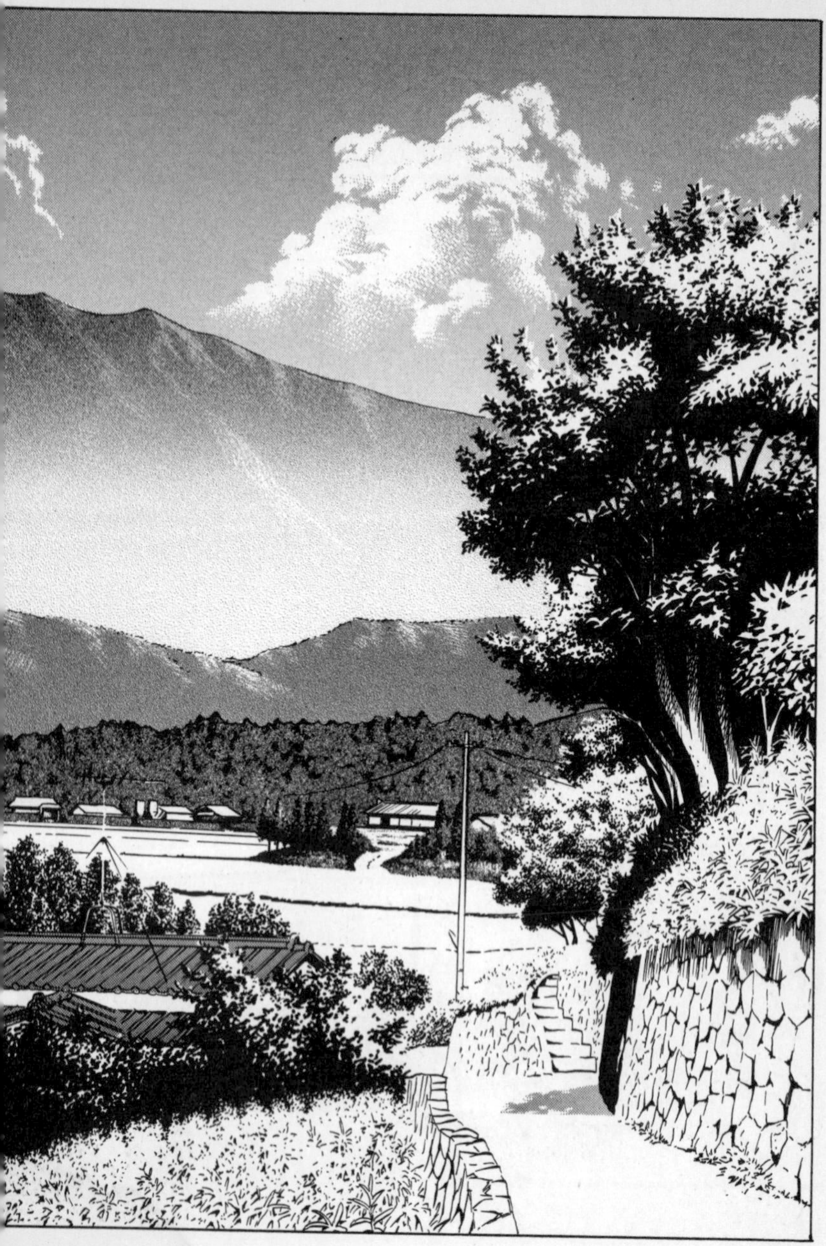

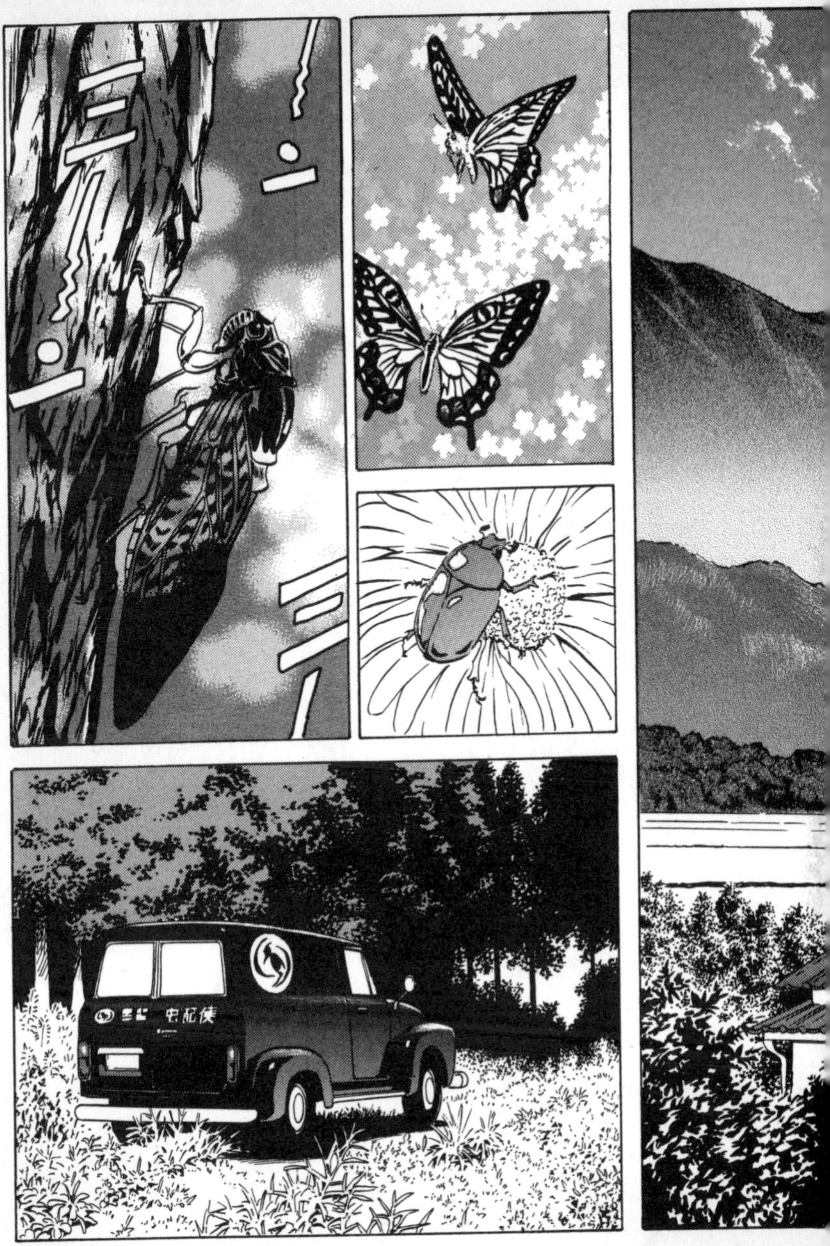

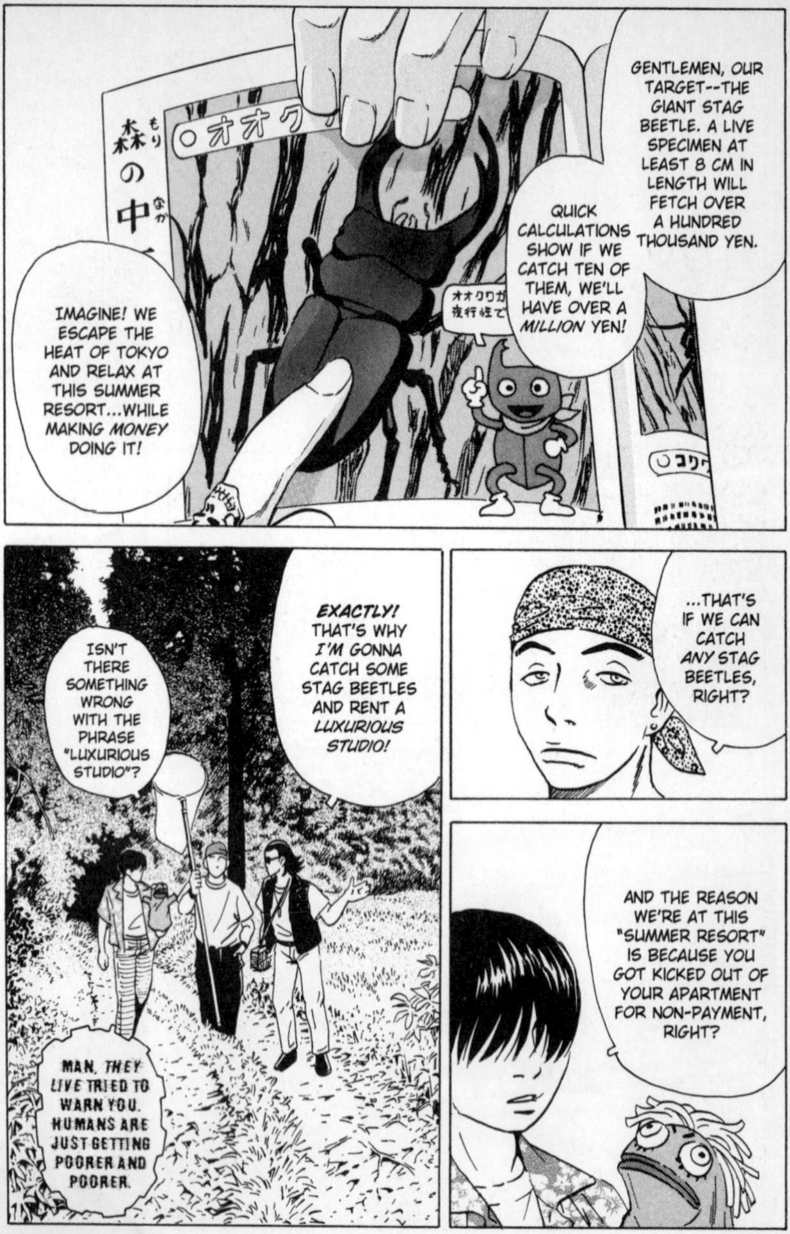

GENTLEMEN, OUR TARGET--THE GIANT STAG BEETLE. A LIVE SPECIMEN AT LEAST 8 CM IN LENGTH WILL FETCH OVER A HUNDRED THOUSAND YEN.
QUICK CALCULATIONS SHOW IF WE CATCH TEN OF THEM, WE'LL HAVE OVER A *MILLION* YEN!
森の中
オオク
IMAGINE! WE ESCAPE THE HEAT OF TOKYO AND RELAX AT THIS SUMMER RESORT...WHILE MAKING *MONEY* DOING IT!
...THAT'S IF WE CAN CATCH *ANY* STAG BEETLES, RIGHT?
AND THE REASON WE'RE AT THIS "SUMMER RESORT" IS BECAUSE YOU GOT KICKED OUT OF YOUR APARTMENT FOR NON-PAYMENT, RIGHT?
EXACTLY! THAT'S WHY *I'M* GONNA CATCH SOME STAG BEETLES AND RENT A *LUXURIOUS STUDIO!*
ISN'T THERE SOMETHING WRONG WITH THE PHRASE "LUXURIOUS STUDIO"?
MAN, *THEY LIVE* TRIED TO WARN YOU. HUMANS ARE JUST GETTING POORER AND POORER.

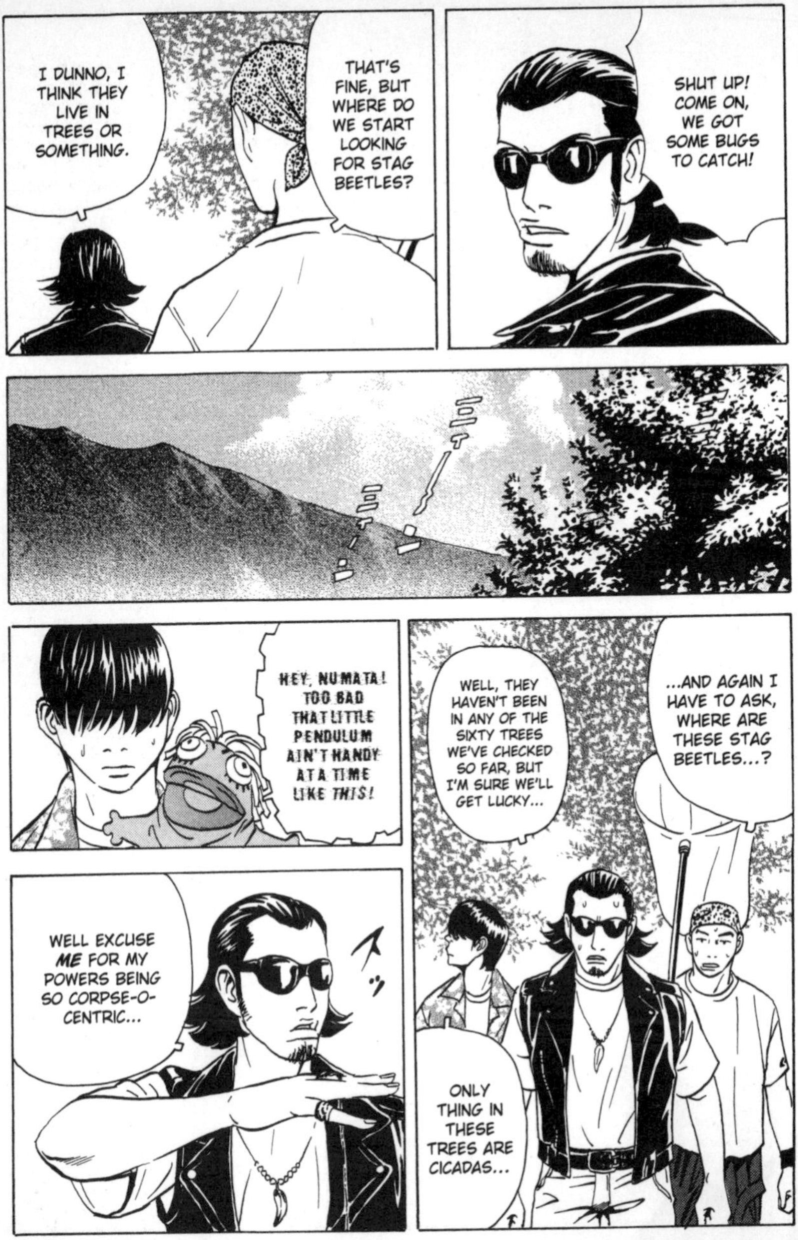
SHUT UP! COME ON, WE GOT SOME BUGS TO CATCH!
THAT'S FINE, BUT WHERE DO WE START LOOKING FOR STAG BEETLES?
I DUNNO, I THINK THEY LIVE IN TREES OR SOMETHING.
...AND AGAIN I HAVE TO ASK, WHERE ARE THESE STAG BEETLES...?
WELL, THEY HAVEN'T BEEN IN ANY OF THE SIXTY TREES WE'VE CHECKED SO FAR, BUT I'M SURE WE'LL GET LUCKY...
ONLY THING IN THESE TREES ARE CICADAS...
HEY, NUMATA! TOO BAD THAT LITTLE PENDULUM AIN'T HANDY AT A TIME LIKE *THIS*!
スッ
WELL EXCUSE ***ME*** FOR MY POWERS BEING SO CORPSE-O-CENTRIC...

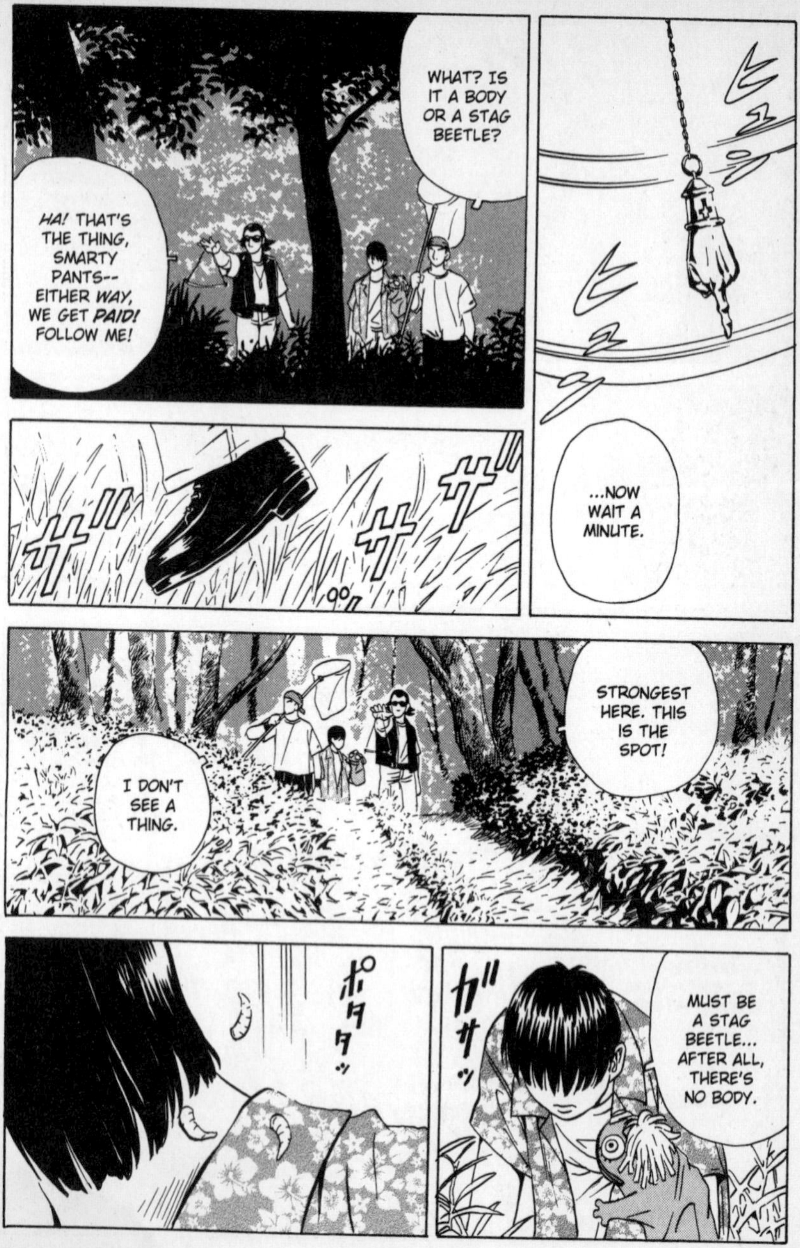
...NOW WAIT A MINUTE.
WHAT? IS IT A BODY OR A STAG BEETLE?
HA! THAT'S THE THING, SMARTY PANTS-- EITHER *WAY*, WE GET *PAID!* FOLLOW ME!
STRONGEST HERE. THIS IS THE SPOT!
I DON'T SEE A THING.
MUST BE A STAG BEETLE... AFTER ALL, THERE'S NO BODY.

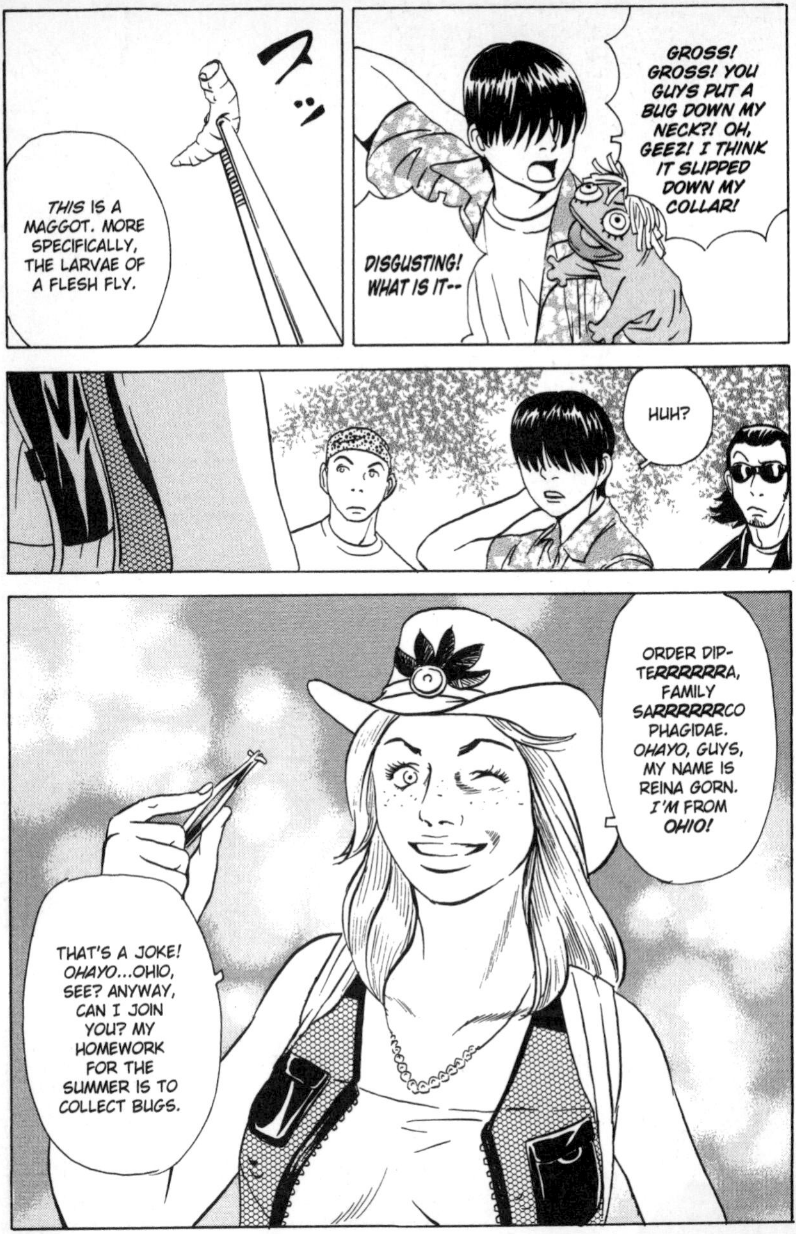
GROSS! GROSS! YOU GUYS PUT A BUG DOWN MY NECK?! OH, GEEZ! I THINK IT SLIPPED DOWN MY COLLAR!
DISGUSTING! WHAT IS IT--
フッ
THIS IS A MAGGOT. MORE SPECIFICALLY, THE LARVAE OF A FLESH FLY.
HUH?
ORDER DIP-TERRRRRRA, FAMILY SARRRRRRCO PHAGIDAE. OHAYO, GUYS, MY NAME IS REINA GORN. I'M FROM OHIO!
THAT'S A JOKE! OHAYO...OHIO, SEE? ANYWAY, CAN I JOIN YOU? MY HOMEWORK FOR THE SUMMER IS TO COLLECT BUGS.

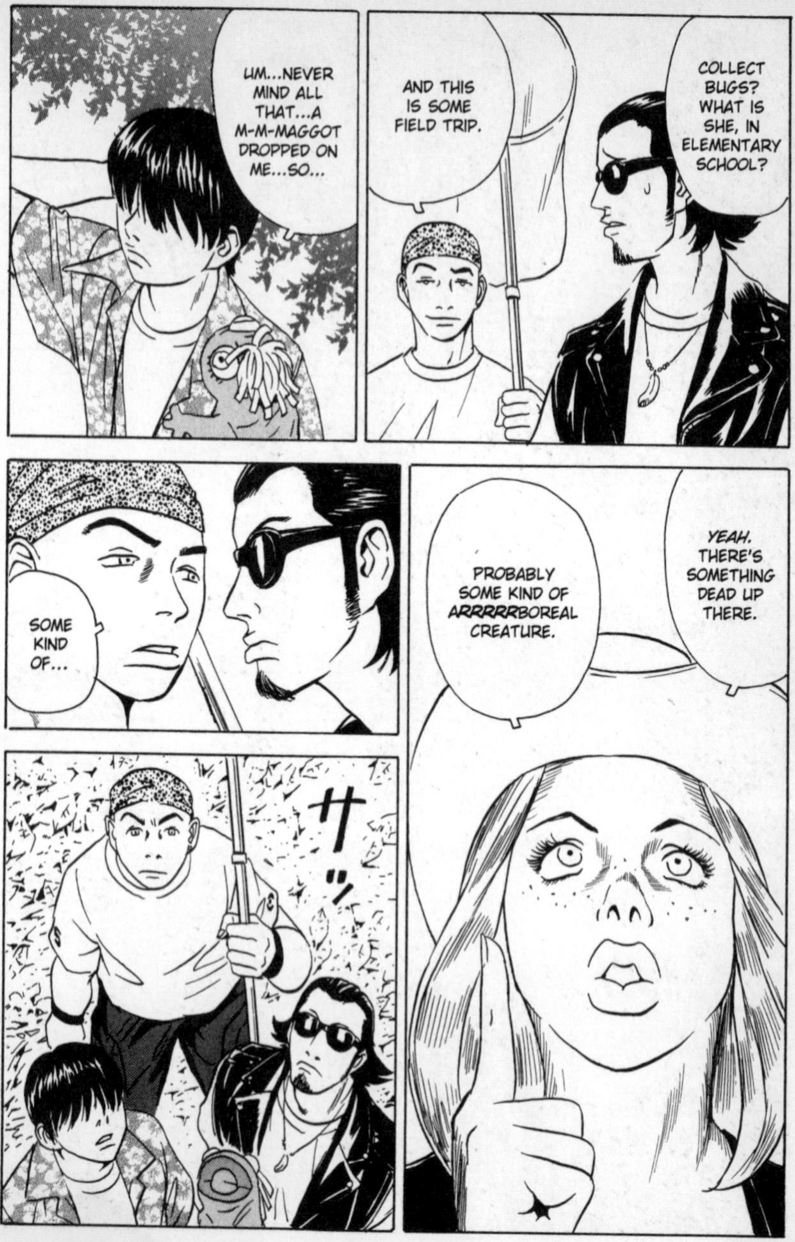
COLLECT BUGS? WHAT IS SHE, IN ELEMENTARY SCHOOL?
AND THIS IS SOME FIELD TRIP.
UM...NEVER MIND ALL THAT...A M-M-MAGGOT DROPPED ON ME...SO...
YEAH. THERE'S SOMETHING DEAD UP THERE.
PROBABLY SOME KIND OF *ARRRRR*BOREAL CREATURE.
SOME KIND OF...
サッ

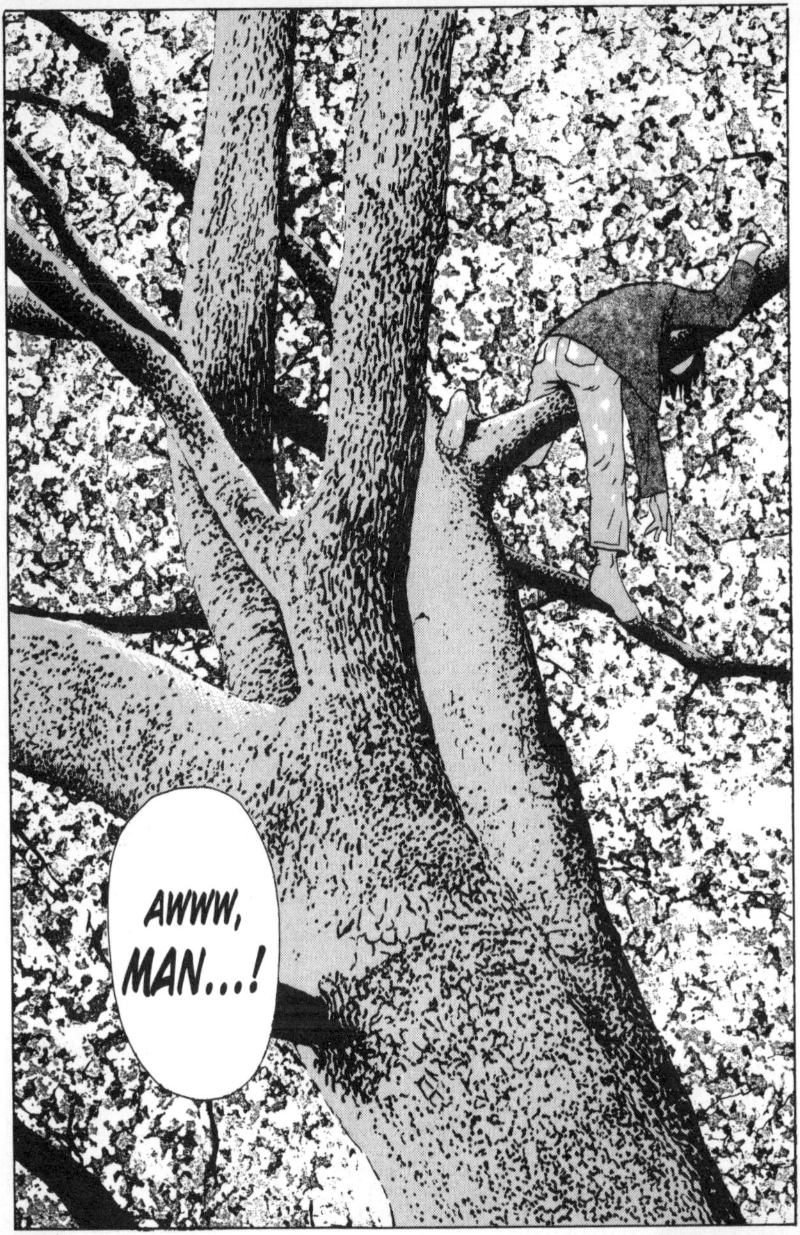
AWWW, MAN...!

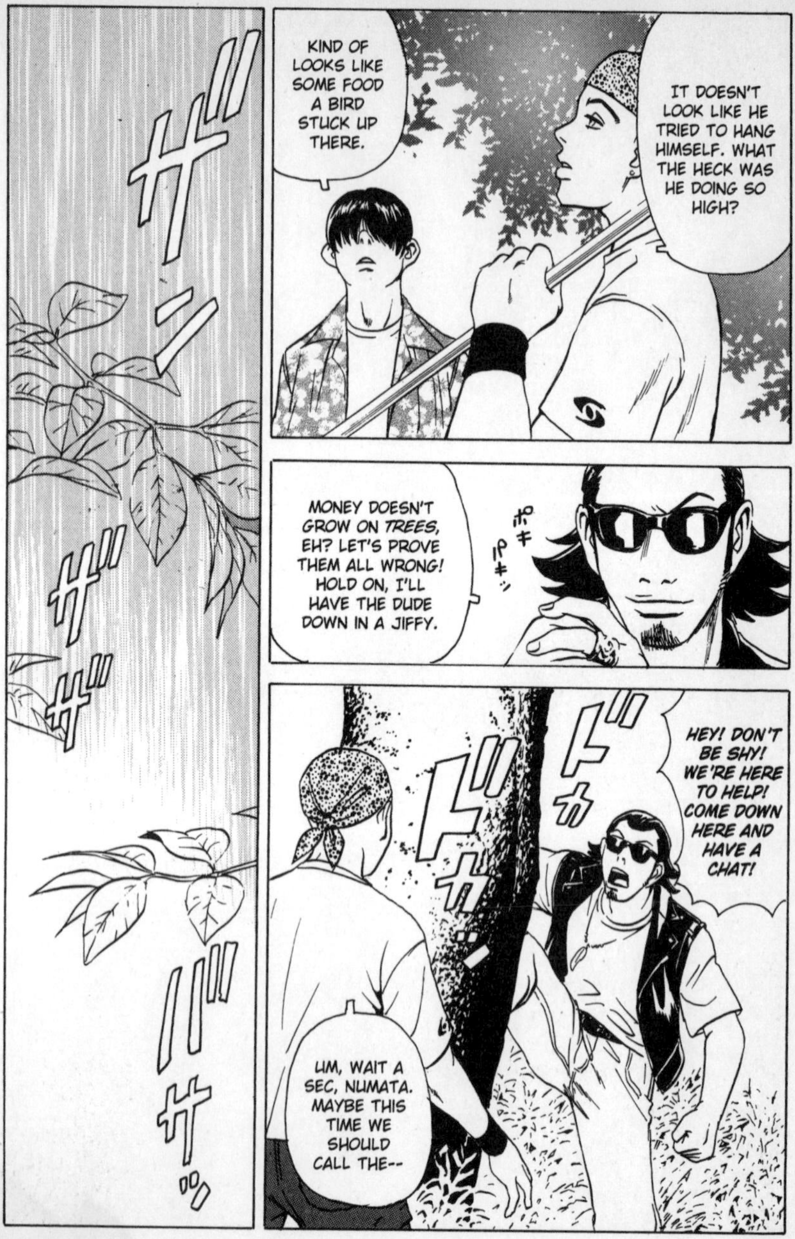
IT DOESN'T LOOK LIKE HE TRIED TO HANG HIMSELF. WHAT THE HECK WAS HE DOING SO HIGH?
KIND OF LOOKS LIKE SOME FOOD A BIRD STUCK UP THERE.
ポキ パキッ
MONEY DOESN'T GROW ON *TREES*, EH? LET'S PROVE THEM ALL WRONG! HOLD ON, I'LL HAVE THE DUDE DOWN IN A JIFFY.
HEY! DON'T BE SHY! WE'RE HERE TO HELP! COME DOWN HERE AND HAVE A CHAT!
UM, WAIT A SEC, NUMATA. MAYBE THIS TIME WE SHOULD CALL THE--

ドッ

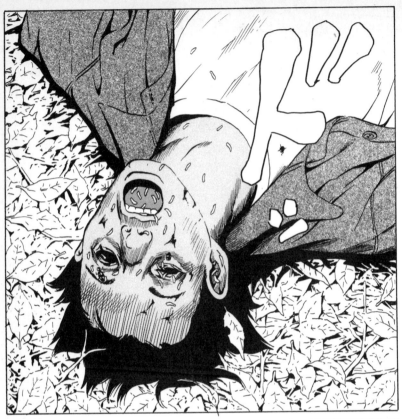

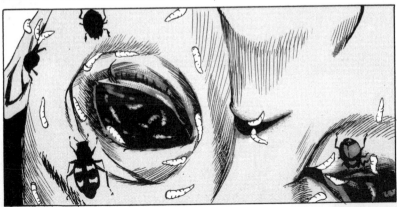

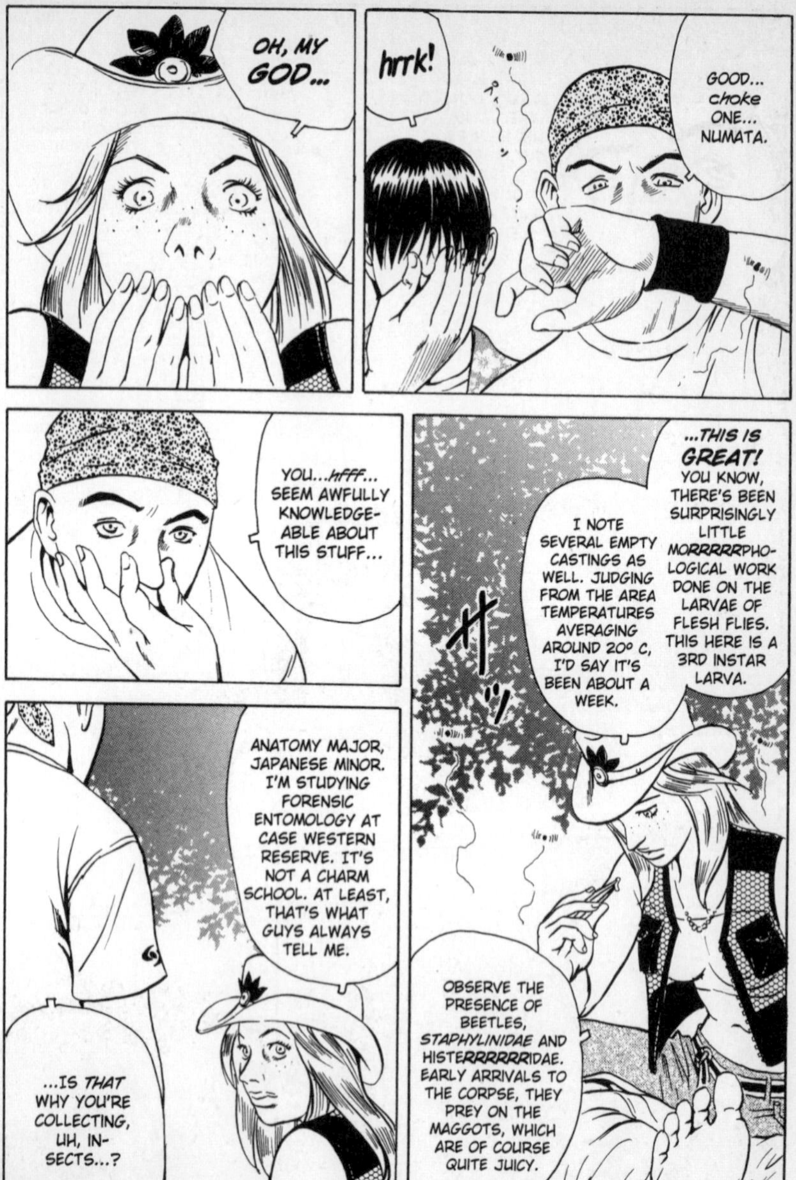
GOOD... choke ONE... NUMATA.
hrrk!
OH, MY GOD...
...THIS IS GREAT! YOU KNOW, THERE'S BEEN SURPRISINGLY LITTLE MORRRRRPHOLOGICAL WORK DONE ON THE LARVAE OF FLESH FLIES. THIS HERE IS A 3RD INSTAR LARVA.
I NOTE SEVERAL EMPTY CASTINGS AS WELL. JUDGING FROM THE AREA TEMPERATURES AVERAGING AROUND 20º C, I'D SAY IT'S BEEN ABOUT A WEEK.
OBSERVE THE PRESENCE OF BEETLES, *STAPHYLINIDAE* AND HISTE*RRRRRR*IDAE. EARLY ARRIVALS TO THE CORPSE, THEY PREY ON THE MAGGOTS, WHICH ARE OF COURSE QUITE JUICY.
YOU...*hfff*... SEEM AWFULLY KNOWLEDGE-ABLE ABOUT THIS STUFF...
ANATOMY MAJOR, JAPANESE MINOR. I'M STUDYING FORENSIC ENTOMOLOGY AT CASE WESTERN RESERVE. IT'S NOT A CHARM SCHOOL. AT LEAST, THAT'S WHAT GUYS ALWAYS TELL ME.
...IS *THAT* WHY YOU'RE COLLECTING, UH, IN-SECTS...?

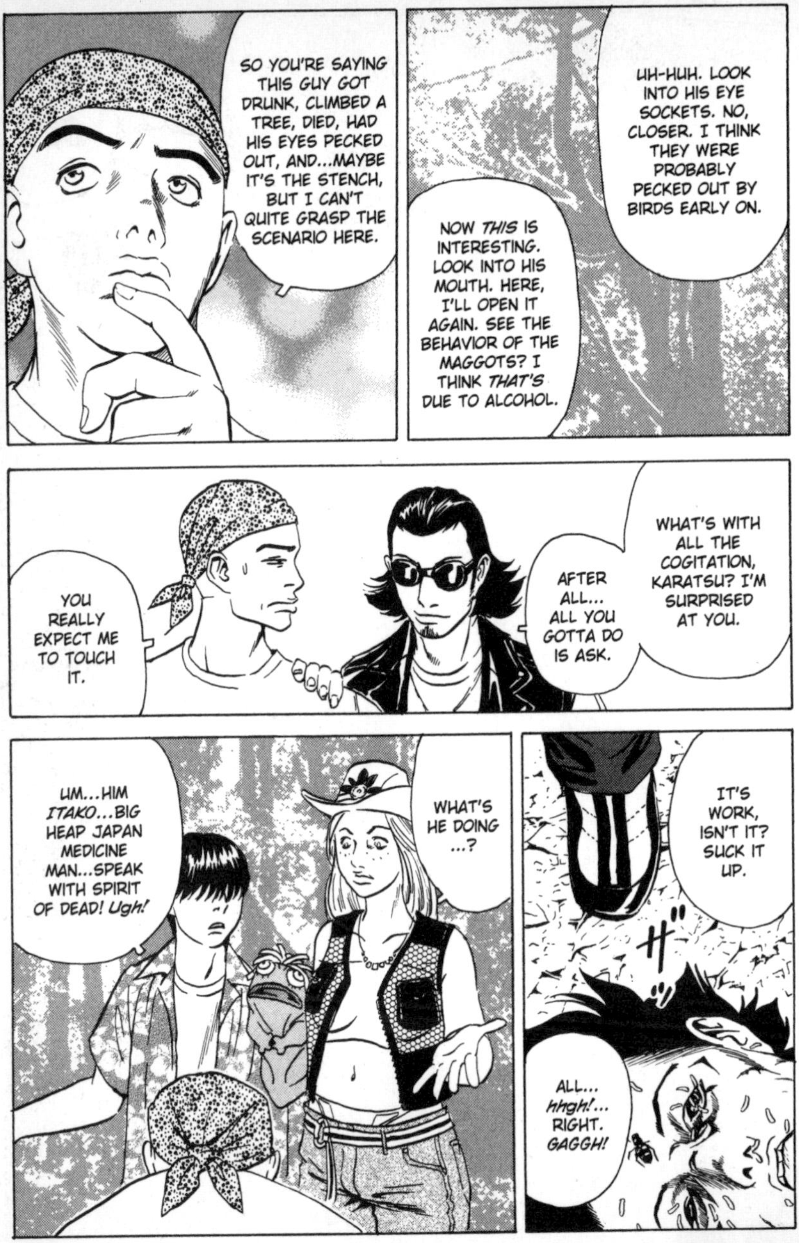
UH-HUH. LOOK INTO HIS EYE SOCKETS. NO, CLOSER. I THINK THEY WERE PROBABLY PECKED OUT BY BIRDS EARLY ON.
NOW *THIS* IS INTERESTING. LOOK INTO HIS MOUTH. HERE, I'LL OPEN IT AGAIN. SEE THE BEHAVIOR OF THE MAGGOTS? I THINK *THAT'S* DUE TO ALCOHOL.
SO YOU'RE SAYING THIS GUY GOT DRUNK, CLIMBED A TREE, DIED, HAD HIS EYES PECKED OUT, AND...MAYBE IT'S THE STENCH, BUT I CAN'T QUITE GRASP THE SCENARIO HERE.
WHAT'S WITH ALL THE COGITATION, KARATSU? I'M SURPRISED AT YOU.
AFTER ALL... ALL YOU GOTTA DO IS ASK.
YOU REALLY EXPECT ME TO TOUCH IT.
IT'S WORK, ISN'T IT? SUCK IT UP.
ALL... *hhgh!*... RIGHT. *GAGGH!*
WHAT'S HE DOING ...?
UM...HIM *ITAKO*...BIG HEAP JAPAN MEDICINE MAN...SPEAK WITH SPIRIT OF DEAD! *Ugh!*

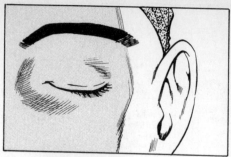

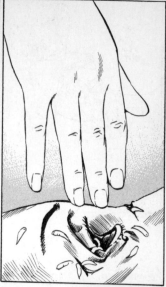

WELL...?
WHAT DOES
HE WANT...?

A BI...RD...
I WA...NT TO
BECO...ME
A BIRD...

...I
WA...NT...TO
BECO...ME A
BIRRRRRRRD!

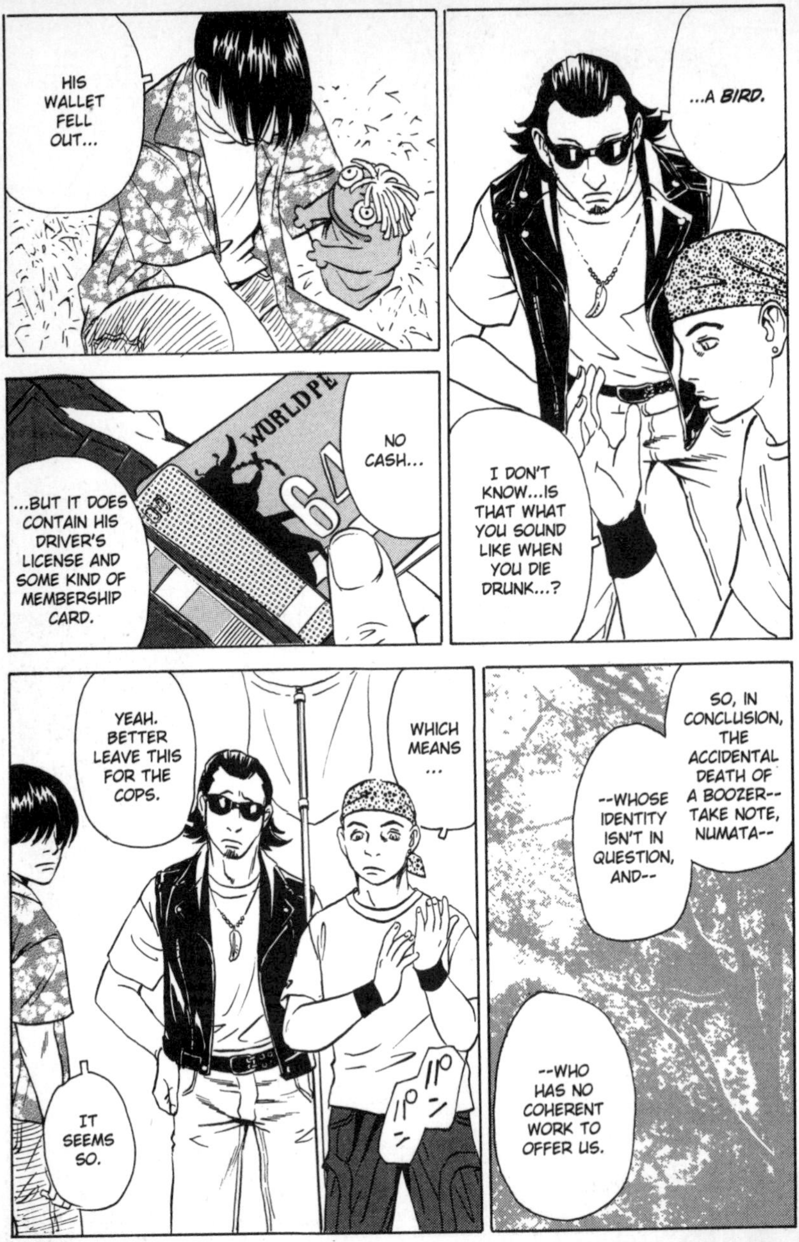

...A *BIRD.*
I DON'T KNOW...IS THAT WHAT YOU SOUND LIKE WHEN YOU DIE DRUNK...?
HIS WALLET FELL OUT...
WORLDPE
NO CASH...
...BUT IT DOES CONTAIN HIS DRIVER'S LICENSE AND SOME KIND OF MEMBERSHIP CARD.
SO, IN CONCLUSION, THE ACCIDENTAL DEATH OF A BOOZER-- TAKE NOTE, NUMATA--
--WHOSE IDENTITY ISN'T IN QUESTION, AND--
--WHO HAS NO COHERENT WORK TO OFFER US.
WHICH MEANS...
YEAH. BETTER LEAVE THIS FOR THE COPS.
IT SEEMS SO.

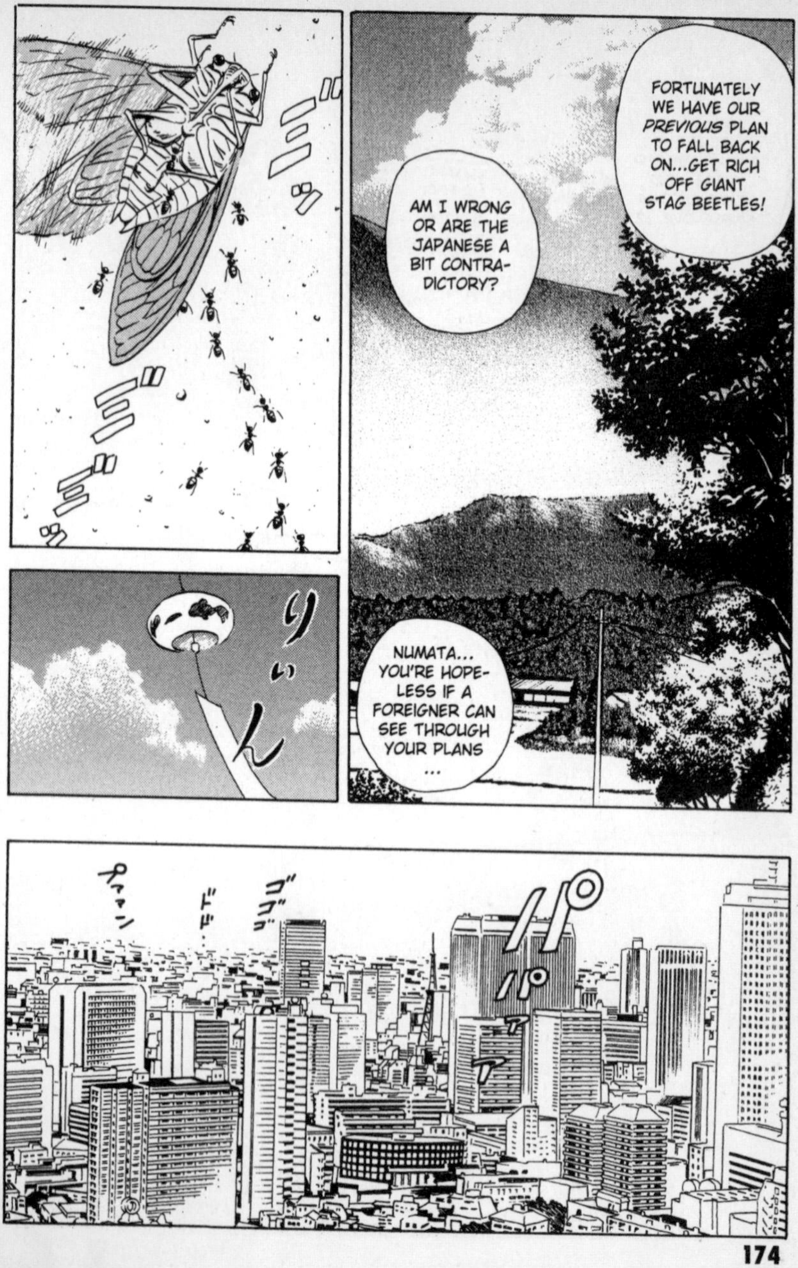
FORTUNATELY WE HAVE OUR *PREVIOUS* PLAN TO FALL BACK ON...GET RICH OFF GIANT STAG BEETLES!
AM I WRONG OR ARE THE JAPANESE A BIT CONTRA-DICTORY?
NUMATA... YOU'RE HOPE-LESS IF A FOREIGNER CAN SEE THROUGH YOUR PLANS ...
りいん
パパァ
ゴゴゴ
ドド

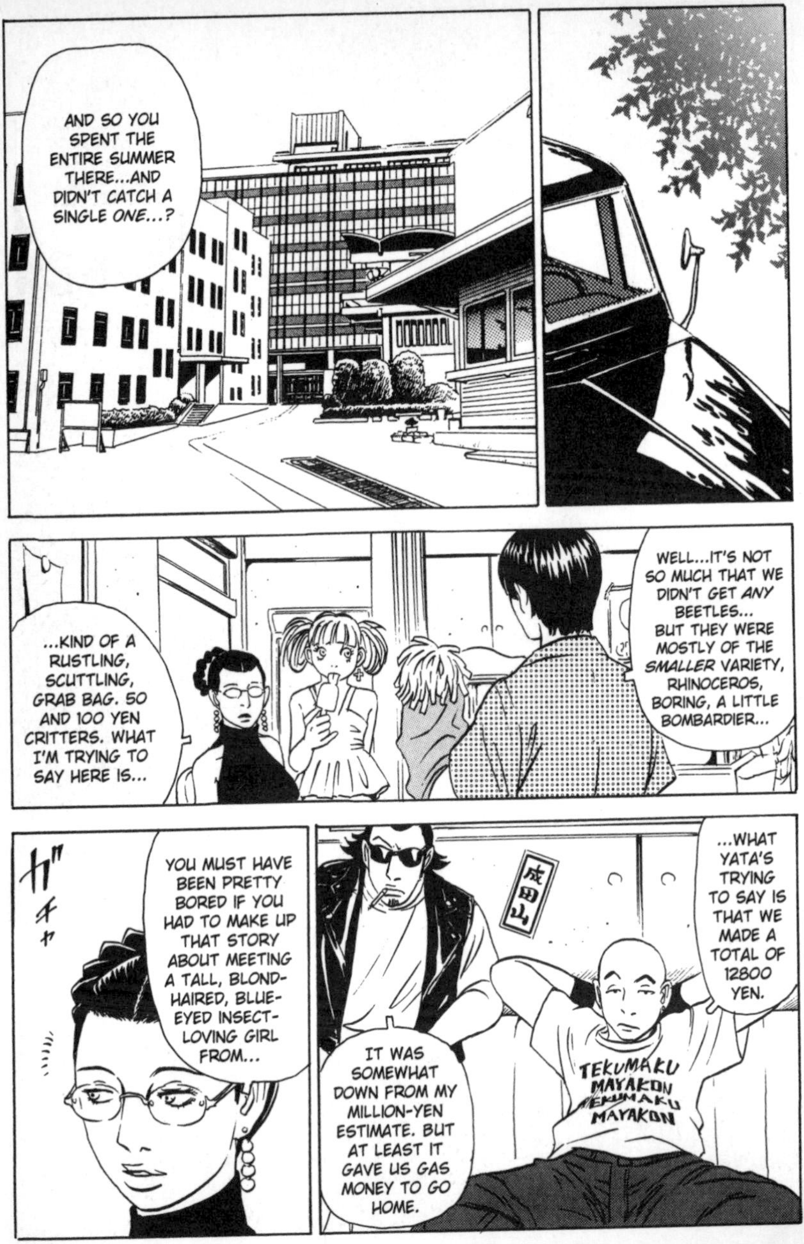
AND SO YOU SPENT THE ENTIRE SUMMER THERE...AND DIDN'T CATCH A SINGLE *ONE*...?
WELL...IT'S NOT SO MUCH THAT WE DIDN'T GET *ANY* BEETLES... BUT THEY WERE MOSTLY OF THE *SMALLER* VARIETY, RHINOCEROS, BORING, A LITTLE BOMBARDIER...
...KIND OF A RUSTLING, SCUTTLING, GRAB BAG. 50 AND 100 YEN CRITTERS. WHAT I'M TRYING TO SAY HERE IS...
成田山
...WHAT YATA'S TRYING TO SAY IS THAT WE MADE A TOTAL OF 12800 YEN.
TEKUMAKU
MAYAKON
MAYAKON
IT WAS SOMEWHAT DOWN FROM MY MILLION-YEN ESTIMATE. BUT AT LEAST IT GAVE US GAS MONEY TO GO HOME.
ガチャ
YOU MUST HAVE BEEN PRETTY BORED IF YOU HAD TO MAKE UP THAT STORY ABOUT MEETING A TALL, BLOND-HAIRED, BLUE-EYED INSECT-LOVING GIRL FROM...

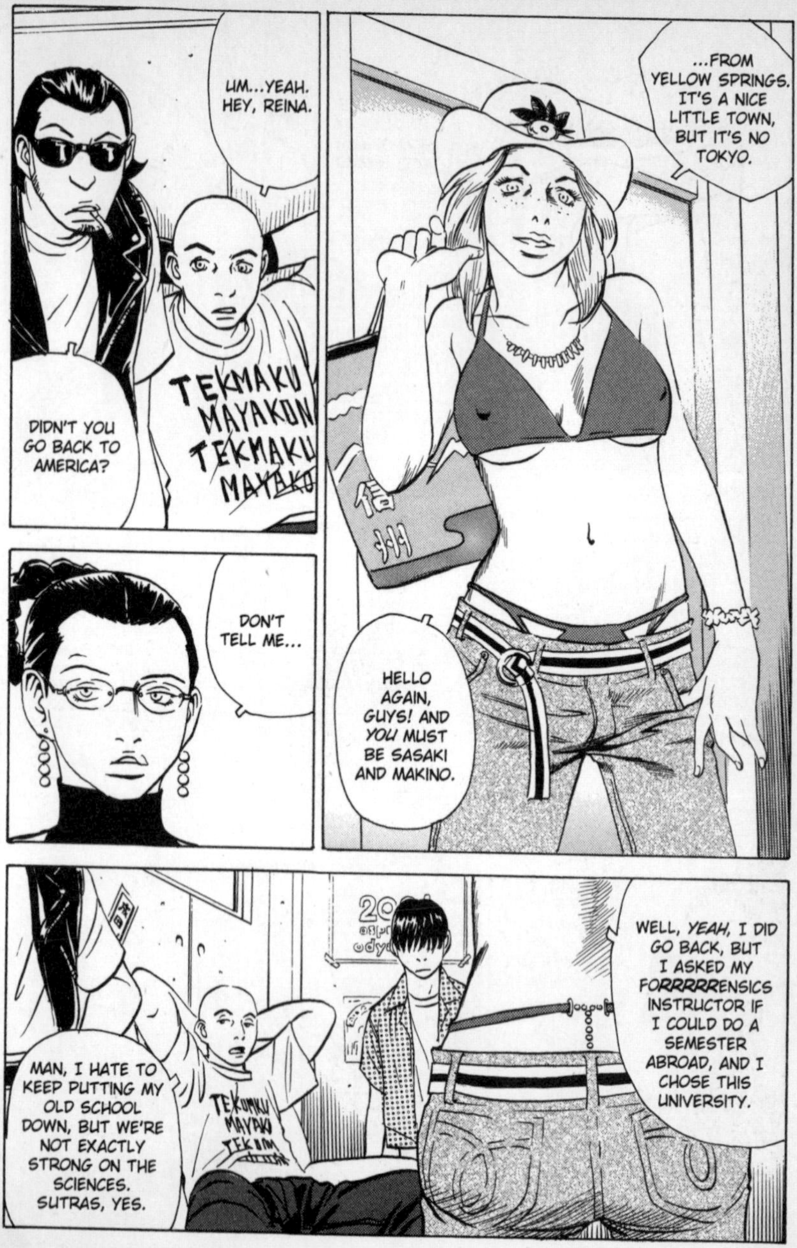
...FROM YELLOW SPRINGS. IT'S A NICE LITTLE TOWN, BUT IT'S NO TOKYO.
HELLO AGAIN, GUYS! AND *YOU* MUST BE SASAKI AND MAKINO.
UM...YEAH. HEY, REINA.
DIDN'T YOU GO BACK TO AMERICA?
DON'T TELL ME...
WELL, *YEAH,* I DID GO BACK, BUT I ASKED MY FO*RRRRR*ENSICS INSTRUCTOR IF I COULD DO A SEMESTER ABROAD, AND I CHOSE THIS UNIVERSITY.
MAN, I HATE TO KEEP PUTTING MY OLD SCHOOL DOWN, BUT WE'RE NOT EXACTLY STRONG ON THE SCIENCES. SUTRAS, YES.

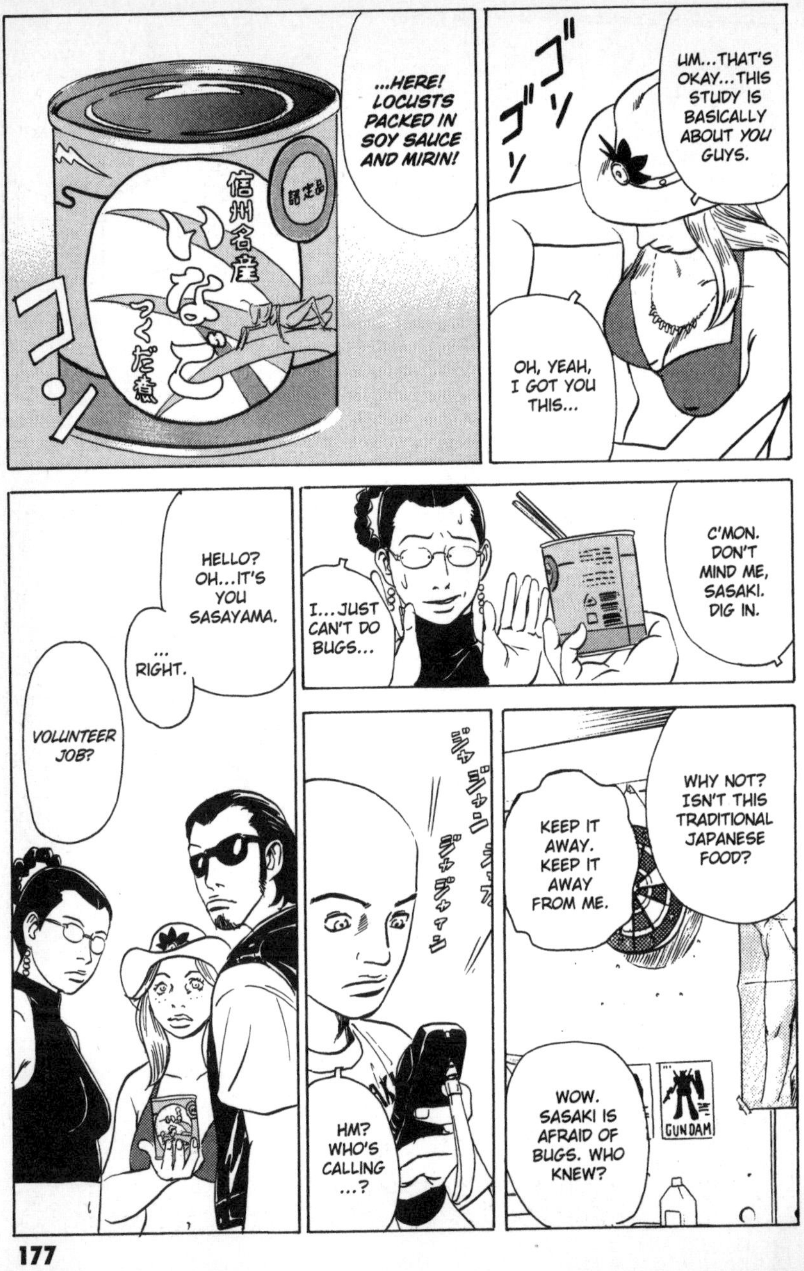

UM...THAT'S OKAY...THIS STUDY IS BASICALLY ABOUT *YOU* GUYS.
OH, YEAH, I GOT YOU THIS...
...HERE! LOCUSTS PACKED IN SOY SAUCE AND MIRIN!
信州名産
いなご
つくだ煮
C'MON. DON'T MIND ME, SASAKI. DIG IN.
I...JUST CAN'T DO BUGS...
WHY NOT? ISN'T THIS TRADITIONAL JAPANESE FOOD?
KEEP IT AWAY. KEEP IT AWAY FROM ME.
WOW. SASAKI IS AFRAID OF BUGS. WHO KNEW?
GUNDAM
HM? WHO'S CALLING ...?
HELLO? OH...IT'S YOU SASAYAMA.
... RIGHT.
VOLUNTEER JOB?

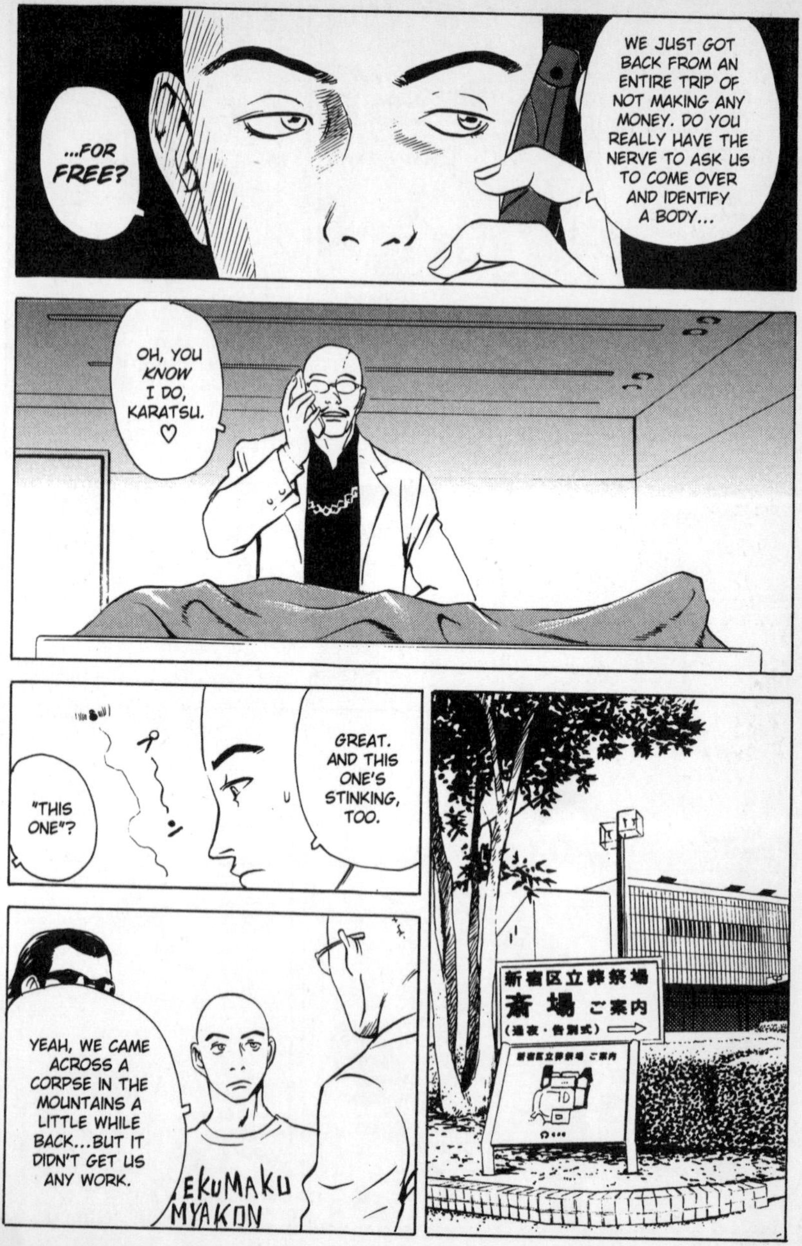
WE JUST GOT BACK FROM AN ENTIRE TRIP OF NOT MAKING ANY MONEY. DO YOU REALLY HAVE THE NERVE TO ASK US TO COME OVER AND IDENTIFY A BODY...
...FOR FREE?
OH, YOU KNOW I DO, KARATSU. ♡
新宿区立葬祭場
斎場 ご案内
(通夜・告別式)
新宿区立葬祭場 ご案内
GREAT. AND THIS ONE'S STINKING, TOO.
"THIS ONE"?
YEAH, WE CAME ACROSS A CORPSE IN THE MOUNTAINS A LITTLE WHILE BACK...BUT IT DIDN'T GET US ANY WORK.
EKUMAKU MYAKON

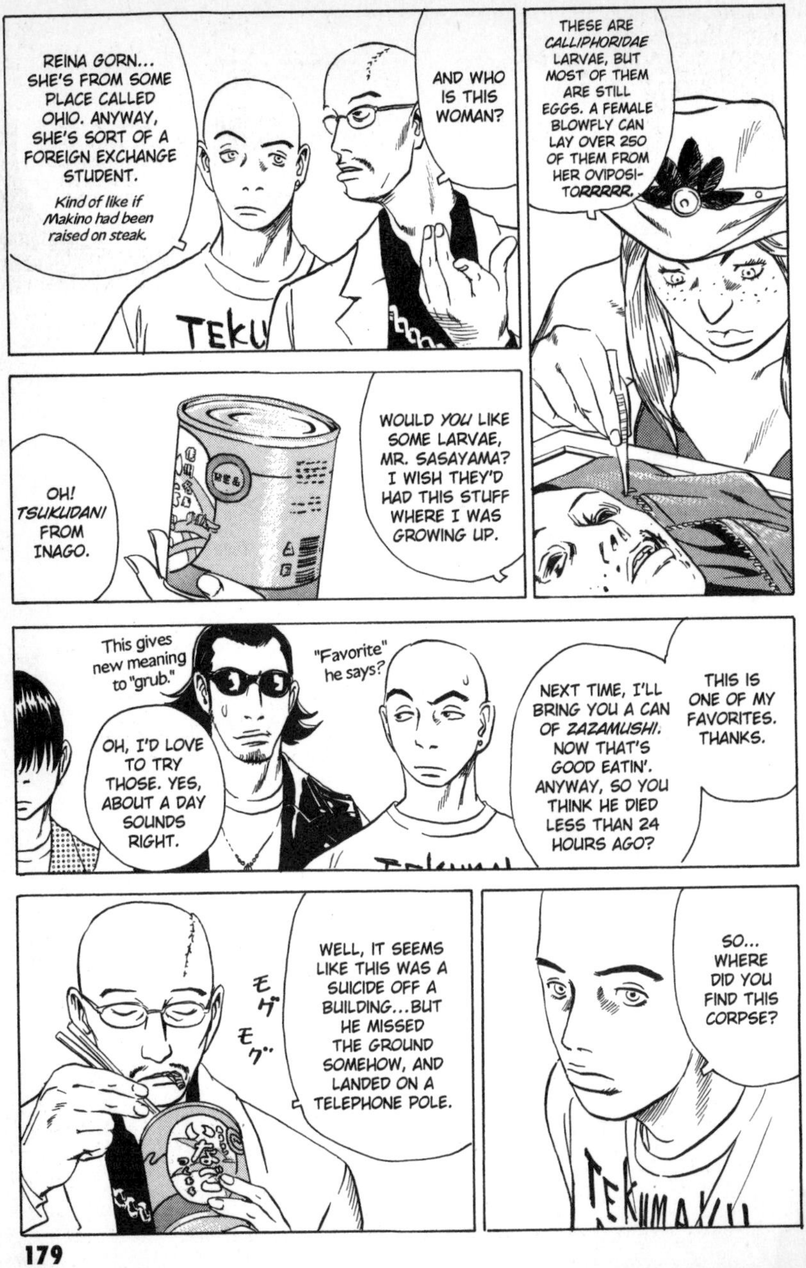
THESE ARE *CALLIPHORIDAE* LARVAE, BUT MOST OF THEM ARE STILL EGGS. A FEMALE BLOWFLY CAN LAY OVER 250 OF THEM FROM HER OVIPOSI-TORRRRR.
AND WHO IS THIS WOMAN?
REINA GORN... SHE'S FROM SOME PLACE CALLED OHIO. ANYWAY, SHE'S SORT OF A FOREIGN EXCHANGE STUDENT.
Kind of like if Makino had been raised on steak.
TEKU
WOULD *YOU* LIKE SOME LARVAE, MR. SASAYAMA? I WISH THEY'D HAD THIS STUFF WHERE I WAS GROWING UP.
OH! *TSUKUDANI* FROM INAGO.
THIS IS ONE OF MY FAVORITES. THANKS.
NEXT TIME, I'LL BRING YOU A CAN OF *ZAZAMUSHI*. NOW THAT'S GOOD EATIN'. ANYWAY, SO YOU THINK HE DIED LESS THAN 24 HOURS AGO?
"Favorite" he says?
This gives new meaning to "grub."
OH, I'D LOVE TO TRY THOSE. YES, ABOUT A DAY SOUNDS RIGHT.
SO... WHERE DID YOU FIND THIS CORPSE?
TEKUMAKU
WELL, IT SEEMS LIKE THIS WAS A SUICIDE OFF A BUILDING...BUT HE MISSED THE GROUND SOMEHOW, AND LANDED ON A TELEPHONE POLE.
モグモグ

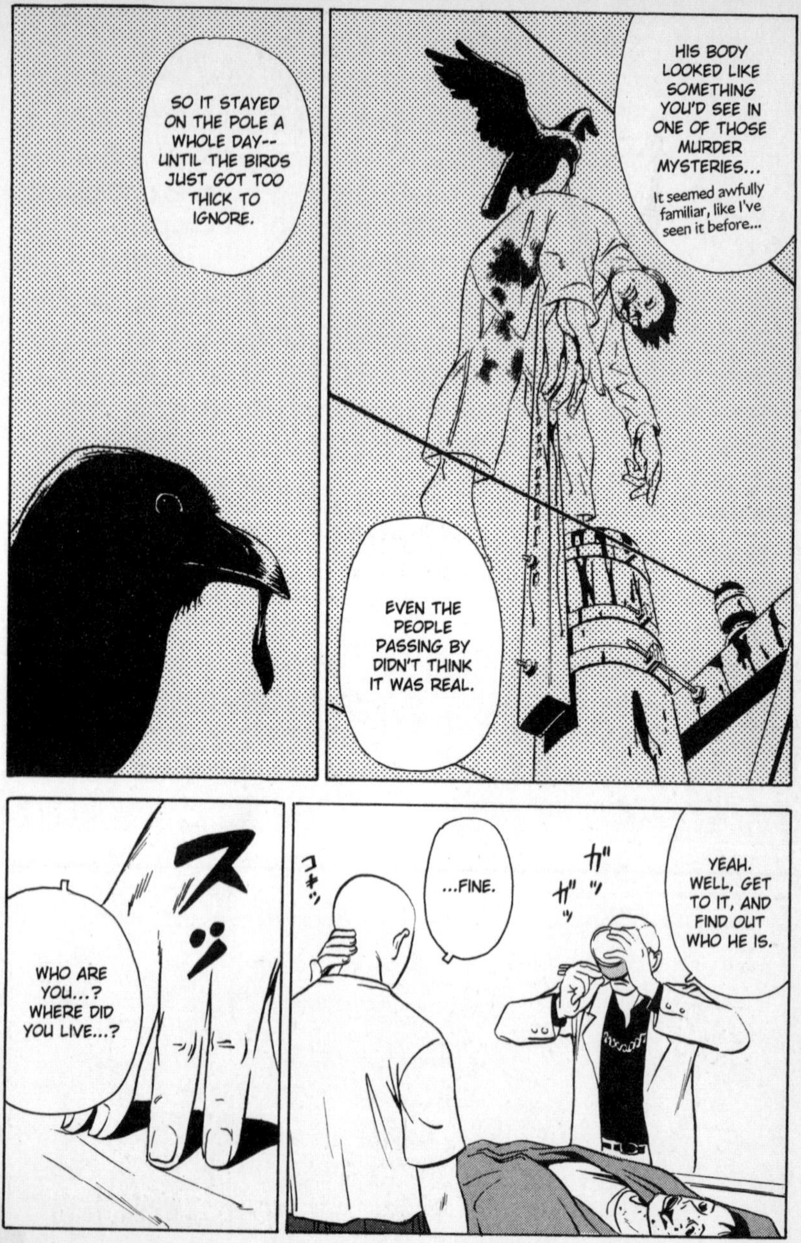
HIS BODY LOOKED LIKE SOMETHING YOU'D SEE IN ONE OF THOSE MURDER MYSTERIES...
It seemed awfully familiar, like I've seen it before...
EVEN THE PEOPLE PASSING BY DIDN'T THINK IT WAS REAL.
SO IT STAYED ON THE POLE A WHOLE DAY--UNTIL THE BIRDS JUST GOT TOO THICK TO IGNORE.
YEAH. WELL, GET TO IT, AND FIND OUT WHO HE IS.
ガッ ガッ
...FINE.
コキッ
スッ
WHO ARE YOU...? WHERE DID YOU LIVE...?

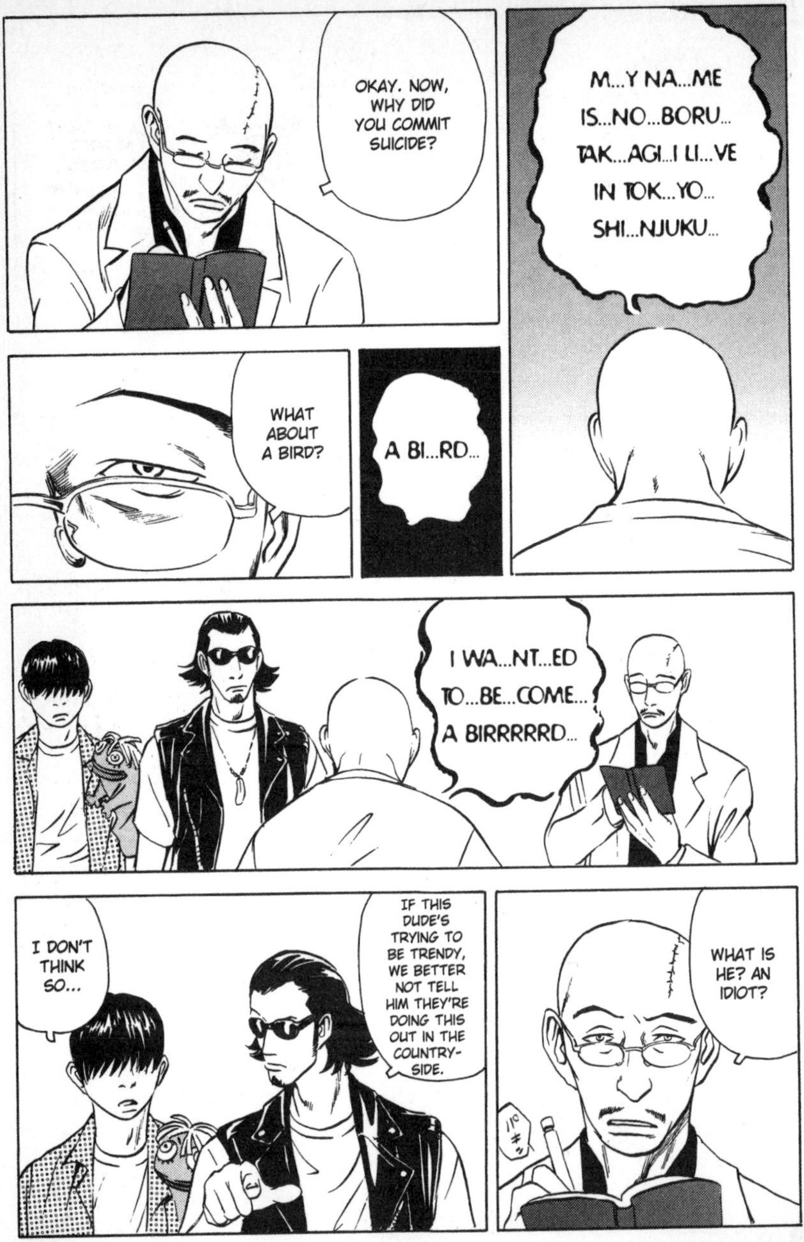
M...Y NA...ME IS...NO...BORU... TAK...AGI...I LI...VE IN TOK...YO... SHI...NJUKU...
OKAY. NOW, WHY DID YOU COMMIT SUICIDE?
A BI...RD...
WHAT ABOUT A BIRD?
I WA...NT...ED TO...BE...COME... A BIRRRRRD...
WHAT IS HE? AN IDIOT?
IF THIS DUDE'S TRYING TO BE TRENDY, WE BETTER NOT TELL HIM THEY'RE DOING THIS OUT IN THE COUNTRY-SIDE.
I DON'T THINK SO...

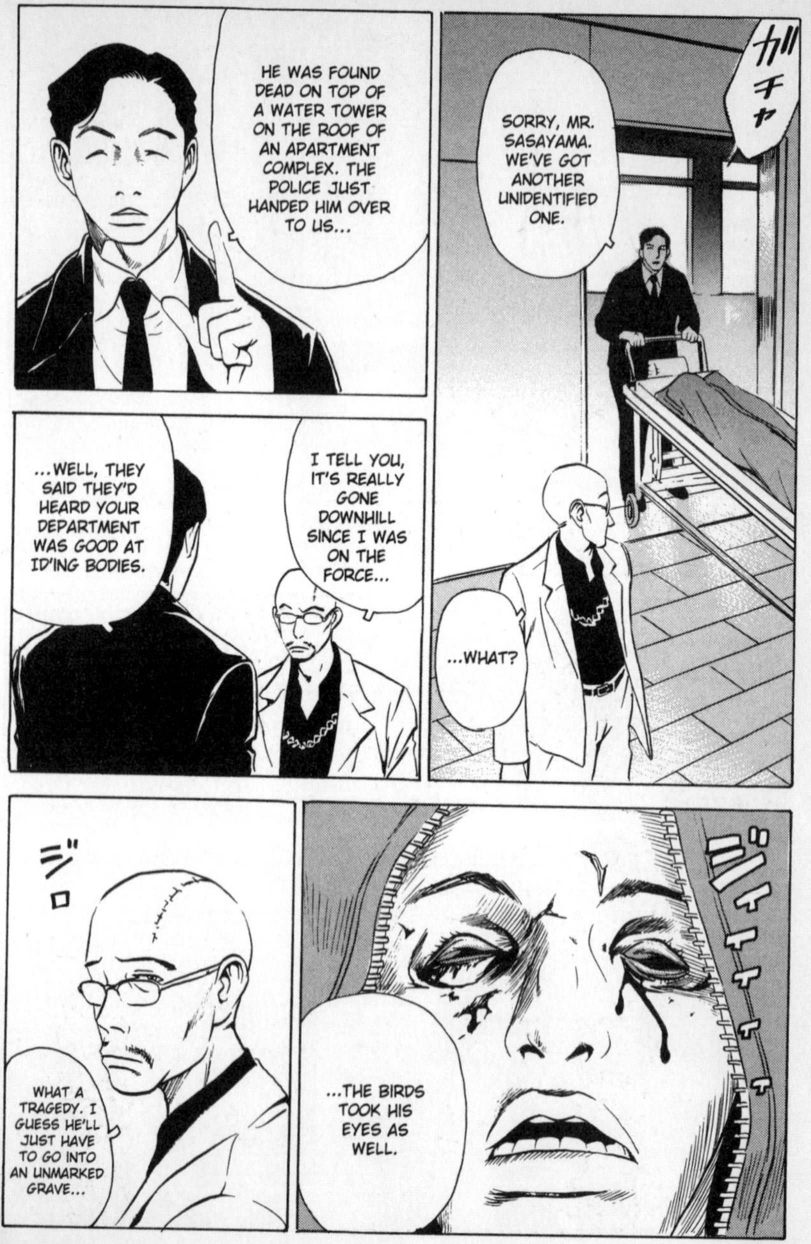

ガチャ
SORRY, MR. SASAYAMA. WE'VE GOT ANOTHER UNIDENTIFIED ONE.
...WHAT?
HE WAS FOUND DEAD ON TOP OF A WATER TOWER ON THE ROOF OF AN APARTMENT COMPLEX. THE POLICE JUST HANDED HIM OVER TO US...
I TELL YOU, IT'S REALLY GONE DOWNHILL SINCE I WAS ON THE FORCE...
...WELL, THEY SAID THEY'D HEARD YOUR DEPARTMENT WAS GOOD AT ID'ING BODIES.
...THE BIRDS TOOK HIS EYES AS WELL.
ジロ
WHAT A TRAGEDY. I GUESS HE'LL JUST HAVE TO GO INTO AN UNMARKED GRAVE...

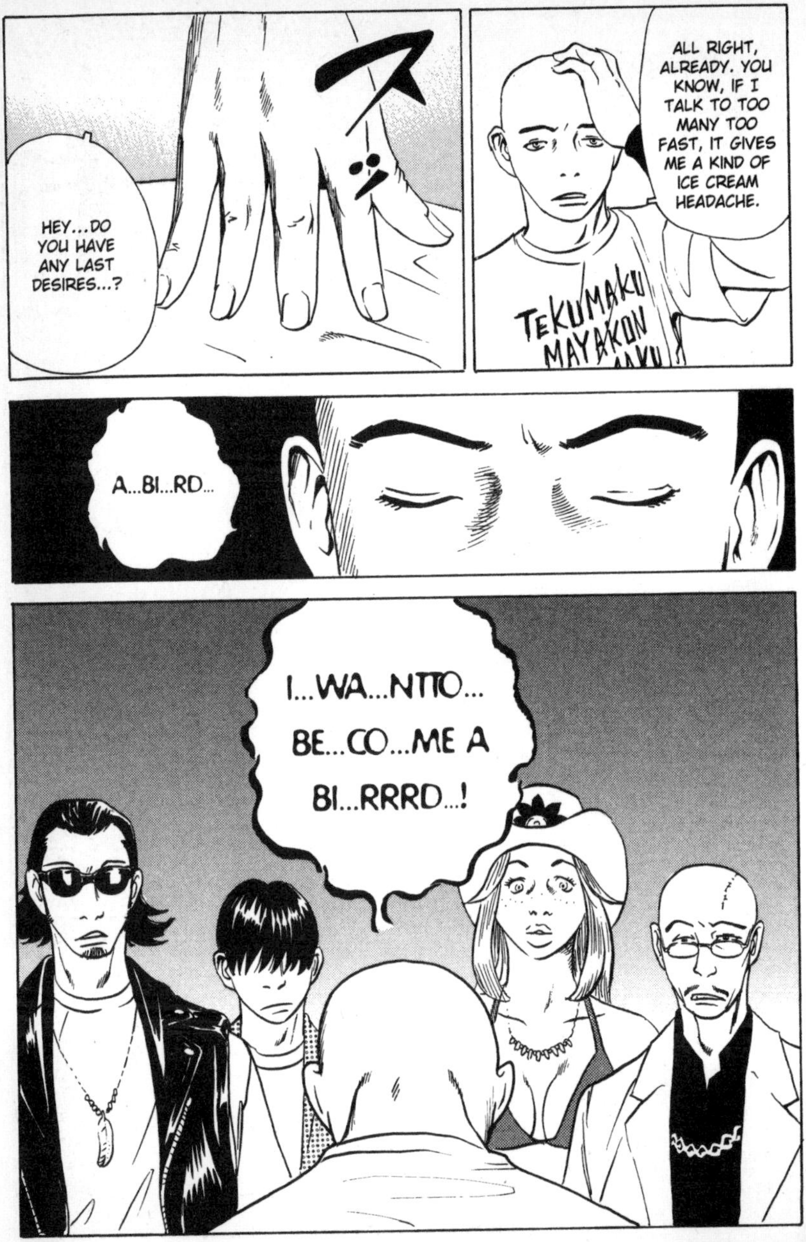
ALL RIGHT, ALREADY. YOU KNOW, IF I TALK TO TOO MANY TOO FAST, IT GIVES ME A KIND OF ICE CREAM HEADACHE.
TEKUMAKU MAYAKON
ス
HEY...DO YOU HAVE ANY LAST DESIRES...?
A...BI...RD...
I...WA...NTTO... BE...CO...ME A BI...RRRD...!

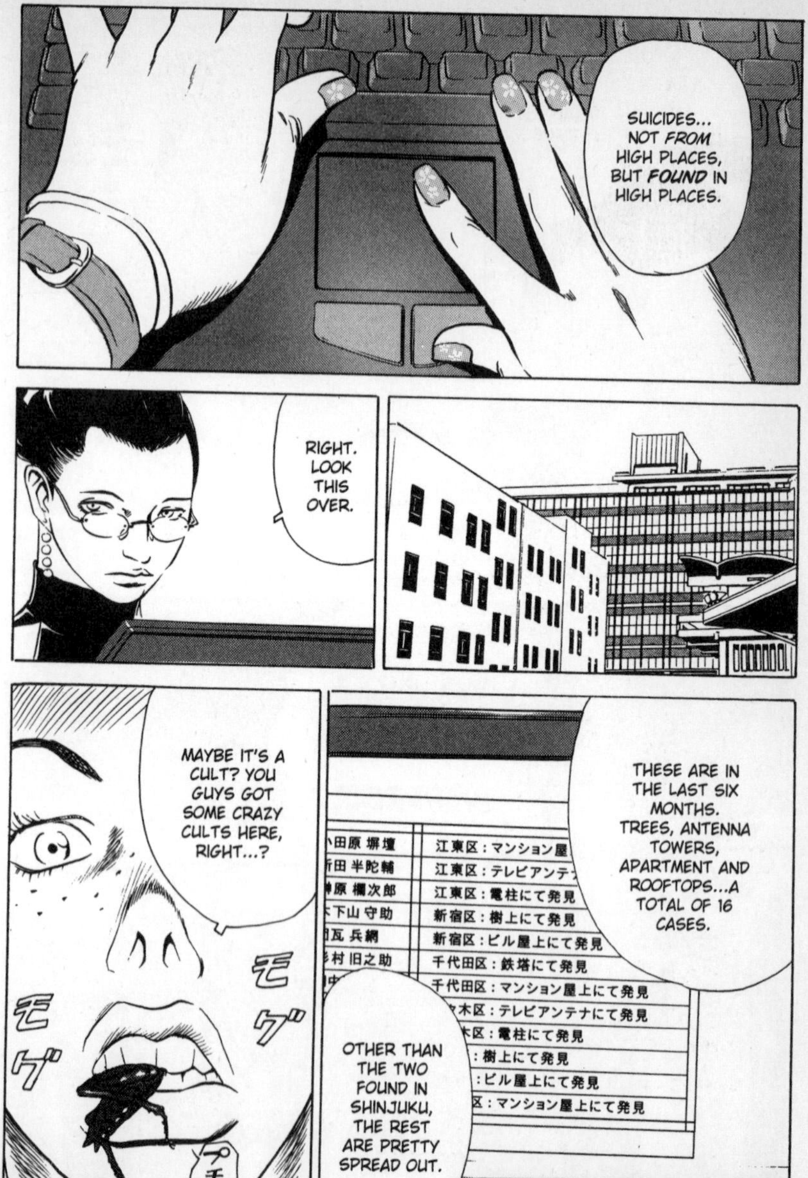
SUICIDES... NOT *FROM* HIGH PLACES, BUT ***FOUND*** IN HIGH PLACES.
RIGHT. LOOK THIS OVER.
THESE ARE IN THE LAST SIX MONTHS. TREES, ANTENNA TOWERS, APARTMENT AND ROOFTOPS...A TOTAL OF 16 CASES.
江東区：電柱にて発見
新宿区：樹上にて発見
新宿区：ビル屋上にて発見
千代田区：鉄塔にて発見
千代田区：マンション屋上にて発見
OTHER THAN THE TWO FOUND IN SHINJUKU, THE REST ARE PRETTY SPREAD OUT.
MAYBE IT'S A CULT? YOU GUYS GOT SOME CRAZY CULTS HERE, RIGHT...?
モグモグ
プチュ

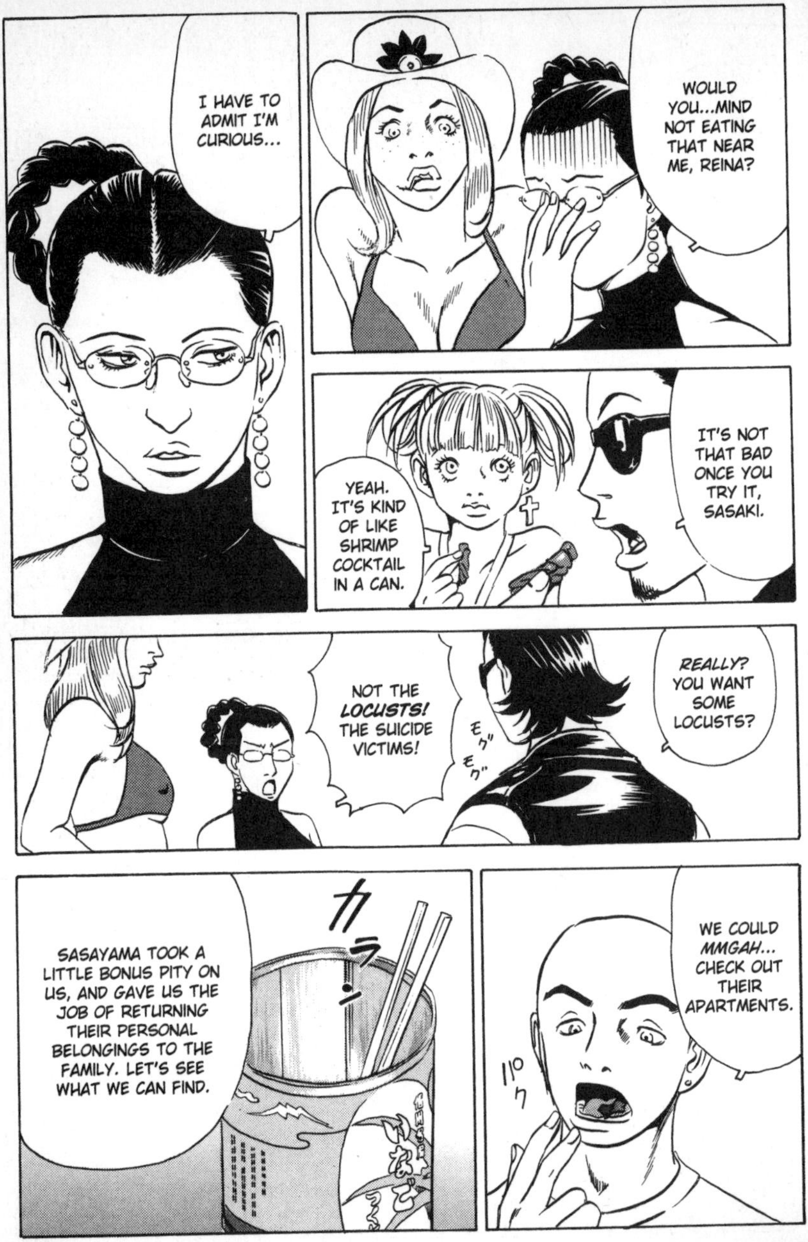
WOULD YOU...MIND NOT EATING THAT NEAR ME, REINA?
IT'S NOT THAT BAD ONCE YOU TRY IT, SASAKI.
YEAH. IT'S KIND OF LIKE SHRIMP COCKTAIL IN A CAN.
I HAVE TO ADMIT I'M CURIOUS...
REALLY? YOU WANT SOME LOCUSTS?
モグ モグ
NOT THE ***LOCUSTS!*** THE SUICIDE VICTIMS!
WE COULD *MMGAH...* CHECK OUT THEIR APARTMENTS.
パク
カラン
SASAYAMA TOOK A LITTLE BONUS PITY ON US, AND GAVE US THE JOB OF RETURNING THEIR PERSONAL BELONGINGS TO THE FAMILY. LET'S SEE WHAT WE CAN FIND.

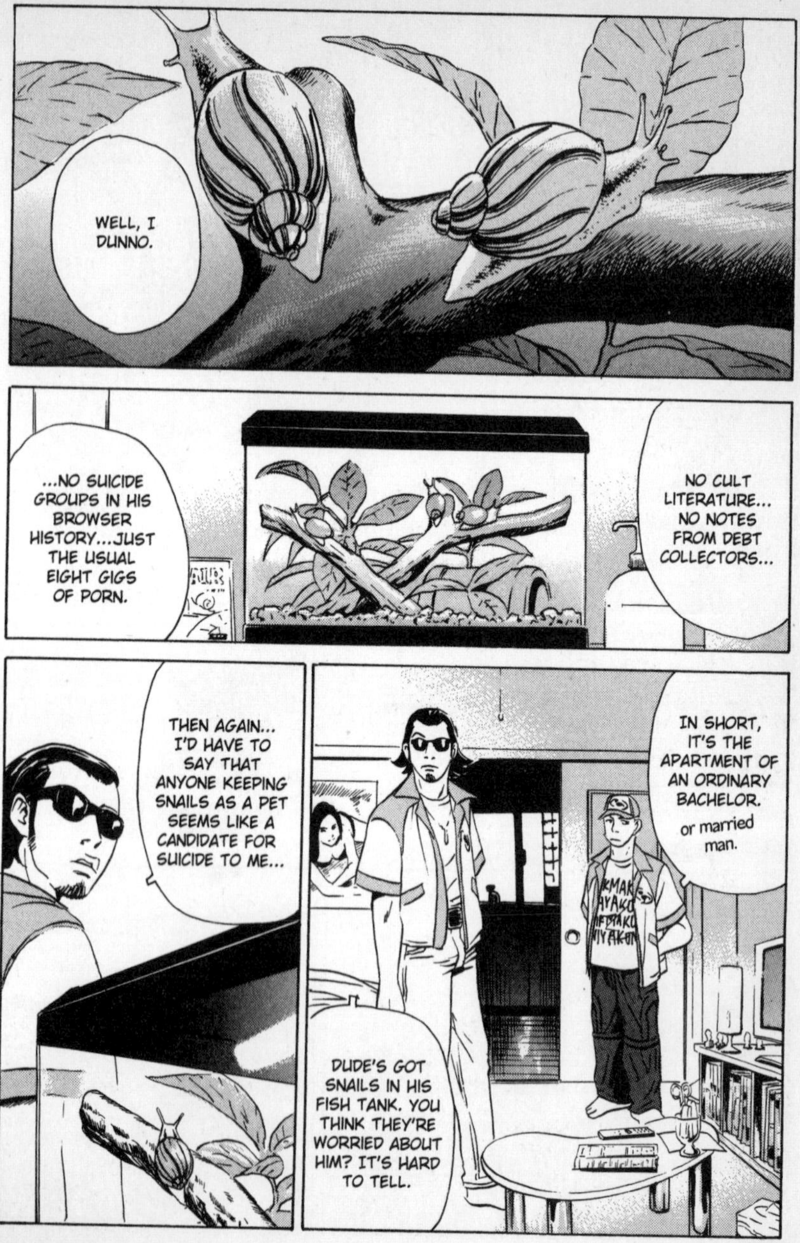
WELL, I DUNNO.
NO CULT LITERATURE... NO NOTES FROM DEBT COLLECTORS...
...NO SUICIDE GROUPS IN HIS BROWSER HISTORY...JUST THE USUAL EIGHT GIGS OF PORN.
IN SHORT, IT'S THE APARTMENT OF AN ORDINARY BACHELOR.
or married man.
DUDE'S GOT SNAILS IN HIS FISH TANK. YOU THINK THEY'RE WORRIED ABOUT HIM? IT'S HARD TO TELL.
THEN AGAIN... I'D HAVE TO SAY THAT ANYONE KEEPING SNAILS AS A PET SEEMS LIKE A CANDIDATE FOR SUICIDE TO ME...

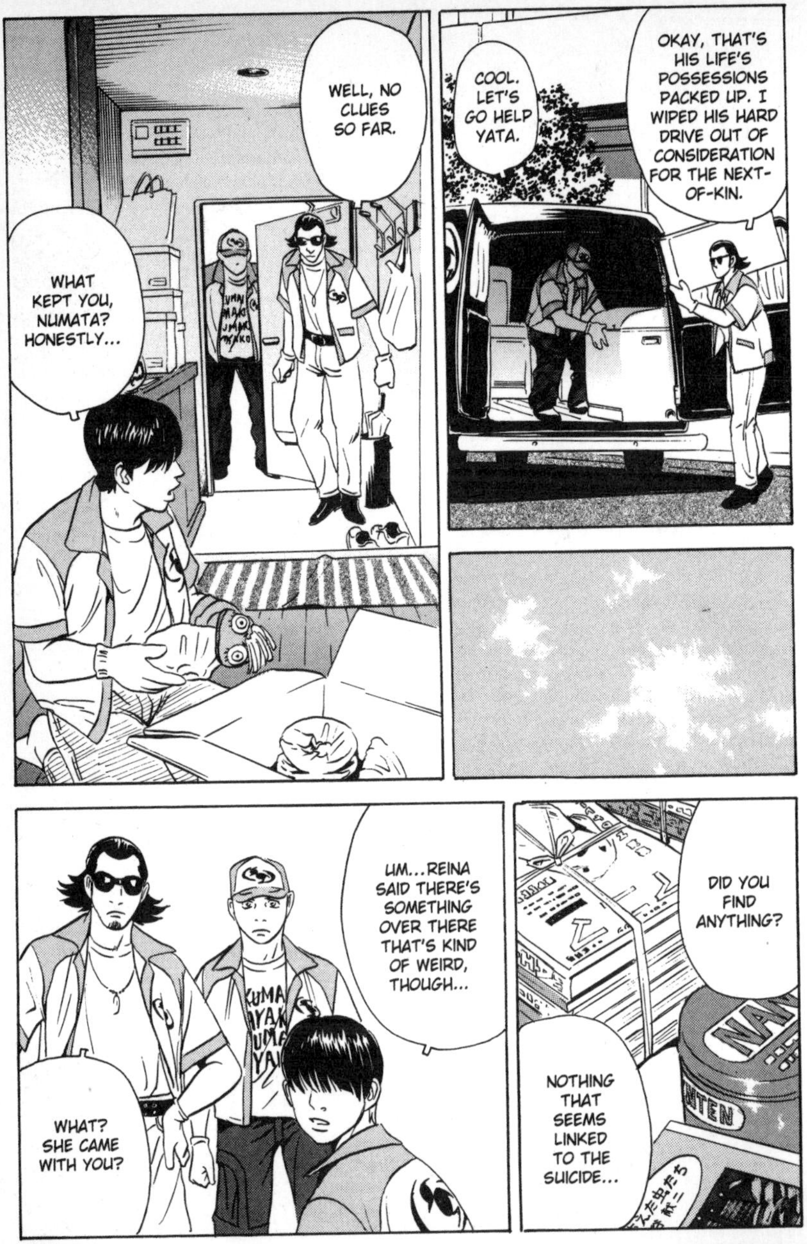
OKAY, THAT'S HIS LIFE'S POSSESSIONS PACKED UP. I WIPED HIS HARD DRIVE OUT OF CONSIDERATION FOR THE NEXT-OF-KIN.
COOL. LET'S GO HELP YATA.
WELL, NO CLUES SO FAR.
WHAT KEPT YOU, NUMATA? HONESTLY...
DID YOU FIND ANYTHING?
NOTHING THAT SEEMS LINKED TO THE SUICIDE...
NAN
NTEN
UM...REINA SAID THERE'S SOMETHING OVER THERE THAT'S KIND OF WEIRD, THOUGH...
WHAT? SHE CAME WITH YOU?

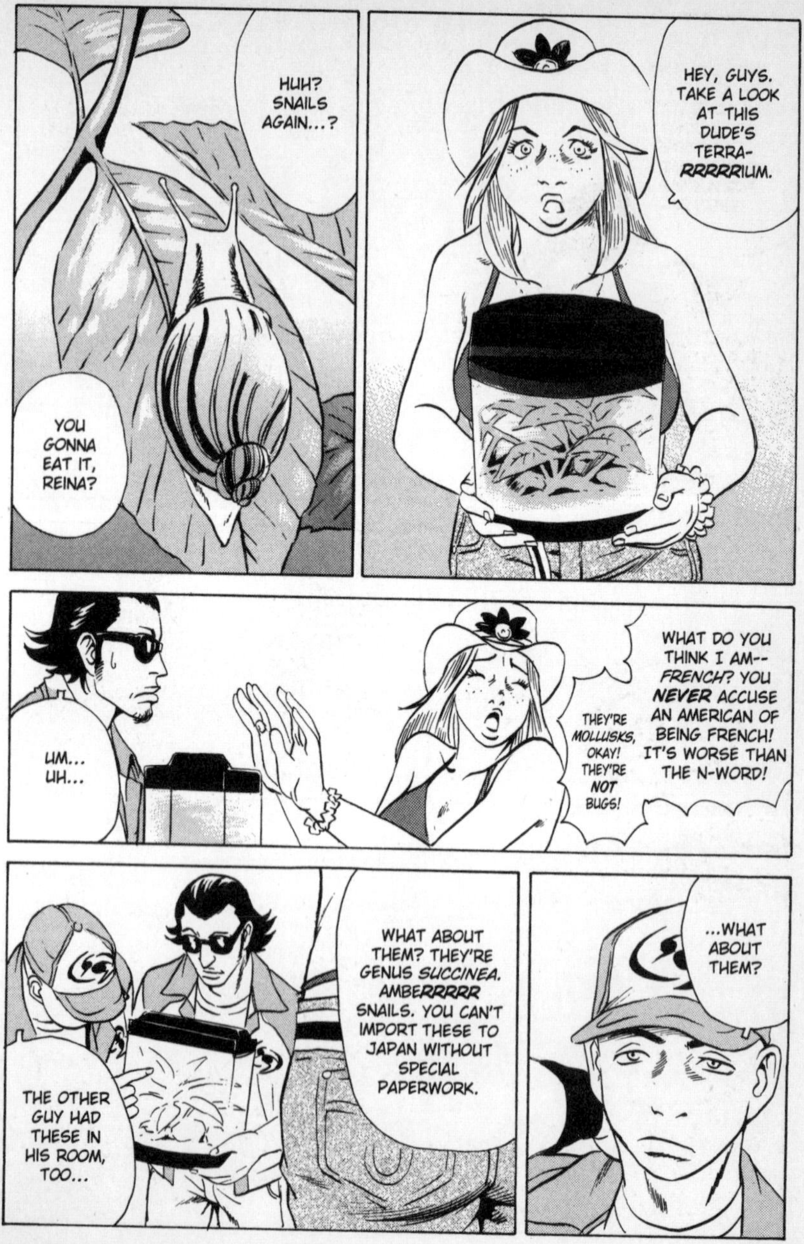
HEY, GUYS. TAKE A LOOK AT THIS DUDE'S TERRA-RRRRRIUM.
HUH? SNAILS AGAIN...?
YOU GONNA EAT IT, REINA?
WHAT DO YOU THINK I AM-- FRENCH? YOU NEVER ACCUSE AN AMERICAN OF BEING FRENCH! IT'S WORSE THAN THE N-WORD!
THEY'RE MOLLUSKS, OKAY! THEY'RE NOT BUGS!
UM... UH...
...WHAT ABOUT THEM?
WHAT ABOUT THEM? THEY'RE GENUS SUCCINEA. AMBERRRRR SNAILS. YOU CAN'T IMPORT THESE TO JAPAN WITHOUT SPECIAL PAPERWORK.
THE OTHER GUY HAD THESE IN HIS ROOM, TOO...

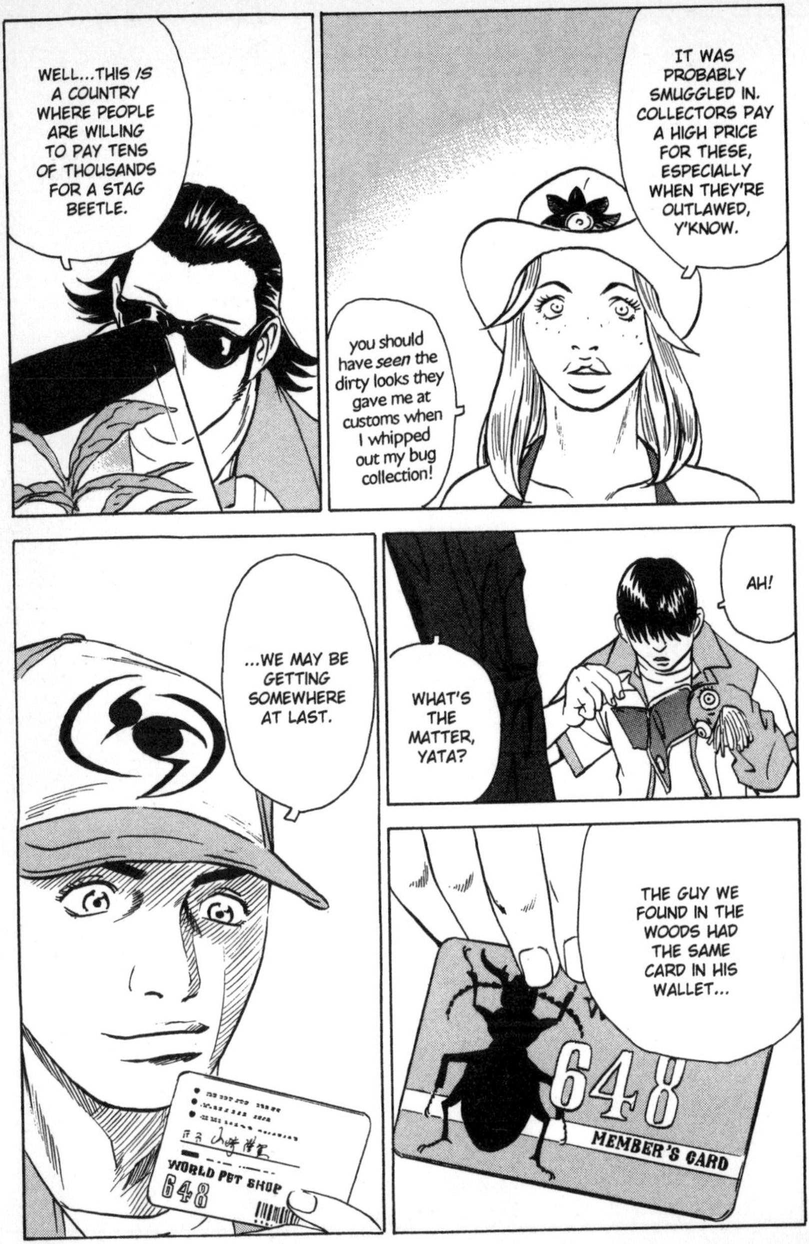
IT WAS PROBABLY SMUGGLED IN. COLLECTORS PAY A HIGH PRICE FOR THESE, ESPECIALLY WHEN THEY'RE OUTLAWED, Y'KNOW.
you should have *seen* the dirty looks they gave me at customs when I whipped out my bug collection!
WELL...THIS *IS* A COUNTRY WHERE PEOPLE ARE WILLING TO PAY TENS OF THOUSANDS FOR A STAG BEETLE.
AH!
WHAT'S THE MATTER, YATA?
THE GUY WE FOUND IN THE WOODS HAD THE SAME CARD IN HIS WALLET...
648
MEMBER'S CARD
...WE MAY BE GETTING SOMEWHERE AT LAST.
WORLD PET SHOP
648

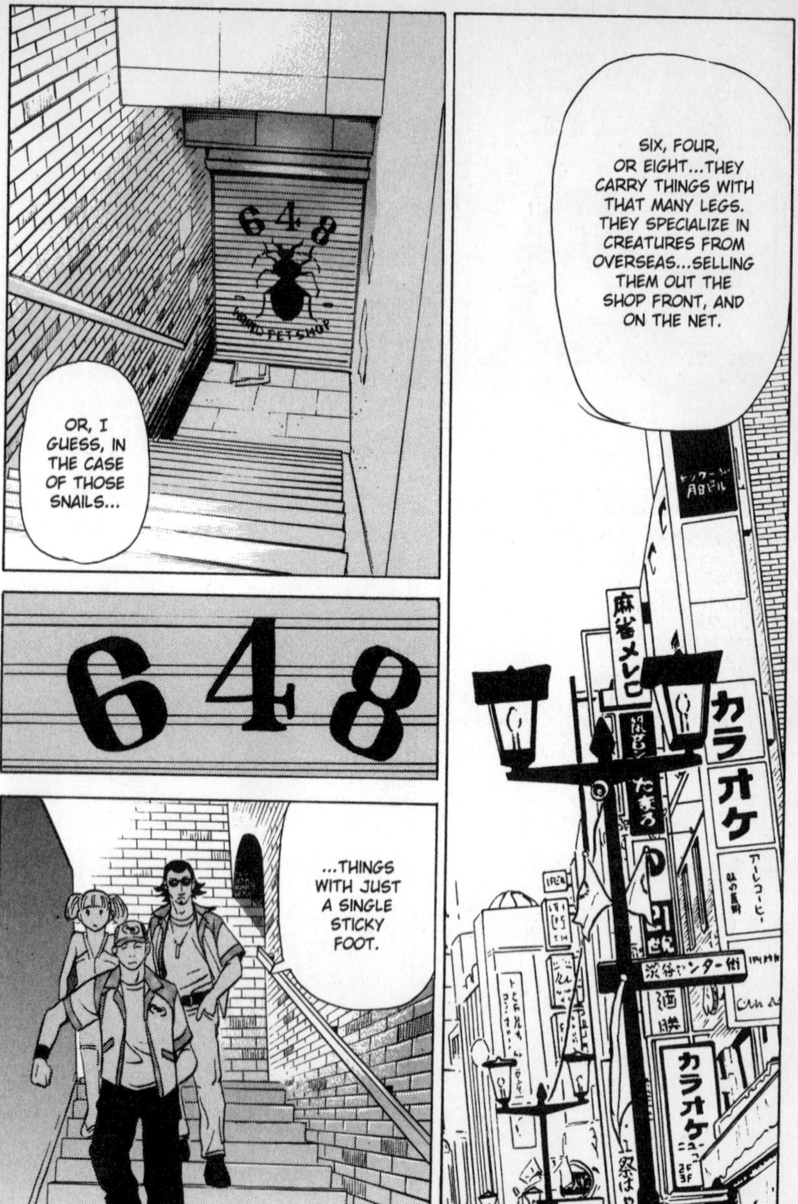
SIX, FOUR, OR EIGHT...THEY CARRY THINGS WITH THAT MANY LEGS. THEY SPECIALIZE IN CREATURES FROM OVERSEAS...SELLING THEM OUT THE SHOP FRONT, AND ON THE NET.
カラオケ
カラオケ
648
OR, I GUESS, IN THE CASE OF THOSE SNAILS...
648
...THINGS WITH JUST A SINGLE STICKY FOOT.

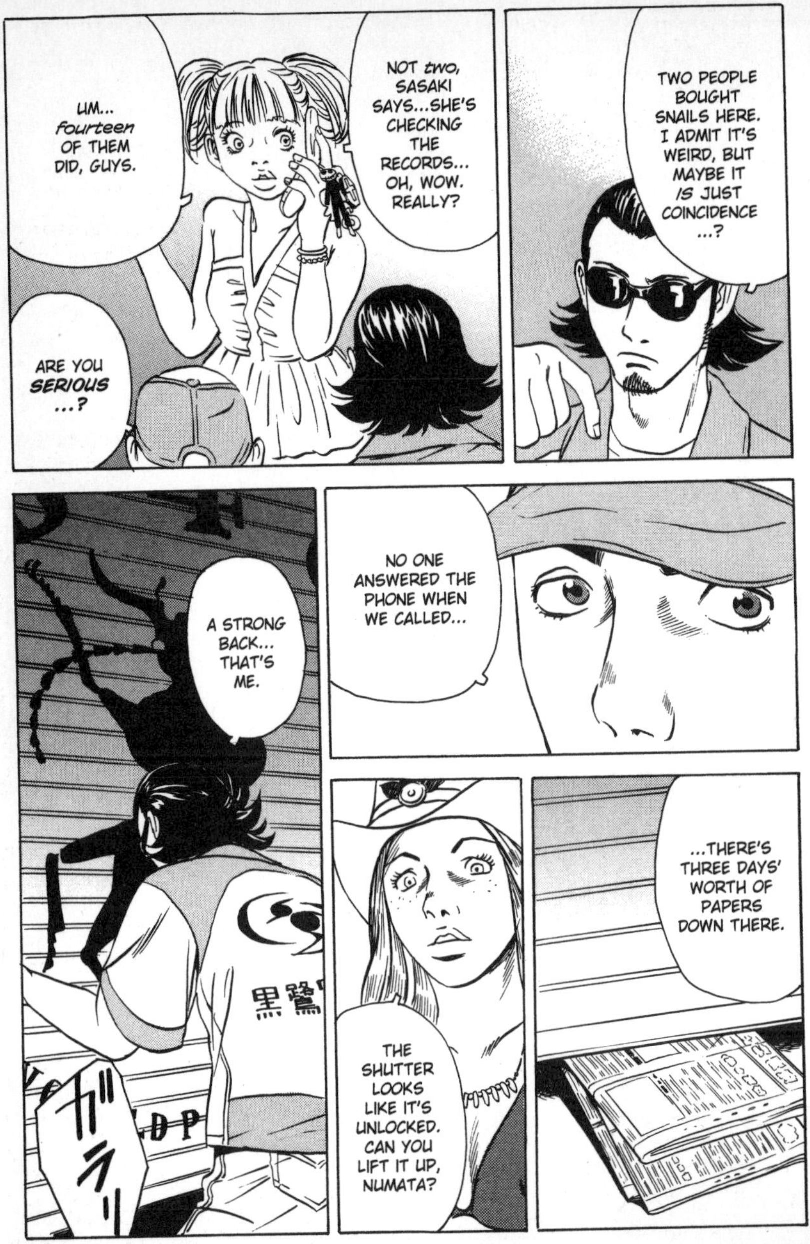

TWO PEOPLE BOUGHT SNAILS HERE. I ADMIT IT'S WEIRD, BUT MAYBE IT *IS* JUST COINCIDENCE ...?
NOT *two*, SASAKI SAYS...SHE'S CHECKING THE RECORDS... OH, WOW. REALLY?
UM... *fourteen* OF THEM DID, GUYS.
ARE YOU **SERIOUS** ...?
NO ONE ANSWERED THE PHONE WHEN WE CALLED...
...THERE'S THREE DAYS' WORTH OF PAPERS DOWN THERE.
THE SHUTTER LOOKS LIKE IT'S UNLOCKED. CAN YOU LIFT IT UP, NUMATA?
A STRONG BACK... THAT'S ME.

HUMID AS ALL HELL IN HERE. WHERE ARE THE LIGHTS?

OH...I FOUND IT.

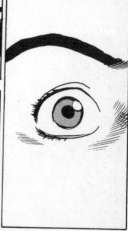

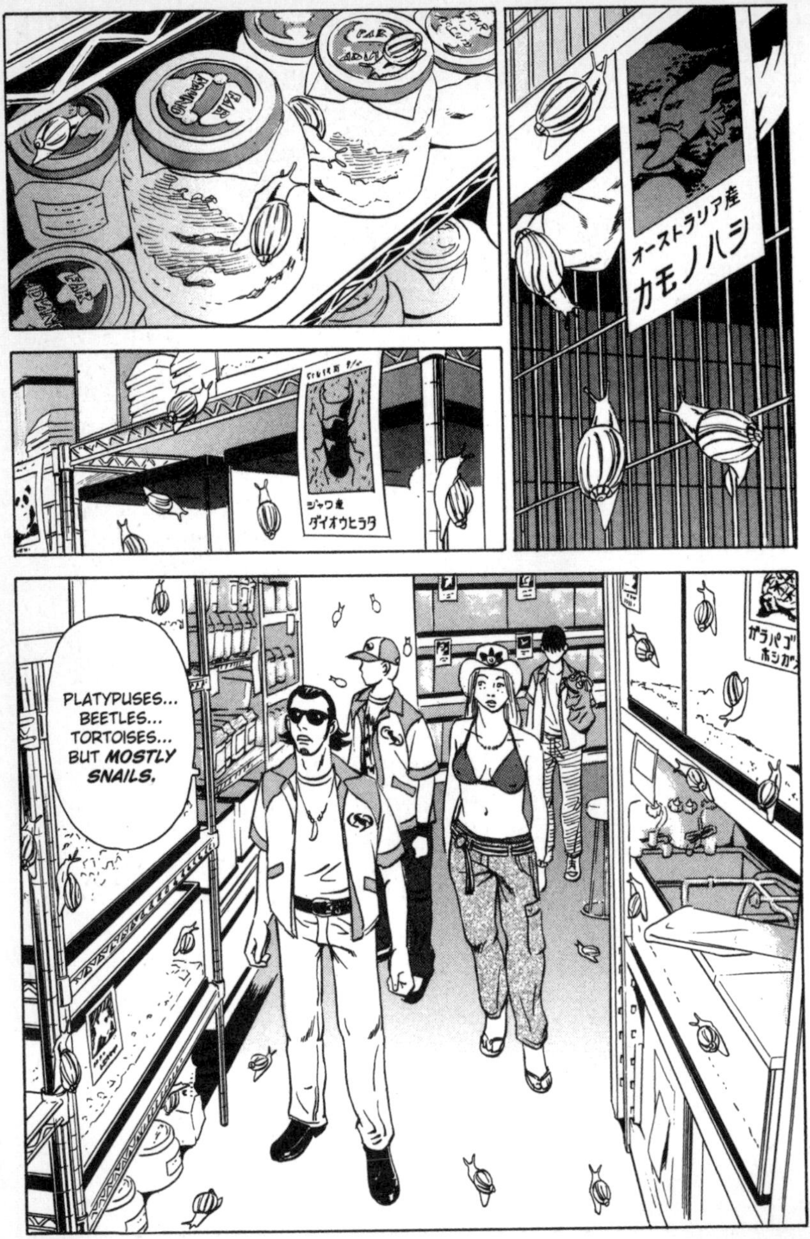
オーストラリア産
カモノハシ
ジャワ産
ダイオウヒラタ
PLATYPUSES... BEETLES... TORTOISES... BUT *MOSTLY SNAILS.*

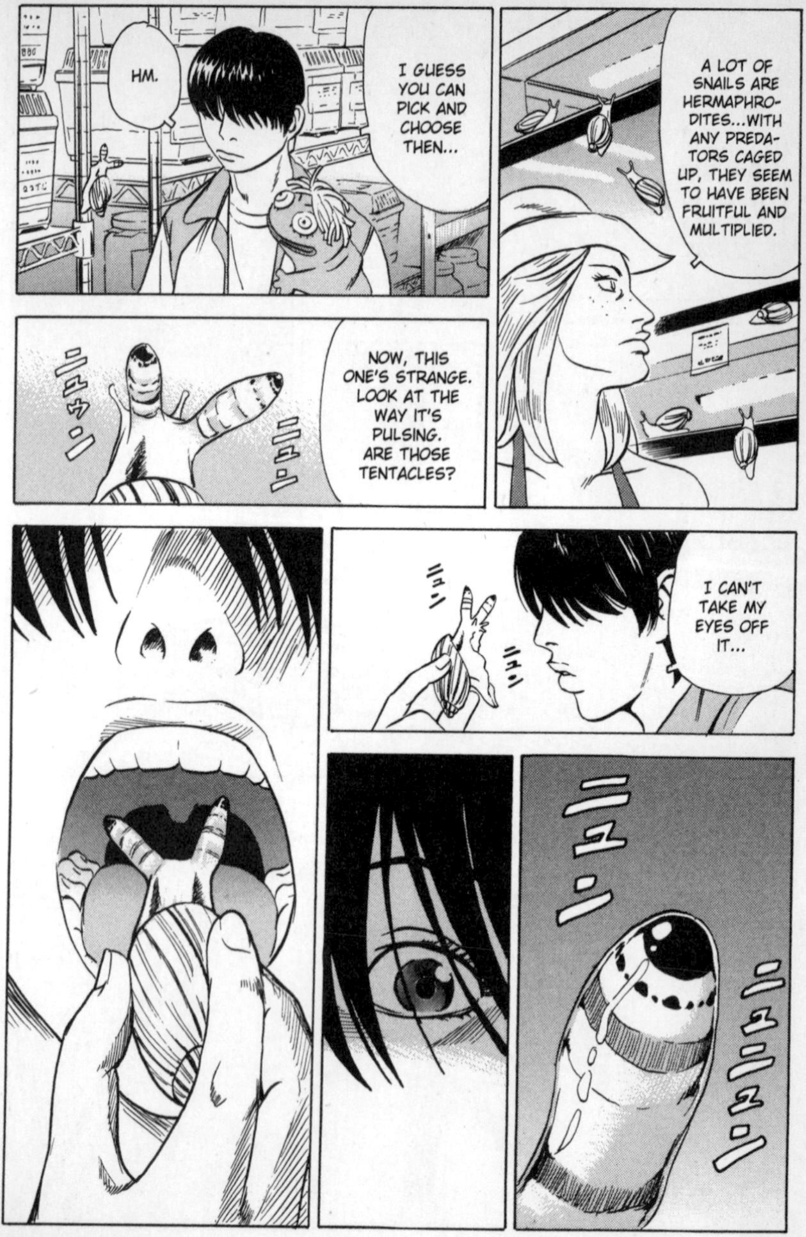

A LOT OF SNAILS ARE HERMAPHRODITES...WITH ANY PREDATORS CAGED UP, THEY SEEM TO HAVE BEEN FRUITFUL AND MULTIPLIED.
HM.
I GUESS YOU CAN PICK AND CHOOSE THEN...
NOW, THIS ONE'S STRANGE. LOOK AT THE WAY IT'S PULSING. ARE THOSE TENTACLES?
ニュウン
ニュニ
I CAN'T TAKE MY EYES OFF IT...
ニュン
ニュン
ニュン
ニュニュニュニュン

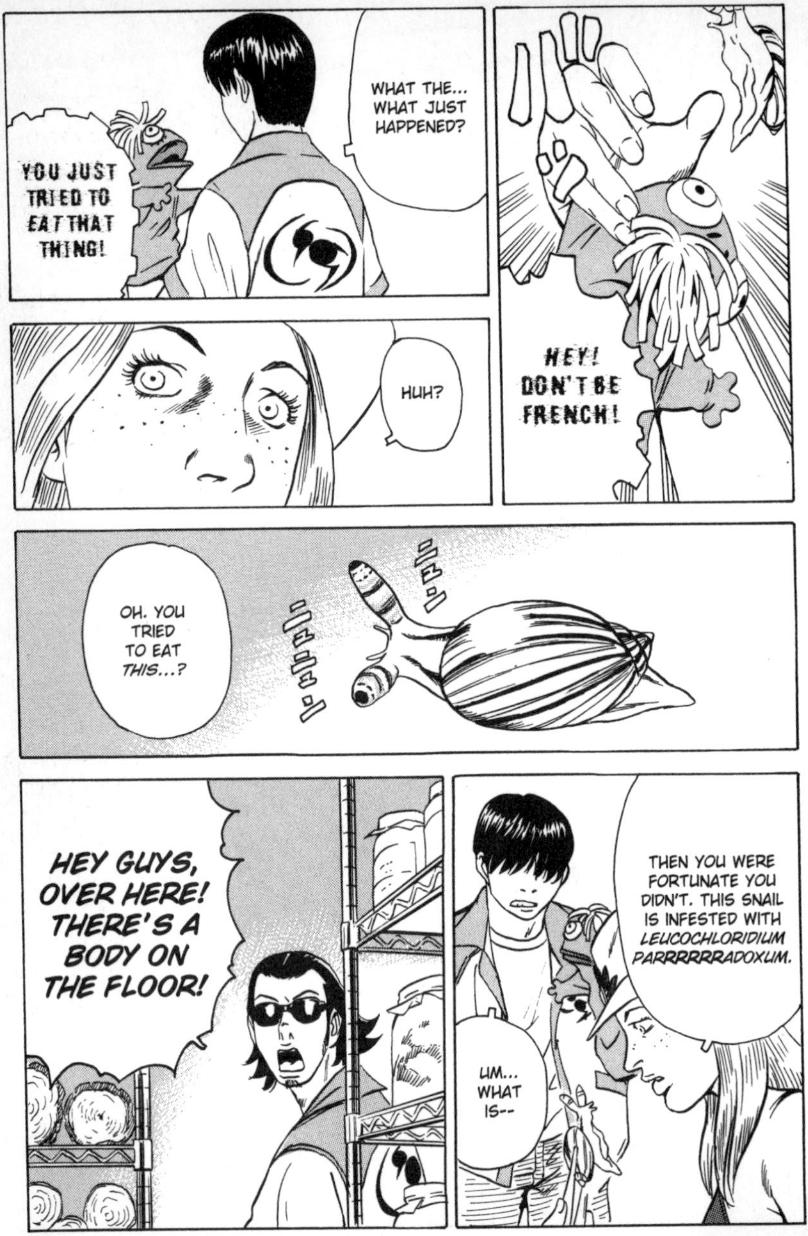
HEY! DON'T BE FRENCH!
WHAT THE... WHAT JUST HAPPENED?
YOU JUST TRIED TO EAT THAT THING!
HUH?
OH. YOU TRIED TO EAT *THIS...?*
THEN YOU WERE FORTUNATE YOU DIDN'T. THIS SNAIL IS INFESTED WITH *LEUCOCHLORIDIUM PARRRRRRADOXUM.*
UM... WHAT IS--
HEY GUYS, OVER HERE! THERE'S A BODY ON THE FLOOR!

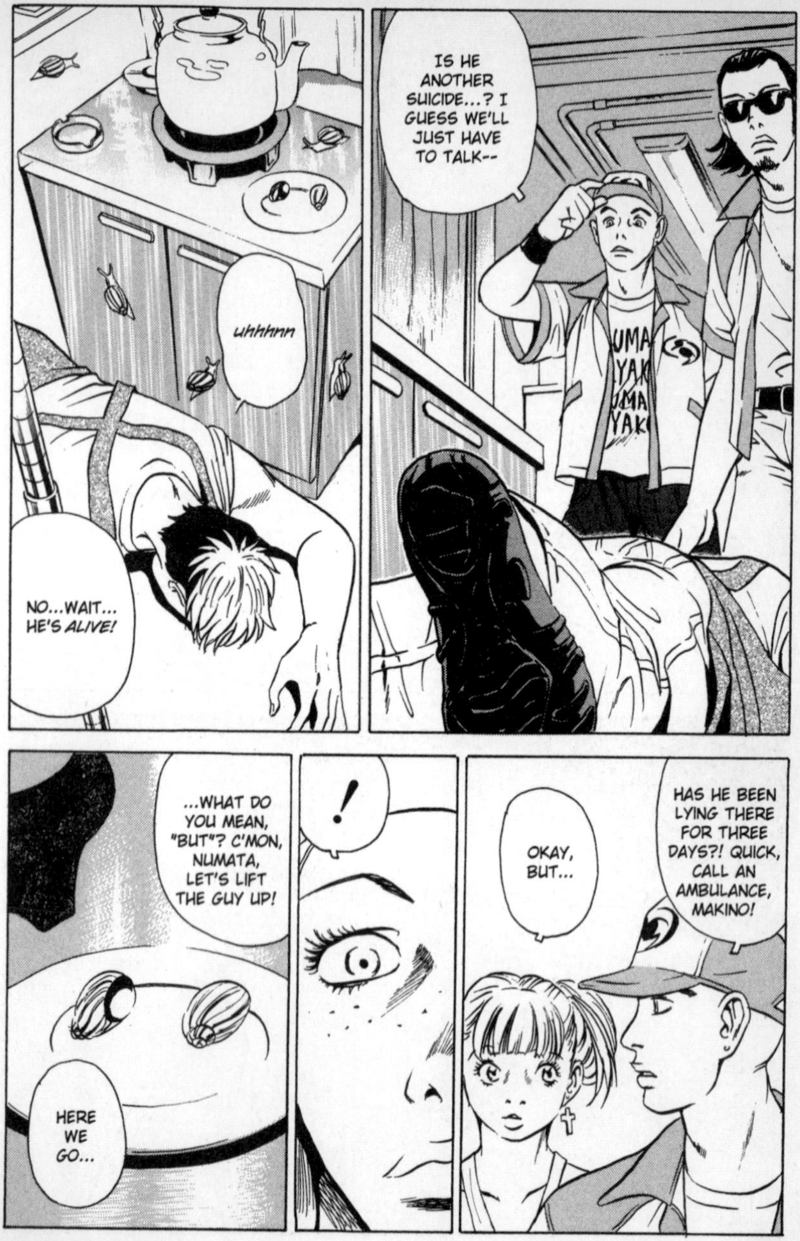
IS HE ANOTHER SUICIDE...? I GUESS WE'LL JUST HAVE TO TALK--
uhhhnn
NO...WAIT... HE'S *ALIVE!*
HAS HE BEEN LYING THERE FOR THREE DAYS?! QUICK, CALL AN AMBULANCE, MAKINO!
OKAY, BUT...
!
...WHAT DO YOU MEAN, "BUT"? C'MON, NUMATA, LET'S LIFT THE GUY UP!
HERE WE GO...

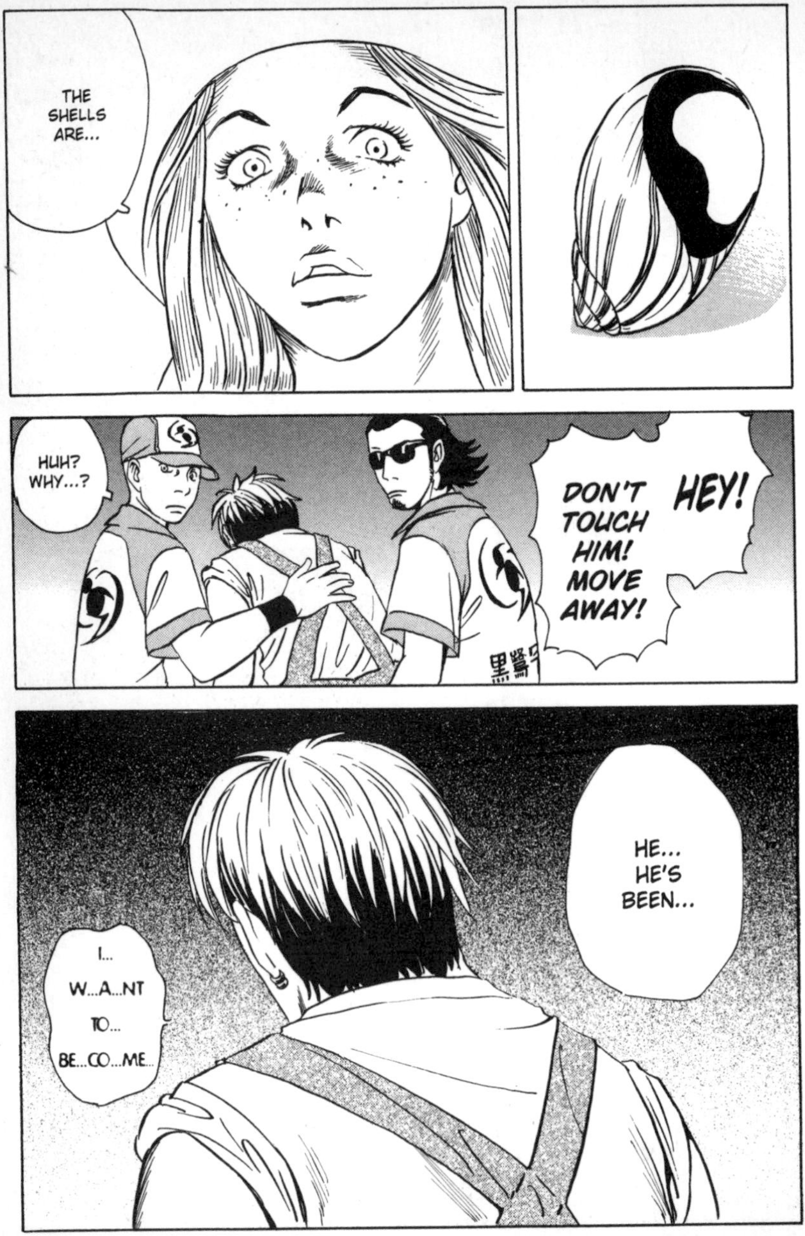
THE SHELLS ARE...
HEY!
DON'T TOUCH HIM! MOVE AWAY!
HUH? WHY...?
HE... HE'S BEEN...
I... W...A...NT TO... BE...CO...ME...

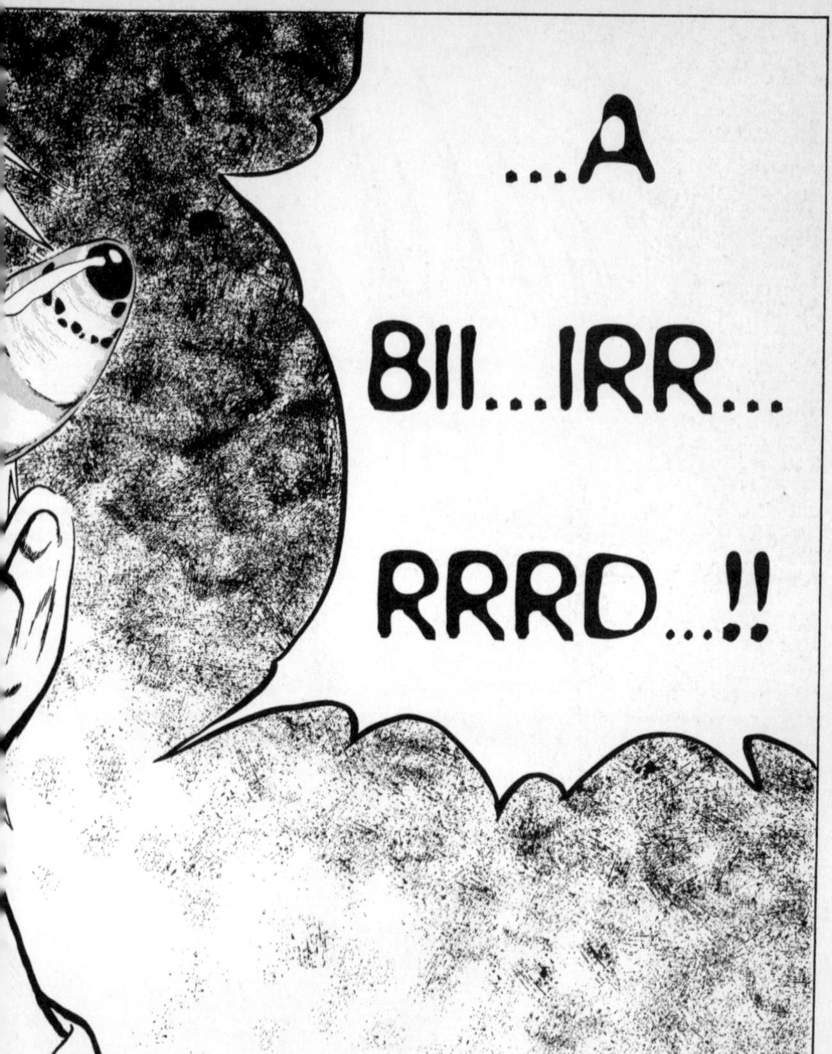
...A BII...IRR... RRRD...!!

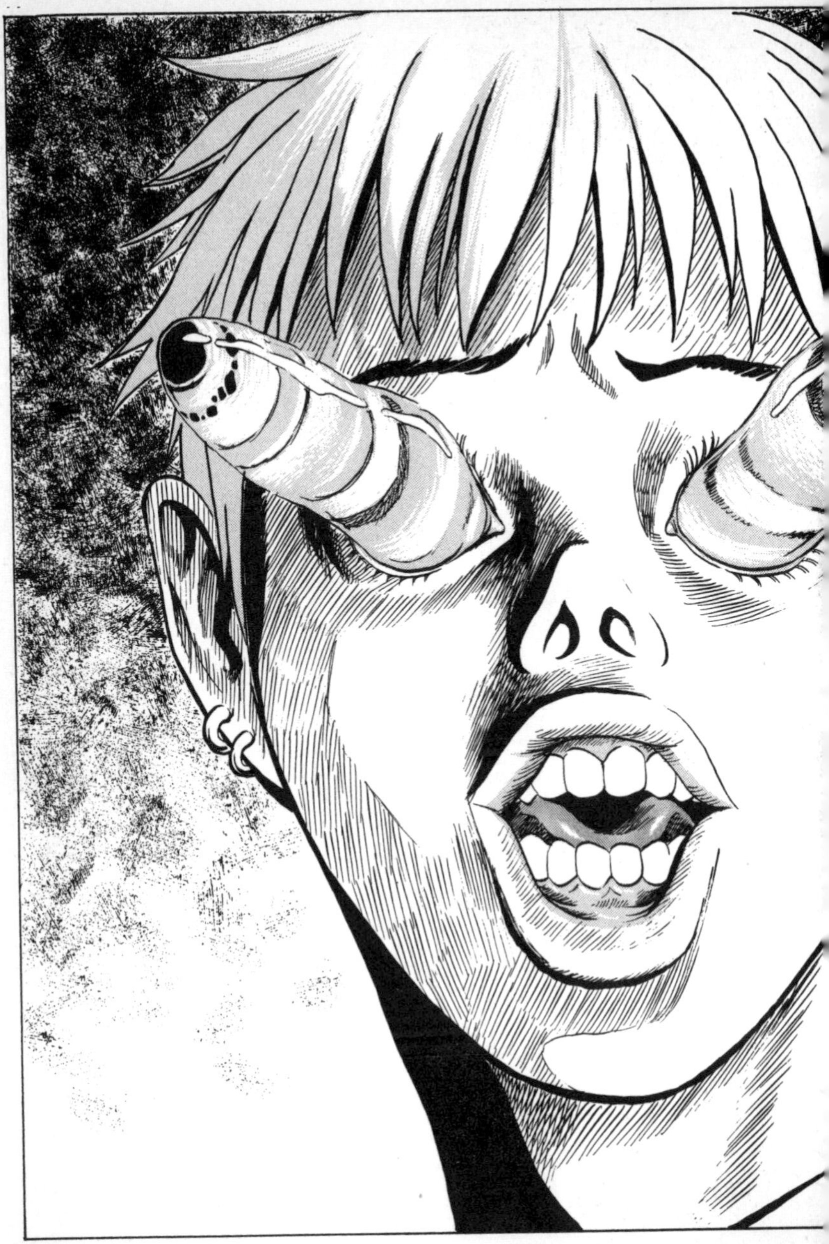

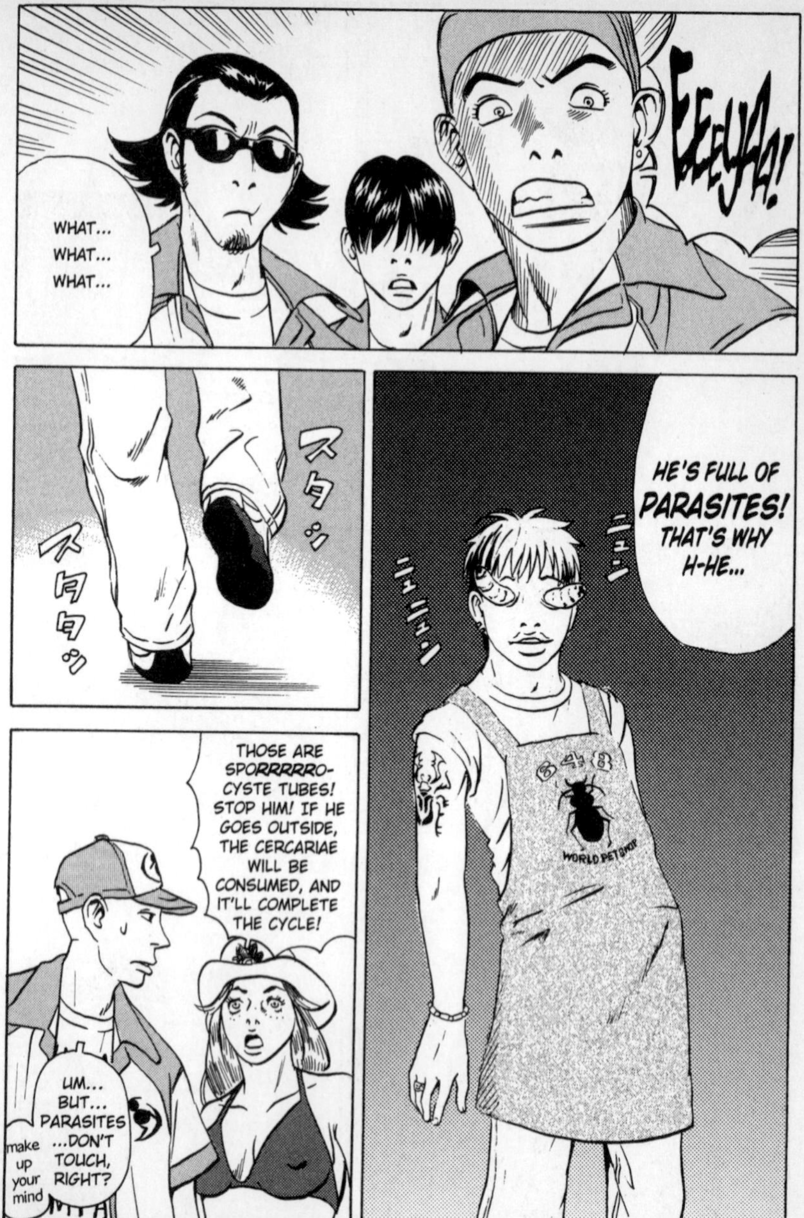
EEEYAA!
WHAT... WHAT... WHAT...
HE'S FULL OF PARASITES! THAT'S WHY H-HE...
848
WORLD PET SHOP
スタッ
スタタッ
THOSE ARE SPORRRRRRO-CYSTE TUBES! STOP HIM! IF HE GOES OUTSIDE, THE CERCARIAE WILL BE CONSUMED, AND IT'LL COMPLETE THE CYCLE!
UM... BUT... PARASITES ...DON'T TOUCH, RIGHT?
make up your mind

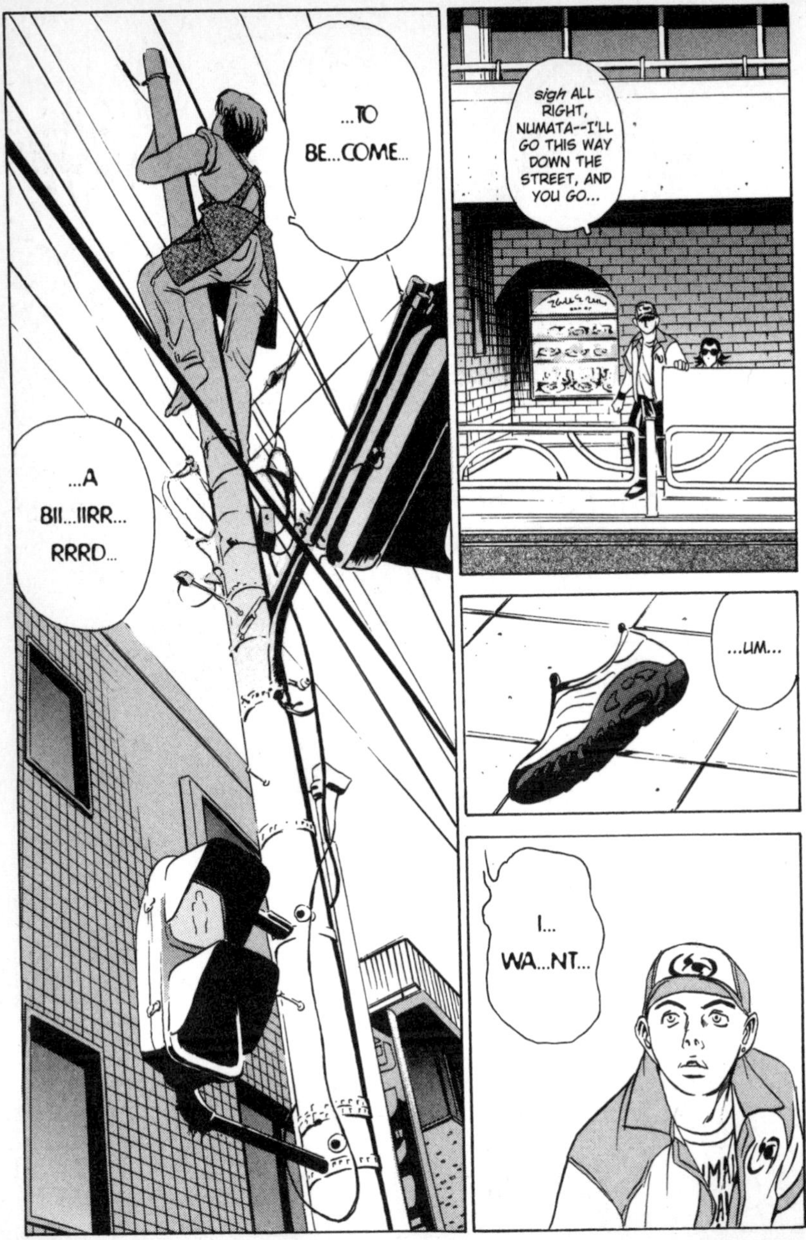
sigh ALL RIGHT, NUMATA--I'LL GO THIS WAY DOWN THE STREET, AND YOU GO...
...UM...
I... WA...NT...
...TO BE...COME...
...A BII...IIRR... RRRD...

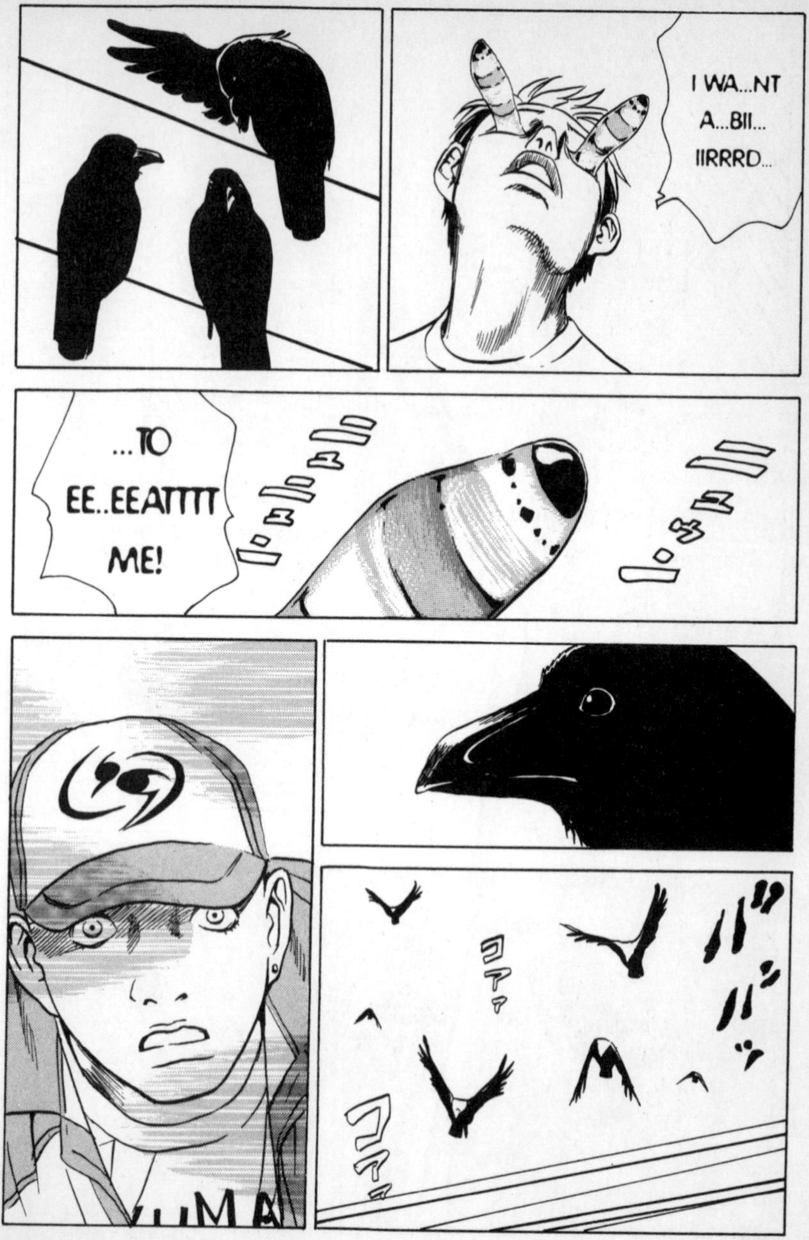

I WA...NT
A...BII...
IIRRRD...
...TO
EE..EEATTTT
ME!

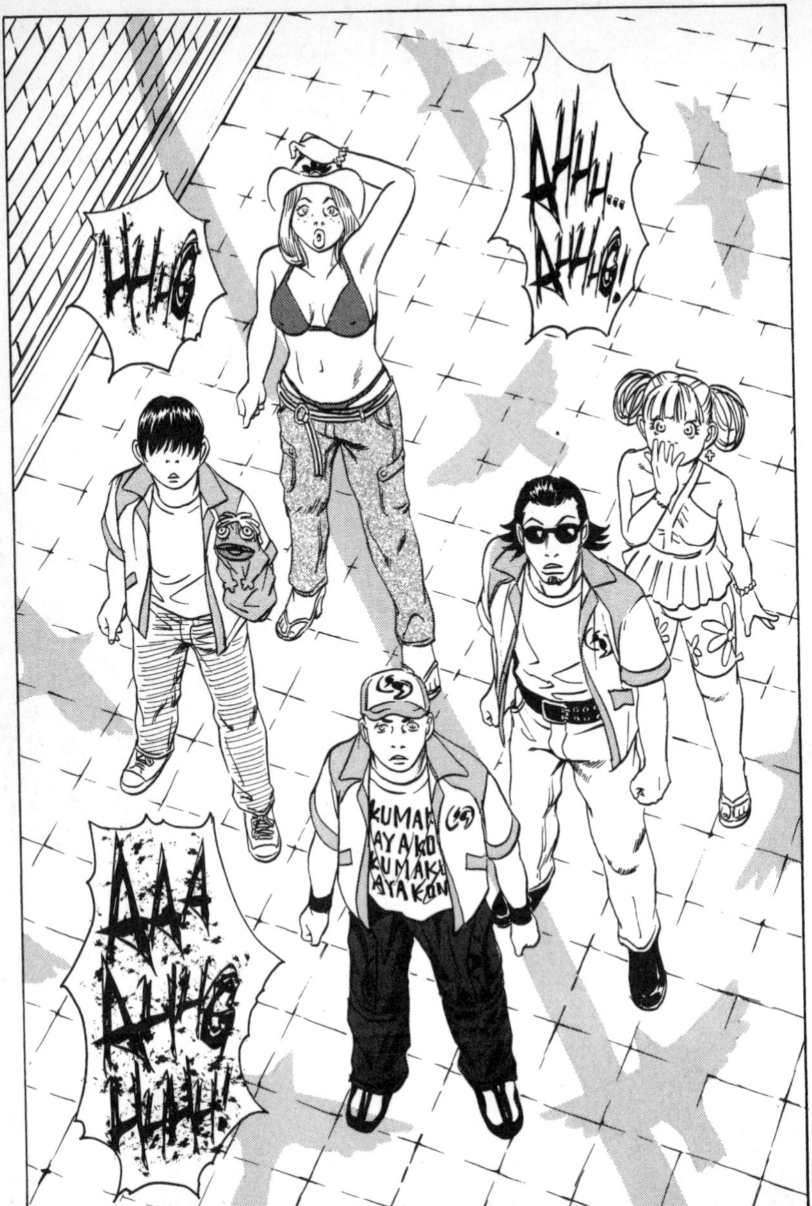
AHHH... AHHG!
HHHG
AAA AHHG HHHH!

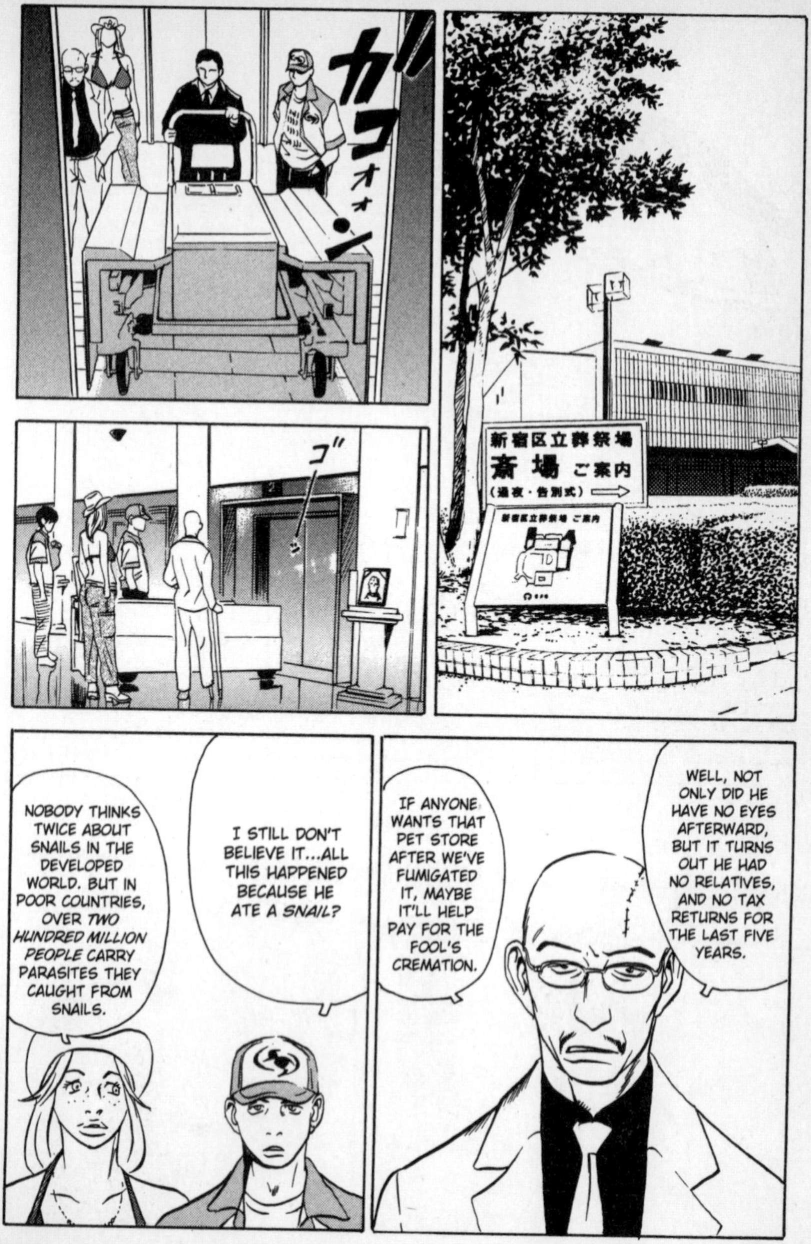

新宿区立葬祭場
斎場 ご案内
(通夜・告別式)
新宿区立葬祭場 ご案内
ガコォォン
ゴ
WELL, NOT ONLY DID HE HAVE NO EYES AFTERWARD, BUT IT TURNS OUT HE HAD NO RELATIVES, AND NO TAX RETURNS FOR THE LAST FIVE YEARS.
IF ANYONE WANTS THAT PET STORE AFTER WE'VE FUMIGATED IT, MAYBE IT'LL HELP PAY FOR THE FOOL'S CREMATION.
I STILL DON'T BELIEVE IT...ALL THIS HAPPENED BECAUSE HE ATE A *SNAIL?*
NOBODY THINKS TWICE ABOUT SNAILS IN THE DEVELOPED WORLD. BUT IN POOR COUNTRIES, OVER *TWO HUNDRED MILLION PEOPLE* CARRY PARASITES THEY CAUGHT FROM SNAILS.

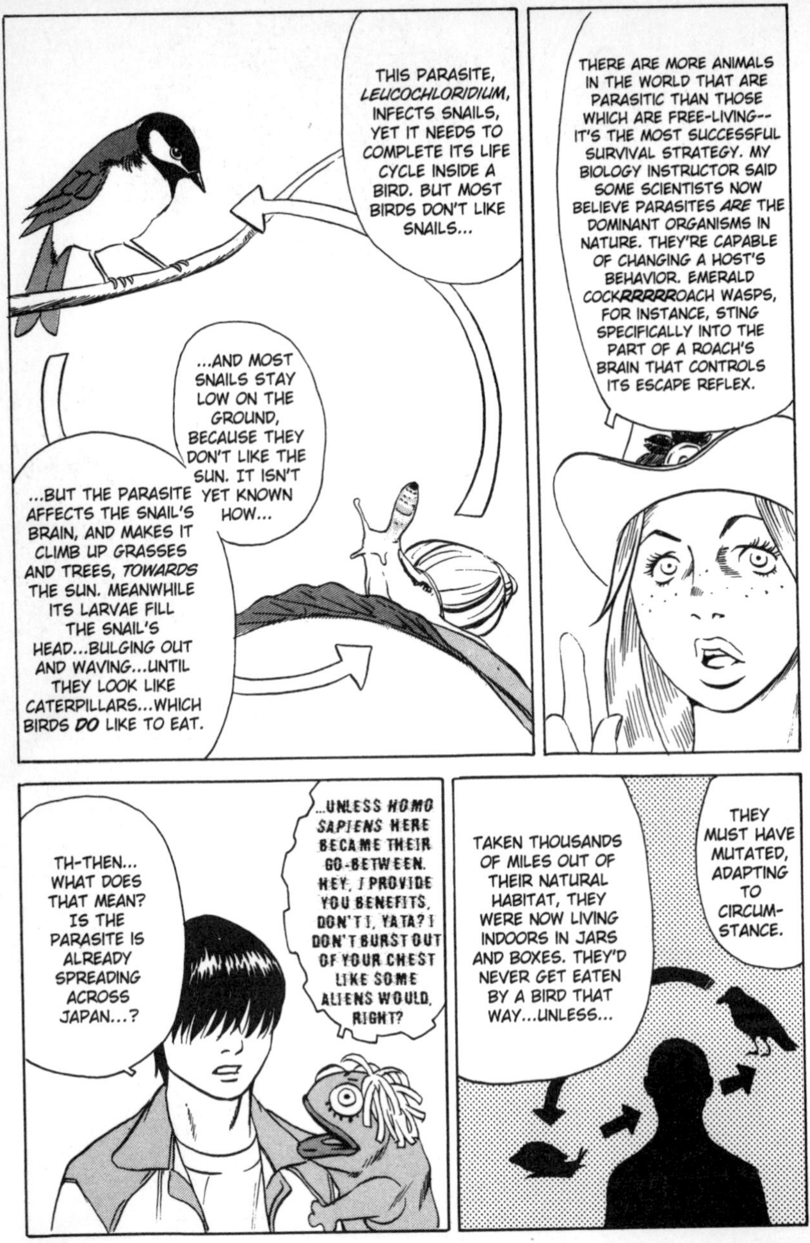

THERE ARE MORE ANIMALS IN THE WORLD THAT ARE PARASITIC THAN THOSE WHICH ARE FREE-LIVING--IT'S THE MOST SUCCESSFUL SURVIVAL STRATEGY. MY BIOLOGY INSTRUCTOR SAID SOME SCIENTISTS NOW BELIEVE PARASITES *ARE* THE DOMINANT ORGANISMS IN NATURE. THEY'RE CAPABLE OF CHANGING A HOST'S BEHAVIOR. EMERALD COCK*RRRRR*OACH WASPS, FOR INSTANCE, STING SPECIFICALLY INTO THE PART OF A ROACH'S BRAIN THAT CONTROLS ITS ESCAPE REFLEX.
THIS PARASITE, *LEUCOCHLORIDIUM*, INFECTS SNAILS, YET IT NEEDS TO COMPLETE ITS LIFE CYCLE INSIDE A BIRD. BUT MOST BIRDS DON'T LIKE SNAILS...
...AND MOST SNAILS STAY LOW ON THE GROUND, BECAUSE THEY DON'T LIKE THE SUN. IT ISN'T YET KNOWN HOW...
...BUT THE PARASITE AFFECTS THE SNAIL'S BRAIN, AND MAKES IT CLIMB UP GRASSES AND TREES, *TOWARDS* THE SUN. MEANWHILE ITS LARVAE FILL THE SNAIL'S HEAD...BULGING OUT AND WAVING...UNTIL THEY LOOK LIKE CATERPILLARS...WHICH BIRDS ***DO*** LIKE TO EAT.
THEY MUST HAVE MUTATED, ADAPTING TO CIRCUM-STANCE.
TAKEN THOUSANDS OF MILES OUT OF THEIR NATURAL HABITAT, THEY WERE NOW LIVING INDOORS IN JARS AND BOXES. THEY'D NEVER GET EATEN BY A BIRD THAT WAY...UNLESS...
...UNLESS *HOMO SAPIENS* HERE BECAME THEIR GO-BETWEEN. HEY, I PROVIDE YOU BENEFITS, DON'T I, YATA? I DON'T BURST OUT OF YOUR CHEST LIKE SOME ALIENS WOULD, RIGHT?
TH-THEN... WHAT DOES THAT MEAN? IS THE PARASITE IS ALREADY SPREADING ACROSS JAPAN...?

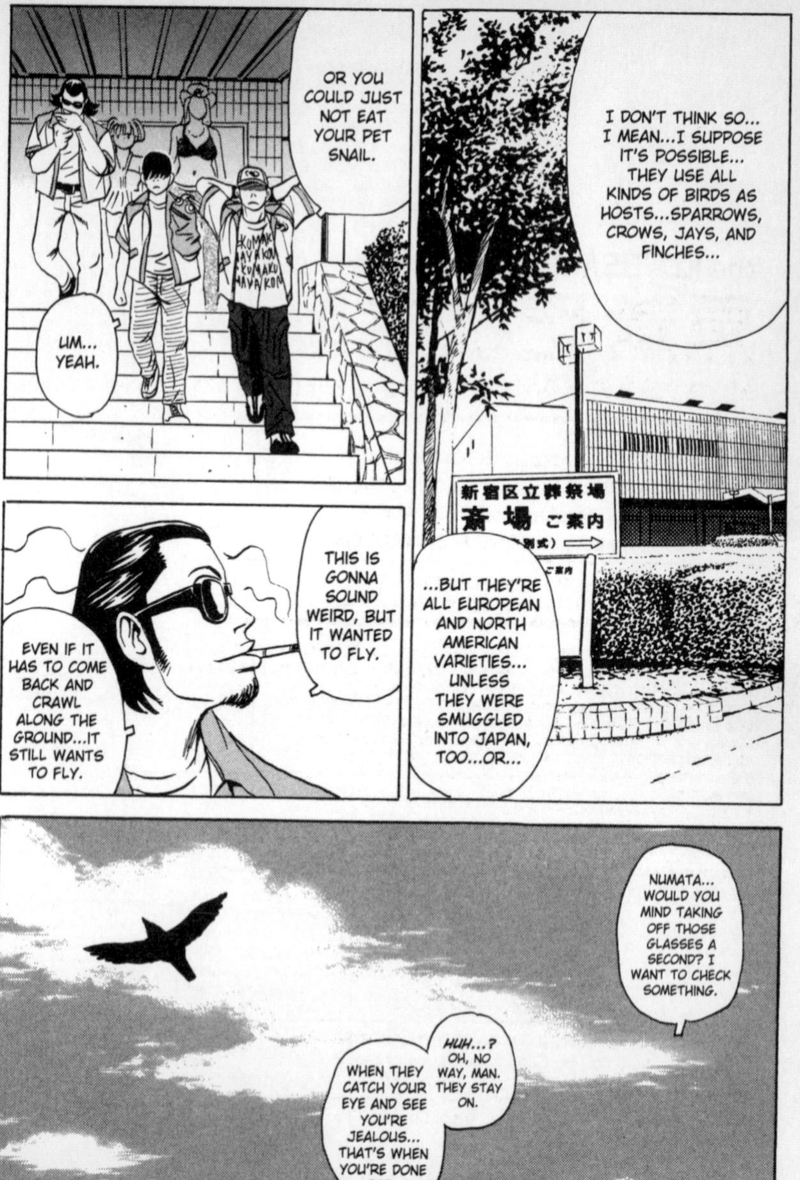
I DON'T THINK SO... I MEAN...I SUPPOSE IT'S POSSIBLE... THEY USE ALL KINDS OF BIRDS AS HOSTS...SPARROWS, CROWS, JAYS, AND FINCHES...
新宿区立葬祭場
斎場 ご案内
...BUT THEY'RE ALL EUROPEAN AND NORTH AMERICAN VARIETIES... UNLESS THEY WERE SMUGGLED INTO JAPAN, TOO...OR...
OR YOU COULD JUST NOT EAT YOUR PET SNAIL.
UM... YEAH.
THIS IS GONNA SOUND WEIRD, BUT IT WANTED TO FLY.
EVEN IF IT HAS TO COME BACK AND CRAWL ALONG THE GROUND...IT STILL WANTS TO FLY.
NUMATA... WOULD YOU MIND TAKING OFF THOSE GLASSES A SECOND? I WANT TO CHECK SOMETHING.
HUH...? OH, NO WAY, MAN. THEY STAY ON.
WHEN THEY CATCH YOUR EYE AND SEE YOU'RE JEALOUS... THAT'S WHEN YOU'RE DONE FOR.

4th delivery: humble desires—the end

the KUROSAGI corpse delivery service

黒鷺死体宅配便

eiji otsuka 大塚英志 housui yamazaki 山崎峰水

designer **HEIDI FAINZA**
editorial assistant **RACHEL MILLER**
art director **LIA RIBACCHI**
publisher **MIKE RICHARDSON**

English-language version
produced by Dark Horse Comics

Published by
Dark Horse Manga
A division of Dark Horse Comics, Inc.
10956 SE Main Street
Milwaukie, OR 97222
www.darkhorse.com

To find a comics shop in your area,
call the Comic Shop Locator Service
toll-free at 1-888-266-4226

First edition: September 2007

ISBN: 978-1-59307-595-8

3 5 7 9 10 8 6 4

PRINTED AT TRANSCONTINENTAL GAGNÉ, LOUISEVILLE, QC, CANADA

DISJECTA MEMBRA

SOUND FX GLOSSARY AND NOTES ON *KUROSAGI* VOL. 4 BY TOSHIFUMI YOSHIDA
introduction and additional comments by the editor

TO INCREASE YOUR ENJOYMENT of the distinctive Japanese visual style of this manga, we've included a guide to the sound effects (or "FX") used in this manga-style adaptation of the anime film. It is suggested the reader *not* constantly consult this glossary as they read through, but regard it as supplemental information, in the manner of footnotes. If you want to imagine it being read aloud by Osaka, after the manner of her lecture to Sakaki on hemorrhoids in episode five, please go right ahead. In either Yuki Matsuoka or Kira Vincent-Davis's voice—I like them both.

Japanese, like English, did not independently invent its own writing system, but instead borrowed and modified the system used by the then-dominant cultural power in their part of the world. We still call the letters we use to write English today the "Roman" alphabet, for the simple reason that about 1600 years ago the earliest English speakers, living on the frontier of the Roman Empire, began to use the same letters the Romans used to write their Latin language to write out English.

Around that very same time, on the other side of the planet, Japan, like England, was another example of an island civilization lying across the sea from a great empire, in this case, that of China. Likewise the Japanese borrowed from the Chinese writing system, which then as now consists of thousands of complex symbols—today in China officially referred

to in the Roman alphabet as *hanzi*, but which the Japanese pronounce as *kanji*. For example, all the Japanese characters you see on the front cover of *The Kurosagi Corpse Delivery Service*—the seven which make up the original title and the four each which make up the creators' names—are examples of kanji. Of course, all of them were hanzi first; although the Japanese did invent some original kanji of their own, just as new hanzi have been created over the centuries as Chinese evolved.

Note that whereas both *kanji* and *hanzi* are methods of writing foreign words in Roman letters, "kanji" gives English-speakers a fairly good idea of how the Japanese word is really pronounced—*khan-gee*—whereas "hanzi" does not—in Mandarin Chinese it sounds something like *n-tsuh*. The reason is fairly simple: whereas the most commonly used method of writing Japanese in Roman letters, called the Hepburn system, was developed by a native English speaker, the most commonly used method of writing Chinese in Roman letters, called the *Pinyin* system, was developed by native Mandarin speakers. In fact Pinyin was developed to help teach Mandarin pronunciation to speakers of other Chinese dialects; unlike Hepburn, it was not intended as a learning tool for English-speakers *per se*, and hence has no particular obligation to "make sense" to English speakers or, indeed, users of other languages spelled with the Roman alphabet.

Whereas the various dialects of Chinese are written entirely in hanzi, it is impractical to render the Japanese language entirely in them. To compare once more, English is a notoriously difficult language in which to spell properly, and this is in part because it uses an alphabet designed for another language, Latin, whose sounds are different. The challenges the Japanese faced in using the Chinese writing system for their own language were even greater, for whereas spoken English and Latin are at least from a common language family, spoken Japanese is unrelated to any of the various dialects of spoken Chinese. The complicated writing system Japanese evolved represents an adjustment to these differences.

When the Japanese borrowed hanzi to become kanji, what they were getting was a way to write out (remember, they already had ways to *say*) their vocabulary. Nouns, verbs, many adjectives, the names of places and people—that's what kanji are used for, the fundamental data of the written language. The practical use and processing of that "data"—its grammar and pronunciation—is another matter entirely. Because spoken Japanese neither sounds nor functions like Chinese, the first work-around tried was a system called *manyogana*, where individual kanji were picked to represent certain syllables in Japanese (a similar method is still used in Chinese today to spell out foreign names).

The commentary in *Katsuya Terada's The Monkey King* (also available from Dark Horse, and also translated by Toshifumi Yoshida) notes the importance that not only Chinese, but Indian culture had on Japan at this time in history—particularly, Buddhism. It is believed the Northeast Indian *Siddham* script studied by Kukai (died 835 AD), founder of the Shingon sect of Japanese Buddhism, inspired him to create the solution for writing Japanese still used today. Kukai is credited with the idea of taking the manyogana and making shorthand versions of them now known simply as *kana*. The improvement in efficiency was dramatic—a kanji, used previously to represent a sound, that might have taken a dozen strokes to draw, was now reduced to three or four.

Unlike the original kanji it was based on, the new kana had *only* a sound meaning. And unlike the thousands of kanji, there are only 46 kana, which can be used to spell out any word in the Japanese language, including the many ordinarily written with kanji (Japanese keyboards work on this principle). The same set of 46 kana is written two different ways depending on their intended use: cursive style, *hiragana*, and block style, *katakana*. Naturally, sound FX in manga are almost always written out using kana.

Kana works somewhat differently than the Roman alphabet. For example, while there are separate kana for each of the five vowels (the Japanese order is not A-E-I-O-U as in English, but A-I-U-E-O), except for "n," there are no separate kana for consonants (the middle "n" in the word *ninja* illustrates this exception). Instead, kana work by grouping together consonants with vowels: for example, there are five kana for sounds starting with "k," depending on which vowel follows it—in Japanese vowel order, they go KA, KI, KU, KE, KO. The next set of kana begins with "s" sounds, so SA, SHI, SU, SE, SO, and so on. You will observe this kind of consonant-vowel pattern in the FX listings for *Kurosagi* Vol. 4 below.

Katakana are almost always the kind that get used for manga sound FX, but on occasion (often when the sound is one associated with a person's body) hiragana are used instead. In *Kurosagi* Vol. 4 you can see one of several examples on page 103, when Nunokusa screams with a "WAAA" sound, which in hiragana style is written わあああ. Note its more cursive appearance compared to the other FX. If it had been written in katakana style, it would look like ワアアア.

To see how to use this glossary, take an example from page 4: "4.2 FX: ZA—sound of a board being pressed down on grass." 4.2 means the FX is the one on page 4, in panel 2. ZA is the sound these kana—ザ ツ—literally stand for. After the dash comes an explanation of what the sound represents (in some cases, such as this one, it will be less obvious than others). Note that in cases where there are two or more different sounds in a single panel, an extra number is used to differentiate them from right to left; or, in cases where right and left are less clear, in clockwise order.

The use of kana in these FX also illustrates another aspect of written Japanese—its flexible reading order. For example, the way you're reading the pages and panels of this book in general: going from right-to-left, and from top to bottom—is similar to the order in which Japanese is also written in most forms of print: books, magazines, and newspapers. However, many of the FX in *Kurosagi* (and manga in general) read left-to-right. This kind of flexibility is also to be found on Japanese web pages, which usually also read left-to-right. In other words, Japanese doesn't simply read "the other way" from English; the Japanese themselves are used to reading it in several different directions.

As might be expected, some FX "sound" short, and others "sound" long. Manga represent this in different ways. One of many instances of "short sounds" in *Kurosagi* Vol. 4 is to be found in the example from 4.2 given above: ZA. Note the small ツ mark it has at the end. This ordinarily represents the sound "tsu," but its half-size use at the end of FX like this means the sound is the kind which stops or cuts off suddenly; that's why the sound is written as ZA and not ZATSU—you don't "pronounce" the TSU in such cases. Note the small "tsu" has another occasional use *inside*, rather than at the end, of a particular FX, where it indicates a doubling of the consonant sound that follows it.

There are three different ways you may see "long sounds"—where a vowel sound is extended—written out as FX. One is with an ellipsis, as in 66.1's GOGOGO. Another is with an extended line, as in 42.1's BIII. Still another is by simply repeating a vowel several times, as in 75.1's KIIIIN. You will note that 42.1 has both the "tsu" and an ellipsis at its end, suggesting an elongated sound that's suddenly cut off; the methods may be combined within a single FX. As a visual element in manga, FX are an art rather than a science, and are used in a less rigorous fashion than kana are in standard written Japanese.

The explanation of what the sound represents may sometimes be surprising; but every culture "hears" sounds differently. Note that manga FX do not even necessarily represent literal sounds; for example 39.5 FX: KIRA—in manga this is the figurative "sound" of a gleam of light, in this case off Sasaki's glasses (anyone who's been around manga or anime a while recognizes this particular example as a classic—usually accompanied by the hand pushing up to adjust the specs, it suggests the character with glasses has just scored a point). Such "mimetic" words, which represent an imagined sound, or even a state of mind, are called *gitaigo* in Japanese. Like the onomatopoeic *giseigo* (the words used to represent literal sounds—i.e., most FX in this glossary are classed as giseigo), they are also used in colloquial speech and writing. A Japanese, for example, might say that something bounced by saying PURIN, or talk about eating by saying MUGU MUGU. It's something like describing chatter in English by saying "yadda yadda yadda" instead.

One important last note: all these spelled-out kana vowels should be pronounced as they are in Japanese: "A" as *ah*, "I" as *eee*, "U" as *ooh*, "E" as *eh*, and "O" as *oh*.

2.1 Once again, the chapter titles in *Kurosagi* are those of old Japanese pop songs—in this case of Vol. 4, all by Momoe Yamaguchi, an idol who had her debut in 1972 and retired in 1980.

4.2 FX: ZA—sound of a board being pressed down on grass

4.3 FX: ZA—sound of a board being pressed down on grass

5.3 The editor and translator's generation mostly knows the Mandelbrot Set from its 1.) ubiquitous appearance on the walls of late '80s computer labs, and 2.) ubiquitous appearance on the ads of early '90s dance parties. By the way, those "energy drinks" around now were marketed unsuccessfully as "smart drinks" fifteen years ago, which makes you think about the power of words.

6.1 Note that in Japan, a crop circle is called a *misuterii saakuru*; i.e., the English words "mystery circle." The early '90s were also associated with something of a crop circle craze, and even though the methods by which they can be made are shown here, some enthusiasts of the paranormal took them somehow as evidence of alien visitation, an idea on which local farmers did in fact cash in, sometimes earning much more charging tourists to see the circles than they could have selling the crop itself. Carl Sagan discussed the phenomenon in *The Demon-Haunted World*, noting that so much of the traditional "evidence" put forth for alien visitation are things, however complex or mysterious-appearing, that human beings can do themselves.

9.1 FX/balloon: KIN—sound of metal tip on cane clinking on floor

9.2 Readers of Dark Horse's manga *Club 9* will be aware that Japan has plenty of hicks and rubes, and that not everybody in Japan is a fifteen-year-old girl going to high school in Shibuya, who's secretly the princess of a mysterious kingdom/clumsy but good-hearted/one of several females vying for a boy's affection/running an escort agency/etc.

10.1.1 FX/balloon: PIRURURU PIRURURU—phone ringing

10.1.2 FX/balloon: KACHA—picking up phone

11.4 Yes, they have the 4-H in Japan. Japan already has the most aged population on Earth (it is estimated 40% of the population will be over 65 by the middle of this century, suggesting the moé phenomenon is a society's attempt to cup its sweaty palms around an ever-diminishing flame), and such demographics are even more evident in small towns and villages, as younger people who leave in search of opportunity rarely return. Attempts to drum up the local economy by promoting a theme to tourists are not uncommon. This sort of thing, of course, also happens in the United States—the mountain town of Leavenworth, WA successfully went Bavarian in the 1960s—Gothic lettering on the signs, edelweiss, lederhosen—the whole *verdammtneun*.

12.3 In this particular case, *Oryzias latipes*, the ricefish known in Japanese as *medaka*. Only about 4cm long, they are commonly found in rice fields in Asia—hence their name.

13.2 *Manju* are buns made with sweet bean paste, and are a ubiquitous Japanese snack. If you will observe closely, you will note the tiny flying saucer stamped on these, evidently qualifying them as "UFO-Manju."

15.4 FX: TSUN TSUN—poke poke

15.5 In the original Japanese, Makino said ". . . as Kussie, Hibagon, and Tsuchinoko," all referring to *cryptids*, or animals which exist in legend or folklore (to which there might possibly be some truth). The Japanese also

use the term UMA ("Unidentified Mysterious Animal," which was a show of the same name on Japan's NTV network). "Kussie," an obvious variation on "Nessie" (nickname of the Loch Ness Monster), is likewise said to live in Lake Kussharo in eastern Hokkaido. Some believe it is the giant snake spoken of in the legends of the Ainu, Japan's indigenous people. "Hibagon" is another: an ape-like man said to have been spotted in the region of Mount Hiba in Hiroshima Prefecture. Tsuchinoko are popular creatures in Japanese mythology and pop culture; although often described as "snakes" a foot or two long, they're conceived of as rather thick, like a banana slug.

18.6 FX: KATA KATA KATATA KATA—mummy rattling

19.1 FX: BA—fingers spreading

19.2.1 FX/right: MISHI MISHI—sound of dry bones creaking

19.2.2 FX/left: POKI—small snapping sound

20.3 FX/balloon: KUWA—sitting up suddenly

20.4 FX: SHU—leaping sound

20.5 FX/balloon: GASHAAN—crashing window

22.5 FX/balloon: KIRA—something glinting in the sky

23.5 You are going to have to take the editor's word for it that everything Yata said in this panel was untrue.

24.3 FX/balloon: GACHA—door opening

25.5 The editor still has a distinct memory of his Russian teacher, Mrs. Knirck, saying *"ess ess ess errrrrrrrrrr."* This was back in the Andropov era, so studying it still had that hardcore, spy-thriller vibe. Not that life in the Soviet Union was portrayed as glamorous by any means; the textbook featured conversation practice between a "Yuri" and "Alexei," whose dialogues revealed their two choices in life were to watch the *futbol* teams *Spartak* and *Dynamo* play on their *Televisor*, or to listen to some *kulturny jazz* on the radio.

26.1 The Soviet Union, in a sort of kick-'em-when-they're-down gesture, declared war on Japan two days after the dropping of the atomic bomb on Hiroshima, seizing four of the Kurile Islands north of Hokkaido that had been previously regarded as Japanese territory; they are held by Russia to this day and remain a strain in the relationship between the two nations. There is considerable reason to believe that if the war had gone on for only a few more weeks, the USSR would have invaded Hokkaido as well, leaving Japan to be divided much as the fate which befell Korea (such a scenario is alluded to in Makoto Shinkai's 2004 anime *The Place Promised in Our Early Days*).

26.5 The comparison was first made by Patrick Macias, editor of the much talked-about new magazine *Otaku USA* (otakuusamagazine.com).

28.5 FX: DON—putting down boom box

28.6 Real name Kiyoto Nagai; the tragic '50s crooner borrowed his first (stage) name from Frank Sinatra.

30.2 FX: BURU BURU—puppet trembling

31.6 FX/balloon: GOKU—swallowing sound

33.1 FX: GOTOTO GOTOTO—sound of bus rattling as it pulls away

33.3 FX/balloon: BURORORORO—sound of bus driving away

34.1 FX: KATA—CD case being put down

34.3 FX/balloon: KAPA—opening laptop

34.4 FX/balloon: KACHI—plugging in outlet

35.1 Seti@home is a real project with over five million participants worldwide, and you can download the program and get involved by going to http://setia-thome.berkeley.edu/. The stuff about dead idols is just Sasaki. Probably.

35.6 FX/balloon: KAKO—hitting return key

36.4 FX: KOTO—putting down microphone

36.5 FX: CHII—CD-ROM closing

38.2 FX: CHUII KO KO—sound of drive accessing data

38.4 FX: PON—computer beep

38.7 FX: KAPA—puppet's mouth opening

39.3 FX: POON—computer beep

39.5 FX: KIRA—glint of light on glasses

41.4.1 FX/monkey: OOOKIKI—monkey sounds

41.4.2 FX/monkey: UO . . .KIKI—monkey sounds

42.1.1 FX/balloon: BIII—alarm sound

42.1.2 FX/balloon: BIII—alarm sound

42.1.3 FX/balloon: BIII—alarm sound

42.2.1 FX/Monkey: KIII—panicked monkey sound

42.2.2 FX/Monkey: GYAA—monkey scream

42.2.3 FX/Monkey: KII—more monkey sounds

46.2 FX: GOBA—rockets firing

47.1 FX: GOGOGOGO—sound of space shuttle lifting off

48.2 This is a bit of an exaggeration; a space shuttle mission generally costs no more than nine hundred million dollars. This story originally appeared in *Shonen Ace* magazine in June of 2004, during the two-and-a-half years between the loss of the shuttle *Columbia* and America's return to space with the launch of the *Discovery* on July 26, 2005. *Discovery*'s crew in fact included a guest Japanese astronaut, engineer Soichi Noguchi, who conducted three spacewalks during the mission.

48.5 FX/balloon: KIN—metal cane tip hitting floor

50.2 The Arecibo Radio Telescope, from which the information processed through Seti@home is received, was prominently featured in the 1997 film *Contact*, based on the novel by Carl Sagan. In 1974, Sagan was involved in the first known deliberate attempt to send a signal from Earth to any alien civilizations which might be listening, transmitting from Arecibo an encoded image containing such information as the formula of the DNA molecule and the makeup of our solar system. In 2001, an ostensible "reply" in the form of a crop circle image appeared in the fields outside Chilbolton Observatory in England, neatly wrapping up the themes of this chapter.

52.1 FX: CHAN CHANCHA CHA CHAKA—jingle playing

59.3 The crew is headed for Tokyo Big Sight, nickname of the Tokyo International Exhibition Center, and home to among other things of the world's largest comics fan convention, Comic Market, which draws well over 350,000 attendees not once, but twice a year (compare to the annual San Diego Comic-Con, whose attendance in 2006 was 125,000).

61.1 "Mysteries of the Corpse" is inspired by the actual "Mysteries of the Human Body" exhibit that began in Tokyo in September of 2004 (although in Rafael Vinoly's magnificent downtown Tokyo International Forum rather than at Tokyo Big Sight). North American readers may have seen one of the "Body Worlds" traveling exhibitions using a similar process to display "plastinated" corpses (in fact the exhibit is currently on display just a few miles away in Portland as the editor types this . . . in the dead of night . . .), either in person, or through their appearance in the Miami museum scene of *Casino Royale*. The official website of "Body Worlds" is www.bodyworlds.com/en.html.

61.2 FX: HYUN HYUN—sound of pendulum

61.5 FX: SU—reaching out to touch

61.6 The dialogue here—as it will be several times in this chapter—is a phonetic rendering of Mandarin Chinese.

62.2 FX: SU—touching another display

62.5 Although this type of preservation is generally known as *plastination*, the "Mysteries of the Human Body" exhibit seems to have in fact preferred the term *plastomic* (the "-tomic" in this case referring to cutting or dissection), perhaps because the exhibit was seen in competition to "Body Worlds."

63.2 FX: KO—footstep

65.2 FX: SU—touching head

65.3 FX: PA—lifting hand off

65.6 Usually in *Kurosagi* this exclamation is rendered in English as "Huh?" and while Makino is in fact a "Huh?" sort of person, the original Japanese is pronounced "Eh?" and is ultimately much cuter, especially in a drawn-out phrase such as *eeeeeeeee?! sugoi na!!!* ("Huhhhhhhhh? That's so cool!")

66.1 FX: GOGOGO—car moving

66.2 FX: GOTON GATA—sound rattling inside the car

68.3 It's somewhat unusual in a manga to have a character portrayed as fluent in foreign languages as a responsibility of their job (rather than because of travel abroad or mixed parentage) and is perhaps a healthy sign of a more cosmopolitan attitude toward being Japanese.

68.5 FX: SU—touching head

69.2 The text here—as will be several times in this chapter—is hanzi, i.e., written Chinese.

72.1 The real-life inventor of the plastination process is a German anatomist named Dr. Gunther von Hagens, who, between his movie-scientist name, habitual black fedora and suit, penchant for theater (in 2002 he conducted the first public autopsy in England since the days of Charles Dickens), and family background (his father was in the Nazi SS) is hardly less dramatic, if less sinister than the fictional Takashi Nunokusa. Von Hagens does in fact run a plastination center in Northeastern China, in the city of Dalian, and the German magazine *Der Spiegel* has accused him of using the bodies of executed prisoners, although not necessarily for those on display in "Body Worlds."

75.1 FX: KIIIIIN—sound of a jet plane

77.2 A photograph of the actual site can be seen at www.h5.dion.ne.jp/~nkusu/asiaphoto/china/photopage/haerbin6.html. This is also the first time the editor has ever seen Unit 731 mentioned in a manga. The humans experimented on here were euphemistically referred to as *maruta*, or "logs," supposedly due to the cover story that the camp was a "lumber mill." Infected fleas bred by Unit 731 (and other Japanese biological warfare units) were deliberately released over Chinese cities to spread bubonic plague. Testimonies from two of the Japanese doctors involved can be found in the much-recommended *Japan at War: An Oral History*, by Haruko and Theodore Cook. "I am a war criminal because of the things I actually did. Not in theory," said one, whereas the other recalled of a nurse in the unit bearing a lethal syringe, "She was even prouder than me. She giggled. The demon's face is not a fearful face. It's a face wreathed in smiles."

79.1 The Yasukuni Shrine, which is treated as the Japanese national war memorial (somewhat analogous to Arlington National Cemetery, although Yasukuni is privately funded) enshrines the spirits of those WWII leaders convicted as war criminals, as well as millions of ordinary soldiers. Moreover the attached Yasukuni museum describes Japan as being "forced into conflict," its motives being "the independence and peace of the nation and for the prosperity of all of Asia." Although millions of Chinese died in the 1930s and 40s due to the Japanese desire for an empire in Asia (which was in fact officially described as the "Co-Prosperity Sphere") the editor cannot help but regard such modern-day protests with *some* dubiousness, owing to the fact in the decades since the war millions more Chinese have been murdered by their own government, which has remained authoritarian, whereas Japan's has achieved democracy.

80.2 FX: CHIN—hanging up sound

81.5 FX/balloon: SHA—sound of a curtain being closed

81.6.1 FX/balloon: FUN FUN FUFUN FUN FUN—happy humming

81.6.2 FX: SUTO—sound of the skirt hitting floor

82.1 Between Kenji Tsuruta's *Spirit of Wonder* and Hiroaki Samura's *Ohikkoshi*, we seem to have a thing here at Dark Horse for manga involving Chinese dresses, or *cheongsam* as they're sometimes called (from the Cantonese term, which technically refers both to male and female versions of the outfit). If I may quote Ian Fleming, "The high, rather stiff collar of the cheongsam gives authority and poise to the head and shoulders, and the flirtatious slits from the hem of the dress upwards, as high as the beauty of the leg will allow, demonstrate that the sex appeal of the inside of a woman's knee has apparently never occurred to Dior or Balmain."

82.2 FX/balloon: PU—sound of a knife piercing curtain

82.3 FX: TSUUU—sound of knife slicing curtain

82.4 FX: SU—curtain being pushed aside

83.2 FX/Kuro: MOGU MOGU—chewing sound

83.3 FX: KARAN KAN—sound of dropped chopsticks clinking on bowl

83.5 FX: SHA—sound of a curtain being moved aside

84.2 FX/balloon: GASHAN—sound of breaking glass

84.6 FX/balloon: SA—sound of a knife being put to throat

84.7 FX/balloon: KOKI KOKI—cracking knuckles

85.1 FX/Makino: MOGA MOGO AGA—trying to talk through covered mouth

86.1.1 **FX/black: GOGOGOTO GOTOTON**—sound of truck going down dirt road

86.1.2 **FX/balloon: BASHA**—sound of tires hitting puddle

86.3 **FX: MUSUU**—sound of Kuro frowning

86.4 **FX: GOGOGO**—sound of the truck

87.3 **FX/balloon: KII**—sound of brakes

87.5 **FX: KO**—footstep

90.5 The hideous punchline is that most of the members of Unit 731, including Dr. Shiro Ishii, did escape prosecution or judgment—not thanks to the sinister Russians or Chinese, but the good old U.S. of A., whose occupation authorities in Japan granted them immunity in exchange for their data. The reasoning at the time was that this expertise was better in American hands than Soviet, a case not unlike those Nazi V-2 rocket scientists brought into the U.S. space program (the V-2 had in fact been built with concentration camp labor; far more people died constructing the rockets than were actually killed by the rocket attacks themselves). The immunity—indeed secrecy—given to the affair by the U.S. in the 1940s had the collateral effect of allowing many in Japan sixty years later to deny their biological warfare program ever happened. The first Japanese expose of Unit 731 was, however, was *The Devil's Gluttony* by Seiichi Morimura, a series of articles collected in book form in 1983 by Kadokawa, who is of course the original publisher of this manga.

91.1 **FX: JYARI**—sound of gravel moving underfoot

91.3 **FX/balloon: GAKOON**—metal door slamming shut

92.1 **FX: PARA**—rope falling off

93.3 Nunokusa is referring to Raimondo de Sangro VII (1710–1771) Prince of Sansevero, known for his macabre experiments and inventions. You can see the "marvelous achievements" on the museum's official site at www.museosansevero.it/eng/sperimentazioni.htm

94.1 **FX: KYU**—pulling on rubber gloves

94.2 **FX: PU**—needle piercing skin

94.3 **FX: TSUU**—sound of blood traveling down tube

94.5 **FX: BAN**—firmly pressing hand onto head

96.2.1 **FX/balloon: PIKU**—eyelid twitching

96.2.2 **FX/balloon: PIKU**—eyelid twitching

96.3 **FX/balloon: PAKA**—eyelid popping open

97.1.1 **FX/balloon: KATA**—rattle

97.1.2 **FX/balloon: KATA**—rattle

97.2.1 **FX/balloon: GATA**—sound of something moving inside box

97.2.2 **FX/balloon: GOTO**—sound of something moving inside box

97.2.3 **FX/balloon: BAN**—sound of something hitting inside the box

97.3 **FX: BAKO**—sound of lid popping open

97.6 **FX: BATAN**—door closing

98.2 **FX: PAN PAPAAN**—gunshots

98.3   **FX: GOTO**—picking up gun

98.5   **FX: KII**—door creaking open

99.3   **FX: YURA YURARI**—wobbly movement sound

99.5   **FX: KURU**—sound of figure turning

100-101.2 FX: PETA PETA—sound of bare feet on tile

102.1   **FX: PAAN PAN PAAN**—gunshots

102.2.1 FX/balloon: PAKI—sound of plastic breaking

102.2.2 FX/balloon: PAKA—sound of plastic cracking open

102.3   **FX: GIRO**—glare

103.1   **FX: WAAAA**—scream

104.1   **FX: BAKAAN**—lock being kicked open

104.4   **FX: YURA YURARI**—wobbly movement

106.3   **FX/balloon: BOWU**—sound of a fire catching

106.4.1 FX/balloon: PAKI—cracking sound

106.4.2 FX/balloon: BACHI—crackling sound

106.5   **FX: DOSA**—thud

108.3   **FX: PACHIN**—clapping hand in prayer

110.4   Note that nowhere in this story is the actual gender of the baby given, so the translator has chosen to avoid personal pronouns.

112.2   Risa Wataya was 19 when she won Japan's top literary award, the Akutagawa Prize, in 2004, for her short novel *Keritai Senaka* ("A Backside I Want to Kick"), which has reportedly sold over one million copies since. The current governor of Tokyo, Shintaro Ishihara, who remarked last year "I hate Mickey Mouse—he has nothing like the unique sensibility that Japanese animation has" himself won the Akutagawa Prize as a young novelist fifty years before.

111.3.1 FX: HAA—panting

111.3.2 FX: HAA—panting

113.3   *Hanami* is literally "flower viewing" (it is also, of course, the name of the Japanese heroine of Dark Horse's *manhwa*—Korean graphic novel—*Hanami: International Love Story*). If you haven't bought it yet, the editor will smoke a Gitanes *Filtre* while you go out and do so. Michael Gombos, DH's Director of Asian Licensing, bought me a pack of them on his latest trip to Japan, because they're the brand that Lupin III smokes. Don't ask me how he knew that. Anyway, there was a time when I was trying out all the cigarettes in my favorite anime, and everybody in *Lupin III* smokes, except for Goemon. When I was a kid, I thought Lupin was passing Zenigata a joint in that scene in *The Castle of Cagliostro* where they're trapped together in the dungeon, but looking again, what I took to be a roach clip was likely just a Gitanes butt with a wire poked through it. Are you back yet? Okay, now that you have Vol. 1 of *Hanami*, you'll notice both the front and back covers show the most famous form of Japanese flower viewing, namely, watching cherry blossoms in the spring. This is traditionally done by laying out a blanket in the park (if a company party, a low-ranking employee may be sent out to claim a prime space ahead of time, even if that means in the dead of night) and regarding the flowers whilst imbibing food and drink, especially drink. There are those ladies and gentlemen of leisure who even make this a month-long party, by starting in the south of Japan early in the season and moving gradually northward each day, following the flowers in full bloom.

113.5 Saigoyama Park was the original site of the residence of Judo Saigo (1843–1902), an influential politician of the Meiji Period.

114.4 FX: ZUPIPIPI—sipping beer from a can

115.1 FX: KARAN KARARAN—empty cans getting kicked

115.5 FX: YURARI—pendulum starting to waver

116.2 FX: TA—footstep

117.3 FX: BASA—pulling up plastic sheet

118.2 FX/balloon: POTO—key landing on ground

120.2 FX: HYUN HYUN HYUN—sound of the pendulum swinging

122.2 FX: HYUN HYUN—pendulum swinging

123.2 FX: KASHAN—sound of the locker being unlocked

123.3 FX: KII—locker creaking open

123.4 FX/balloon: PORO—sound of something starting to fall out

123.5.1 FX: KOON—sound of the rattle bouncing on tile

123.5.2 FX/balloon: PORON—rattle noise

123.5.3 FX/balloon: KORON—rattle noise

123.7.1 FX/balloon: KARAN—rattle noise

123.7.2 FX/balloon: KORON—rattle noise

124.3 FX: ZUSHIRI—sound denoting heaviness of the bag

125.2.1 FX/balloon: KASHA—camera shutter click

125.2.2 FX/balloon: KASHA—camera shutter click

126.1 FX: JI JI JI JI—sound of a zipper being pulled

126.4 Numata's allusion to a "Final Form" here is thought to be a reference to Cell from *Dragonball Z*, who gradually evolves from an "imperfect" to a "perfect" form.

129.5 FX: GU—making a fist sound

130.1 FX/balloon: TSUN TSUN—poking chest sound

132.1 FX/balloon: GACHA—door opening

132.3 FX/balloon: PACHIN—breaking wooden chopsticks apart

133.1 FX/balloon: PWOON—alarm beep going off

133.4.1 FX/balloon: PA—grid lines appearing

133.4.2 FX/balloon: PA—grid lines appearing

133.4.3 FX/balloon: PA—grid lines appearing

133.6 FX/balloon: PWOON—alarm beep going off

133.7 FX: GA GA—shoveling food into mouth

134.3 FX: TA—running off

134.4.1 FX: GACHA—opening car door

134.4.2 FX/balloon: SA—getting into car sound

134.5 FX: BAN—slamming car door sound

134.6 FX: BURORO—car engine sound

135.4 FX/balloon: BUROROR0—car sound

135.5 That is, she's driving a Nissan March, a popular subcompact sold overseas as the Micra. It was reportedly available in the U.S. from 1985 to 1991, but not at present.

135.6 FX: GU—Numata's foot pressing down on Yata's foot on the accelerator

135.7 FX: GYURURURU—sound of the tires peeling out

136.1 FX: GWOOO—sound of cars speeding along

137.3 FX: CHIKA CHIKA—sound of blinkers flashing

137.4 FX: GU GU—sound of a truck changing lanes in front of the car

137.5 In the original version, Numata tells Yata to do *passhingu*—that is, the English word "passing," which the Japanese have adopted to refer to the act of flashing your lights at a car ahead of you, requesting to pass. As with the car horn, of course, this however is often not meant as a polite request, but a sort of assertion of dominance, especially in situations where one could pass simply by switching lanes.

137.6 FX: IRA IRA—sound of irritation

138.1 FX: BA—sound of a moped moving in front of the car

138.4 FX/balloon: KUI KUI—gesturing to follow

139.2 FX/balloon: BIIIIII—sound of a moped motor

139.4 FX/balloon: KII—sound of brakes

140.3 FX: BAN—closing car door

143.4 FX: KACHA—putting down teacup into saucer

143.6 FX/balloon: SURU—sound of a rope being pulled out

144.1 FX: DOTAN BATA—sound of the two wrestling about

144.5 FX: SU—fingers falling from the rope

144.6 FX/balloon: KAKUN—body going limp

144.7 FX: JIWA—liquid starting to soak through skirt

145.1 FX: DOSA—sound of body hitting floor

145.4 FX: DOKA—kicking sound

145.7.1 FX/black: ONGYAA ONGYAA ONGYAA—baby crying

145.7.2 FX/white: NU—sound of hand appearing from below skirt

146.1 FX: ONGYAA ONGYAA—baby crying

146.2 FX: ONGYAA ONGYAA—baby crying

147.1 FX/balloon: PWOON—elevator arrival bell

147.2 FX: GAAA—elevator door opening

147.4 *Ko Sodate Yurei* literally translates to "child-raising ghost"—it is a

Japanese folk tale also known as the story of the *Ame Kai Yurei* ("candy-buying ghost"). A candy vendor is visited by a pale woman with messy hair every night for a week, who asks to buy a piece of candy and then disappears. On the last night, she claims she has no more money, and trades her kimono for the candy. The next day, a passing priest sees the kimono and asks the vendor where he got it, saying it appears to be the same kimono as a young woman who passed away recently. They go to the cemetery, and at the site of the woman's grave, they hear a crying baby. Exhuming the coffin (quite rare in Japanese burials), they find an infant in the arms of the woman along with the pieces of candy. The priest informs the vendor that the young woman had died just before giving birth. They speculate that the baby was born after the death of the mother, and that the spirit of the mother cared for the newborn. The priest tells the dead mother that he would take care of the baby in her place and as if in acknowledgment, the head of the woman seems to move slightly in a nod. The child is said to have grown up to become a priest of high standing. The very old *Ko Sodate Yurei* story is still invoked in Japanese pop culture (for example, in the game *Fatal Frame II*) and reflects particular spiritual beliefs among Japanese women regarding the unborn, including the desire to pray for and protect the spirits of stillborn and aborted children.

148.4 FX/balloon: KACHA—opening door

148.5 FX/balloon: KII—door creaking open

148.6 FX: GASA GOSO—sound of someone moving around amongst the litter

149.4 FX: KASA—rustling

151.4 FX: DA DA DA DA TA—padding forward

152.1.1 FX/white: BA—raising arm quickly

152.1.2 FX/black: SUCHA—readying gun sound

152.3 FX: DWOON—bang

153.2 FX: DOTA BATAN—body writhing on the floor

153.4 FX/balloon: GYU KYUN—spirit being pulled into the bullet

153.5 FX/balloon: KYUN—last bit of the spirit being pulled in

153.6 FX: KOON KON KORON—bullet bouncing and then rolling to a stop

154.1 FX: SU—reaching out

154.6 FX: ZA—turning around

155.6 The kanji *tsuku* used by Akiba means "haunt," but it sounds the same as another kanji that could mean "be with" or "stand with," so the translator has wished to preserve an ambiguity here.

156.1 FX: PORI—scratching head

156.3 FX: SU—handing over photo

156.7 FX: BIRI BIRI—tearing sound

160-161.4 FX: MEEN MEEN MEEN—sound of cicadas

162.1 Collecting live beetles is a traditional hobby in Japan, especially among kids (hence

Numata's remark in 166.1) although a rather dubious way to supplement one's income.

163.3 FX: MEEN MEEN—cicadas

163.6 FX: SU—raising arm

164.1 FX: HYUN HYUN—pendulum swinging

164.3 FX: ZA SA—sound of walking through tall grass

164.5 FX: GASA—moving leaves out of the way

164.6 FX: POTATA—maggots falling on neck and back

165.2 FX: SU—maggot being picked up

165.4 "Reina Gorn" somehow seems a name that is no more than feasible, but there it is. Her Japanese is just slightly off in the original, reflected here by a tendancy to say her "R"s too strongly. Personally, the editor would like to see a Caucasian female character in manga who happens to be short, dark-haired, and flat-chested (Reina could be the sister of Diana Lockheed in *Oh My Goddess!* Vol. 3, even down to the freckles and tank top) but is sympathetic to Japanese creators' desire to share the fantasy, like Chanel No. 5. Manga are supposed to be for fun, you know. Except the manga of Yoshihiro Tatsumi.

166.5 FX: SA—looking up sound

168.2 Some types of shrikes are known as "butcher birds," as they will store the corpse of an insect or lizard for later consumption by skewering it upon a branch. In Japanese the practice is referred to as a *mozu no hayanie*, literally "the swift sacrifice (as in sacrificial offering) of a bull-headed shrike."

168.3 FX: POKI POKI—cracking knuckles

168.4 FX: DOKA DOKA—kicking tree

168.5 FX: ZAN ZAZA BASA—sound of body falling through the branches and leaves

169.1 FX: DO—sound of body hitting ground

170.1 FX: PWOON—fly buzzing around

170.3 FX: SA—lifting arm up to look

171.4 FX: ZA—footstep

171.5 Yata is speaking a bit of broken English here in an attempt to explain the concept.

173.5 FX/balloon: PAN PAN—dusting self off

174.2 FX: JI JI JI—sound of cicadas

174.3 FX: RIIIN—sound of a wind chime

174.4.1 FX/white: PAPAA—sound of car horns

174.4.2 FX/black (r.): GO GO GO—rumbling construction sound

174.4.3 FX/black (m.): DODO—more construction sounds

174.4.4 FX/black (l.): PUWAAN—car horn sound

175.5 FX: GACHA—door opening

177.1 FX: GOSO GOSO—sound of Reina digging around in her bag

177.2 FX: KON—canned food hitting top of table
Local specialties, particularly food, are a common gift in Japan, especially when returning from a journey (and of course, this type of

gift can be found in U.S. airports as well, such as sourdough in San Francisco or crab cakes in Baltimore). This particular can bears the legend "Shinshuu Local Food—INAGO—Tsukudani." Inago are, of course, a type of locust; *tsukudani* is a style of cooking by boiling in soy sauce and *mirin* (which is sort of to saké as cooking sherry is to wine).

177.5 FX: JAJAN SHAKA JAJAAN—ringtone of mobile phone

178.4 FX: BUUUN—sound of a fly

179.4 *Zazamushi* are aquatic insects inhabiting gravel beds in rivers; usually consisting mainly of larval *Trichoptera*.

179.6 FX: MOGU MUGU—munching sound

180.3.1 FX/Sasayama: GA GA—shoveling food into mouth

180.3.2 FX/Kuro: KOKI—cracking neck

180.4 FX: SU—placing hand on corpse

181.6 FX/balloon: POKI—sound of pencil lead breaking

182.1 FX/balloon: GACHA—door opening

182.4 FX: JIIII—zipper sound

182.5 FX: JIRO—glaring sound

183.2 FX: SU—touching corpse

184.5.1 FX: MOGU MOGU—munching sound

184.5.2 FX/balloon: PUCHU—sound of locust popping between teeth

185.4 FX: MOGU MOGU—munching sound

185.5 FX: PAKU—tossing locust into mouth

185.6 FX: KARAN—sound of chopsticks thrown into empty can

188.3 In a shocking breach of humor, the editor would like to say he personally admires France and has always enjoyed visiting. You know, there, it's called *Kurosagi—Livraison de Cadavres.*

191.6 FX/balloon: GARARI—sound of shutter being slid up

192.1 FX: GARAGARARA—shutter being slid up

192.3 FX: PI—hitting button

194.3 FX: NYUN NYUN—sound of the eyes wiggling and pulsing

194.4 FX: NYUN NYUN—sound of the eyes wiggling and pulsing

194.5 FX: NYUN NYUN—sound of the eyes wiggling and pulsing

195.1 FX: BA—puppet moving other hand away

195.4 FX: NYUN NYUNYUN—sound of the eyes wiggling and pulsing

200.2 FX: NYUN NYU NYUN—sound of the eyes wiggling and pulsing

200.3 FX: SUTA SUTATA—pet shop employee starting to walk away

202.3 FX: NYUN NYUNYUN—sound of the eyes wiggling and pulsing

202.5.1 FX/black: BABA—birds taking flight

202.5.2 FX/white: KOAA KOAA—cawing birds

204.2 FX: GAKOON—elevator doors opening

204.3 FX: GWOOO—sound of flames inside incinerator

STOP!

THIS IS THE BACK OF THE BOOK!

This manga collection is translated into English, but arranged in right-to-left reading format to maintain the artwork's visual orientation as originally drawn and published in Japan. If you've never read comics this way before, take a look at the diagram below to give yourself an idea of how to go about it. Basically, you'll be starting in the upper right-hand corner, and will read each word balloon and panel moving right-to-left. It may take a little getting used to, but you should get the hang of it very quickly. Have fun! If this is the millionth manga you've read this way, never mind. ^_^

1
...
2
THEY TALK TO YOU BECAUSE YOU'RE THE KIND OF GUY WHO CAN'T SAY NO.
3
...YES.
4
RIGHT. SO LET'S TAKE THIS HORRIBLE, STINKING, ROTTING THING BACK TO CAMPUS. QUICK, BEFORE THE COPS NOTICE.
5
BACK TO CAMPUS?!
6
KARATSU, THERE'S NOTHING IN THE HANDBOOK THAT SAYS STUDENTS CAN'T POSSESS CORPSES--OR, IN YOUR CASE, VICE-VERSA.

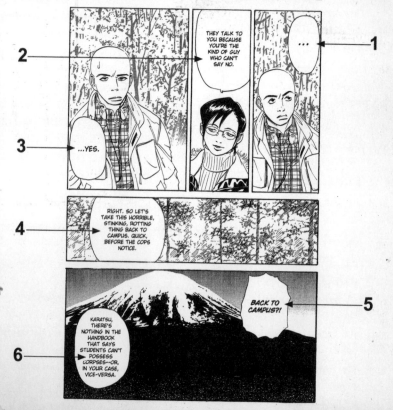